The Evening Stars

Barbara Matusow

THE EVENING STARS

THE MAKING OF THE
NETWORK NEWS ANCHOR

Houghton Mifflin Company
Boston

Library of Congress Cataloging in Publication Data

Matusow, Barbara.
   The evening stars.

   Bibliography:
   Includes index.
   1. Television broadcasting of news — United States.
I. Title.
PN4888.T4M37   1983   070'.92'2   83-321
ISBN 0-395-33968-5

Printed in the United States of America

D   10   9   8   7   6   5   4   3

For Jack

One of the basic troubles with radio and television news is that both instruments have grown up as an incompatible combination of show business, advertising, and news. Each of the three is a rather bizarre and demanding profession, and when you get all three under one roof, the dust never settles.

— Edward R. Murrow

Acknowledgments

THE EVOLUTION OF network television news — so distinct from broad-cast news in other countries — has hardly been examined by scholars, political scientists, or the industry itself, despite the pervasiveness of the medium in our society. Although the early days of radio were chronicled in loving and exhaustive detail, a written record of the origins of television news is virtually nonexistent. Rarer still are examples of early broadcasts. On the subject of that uniquely American personage, the network news anchor, a great deal has been written, of course, but the discussion has tended to center on salaries and personality. Of the role anchors play and the influence they wield within their respective networks much less has been said. While I am acknowledging my debt to certain historians and writers, such as Eric Barnouw, Les Brown, Gary Paul Gates, David Hal-berstam, Alexander Kendrick, Robert Metz, Ron Powers, and others, oral interviews, personal correspondence, and other unpublished documents necessarily form the backbone of this book. Fortunately, network news is such a young institution — only thirty-five years of age in 1983 — that most of the principals are still around, and most were exceedingly gener-ous about sharing their insights, their recollections, and their time.

Literally hundreds of people helped me in one way or another — executives, reporters, producers, librarians, photo researchers, and others; but even leaving aside a great number of them, I find I am left with a staggeringly long list of people to thank.

First and foremost, I am indebted to that select group of people, the current and former anchors of the network evening news, all of whom consented to be interviewed, many of them two, three, or more times:

David Brinkley, Tom Brokaw, John Chancellor, Ron Cochran, Walter Cronkite, John Daly, Douglas Edwards, Peter Jennings, Roger Mudd, Dan Rather, Harry Reasoner, Frank Reynolds, Max Robinson, Howard K. Smith, John Cameron Swayze, and Barbara Walters.

I would also like to thank the many network executives, past and present, who aided me so materially, including Roone Arledge, David Burke, Lester Crystal, Edward Fouhy, Reuven Frank, Fred Friendly, Julian Goodman, Lee Hanna, Ernest Leiser, William Leonard, Elmer Lower, Sig Mickelson, Richard Salant, Van Gordon Sauter, Herbert Schlosser, William Sheehan, Frank Stanton, Arthur Taylor, Richard C. Wald, Sylvester ("Pat") Weaver, Av Westin, and Robert Wussler.

Others who generously contributed their knowledge to this book include Bob Abernethy, Joseph Angotti, John Armstrong, Robert Asman, Joe Bartelme, Christie Basham, Steve Bell, Joel Bernstein, Robert Blackwood, Bob Blum, Don Bowers, Ben Bradlee, Ed Bradley, Rita Braver, Hal Bruno, Art Buchwald, John Carmody, Blair Clark, Carole Cooper, Bill Crawford, Lester Crystal, Bruce Cummings, James Dickenson, Sam Donaldson, Robert Doyle, Herb Dudnick, Willis Duff, Paul Duke, Betty Endicott, Ray Farkas, Don Farmer, Dick Fisher, Paul Friedman, Steve Friedman, Vincent Gaito, Gary Paul Gates, Robert Goralski, Fred Graham, Paul Greenberg, Jim Griffin, David Halberstam, David Hartman, Jim Hartz, Brian Healy, Don Hewitt, Peter Hoffman, E. Gregory Hookstratten, Richard C. Hottelet, Brit Hume, Barry Jagoda, Marvin Josephson, Rick Kaplan, Herbert Kaplow, Michael Keenan, Douglas Kiker, Jim Kitchell, Ted Koppel, Bob Kur, Charles Kuralt, Richard Leibner, Larry LeSueur, Robert MacNeil, Frank Magid, Ralph Mann, Robert McCormick, Charles McDowell, Bill McSherry, Susan Mercandetti, John Miller, Gilbert Millstein, Bill Monroe, Robert "Shad" Northshield, David Nuell, Bill Overend, John Palmer, Ralph Paskman, Jane Pauley, Tom Pettit, Robert Pierpoint, Bill Plante, Walter Porges, Jody Powell, Gerald Rafshoon, Bryson Rash, Joan Richmond, Merle Rubine, Hughes Rudd, Marlene Sanders, Jessica Savitch, Diane Sawyer, Ray Scherer, Bob Schieffer, Max Schindler, David Schoumacher, Willard Scott, Eric Sevareid, Bill Shadel, Lynn Sherr, Charles Sieg, Robert Siegenthaler, Dorrance Smith, James Snyder, Sanford Socolow, Gerry Solomon, Lesley Stahl, Carl Stern, Neil Strawser, Howard Stringer, Ken Tiven, Lee Townsend, Patrick Trese, Tom Turley, Richard Valeriani, Jim Vance, Sander Vanocur, Mike Wallace, George Watson, Joe Wershba, Don West, Wallace Westfeldt, Roy Wetzel, Bill Wheatley,

Kay Wight, James Wooten, and Sam Zelman. A number of others who prefer not to be named similarly have my thanks.

I am also grateful for the assistance of Terrence Adamson, Josephine Franklin-Trout, Sandra Goroff, George Herman, Walter Isaacson, Marlene Marmo, Steve Neal, Arlie Schardt, Desmond Smith, and Abraham Wilner, and for the unflagging support of my agents, Arnold and Elise Goodman. To Terrell Lamb and Diana Pabst, who ably and cheerfully assisted me in researching this book, and to Carolyn Shields, who typed it, I owe a special debt of gratitude.

A number of editors associated with Houghton Mifflin played a major role in shaping the finished work: Ellen Joseph, who first saw the possibilities in this project and never wavered in her enthusiasm; Nan Talese, who encouraged me to undertake a work of broader significance; Gerard Van Der Leun, whose creative suggestions helped to improve the finished product beyond measure; and Lois Randall, who so skillfully copy edited the final manuscript. Richard C. Cooper, news editor of the Washington Bureau of the *Los Angeles Times*, also performed wonders, suggesting ways to sharpen my ideas and my prose. In addition, a number of people read the manuscript at various stages, offering valuable advice and criticism: Steve Weinberg, Dawson "Tack" Nail, my brothers, Allen Matusow and Donald Matusow, and my aunt, Catherine Korin.

Finally, I would like to thank my husband, Jack Nelson, whose advice and enthusiastic support sustained me through the long and occasionally daunting process of completing this book.

★ Contents ★

The Evening Stars

Introduction

ON AUGUST 17, 1982, the Reagan administration declared its intention to reduce arms sales to Taiwan, a decision that offended conservative members of Congress already angry with the President over his insistence on raising taxes. That night on the CBS Evening News, Dan Rather led off his broadcast by telling viewers that, taken together, the arms sale decision and the proposed tax increase constituted a "reversal of policy" that had infuriated members of the President's own party.

Watching the six-thirty "feed" of the broadcast in his private quarters in the White House, Ronald Reagan became so agitated by Rather's characterization of his Taiwan policy that at two minutes after seven, in the midst of the second evening news feed, the President put through a phone call to the CBS newsroom to discuss the matter with Rather directly. A few minutes later, Rather reported the conversation to viewers, quoting Mr. Reagan as saying, "There has been no retreat by me, no change whatsoever," on the issue of Taiwan.

For the President of the United States to call a network newscaster in the middle of a broadcast, asking in effect for a correction, is a mark of the influence wielded by the network news anchor — a relatively new phenomenon. After decades of being little more than "personalities" or celebrities, the handful of men and women who present the evening news on the three major commercial networks has now joined the pantheon of individuals who profoundly influence the world in which we live. Uninvited, unelected, and with almost no public debate, they have taken their place beside presidents, congressmen, labor leaders, industrialists, and others who shape public policy and private attitudes.

Of all these influential figures, however, only the anchor is in a position to exert personal control over the nation's primary medium of communications, the evening news. It was Walter Cronkite alone, for instance, who decided to end his broadcast each night with a reminder of how many days the American hostages had been imprisoned in Iran — a decision that helped focus attention on the story even after camera crews and reporters were banned from Iran and despite the Carter administration's best efforts to bury the issue. Cronkite's decision was, in effect, a decision that the hostages — unlike the crew of the U.S.S. *Pueblo,* held captive by the North Koreans in 1968, or the POWs in Vietnam — were so important that the spotlight of national attention should not stray from them, even for a single night. These constant reminders, political scientists have since concluded, underlined the U.S. government's inability to resolve the issue quickly and thus played no small part in the voters' eventual rejection of President Jimmy Carter as an ineffectual chief executive. In the long view of history, the national obsession with a small number of hostages in a remote country may seem incomprehensible, especially since it shifted attention away from developments in Europe, the Soviet Union, and Asia that were to have far more important consequences for this country's vital interests. Yet such is the inevitable potential for distortions in a system that elevates a single individual to a position of such power.

In general, of course, the networks rarely stray far from the broad, general consensus that marks American news coverage. But notable differences emerge in the way the three networks cover a particular story on any given night, more so than is commonly believed. In any news operation, one individual ultimately has the last word on what items to include or exclude, how much emphasis each story should get, or how to treat an especially controversial or sensitive subject. In TV news, traditionally, that person was the executive producer — acting as the representative of management, although in actual practice management seldom intervened in editorial decisions. Increasingly, however, it is the anchors who are running the show.

This ascension of the anchor, both on the world stage and within the networks, has been a gradual, evolutionary process. In the early days of television, the evening newscast was so primitive technically, so lacking in journalistic credibility, that the men who read the news were relatively humble figures. They were popular with the public, somewhat in the manner that game show hosts develop a following.

Then, in the sixties, network anchors began to assume an aura of moral and intellectual authority, a process abetted by the networks in the hope that the anchor's prestige would rub off on the organization as a whole, i.e., boost ratings and advertising revenues. At the same time, anchors began to take charge of their own programs, gaining the upper hand over producers. Unconsciously, perhaps, the networks were beginning to create their own monsters.

Today, the anchors of the evening news have become so powerful that they can cause the careers of correspondents to blossom or fade or they can derail the careers of executives to whom they nominally report. European observers of our "strong anchor" system find it astonishing — and disturbing. Virtually every other country has taken deliberate steps to ensure that the individual who gives the news does not have the last word over its content.

Indeed, there are some potentially grave consequences, first because television news has become one of the basic institutions of American society, and second, because the anchors are not quite what they seem. Outwardly the steady, dispassionate eyes and ears of Everyman, anchors live in a world far different from that of their viewers — or for that matter, from the world of most of those they report about. It is a world of enormous, abrupt wealth, of instant fame that isolates the anchor from the world he is responsible for describing, even as it feeds his sense of being at the vortex of events. In their dealings with the ouside world, for example, men like Dan Rather and Tom Brokaw find that high government officials are as near as the telephone, far more accessible to them than such officials are to ordinary correspondents. For all the intimate lunches and background chats, however, anchors are hopelessly cut off from the close, steady contact and observation of government leaders and their policies that are the indispensable foundation for sound judgments. As a result, day after day, the anchors make decisions about what should be emphasized, played down, or kept off the air entirely, from positions as remote as those of Tibetan monks.

And what of the anchor who turns out to be lacking in personal integrity? What is to stop him, if, in the quest for higher ratings or personal aggrandizement, he sensationalizes the news or ignores dull but vital stories for fear of driving viewers away? The sobering reality is that very little *can* be done; increasingly, the anchor today is answerable to nothing but the dictates of his own conscience.

The past few years have seen a tremendous acceleration in the wealth

and influence that anchors enjoy — a situation resulting from the intensified commercial pressures on network news. The stakes are now so
high, and star-quality journalists in such short supply, that desperate
networks are giving away salaries and editorial prerogatives that could not
have been fantasized a decade ago. But the seeds of the current situation
have been present since the birth of American broadcasting. The triumph
of the anchor is, in fact, the logical outgrowth of a system almost totally
unfettered by any considerations except the need to maximize profits.
This book is an attempt to trace the rise of both the anchor and the evening
news, beginning with the episode that reveals the most about the status of
star newscasters in the eighties.

I
Dan Rather's Dilemma

It's hard to put a value on Dan Rather. If he turns out to be the catalyst that brings viewers to the "World News Tonight," how much he is worth over ten years is incalculable.
— Roone Arledge
President, ABC News

BY THE FALL of 1979, Dan Rather was feeling tired, restless, and frustrated. After three years of careening around the world for "60 Minutes," he was getting fed up with airport terminals and rented beds. Worse, he saw himself, after three decades of unremitting hard labor in broadcasting, being denied the one prize he sought: to be named anchor of the CBS Evening News.

It was ironic that Rather should be feeling insecure about his future, because a heated contest was shortly to develop over his services that would send salaries for network anchors into a new, almost unbelievable stratosphere. It was a battle that would also precipitate a number of changes that were more profound — and troubling — about the way news would be reported in the years to come.

CBS kept Rather, of course, but it was a costly — even damaging — victory. Beyond the huge concessions Rather won, Walter Cronkite, still vigorous at sixty-four and a proven ratings winner, would be forced into semiretirement; and Roger Mudd, the network's most experienced and prestigious political reporter, would angrily defect to another network.

Even before the opening skirmishes in the bidding war, all three networks were eyeing Rather with longing. "He was the biggest blue chip around," says his agent, Richard Leibner. Rather, then forty-eight, was still youthful-looking and handsome, but his black hair was flecked with gray, giving him the look of a battle-scarred matinee idol. He projected what seemed to be the ideal combination for television in the eighties — maturity, authority, and sex appeal.

As a journalist, he had unassailable credentials. He had covered civil rights, Europe, Vietnam, and the White House under two different presidents. During Watergate, he took on Richard Nixon and stood his ground despite enormous pressures. He rounded out his résumé as a reporter on "60 Minutes," interviewing politicians and foreign leaders, exposing fraud and corruption. In the process, he became a celebrity of the first rank.

Yet Rather was by no means the automatic choice for Cronkite's seat, and he knew it. For years, Roger Mudd had been considered the heir apparent. (The phraseology at CBS tended to be royal; people spoke of "the Cronkite succession," as if the anchor chair were a throne. In a way, it was.)

The view that Mudd would get the job had been building for a long time. Since 1972, he had been the regular — almost the only — substitute for Cronkite on the evening news. In the early seventies, Richard Salant, then president of the news division, once remarked that if Walter Cronkite were ever hit by a truck, he guessed his successor would be Roger Mudd. It was the only comment ever uttered publicly on the subject by CBS management.

The selection of a successor was further complicated by Cronkite himself; management could never be sure when he would step down. For years, he had been talking about slowing down, even quitting, especially when the ratings dipped; but each time he would change his mind and bounce back. Certainly, no one had the effrontery to try to pin him down for a definite departure date, not at that stage, anyway.

The question of who would replace Cronkite could not be ignored indefinitely. Audience studies showed that his viewers were aging with him; he did not have as much appeal among younger viewers — the group most prized by advertisers — as he did among people over fifty-five. Still, the prospect of replacing Cronkite had always filled executives with dread. Salant, who presided over CBS News for sixteen years, recalls that he resolutely ducked the problem. "Walter used to come in about every six months and say, 'Dick, I've just got to phase out. I ought to go on three times a week, and you ought to put my successor on two times a week.' And each time I replied, 'Walter, please don't make me make this decision. I've only got three, or two, then finally, one year to go before I retire. Stick my successor with this one.' ''*

It was a decision that would have given anyone pause. The anchor is considered the most important factor in the popularity of a news program, and Cronkite, who had anchored since 1962, had kept CBS News ratings on top for over a decade. If his successor caused the ratings to slip by even a fraction of a point, the financial losses would be serious. On early evening network news, a single rating point — representing about 833,000 TV households — accounts for upwards of $25 million a year in revenue.

Some of the consequences were less tangible. At CBS, the anchor is in many ways the spiritual leader of the news division. Over 1000 people look to him to set the tone, not only for his own broadcast, but for the organization as a whole; in turn, he needs their support to succeed. Cronkite came from the "get it fast, get it first, get it right" school of journalism, and he demanded no less from others. Would the new anchor send out equally strong, consistent signals? Would he set a standard that the employees of the news division would be proud to follow?

CBS — and the public — were fortunate that the two top contenders for the job, Dan Rather and Roger Mudd, were exceptional journalists who had proven themselves many times under fire. They belonged to the same generation of reporters and were exposed to the same standards and practices during their long apprenticeship with CBS. There were differences, of course. Mudd was clearly the better writer of the two. Rather could turn out copy much faster and was less likely to get flustered when working close to deadline. Their priorities as newsmen were different, too. The staff noticed that when Rather sat in for Cronkite on the Evening News, nothing got his adrenaline going like a good scoop. When Cyrus Vance resigned in protest over the aborted mission to rescue the American hostages in Iran, Rather put out the word that he wanted CBS to be the first to identify Vance's replacement. White House correspondent Lesley Stahl quickly obliged by reporting that Senator Edmund Muskie had been chosen to succeed Vance. Both Stahl and Marya McLauglin, who helped track down the story, were rewarded with bottles of champagne from Rather.

Mudd was more apt to be stirred by a finely crafted, well-written piece than he was by beating the opposition. He was also more interested in

*All quotes are taken from interviews with the author, unless otherwise noted.

intellectual substance than Rather. A good illustration of the kind of story that excited Mudd occurred when he was sitting in for Cronkite during the summer of 1978 and President Carter gave his famous speech lamenting the "spiritual malaise" he perceived to be gripping the country. A young producer, Rita Braver, learned that Carter had taken his inspiration for the speech from two books that were current at the time, *Leadership* by James MacGregor Burns and *The Culture of Narcissism* by Christopher Lasch. After finding the relevant passages, Braver passed the information on to Mudd. He was fascinated, and asked Braver to work up a full-fledged report with one of the correspondents. It was not an easy story to do on television, and Lesley Stahl, who began work on the project, kept getting distracted by other assignments. Mudd persisted, however, hounding Braver for days to get the piece done. Finally, in desperation, she turned to correspondent Bruce Morton for help. Together, they produced a highly praised piece that both were proud of, one they realized would never have been done without Mudd's insistence.

There were differences between Mudd and Rather as broadcasters, as well. Mudd was generally considered to be the better reader; his delivery seemed more natural, à la Cronkite. Rather's manner seemed studied, almost theatrical at times, and he came across as slightly grim.

On the other hand, Rather is better at ad libbing. He was originally hired by CBS because of the outstanding job he did as a Houston anchorman covering Hurricane Carla, a killer storm that devastated the Texas coast in 1961. Operating alone from the weather bureau in Galveston, with flood waters rising to the second floor of the building, Rather stayed on camera almost nonstop for three days. When it comes to displaying grace under pressure, in fact, he has few peers in the business, as he demonstrated at the 1968 Democratic convention in Chicago. The moment is usually remembered because Walter Cronkite, in a rare show of emotion, got angry when he saw Rather pushed to the floor by Mayor Richard Daley's overzealous security forces. "I think we've got a bunch of thugs here, Dan, if I may be permitted to say so," Cronkite snapped. But Rather never lost his cool. Picking himself up off the floor, obviously winded from the punch he had taken to the stomach, he replied, smiling, "Mind you, Walter, I'm all right. It's all in a day's work," and proceeded about his business.

Mudd hates to be put in a situation he can't control and does not fly by the seat of his pants as well as Rather. A creature of Washington, Mudd ad libs easily in his own milieu, where he can call on his extensive store of political lore, but he is uncomfortable talking off-the-cuff about matters outside his specialty.

In terms of personality, interests, and attitudes toward the job, all of which affect an anchor's performance, the contrasts between the two are even more striking. Rather is a hard-driving, tireless worker who has put almost everything in his life second to his career. Calculating and strong-willed, he nevertheless displays a need to be loved and admired, as well as a certain insecurity about his family background and education.

Mudd has never cared what anybody thinks. Something of a patrician, he moves comfortably among Washington's political and social elite. He is considerably less driven than Rather, putting home and family ahead of the demands of the job.

The first thing that strikes most people about Rather is the care with which he has cultivated his image, a curious mixture of elegant city slicker and simple country boy. His suits are tailor-made in London by the same house that used to outfit Edward R. Murrow, a man whose career Rather has used as a model for his own. The silk ties and pocket handkerchiefs match. Preoccupied with his looks, he is always immaculately groomed and barbered, often trying out new hair styles.

Somehow though, he never seems to have traveled far from his humble Texas origins. His talk is sprinkled with down-home expressions — "I didn't know whether to bark at the moon or wind my watch." And he frequently reminds listeners that he grew up poor, in the midst of the Depression. His father, Irwin "Rags" Rather, was a ditchdigger on a pipeline in East Texas; his mother was a waitress. The family moved around a lot when Dan was a child, eventually settling in a working-class neighborhood in Houston.

Rather was the oldest of three children and the first member of his family to finish college. Like most who have served as network news anchors, his education was spotty. He worked his way through Sam Houston State College in Huntsville, where he majored in journalism, but he put in more time as a writer and sportscaster at the local radio station than he did on his studies. He also pumped gas and worked on an oil rig.

Called "Driven Dan" by his colleagues, Rather never took time to develop leisure activities, apart from an occasional hunting or fishing trip. He and his wife, Jean, live in an unpretentious six-room cooperative apartment in Manhattan, the only property they owned when he was chosen for the anchor job. On those rare occasions when he isn't working, he and Jean like to go to the theater or spend a quiet evening with close friends.

Although Rather stays well informed on a wide variety of subjects, he is by no stretch of the imagination an intellectual, nor does he pretend to be. Conscious of the gaps in his education, he has tried to catch up by reading books suggested by his wife, whose judgment he values, or by mentors such as Eric Sevareid, for decades the resident intellectual at CBS.

Relaxing among friends, Rather is down-to-earth, warm, and funny. Most of the time, though, his manner is guarded. He seems to monitor his own performance constantly, looking for flaws in his personality, which he goes out of his way to point out to other people — a technique perhaps calculated to win them over or ward off jealousy.

All his life he has been an overachiever, the "I-can-do-it–send-me-in-Coach" type. In college, even though he was told he wasn't big enough, fast enough, or good enough, he was determined to make the football team and win a scholarship. In his autobiography, *The Camera Never Blinks,* Rather tells how the coaches looked at him "with a weary respect. I was like the bastard cat you keep throwing off the end of the dock, and by the time you drive home, he's waiting on the doorstep. But I stuck it out, long after all the others who didn't have scholarships had quit, and one or two more had given theirs back." Rather would go to practice, day after day, taking a fearful physical beating, until one day, the coach finally called a halt and sent him home. Rather was heartbroken. "I can remember walking out of his office and into the rain," he wrote. "Tears streamed down my face. It was one of the few times in my life I can remember crying."

This doggedness and willingness to take punishment have served him well in the television news business, which can be grueling in the extreme. He established a pattern of ferocious working hours in his first full-time broadcasting job in the midfifties at KTRH, the CBS radio affiliate in Houston. His workday began at 5:00 A.M., and ended officially at 1:00 P.M., but he often stayed on to do the evening news. While at KTRH, he met and married the former Jean Goebel, a petite, vivacious secretary at the station. But so driven was he that many nights he never left the station at all. In the late fifties, he moved on to KHOU, the CBS television station in Houston. There, as news director and anchor of the early and late news, he showed the same willingness to put the job first. He had a rule that whenever an important story broke, he was to be called at home, whatever the hour. The phone often rang before dawn.

The addition of children — a daughter, Robin, and a son, nicknamed Danjack — did little to alter the pattern. When Rather joined CBS in 1962, he was home only forty-one days the first year, thirty-two the second. Once, when he showed up for one of his brief layovers at home, a small playmate asked Danjack who the stranger was. "Oh," the boy replied, "that's Dan Rather."

In the limited time he was at home, Rather was a loving father who did as much with the children as he could, taking Danjack fishing and encouraging his daughter's interest in basketball. But there was so little time that he sometimes felt he didn't know his own children. For a while, his marriage looked shaky. "I made some grievous errors when the children were young," Rather once told a magazine interviewer, "but we're very close now. Mostly thanks to Jean."

The Rathers were luckier than most. Although no precise figures are available, divorce among network correspondents is common. The long hours, the weeks and months away from home, the opportunity for sexual encounters on the road, the frequent uprooting of the family are devastating to all but the strongest marriages.

Rather was the ultimate good soldier, doing whatever the company asked, going wherever he was told, no matter what the personal inconvenience. In 1964, for example, less than a year after moving from Dallas to Washington to cover the White House, he was asked to go to London. He was reluctant to move his family again so soon, especially after he learned management's real reason for wanting to send him to London was to free up his spot at the White House for Harry Reasoner. Yet he swallowed his pride and went. Back at the White House ten years later, he had to swallow hard again, For the second time, he was taken off the beat under suspicious circumstances. As long as Richard Nixon was in office, CBS had resisted administration pressure to reassign him, but only days after Gerald Ford was sworn in, Rather was ordered to return to New York. For a while, he considered quitting; he had been offered the anchor slot at the ABC station in New York, which would have made him rich. But money never meant as much to Rather as rising to the top at CBS; he reported to headquarters, accepting the position of chief correspondent of the documentary series "CBS Reports."

Wherever he was, Rather seldom had to be prodded to take a reporting assignment — and the more dangerous, the better. The riskier the circumstances, he figured, the better the story, and the more exposure he would get. He *begged* the company to send him to Vietnam, an assignment that was hazardous but clearly enhanced his career.

On or off the job, Rather is something of an eager beaver. He finds it almost impossible to say no to anyone and is constantly overextending himself, accepting engagements that he later has to break. Polite to a fault, he punctuates his conversations with ''ma'am'' and ''sir,'' even thanking people for recognizing him when they stop him on the street.

Professionally, he is generous with his time and information and goes out of his way to help people. Jim Vance, now a highly successful anchorman at WRC, the NBC station in Washington, remembers the time when as a young, inexperienced black reporter, he was sent to the White House to cover a story about Nixon. ''I was so scared, I felt like peeing in my pants,'' says Vance. ''I was standing in a corridor outside the press area, and a lot of people passed by me without paying any attention. Rather walked past, and I guess he noticed that I looked like a frightened puppy, because he came back and said, 'You sure look like you could use a little help.' And he took about five or ten minutes to explain the lay of the land. I'll never forget it.''

Rather is so solicitous of others, in fact, that it attracts notice in the gruff world of television newsrooms, where ''please'' and ''thank you'' have largely been dispensed with. ''When Rather sat in for Cronkite, he tried too hard to be nice, to be liked,'' says Bill Overend, a former writer on Cronkite's staff. ''If he was going to the cafeteria for coffee, for example, he would go around the room taking orders first and come back with a whole tray full. It got a little ridiculous.''

Rather is a firm believer in recognizing others for their work, another departure from the customary lack of civility in a newsroom where people are fighting to make their deadlines. His little notes of appreciation are so frequent the staff refers to them as ''Rathergrams.'' Many of the recipients are grateful; others find his method of operation too studied, even phony.

People who know Rather insist his ''Texas humbles'' and his elaborate manners are sincere. One friend claims the trouble is that Dan has a kind of Boy Scout mentality, always wanting to do the right thing but not necessarily knowing by instinct what the right thing is. Whatever the reason, he goes overboard at times. He sends a plant that is just a little too big and expensive to a functionary in the newsroom who has been given a minor promotion, or he writes a thank-you note to a photographer or a soundman who has actually done a poor job. Right or wrong, Rather is always trying to find favor.

In contrast to Rather — and to most other television correspondents — Roger Mudd is an intellectual, well-read, even erudite. He grew up in a middle-class home in Washington, D.C. His father, Kostka, was an engineer and mapmaker who worked for the government.

Roger Mudd is a tall (six feet two), powerfully built man who weighs well over 200 pounds. In this respect he is not unusual; a surprising number of network anchors have been physically large and imposing. Mudd has a commanding presence, intensified by his massive shoulders and large head. If Rather is movie-star handsome, Mudd has craggy good looks, with thinning brown hair and piercing blue eyes that look on the world with a perpetual air of detached amusement. He is indifferent about his clothes, partial to tennis shorts and baggy corduroys.

Mudd comes across as a man who is comfortable with himself. (Detractors call it arrogance.) Of the two men, colleagues consider Mudd to have a keener intellect and more depth. He got his B.A. at Washington and Lee University in Lexington, Virginia, and a master's degree in American history and literature from the University of North Carolina. His advisers were so impressed with his master's thesis (on the Roosevelt administration, entitled ''The Press and the Brain Trust'') that they wanted him to go on for his doctorate and become a historian.

Everything has always come easily to Mudd. He was a star on the campus in Lexington, where he was known as ''Boomer,'' because of his stentorian voice, which one schoolmate claims could be heard for miles. A mainstay on the varsity crew, he was also a standout in campus theatrical productions.

One of the few times he ever ran into difficulties in his career was the summer he worked as a reporter for the *Richmond News Leader.* ''He was famous for being a literate writer,'' recalls Charles McDowell, a colleague of that era working for the jointly owned *Richmond Times-Dispatch.* ''The only thing he was more of than literate was slow. He got to be a legend as the slowest typist who ever received a professional wage. He had these big hands, you see, and huge fingers, and he always claimed his fingers got stuck in the typewriter.''

At the end of the summer, when his contract was not renewed, Mudd went to work for radio station WRNL in Richmond, quickly becoming a local sensation, mainly by doing things that hadn't been tried in that area before, such as covering local events with a tape recorder and using sound excerpts with his reports. (In the fifties, radio reporters were still a rarity; most radio news consisted of announcers reading items straight from the news wires, known in the trade as "rip and read.") Mudd also attracted attention in town for his performances at the local theater company; his portrayal of Duke Mantee, the Bogart role in *The Petrified Forest,* is said to have been a knockout. About that time, too, he met and married an attractive local girl, Emma Jeanne (E. J.) Spears, who shared his interests in the theater, history, and gracious living.

Today, the Mudds preside over a huge, rambling house with wrap-around porches that sits atop several acres of rolling, green lawn on the outskirts of Washington. The house seems warm and inviting, overflowing with children, hockey sticks, and musical instruments. Anyone who has been to Hickory Hill, Ethel Kennedy's estate in the same Virginia suburb, cannot fail to be impressed by the many similarities. Both houses abound with young people (the Mudds have four, three boys and a girl). Family photos and memorabilia are displayed on every available surface.

Like the Kennedys, the Mudds are great party-givers and gracious hosts. Visitors are called upon to *do* things, like square dance or play touch football with the kids. At one time, the Mudds were close to Ethel Kennedy and were frequent guests at Hickory Hill, a connection that E. J. Mudd is known to have enjoyed. (The connection was shattered after Mudd's famous interview with Senator Edward Kennedy just before he announced his intention to run for President in 1980 — an interview that crippled Kennedy's campaign because of the Massachusetts senator's halting, ill-prepared answers to Mudd's blunt questions about Chappaquiddick, Kennedy's marriage, and his reasons for wanting to be President.)

The closeness of the Mudd family is legendary, with Daniel, Jonathan, Maria, and Matthew occupying center stage. If one of the boys has a football game, Mudd is there, and he has never missed a father-daughter field day. Discipline is strict, though; a youngster who doesn't comb his hair is denied the use of the family car. Friends describe the Mudds as cultural and social conservatives, almost nineteenth century in their devotion to family, tradition, and religion. (They are Catholics.) Form counts, too. E. J., although gregarious and fun-loving, does not tolerate the use of bad language in her presence.

Some of the parents' idealism appears to have rubbed off on the children. When Daniel, their eldest, joined the Marines, he said he was doing it because he wanted to serve his country and because he felt his life had been so privileged. The Saturday before he left, the Mudds gave a black-tie dinner in his honor for close family friends. One guest, Jim Dickenson, a Washington newspaperman and an ex-Marine, says it reminded him of the formal, ante-bellum South. "It was like the scene from *Gone With the Wind,*" he says, "when all the young men rode gallantly and romantically off to join the cavalry. Never have I seen a son sent off with such an elaborate and loving ceremony."

As admirable as most people would find such dedication to family, it was not appreciated at CBS, an organization with almost military notions of duty and obedience. Producers complained that Mudd refused assignments if one of the children had a birthday or a graduation. To Mudd, it was a question of values. "You bet my family comes first," he says. "My view is that you owe them the best years of your life. The time you spend with them ought to be total and intense and clear of all other considerations. While it may not be possible to spend every weekend or every night with them, the time you do spend should be quality time. It should be undivided. You should not be fretting, spending most of the time on worrisome things, juggling phone calls from the office."

He acknowledges that he was often unavailable for assignments. "It was a twenty-four-hour job to avoid being run over. They [the company] want you all the time; they want you for everything and for nothing, by which I mean dumb things of no consequence whatever. They don't want to have to say 'Roger's off.' When they say that, some higher-up is going to say, 'Goddamn it, how come he's off again?' So it was always a rear-guard action to maintain some semblance of a private life."

Mudd also developed a bad reputation with some of his superiors because of his attachment to his Washington beat. Unlike most TV reporters, who regard themselves as generalists, Mudd considers himself a specialist in congressional affairs and politics, and he has never wanted to cover anything else. "The Capitol needs someone concentrating full time on it," he says. "It's an important job, which takes professional commitment."

Apart from the three years he spent in Richmond and a brief stint teaching history and English at a prep school in Georgia, Mudd has spent his entire professional career covering Washington, first as a reporter for the CBS television affiliate, and then, starting in 1961, covering Congress for the network. Always, he seemed marked for higher things, but the assignment that sealed his status as a star was the Civil Rights Act of 1964, which was held up by a filibuster that lasted sixty-seven days. Fred Friendly, then president of CBS News, got the bright idea that Mudd ought to provide saturation coverage for the filibuster, filing radio reports every hour on the hour and appearing on every available TV newscast. Although Mudd told Friendly he thought the whole thing sounded like a stunt, he did an outstanding job. Between late March and the middle of June, he filed a total of 867 reports on the debate. Stunt or no stunt, it was the making of Mudd. The *Washington Post*, for example, said his presence at the scene "personalized and dramatized the halting process of our government to the average viewer in a way no amount of words or secondary reports could have."

Capitol Hill continued to be Mudd's major preoccupation in the years that followed; he rarely left town on assignment except to cover political campaigns. When it came to understanding the inner workings of Congress, Mudd was almost in a class by himself. It was not so much the legislative process that intrigued him, however, as the behavior of the political animals who inhabited the Hill — the rolling oratory of an Everett Dirksen, the eccentricities of a Bobby Byrd.

At various times, the company tried to persuade him to broaden his sphere of interest, but he always refused. His independence was all the more noteworthy at CBS, where most employees seemed willing to throw themselves in front of a moving train if that's what it took to get ahead. "You couldn't assign Mudd to anything he didn't want to do," complains one long-time CBS News executive. "I never got the feeling he would knock himself out. He never worked on breaking stories, for example. He liked being an honorary member of the Senate club."

Mudd was not at all interested in going to Vietnam, a point that is frequently brought up against him at CBS. A year after his marathon coverage of the Civil Rights filibuster, Mudd says that Friendly asked him to do the same thing in Vietnam — that is, file reports morning, noon, and night. Mudd and his family were vacationing in the Loire Valley of France when Friendly tracked them down. "I told Friendly I wouldn't do it," Mudd says, "that it was like flagpole sitting. And that furthermore, you could never match a success with a success. That's the last I ever heard about it." Friendly says he doesn't recall asking Mudd to provide marathon coverage. "I can't imagine why I would have proposed that," he says. "We couldn't satellite pictures out of Vietnam at the time, so it wouldn't have been very practical." Friendly does recall that Mudd told him he wasn't interested in going. In any case, he was one of the few CBS correspondents who never covered the war.

For CBS, the Vietnam story became a sacred mission. CBS was the first news organization, with the exception of the *New York Times*, to sense the importance of Vietnam and to commit major resources to covering the conflict. The CBS team felt it was *their* story; they were beating everybody (except the *Times*), and they were proud of it. Eighteen-month rotation tours were set up, and almost every corre-spondent and producer of any standing in the news division went. As CBS continued to score exclusive after exclusive, great esprit developed within the organization, along with considerable resentment against Mudd for not going. Mudd acknowledges he didn't volunteer. "I'm a political reporter covering Congress," he says, adding, "If going to Vietnam is their badge of a reporter, that kind of macho journalism makes me sick."

Mudd's absorption with Washington, in the view of many at CBS, affected his news judgments when he sat in as anchor. Sanford Socolow, a producer of the CBS Evening News for many years, found Mudd's news judgments "peculiar." "He was death on foreign stories," says Socolow. "You had to fight like hell to get him to use them." Space was another bugaboo. "He had a ferocious, antispace bias," Socolow maintains. "You had to bleed to get a space story on." Socolow and the rest of the staff were incredulous when, watching Mudd on TV one night several months after he joined NBC in 1980, they heard him lead off the newscast with a story about the spaceship *Voyager* approaching Saturn. (Even more astounding to them was the fact that when Mudd came back on camera after a report on the mission, he plugged an NBC special on space to be aired later that night. Mudd had always adamantly refused to do "pro-mos" on the ground they were too commercial and had no place in the body of a news program. One CBS writer watching Mudd on TV that night theorized that he had either been lobotomized or somebody at NBC was standing off camera pointing a gun at his head.)

One of the sharpest contrasts between Rather and Mudd is the way they deal with people. Mudd, who is witty and jovial in social situations, is in-clined to be irascible and cantankerous on the job. His relationship with colleagues and friends at CBS seemed oddly adversarial. "He would challenge a person to defend a statement, even in the middle of the most casual conversation,'' says one old friend. ''It got a little exhausting to have lunch with him more than once a week.''

Abrasive and demanding with the support staff, Mudd was frankly contemptuous toward the higher-ups at CBS. One day, when he was substituting for Cronkite on the Evening News, he was in a rage because he had been summoned to New York on short notice; someone had apparently neglected to tell him in advance that Cronkite would be off. Mudd was sitting in the anchor slot, preparing to go on the air, when Richard Salant walked into the room. ''Dick, come here,'' Mudd called brusquely, and he proceeded to lecture the president of CBS News in a loud, angry voice, as other staff members looked on aghast. He finished up by telling Salant, ''And don't let anything like this happen again.''

''Roger always got away with murder,'' says a producer who knows him well. ''He never did what management asked him; he thought they were all a bunch of pygmies. He would make them charter planes for him so he wouldn't miss one hour of his weekend at the beach with his family. No one wanted to deal with him, he was so difficult.''

Allowances are made for temperament and ego in television news, however, and Mudd was genuinely liked by many people in the news division who admired his wit, intelligence, and integrity. Overall, he was probably even something of the in-house favorite for Cronkite's job. Reporters and producers liked the firm, competent leadership he provided when he sat in for Cronkite, who had become less and less involved in the broadcast. Mudd would screen all reports and question the correspondents closely, offering pertinent comments and suggestions. Many at CBS also felt that Mudd better exemplified the organization's finer traditions, that he would make a better guardian of the honesty and sanctity of the Evening News than Rather, who was seen in some corners as a little too flashy and theatrical.

But the decision of who would replace Cronkite was not up to the rank and file. The job fell to William Leonard, a lame-duck executive who was tapped for the CBS News presidency two years before he was scheduled to retire. How was he to choose between a Rather and a Mudd? According to Leonard, in order to understand what happened, you have to start with the qualifications for the job.

''There are four things you look for in an anchorman,'' he says. ''Three are journalistic. One is not. First, you have got to be able to communicate on television; you have to be able to broadcast, write, and look well.

"Number two is your ability as a journalist behind the screen. What kind of story judgment do you have? How good a reporter are you? How well do you run your staff, if you run it at all? Can you smell a story? Can you recognize something that will *become* a story?

"Number three relates to moments of crisis, when you are on the air in a live situation, when you are under fire — elections, conventions, space shots, and things that come out of nowhere that you can't prepare for, like the shooting of a President. How well can you ad lib intelligently?

"Number four I like to think of as the least important of the four, but it does count: the public and private personality of the man. The anchor is, after all, the most apparent symbol of what CBS News and CBS itself stand for to the public. What is he like, not on the air, but as a guy? As someone who makes speeches, says hello at a party, as a man who will suffer fools with some kind of gladness, whether they are in or outside of the company. Cronkite was marvelous at this, of course."

Mudd's principal drawback, in Leonard's estimation, was his unbending attitude toward the job, but Rather was open to criticism, too, because of his willingness to play the celebrity. For this reason, a number of executives felt that the best solution was to put them together. "I always thought they would make a terrific team," says Leonard. "They're physically, temperamentally, a good contrast. Here you had two superb journalists and broadcasters, one of whom would like to be in Washington, the other who is willing to go anywhere. It would have been ideal."

Beyond the qualifications Leonard mentioned, the two candidates met another, absolutely crucial requirement: They had great credibility within both the print and the broadcast news establishment. TV news has always been viewed as a kind of journalistic stepsister, a blend of showmanship and news that makes it, in the eyes of many, a less legitimate medium of information than newspapers. With a credible anchor "fronting" the evening news, however, the entire product appears more believable, more serious somehow — an important consideration to TV executives who are trying to counter the impression that the networks are greedy, immoral entities who contribute nothing to the public welfare.

But attractive performers who command national respect are rare, so the one thing Bill Leonard hoped to prevent as negotiations got under way in the fall of 1979 was losing either man — a possibility that had begun to worry him. For many years, CBS had enjoyed the reputation as the best place for a television journalist to work — the Cadillac of networks. Those who succeeded in meeting its demanding standards seldom left. CBS was even secure enough in its supremacy to punish the wayward. "Once they left," says Ralph Paskman, who ran the day-to-day operation of CBS News for almost fifteen years, "we never let them back. Loyalty used to mean something."

By the late seventies, though, a number of changes had rocked the lofty serenity of CBS News. Richard Salant, who had led the news division through rough times with great dedication and skill, was forced to retire in 1978, despite his desire to stay on past the age of sixty-five. His loss was bad enough, but it came as a great shock when he went across the street to become vice chairman of NBC in charge of news. A year later, William Small, at one time head of the CBS bureau in Washington and later passed over for the presidency of the news division, followed Salant to NBC to become president of NBC News. Further personnel raids were expected.

ABC News was presenting an even greater challenge. ABC, which had been running last in the news race since the dawn of television, was suddenly coming on strong under the leadership of Roone Arledge.

Arledge, an acknowledged television genius, practically invented the art of covering sports on TV, and he had breathed fire into the troops after becoming president of the news division in 1977. Under his tutelage, the "World News Tonight" was moving up steadily in the ratings until it pulled even with NBC, which had been solidly entrenched in second place for most of the seventies.

Arledge was also successful in luring away first-rate people from other networks. He thought nothing of offering a producer who was making $35,000 a year at CBS an additional $50,000 a year to come to ABC. With on-air personnel (called "talent" in the business), he was even more liberal. When he went after CBS correspondent Charles Osgood, an outstanding writer and radio broadcaster who was earning $120,000 a year, he offered him $500,000, a sum previously reserved for anchors and superstars. In the end, Osgood turned down ABC — he signed a new contract with CBS for more than $400,000 a year — but about twenty-five other top-flight correspondents and producers took the bait, though most were offered considerably less money than Osgood.

Arledge had his lure set for a bigger CBS fish, however: Dan Rather. He first approached Rather about joining ABC in the summer of 1979, but the timing made Rather uneasy. His contract did not expire until September 1981, and he knew it would cause trouble if word got out that he was talking to another network so early in the game. Rather put Arledge off, but he promised to contact him when his contract came up for discussion at CBS.

NBC was interested in Rather, too, but again, it was too early. Rather promised his old boss, Bill Small, that he would talk to him when the time was ripe.

That was where matters stood until late October 1979, when Leonard invited Rather to lunch at the Dorsett Hotel. Leonard and the business affairs people were busy that fall trying to prevent further inroads by other networks on their news staff. People with three-year contracts were being asked to sign for five years; those with five-year terms were being offered ten. In particular, Leonard was anxious to get his two biggest stars, Dan Rather and Roger Mudd, locked up with ironclad, long-term contracts.

As the first round of what quickly became a high-stakes poker game opened, none of the players had a good feel for anybody else's hand. Leonard knew Rather was starting to get restless with the grind at "60 Minutes" and was interested in anchoring, but he did not seem to realize just how hot a property Rather had become. Neither, it developed, did Rather or his agent, Richard Leibner.

When Rather called Leibner with the information that CBS wanted to open negotiations, Leibner went through the roof. "It's much too early for this," he said. "What if we start talking to the other nets and they make us an offer we can't refuse? CBS could keep you off the air for the next two years." On the other hand, Leibner reasoned, this *could* be a good time to find out what the competition had to offer. Leibner, a cagey character with a fast stream of patter, has a stable of big-name news clients, including Mike Wallace, Jessica Savitch, and Ed Bradley. He, like Rather, believed Mudd was the leading candidate at CBS, and he reasoned that if Mudd were tapped for Cronkite's job, Rather would lose considerable bargaining power. Leibner also wanted to find out if there was any "real money" out there this time. He had always lectured Rather about being too easy at contract time, telling him other TV news personalities earned two and three times as much as he did. Leibner had an idea this go-round could be different.

Leonard's first offer was not exactly overwhelming. He proposed a big raise but no change in Rather's status in exchange for signing a long-term contract. He did mention one intriguing possibility, however: a Rather-

Mudd anchor combination once Cronkite stepped down. But Leonard stressed he could make no promises, since no one knew when Cronkite was leaving, and Leonard himself might be retired by that time and not around to guarantee any arrangement.

Rather was pleased but doubtful. It was the first time any executive had ever formally raised the possibility that he might be in contention for Cronkite's job. At the same time, he was dubious about the workability of a dual anchor arrangement with Mudd. The chemistry might be wrong, he told Leonard, and besides, he didn't think Mudd would go for it. Forget about Mudd for a moment, Leonard said. How did he, Rather, feel about it? Rather said he thought he could live with it, provided of course that Mudd agreed.

Rather was almost positive Roger wouldn't buy it. As the leading contender for Cronkite's job, why should he? Rather might have insisted on the right to anchor alone, too, except for his belief that Mudd had the upper hand.

Also, he knew there was personal bitterness between them that would complicate matters. At one time, the two men had been friends, but no longer.

Back in the sixties, when Rather was still a young, hungry recruit, anxious to make the grade at CBS, Mudd was one of the first correspondents to befriend him after he moved to Washington. The two men and their wives saw each other socially, and the Mudds even threw a going-away party for the Rathers when Dan was transferred to London. Yet, as each grew in stature within the organization, seeds of rivalry began to sprout. Inevitably, they were pitted against each other by separate Rather and Mudd camps at the executive level and among the lower echelons. One incident, more than any other, helped destroy the friendship, especially where Mudd was concerned.

The episode was rooted in the famous speech delivered by Spiro Agnew in Des Moines, Iowa, in November 1969, in which he accused the three commercial networks of unfair, biased, and negative coverage. The speech, delivered live on all three networks, had an electrifying effect on an industry that depends on government licenses for its existence. In particular, Agnew bore down on instant analysis, the practice of assembling a panel of newsmen to comment on the President's speech immediately after it is delivered. Just ten days earlier, President Nixon had felt he had been cut up by network commentators after delivering an address defending his policies in Vietnam. It was obvious the administration hoped to muzzle the nay-sayers.

Nothing was done about instant analysis at CBS, however, until 1973, when chairman William Paley ordered that it be stopped. The Paley pronouncement was viewed by many at CBS as a case of bowing to administration pressure, even if the response was belated. In Washington, a group of correspondents, including Rather, Mudd, Bernard Kalb, Daniel Schorr, and George Herman, decided to send a letter to Paley protesting the decision. Mudd was one of the drafters of the letter, which turned out to be a strongly worded document. When Rather saw the letter, he backed off. The wording did not accurately portray how he felt, he told the group; he would write a letter of his own.

Salant, who was still president of the news division, was also unhappy with Paley's instant analysis directive. He let it be known he was delighted to have the support of the correspondents in Washington, signaling that there would be no penalty for signing. At this point, Rather said he was willing to be a part of the group after all. The group, understandably, turned him down.

Mudd, in particular, was furious, accusing Rather of gutlessness. Ultimately, Rather conceded to friends he was ashamed of his behavior, and he even admitted publicly that it was not his finest hour. But Mudd never forgave him. He told friends he considered Rather an amoral, Texas-style Sammy Glick, a hustler who played office politics and would stop at nothing to get ahead. He was also critical of Rather's penchant for publicity, his willingness to pose for *People* and other popular magazines, conduct Mudd judged unbecoming in a journalist.

Rather, meanwhile, began to accumulate reasons of his own for resenting Mudd, who seemed increasingly to be blocking his career advancement. Mudd had been a kind of fair-haired boy from the time he joined CBS in 1961. By 1964, he was picked, with Robert Trout, one of CBS's best-known and most venerable radio correspondents, to replace Walter Cronkite at the Democratic convention, in the wake of the trouncing NBC gave CBS in the ratings at the Republican convention. It was widely believed Bill Paley himself was behind the move, and in those days, before Walter Cronkite had become a national icon, many at CBS thought it was only a matter of time until Mudd replaced him on the Evening News.

Rather too had been singled out early in his career at CBS, but he had too much Texas dust on his shoes — a certain lack of polish and education that disadvantaged him in the class-conscious atmosphere prevailing at CBS since the tweedy days of Edward R. Murrow.

While Rather's charisma and his value as a reporter were apparent from the start, he was not initially viewed as "the anchor type." When Harry Reasoner left CBS for ABC in 1970, creating an anchor opening on Sunday evenings, Rather applied, only to be told by Gordon Manning, a CBS News vice president, that he was a good enough reporter but didn't have the leadership qualities necessary for anchoring. Rather found it especially galling that Manning favored CBS correspondent John Hart for the job. He had been at CBS longer than Hart, he argued, and had more than paid his dues. After some intense lobbying, Rather finally got the job, but not until he had been subjected to a humiliating trial period.

There were other affronts, and it looked to Rather and his partisans as if Mudd were behind them — not so much Mudd himself as his supporters in higher management, notably Manning and Paul Greenberg, who as executive producer on the Cronkite show in the early seventies was harshly critical of Rather's work.

By 1979, however, both Greenberg and Manning were at NBC, along with other former CBS executives who probably leaned toward Mudd. Mudd's hand, in the form of support at the executive level at CBS, held fewer aces than most people supposed.

When Leonard invited Mudd to New York that October to discuss signing a new contract, the meeting did not go smoothly. Leonard offered to double Mudd's salary of $200,000 a year on the spot, in exchange for his signing a new contract. As with Rather, however, he was unable to give Mudd any guarantees about future assignments. All he could do was suggest that eventually Cronkite would be replaced by a Rather-Mudd team. Mudd asked Leonard to put that in writing, but he declined. Mudd pressed him. Was it possible that CBS would ultimately decide on a single anchor? Leonard admitted that it was a possibility. Might that single anchor be Mudd? Leonard said yes. Might it be Rather? Again, Leonard answered yes. Might Cronkite even stay on for a couple of years longer? The answer, again, was yes.

Knowing Walter Cronkite as he did, Mudd found it hard to imagine his bowing out of the picture completely. Mudd asked for some concrete details on any future Cronkite role on the Evening News. Would Cronkite continue to be a dominant presence on the show? Would he contribute reports? ''You want to know what controls other people will have,'' Mudd explained later. ''It could look like Walter was retiring, but in reality, he might not be. Bill couldn't answer my questions. He kept coming back to his 'best guess.' I told him, 'What you're asking me to do is to surrender all freedom to go elsewhere in case you decide on something I can't live with.' From his standpoint, of course, Leonard couldn't double my salary and then allow me to be a free agent. I told him I'd stay with my present contract, that I didn't want to sign any under 'best-guess' arrangement.''

The conversation was disturbing to Mudd. Although he had never been promised anything in writing, he felt he had earned the right to Cronkite's job. It was his first indication the job might not be his. A fiercely proud man, Mudd gave no indication in public that his hand might be weaker than people believed.

The conversation was equally disturbing to Mudd's agent, William Cooper. He urged Mudd to let him find out what the other networks had to offer, but Mudd refused. Having declined to open negotiations with CBS, he felt it would be dishonorable to talk to the other networks. Besides, Mudd found the whole process of being ''hustled,'' as if he were a piece of meat, distasteful.

Rather's feelers were eagerly snapped at. At NBC, he dealt personally with NBC News president Bill Small. Rather might not have been interested in NBC, since it was perceived as an organization on the way down. But the new men in charge of news, Small and Salant, were the people who had protected him during the dark days of Watergate, when the White House wanted him off the beat. Small was eager to win Rather to NBC, but he couldn't propose anything definite at that time. Just as CBS had a ''Cronkite problem,'' NBC had a Chancellor problem. John Chancellor, a highly respected veteran who had been anchoring the NBC Nightly News for almost ten years, could not be ousted from his job except by mutual agreement. It was a promise made to Chancellor by previous managements, and one that Small felt duty-bound to honor. Small did tell Rather he thought things could be worked out, although it might take a little time.

At ABC, there was no such hesitation. Arledge jumped at the first signal from Leibner. And ABC had a New York slot that was conveniently empty.

When Arledge first started to revamp the ABC Evening News (re-named the ''World News Tonight''), his first priority was to break up the unfortunate team of Barbara Walters and Harry Reasoner. Arledge used to say that watching them on TV was like showing up at someone's house for dinner just after the hosts had had a horrible domestic quarrel. But who could replace them? Arledge tried to lure such respected names as Robert MacNeil and Bill Moyers into the ABC fold, but no agreement was ever reached.

When he finally unveiled his team, it was highly unconventional. Instead of anchors, there were "desks." Frank Reynolds, a well-respected if uncharismatic newsman who had anchored at ABC in the late sixties, was resurrected to report from a "National Desk" in Washington. Peter Jennings, another ABC anchor retread from the sixties, would handle the foreign news from a "desk" in London. And Max Robinson, one of the top black local anchors in the country, was hired away from WDVM in Washington to report from a "Domestic desk" in Chicago.

The solution had a number of advantages, including the fact that it helped disguise the absence of a dominant figure on the broadcast, until then regarded as essential, and it left the New York seat dark. "If we had put anyone in New York," Arledge points out, "he would have been chewed alive by the press before he ever got started." The situation also gave Arledge more flexibility. None of the existing anchors had to be pushed out if and when Arledge acquired a major presence for the broadcast. The new man (there were no women in the running) would simply be added to the existing cast.

It was hoped, though, that the new anchor would not spend that much time in New York. Arledge wanted a *field* anchor, someone who would be out covering major stories, cuing the audience by his presence on the scene that the story was important — lending excitement and drama to the broadcast. Rather, with his years of experience in the field, his image as a dashing correspondent, and his appetite for hard work, was tailor-made for the job.

Arledge lost no time in getting back to Leibner with an offer that was calculated to overwhelm — a kind of pre-emptive strike. Rather would not only be the chief correspondent and principal presence on the "World News Tonight," but he could also anchor "20/20" and contribute as many pieces as he had time to do. He would anchor documentaries, special programs, and all major live events, such as elections, conventions, and inaugurations. Finally, if he chose, Rather could anchor the new late-night news program ABC was planning. (It later became

"Nightline.") As Arledge told Rather, he wanted him to become the *logo* of ABC News, the physical personification of the entire organization.

It was more than any one human being could possibly handle, but there it was, on the table. Arledge and his chief of staff, David Burke, who was heavily involved in the negotiations throughout, agreed to put it all in writing. The money, too, was fantastic, unbelievable: almost $2 million *a year.* Never before had a news division offered money of this kind. The entertainment division of ABC had to ante up half of Barbara Walters's million-dollar salary when she was hired in 1976. Cronkite himself was earning only about $650,000 a year at that time.

But money was not the isue; Roone Arledge was. Rather had never even met Arledge before, and much of what he had read about him in the press was unfavorable.

The television news fraternity had been alarmed by the appointment of a sports impresario as president of a news division, a flamboyant personality who wore open shirts and gold chains around his neck. To the critics, it was only a matter of time before Arledge put dancing girls and circus bears on the ABC Evening News. Even though Arledge's credibility improved as ABC moved up in the ratings, with no appreciable decline in standards, Rather still wondered if he could live with him and his news philosophy.

Rather was prepared to be unimpressed. Instead, he was nearly bowled over by Arledge's charm and intelligence. From the first meeting, the two men found themselves on the same wavelength. Arledge had taken pains to study Rather carefully before he laid out his offer, and he realized he was dealing with a man who wanted to be taken seriously. Therefore, he offered him something that went beyond money and exposure: Rather could help run the news division.

This aspect of the offer sounded unprecedented. Even Walter Cronkite, who held the coveted title of managing editor of his broadcast, was always regarded as "talent" by CBS management, which is another way of saying "performer." When CBS News executives sat down to plan their coverage of major events, Cronkite was not asked to take part. He had veto power in matters that involved him personally, but he was not consulted in the day-to-day running of the news division or on broader policy questions.

Now Arledge was offering Rather a say in who was hired and fired at ABC, which reporters would be assigned to stories, what kinds of stories were covered, the whole philosophy of coverage at ABC News. (Arledge was opening a Pandora's box here; soon other top network news stars would be demanding similar prerogatives.) It was apparent the offer was not mere lip service, either; Rather would be given an office on the fourth floor of ABC's New York headquarters, where the five or six key executives of the news division are located.

Rather was startled to realize how much homework Arledge and Burke had done. When they offered the fourth floor office, for example, they quoted an observation from *The Palace Guard* — Rather's book (co-authored with Gary Paul Gates) on the White House during Watergate — about power being in direct proportion to proximity. They had also learned that he talked of wanting to write a book of standards and practices for television journalists, so they asked him to write such a book for ABC News.

In the ensuing months, Rather met with Arledge and Burke over a dozen times, sometimes separately, sometimes together. It was all handled quietly, though, away from the prying eyes of the press. Sometimes Burke would pick Rather up on a street corner and tell the driver to head up the West Side of Manhattan in search of a quiet place where they could talk. Once, they stopped at a Chinese take-out place and sat down in a rear booth, ordering only a cup of coffee. The waiter told them if they didn't order any food, they couldn't sit in a booth. To avoid the possibility of being seen sitting at the front counter, however, they left. The only other restaurant in the vicinity was another Chinese take-out joint, also with booths in the back, so this time, they discussed the multimillion-dollar deal over egg rolls and coffee. At other times, they met late at night in Arledge's Park Avenue apartment or in rented hotel rooms.

Gradually, Arledge and Burke laid out a convincing case for Rather's moving to ABC. It was the most dynamic operation, they contended, the best run, with the most up-to-date equipment, the most energetic staff — and it had momentum. ABC was more flexible, too, more willing to experiment. There were no ghosts from the past, clanging their chains, forever admonishing, "You can't do this . . . you can't do that." Rather could be his own man at ABC, they argued. People wouldn't expect him to be "Walter Cronkite Junior," forever comparing him unfavorably to the great man. At ABC, if the ratings went up *he* would get the credit. At CBS, if the ratings held, people could claim he owed it all to Cronkite's loyal audience.

Leibner thought the offer was fantastic. "Take it," he urged, "before they change their minds." Soon Rather got swept up in the fabulous vision that Arledge and Burke were conjuring up. He was inclined to accept.

One person who remained slightly dubious was Rather's wife, Jean. She reminded him of the many years he had put in with CBS News, how it stood for quality and tradition — the classiest place to work. She thought it would be splendid for Dan to team up with Roger and urged him not to dismiss that option. (The rivalry between Rather and Mudd did not extend to their families. Jean had always admired E. J., and Robin Rather even dated Daniel Mudd for a while.) But Rather did not believe CBS could begin to match the ABC offer. He thought the best he could hope for was a nice raise, long-term security, and a lecture about the great and glorious traditons of Edward R. Murrow. "Anytime they want to get their hand on your leg," Rather says, "they bring up Murrow."

When Leibner outlined the ABC offer to Bill Leonard, the CBS executive was dumbfounded. He had never heard anything like it. Still, he urged Leibner not to do anything hasty, nor to assume CBS would fail to match the offer. Leonard then did what any prudent executive would have done; he called in his superiors at the corporate level.

Just as the news division had worried for years about Cronkite's replacement, so had a succession of corporate presidents and executives. A number of them, including Arthur Taylor, president of CBS, Inc., from 1972 to 1976, thoroughly disliked Mudd. "It's hard to like someone who doesn't like you," Taylor explains. "One got the feeling from Roger that he wasn't paid enough money to truck with corporate types. He sent very strong signals that he didn't like *anyone,* which of course was his right. But many of us felt that this difficult nature of his would get transmitted to the screen."

Mudd had given his superiors at the corporate level other reasons to dislike him, including his habit of criticizing television news. In a 1970 speech at his alma mater, Washington and Lee, Mudd found fault with TV news for showing a "dangerous and increasing concentration on action which is violent and bloody" in preference to a thoughtful examination of the issues. The television industry at that time was still hunkering down from the attacks by Spiro Agnew and the Nixon administration, which made the speech doubly unwelcome at Black Rock, as CBS corporate headquarters was called.

In other quarters, Mudd's remarks made him a hero. His willingness to turn the same hard eye on television news that he did on politicians and their foibles found favor with TV's many critics, including members of the print press. His standing with Washington's most influential newspapermen — the political reporters and columnists — was enormous. People like David Broder of the *Washington Post,* Curtis Wilkie of the *Boston Globe,* and syndicated columnists Jack Germond and Jules Witcover admired Mudd for getting down in the trenches with them and disdaining the role of celebrity. They especially appreciated the fact that he shared their uneasiness about television's intrusion into the political process.

Mudd did not seem like a man who was entirely comfortable in broadcasting. He was unyielding in his refusal to touch anything that smacked even faintly of commercialism. When he substituted for Cronkite on radio, for example, he would not read the opening "billboard" at the top of the program: "This is Roger Mudd, sitting in for Walter Cronkite, and this broadcast is brought to you by the Prudential Life Insurance Company" — or whoever was sponsoring the commentary at the time. He considered the line "plugola," so an announcer had to be brought in to read it.

He also detested affiliates' meetings and other gatherings where anchormen and prominent correspondents are expected to press the flesh. "What happens at these conventions is you try to please the station owners and all that. So you practically come down the runway in a sequined gown. And that's difficult, you know, because you like to regard yourself as a journalist, not a hoofer," he says. Characteristically, Mudd was the only CBS correspondent who refused to attend the Hollywood gala the company staged for its fiftieth anniversary — an occasion hosted by Walter Cronkite and Mary Tyler Moore. (The only other correspondent who didn't attend was Marvin Kalb, but that was because he was suffering from back trouble.)

Mudd's uncompromising principles made him seem almost an aberration in an age of sliding moral scales and shifting values. At the corporate level, his behavior was considered petty and incomprehensible. In contrast, Rather had no problems wearing the company colors in public, and he willingly mixed with the CBS executives, some of whom are delighted themselves at the opportunity to hobnob with big-time news personalities.

Arthur Taylor maintains that Rather, not Mudd, was the favorite for Cronkite's job — a view Salant vigorously disputes. "Arthur Taylor doesn't know shit about that. He learned after six months to leave me alone and stay out of my business.'' In Salant's view, Mudd's unbending nature and disdain for the commercial aspects of TV news were assets. "No, he wouldn't push the product,'' Salant says. "That's why I wanted him for the anchor job.''

But Mudd was not the only one whose hand had hidden weaknesses. Rather also had his problems on the corporate side, stemming from his hard-edged reporting during Watergate. His reputation as a Nixon-baiter made him too controversial to suit a number of people in the corporate sphere. (Even in the news division some people thought Rather's crusading aura was a self-serving ploy to boost his own career, a bid to inherit the mantle of Edward R. Murrow.)

It wasn't so much *what* Rather reported from the White House as *how* he reported it. In the late sixties and early seventies, it was still unusual for television correspondents to challenge those in authority, especially presidents. (It was all right to knock Congress; David Brinkley had been doing that for years.) But Rather used to put a little edge on his White House reports that gave them a critical tone. His style — the toughly worded, interpretative summaries, delivered with his peculiar intensity — made him a standout during the Nixon years. He made life difficult for his competitors from the other networks, like Herbert Kaplow and Richard Valeriani — less charismatic men who had graduated from a school of journalism that favored facts over personal interpretation. Indeed, it can be argued that Rather's performance at the White House ushered in a whole new style in TV reporting. "Whatever other qualities Rather had,'' says Herbert Kaplow, who covered the beat for NBC from 1969 to 1972, "he was a good-looking guy. It had an impact on those of us who aren't all that good looking. If I were looking for a job at the networks today, I wouldn't be hired.''

Richard Valeriani, who replaced Kaplow at the White House, was also judged wanting by some of his superiors when compared with Rather. Once, Valeriani was having lunch with Dick Fisher, an NBC Nightly News producer. The lunch was a rather long, liquid affair, and toward the end of it, Fisher leaned over to Valeriani and said, "You ought to do a little more of what Rather does, shake them up more at the White House.'' Valeriani protested, "Look, he's wrong fifty percent of the time.'' "I don't care,'' Fisher replied, "twenty-four hours later, who's going to remember he was wrong?'' Fortunately, Fisher's philosophy was not shared by many at NBC, but Valeriani *was* taken off the beat not long afterward and replaced by somebody undeniably more telegenic: Tom Brokaw. And network correspondents hired in the seventies were indisputably better-looking than their predecessors.

Even before Watergate became a national obsession, Rather's performance enraged Nixon and his aides. When Nixon tried to convince the nation he was winding down the war in Vietnam while actually escalating it, Rather hammered home the discrepancy, prompting John Ehrlichman and Bob Haldeman to determine that Rather had to go. Once, at a breakfast meeting with Salant in New York, Ehrlichman suggested that Rather be reassigned, perhaps to a newly created bureau in Texas, or maybe even given a year off. (It was a stupid thing to do; Salant got so angry he promptly leaked details of the meeting to the press.)

Things got considerably hotter for Rather — and CBS — as the Watergate scandal unfolded. The affiliates, too, found his reporting offensive. Many of the affiliated station owners were small businessmen who normally voted Republican and were inclined to give Nixon a break. To them, Rather looked like a left-wing smart aleck. The last straw, for many, occurred at a meeting of the National Association of Broadcasters in Houston in March 1974. Nixon journeyed to the meeting and decided to hold a press conference there, using the station managers as a sympathetic backdrop. When Rather stood up to ask a question, some members of the audience booed; others applauded. Nixon, whether in a clumsy attempt to be funny or to embarrass Rather, asked him if he were running for something. "No, sir, Mr. President," Rather shot back. "Are you?" The retort was widely interpreted as arrogant and combative; CBS was deluged with mail from the affiliates demanding that Rather be fired.

There is evidence the Nixon forces were orchestrating the reaction, at least in part. CBS correspondent Fred Graham recalls an incident a day or two after the Houston exchange, when he was interviewing George Bush, then chairman of the Republican Party. After the interview, Bush casually mentioned to Graham that he heard the affiliates were kicking up a storm over Rather's performance in Houston. Later that day, Graham called Rather to tell him about it, taking Rather by surprise. Rather called Salant immediately. Salant confirmed that, indeed, a lot of mail was coming in from the affiliates, but that he had been trying to protect Rather from the knowledge. The striking fact about the story is that Bush knew more about the mail than Rather did.

When Nixon resigned a few months later and Rather was reassigned, he was chagrined to hear that a number of affiliate people were bragging about how they had torpedoed Rather. Whether it was true or not, his fortunes at the corporate level suffered. No matter that his image as a rough, tough, no-holds-barred reporter was wildly at variance with the soft-spoken, courteous persona Rather presents off the air. From the company's point of view, the appearance of fairness and decency were as important as the substance of it. His left-of-center image was even more damaging. A corporation in the business of appealing to a mass audience is not eager to have its on-air personnel identified with any particular ideology. This would be doubly true for the anchor, the standard-bearer for the entire organization. For a number of years after Watergate, Rather was on shaky ground at CBS.

Mike Wallace remembers that when Rather first joined "60 Minutes," the mail indicated that viewers found him too pugnacious, too controversial. "Over the years, though," Wallace says, "Dan did a sufficient number of noncontroversial pieces, in front of a large enough audience, with enough regularity, so that that kind of reaction to him began to diminish sharply." Wallace didn't say so, but the mail also showed that women, in particular, found Rather irresistible. Corporate executives read the mail, too. (Mail is read avidly at the networks; it's one of the cheapest marketing survey devices available.) They were aware that Rather's image was softening. Scientific market surveys also showed that Rather was immensely popular — the most popular TV news personality after Cronkite.

Even so, when Leonard sat down with Gene Jankowski, the president of the CBS Broadcast Group, and the other corporate members of the selection committee to figure out how they were going to keep Rather, they were not quite willing to abandon their hope of a Rather-Mudd dual anchor team. It sounded too perfect. Nor were they willing to antagonize Cronkite by pressing him for a commitment to step down. Leonard was forced to stall for time.

He continued to meet with Rather — Rather usually handled his own negotiations on matters of job description, while Leibner discussed money and benefits — and tried to persuade him that CBS would do everything in its power to keep him, that in the end he would be happy with the CBS offer. Leibner tended to dismiss such talk. He figured CBS would never come close to matching ABC's offer. Rather was doubtful, too, but what puzzled him even more was the absence of any mention of

Mudd in his sessions with Leonard. Every time he brought Mudd up, Leonard changed the subject. To Rather, it meant they were still trying to hammer out a dual anchor arrangement.

In fact, Leonard had put the Mudd issue on hold. It seemed the prudent course. If he pressed Roger at this stage about co-anchoring with Dan, he risked losing both of them.

About this time, NBC came in with a firmer offer to Rather, albeit one lacking in specifics. Bill Small assured Rather that the "Chancellor problem" could be solved and that NBC would make a competitive bid. But Leibner was unconvinced. He felt NBC had a history of slow decision-making and would be scared off by the big money on the table. In effect, though, NBC never weighed heavily in Rather's decision. He knew it would take several years before the news division came out of its doldrums; it was not the best place for an anchor to shine.

By now, negotiations had been dragging on for almost two months, and Arledge and Burke were getting nervous. What's the holdup, they wanted to know. Leibner was getting nervous, too. He explained that Dan was still leaning toward their offer, but that it was a hard decision for him to make. He had institutional loyalties to consider. "The hell with institutional loyalties," Burke told Leibner. The agent begged Arledge and Burke to be patient; he was sure Rather would come around.

At times, Rather did seem on the verge of accepting. He and Arledge would get to brainstorming, conjuring up dazzling visions of all the things they could accomplish together. "Dan got so turned on when we were talking that he started using 'we,' " Arledge recalls. " 'We could do this,' or 'We could do that.' "

Then, an incident occurred that tipped the scales even more in favor of ABC. The week after Christmas, Mudd was sitting in for Cronkite in New York, and Jean Rather urged Dan to see Roger personally and attempt to work things out. Rather invited Mudd to lunch, but Mudd put him off. Rather then walked across the street from his office at "60 Minutes" to the Evening News area to repeat the invitation in person, but Mudd turned him down coldly, in full view of several people. Furious, Rather told a friend that he almost decided on the spot to go to ABC and "beat Roger's brains out."

About that time, Arledge weighed in with a second offer. This time, according to friends in whom Rather confided, Arledge was prepared to offer a monetary package that would eventually reach $3 million a year. In addition, he tried to address Rather's concern that ABC lacked the depth of talent of CBS. When Iran seized the American hostages, CBS could send any of a dozen competent foreign correspondents to the scene. ABC's list would be considerably shorter. The same was true for producers. Arledge told Rather to list the twenty best producers in the business, and ABC would hire them. How could he guarantee something like that, Rather wanted to know. Arledge offered to put it in writing, and if all twenty weren't hired within two years, Rather would be free to leave. The only point that was not negotiable, as far as Arledge was concerned, was the multiple anchor format. Rather would be *the* star of the news division, but he would have to share the honors on the ABC Evening News.

In the meantime, CBS was putting *its* package together. By January, the committee included Chairman Paley, who interrupted his vacation in Europe to fly home because of the gravity of the situation. The first order of business was to acknowledge that a Rather-Mudd team was out of the question — that Rather would have to be offered the right to anchor alone if there were any hope of keeping him. Of the two, Rather was clearly more valuable as a ratings draw; ''60 Minutes'' had established that.

When ''60 Minutes'' made its debut in prime time in 1968, the critics loved it, but the public was unexcited. At the end of the first season, it wound up fifty-first out of sixty-five shows in the national Nielsens. The ratings improved gradually, but the season Rather joined, buttressing the formidable team of Mike Wallace and Morley Safer, ''60 Minutes'' got a 30 percent share of the audience — unheard of for a regularly scheduled news program opposite non-news fare. The next season, ''60 Minutes'' did so well, winding up the season with a 36 percent share, that it put CBS News in the black for the first time in history. And the audiences continued to grow, until ''60 Minutes'' regularly made the top ten shows of the week, by 1982 commanding the highest advertising rate on primetime TV: $175,000 for a thirty-second ad.

Any way you looked at it, Dan Rather sold. His first book, *The Palace Guard,* did so well, it enabled the publisher, Harper and Row, to turn a profit in an otherwise bad year. *The Camera Never Blinks,* written with Mickey Herskowitz, was also a best-seller. Mudd was good, but he wasn't necessarily money in the bank.

CBS's other major consideration was ABC. To the CBS executives, it looked as if ABC News was only ''one good anchor'' away from surging to the front of the pack; the addition of Rather just might accomplish that. And as they well realized, leadership in news, once lost, is not easily regained. So, while Leonard and the others nourished a faint hope they might yet keep Mudd at CBS, Mudd was dropped from the anchor equation.

The next hurdle was Cronkite. Leonard was handed the unpleasant job of telling him, in essence, "Listen, we don't want to push you in any way, but we need to know what your intentions are so that we can make Dan a firm offer." Cronkite was mindful of the advantages of stepping down as undefeated champ, and Leonard was making the prospect extremely attractive. In addition to making him a member of the CBS Board of Directors, Leonard offered a seven-year contract calling for an annual salary of $1 million for what was, essentially, part-time work, plus office space, secretaries, and researchers. He could continue to play a role in special events coverage, documentaries, and the Evening News and could take on special assignments. In addition, he could continue to anchor "Universe," a prime-time science series that was dear to his heart. The pension aspect was especially interesting. Legally, Cronkite could not be forced to retire at sixty-five, though under company regulations, he could not collect his pension until he did. Leonard proposed making him a "Special Correspondent," which meant that technically, he would no longer be part of the staff, enabling him to draw a salary *and* collect his pension.

By going off staff, he could also skirt the conflict-of-interest restrictions that apply to employees of CBS News, giving him a freer rein to participate in outside business ventures or to sit on the boards of private corporations, such as Pan American World Airways. (The Pan Am connection later prevented him from taking part in space coverage, so he gave it up.)

To Betsy, Cronkite's wife, who shares the important decisions in his life, it sounded like a great offer. Afraid that he was ruining his health, she had been urging him to slow down for years; she thought it was the ideal time for him to bow out. Cronkite was also swayed somewhat by his preference for Rather over Mudd. About eighteen months earlier, he had even signaled Rather, telling him he was getting tired and thinking about easing up — he could never seem to bring himself to retire flat out. He urged Rather to pursue the matter with Leonard.

Cronkite did not have much use for Mudd, a man so obviously champing at the bit to replace him. They disagreed on many matters, too, including, at times, ethical standards. Once Cronkite accepted a free trip from Pan Am and made the mistake of giving the airline a brief plug in one of his radio commentaries. The whole business was quite unlike Cronkite, who was fanatical about his reputation for honesty and integrity, but Mudd was enraged. He thought it was plugola of the worst kind and called New York to complain. It got back to Cronkite, of course, and did little to cement their fragile relationship.

Cronkite understood what was at stake for CBS if the network lost Dan Rather. Ever the good company man, he agreed to fix a definite date for his departure. It would be moved up from the date he had tentatively set, November 1981, to March.

For CBS, there was still the matter of just how much money and how many perks to offer Rather. Paley and the others wanted to keep him, but at what price? Suppose they met the ABC offer? How would it affect future contract negotiations with other correspondents? They feared they were setting a bad precedent, and they worried about the salary stratosphere they were about to enter. "These salaries very quickly become a distortion of the news business," laments Leonard. "It's very difficult to make a case for the anchor being a simple journalist when he earns five times as much as the President of the United States. This is nothing against Dan Rather or Barbara Walters or Bill Kurtis, but it does not further the sincere effort of those who believe that broadcast journalism is as legitimate and serious an arm of journalism as the print media — that it is not show business." The CBS executives went back and forth on the matter and finally decided to bite the bullet. As Paley remarked to Leonard, "It's been my experience in life that the cheapest things turn out to be the most expensive, and the most expensive things turn out to be the cheapest."

When Leibner called on Leonard and Jankowski early in January to inform them of the latest ABC offer, he thought it would be a pro forma visit, almost a courtesy call. In his mind, there was no way they could come close to matching the ABC deal, either in money or position. He was bringing them a message that, in essence, his client had no choice but to accept the ABC offer. As the CBS executives began outlining *their* offer, Leibner was flabbergasted. They were proposing a firm date for Rather to take over the Evening News as sole anchor, plus the number one spot in special events, documentaries, and various other programs. The money, although not quite as much as ABC had offered, was tremendous: According to industry sources, CBS agreed to pay him $20 million, stretched over ten years, plus various deferred tax benefits that brought the value of the pact closer to $25 million.

Now it was Leibner's turn to blanch. Never dreaming that CBS would go this far, he had encouraged the Arledge courtship, stringing him along for almost two months. Besides, Leibner genuinely believed ABC was the best place for his client. Now, if Rather decided to stay with CBS, Arledge would have every right to be furious; no executive likes to go that far out on a limb only to be rejected. No matter how the Rather affair came out, Leibner had dozens of other clients and he still had to live with Arledge.

Immediately after the meeting, Leibner called Rather and said, "We've got problems." He realized the CBS offer would throw Rather into an even greater agony of indecision. But Rather is not the type to agonize alone; as is his custom when faced with a big decision, he asked a number of his friends for advice. Before long, word of his dilemma began to spread. Within CBS, it was the subject of much excited speculation.

Only one person appeared blissfully unaware of the whole situation: Roger Mudd. He seemed so confident of his position, in fact, that he even declined to substitute for Cronkite one week at Christmas and went skiing instead. But rumors of the deal reached him eventually. One day when he was in New York, he went to lunch with Sandy Socolow, the Evening News producer. Socolow broached the subject saying, "You know, I'm proud of my staff. Nobody has said one word to you about all this Rather stuff." Mudd says he was taken by surprise, embarrassed not to know what Socolow was talking about. Socolow, too, remembers that Roger seemed surprised. "I think he was shook up, although he took it calmly." Socolow told Mudd he wasn't privy to any inside information, but the rumors were flying so furiously that he felt there must be something to them. From what he heard, Socolow told Mudd, it appeared Rather would be named Cronkite's successor. Mudd questioned him closely, grilled him, really, and although the conversation remained cordial, Socolow says he came away drained.

The curious thing is that Mudd did not pursue this information with the higher-ups at CBS. Nor did he pass it along to his agent, Bill Cooper, whom he subsequently dismissed on grounds Cooper had done such a poor job of keeping him informed. It appears Mudd did not want to know, at least not by way of the grapevine. Because of his pride, he evidently felt the company had an obligation to apprise him *officially* on the course of its negotiations with Rather.

Leonard has a different view. "Everybody in the business knew what was going on," he maintains. "He made a choice [not to negotiate] that he could have reversed at any time. He and his agent could have said, 'Hey, wait a minute. Are we getting tapped out of the game, or what?' "

People who know Mudd feel that it would have been impossible for him to do that. He considered the whole business of negotiations tawdry in the first place. As Mudd later testified in a proceeding instituted against him by his agent, "They [CBS] knew my reputation and knew what I stood for and knew what my principles were and knew my phone number. I expected them to make the next move."

Mudd acknowledges that it is management's right to pick whoever they wanted for the anchor spot. He says, in fact, that he felt ambivalent about anchoring itself. "It was not a job I hungered for," he maintains, "but it is a powerful position — one in which you can do a lot of good. You can do a lot of bad, too. A major down-side is you become a captive of the bureaucracy, sealed up in an office in New York, a city not well-connected with the rest of the country. You would have to rely on the judgments of an awful lot of people whose judgments might be once or twice removed." People around CBS tend to dismiss such talk. ("Bullshit" is the usual response.) Mudd's ambivalence may have been genuine, they concede, but the real problem was his unwillingness to relocate to New York. Mudd did not want to uproot his children while they were still in school, and E. J., a strong-willed woman, had made it plain to friends she had no intention of moving, nor did she want Roger to go. Mudd says he simply decided to let events take their course. "I chose not to think about it," he says. "I figured I would deal with the problem of moving to New York when the time came, rather than have it be a constant subject of conversation and concern — would we have to sell the house, move the kids, worry about schools and all that. Instead, I decided to let events unfold."

According to friends, Mudd really hoped to persuade CBS to move the Evening News staff to Washington if he became the anchor. But the network is certain to have resisted the idea fiercely on grounds that it was too expensive and would cause too much inconvenience for the entire organization. Mudd must have known he would not necessarily win this battle, but one thing is certain: He felt he deserved to be asked to succeed Cronkite. "I felt I had earned it," he says. So he sat back and waited. His pride would allow him to do nothing else.

In the meantime, CBS began to pull out all the stops to keep Rather. Stroking sessions with Jankowski, John Backe, the corporate president, and Paley himself were arranged. ("You get to see them if you burn down their building or walk into the chairman's office and shoot him," Rather says. "But not otherwise.") One by one, old friends and mentors in the news division came to him and begged him not to desert. Ernie Leiser, a long-time CBS executive and the man who first spotted Rather in Dallas and brought him to CBS, sounded a common theme, stressing that CBS was still the best environment for a TV journalist and had the best chance of staying that way. Cronkite urged him to stay; so did Rather's old friend Eric Sevareid.

Now Leibner was in a position to extract some additional concessions from CBS, including the demand that Rather be given the title of ''Managing Editor'' of the CBS Evening News as soon as he took over, instead of waiting to ''earn'' it, as Leonard wanted him to do. CBS was not prepared to go as far in offering Rather as many management prerogatives as ABC, but they finally agreed to put language into the contract guaranteeing him the right of consultation on all matters pertaining to his broadcasts.

Meanwhile, Rather began to ponder the ramifications of the ABC offer. How could he be part of management, he wondered, if he was anchoring from Mozambique or Poland? He began to envision himself in an airplane, forever circling. Lately, he was feeling exhausted with the pace of ''60 Minutes'' — even Dan Rather has his physical limits — and the ABC job might prove even more grueling. It took him almost two months to make up his mind. After a sleepless night, he got up on February 14, realizing he could not bring himself to leave CBS. How could he, when the torch passed from Murrow to Cronkite was about to be passed to him?

Leibner, who was widely credited with orchestrating the whole scenario (as if anyone could have figured out a script with so many twists and turns in advance), admits he underestimated Rather's attachment to CBS and its traditions. ''I never understood to the very end,'' he says, ''how important it was for Dan to sit in the most honored chair in journalism. For him to be good enough to follow Cronkite was an incredible thing.''

ABC's David Burke put it this way: ''You live in a church called CBS. You go from deacon, to bishop, to cardinal. How are you going to turn down pope? Replacing Walter Cronkite was like getting the ring, the mitre, the sword. Rather had lived his entire life waiting for the day that miracle might take place. How could you expect him to walk away from the Church at that moment and become a Baptist?''

Interestingly, neither Burke nor Arledge believes that Rather knowingly used the ABC offer as a negotiating ploy to get what he wanted at CBS, the prevailing view among industry cynics. Both feel he came close to accepting their offer. Arledge does concede, though, that Leibner was able to make the most of the situation in his dealings with CBS, negotiating a better deal for his client than would otherwise have been possible.

In spite of all the rumors surrounding Cronkite's replacement, the news that Rather was in and Mudd out rocked the organization. The announcement was made the same day that Rather reached his decision, a day that one staff member in Washington — a Mudd admirer — remembers as the saddest day of his life. ''We were told the announcement about Cronkite's successor would be made that afternoon in New York. I looked around and saw Mudd was in Washington, which meant that Rather had been chosen. Word started going around; everybody realized it. Roger was sitting at his desk, and it was really strange; nobody went near him. It was almost as if everybody was afraid. The tension was incredible.'' The staff watched with apprehension as Mudd was informed that Leonard, who had flown down from New York, was waiting to see him. It was a little after 2:00 P.M., less than two hours before the Rather announcement was made to the press. The meeting was a stormy one, despite Leonard's assurances to Mudd that CBS still valued him and hoped to retain his services. After it was over, Mudd returned to his desk, picked up his coat, and left the building without saying a word to anyone. His fury can be gauged, however, from the brief, tersely worded statement he put out later that afternoon: ''The Management of CBS and CBS News has made its decision on Walter Cronkite's successor according to its current values and standards. From the beginning, I've regarded myself as a news reporter and not as a newsmaker or celebrity.'' Although CBS did not release Mudd from his contract for another eight months, it was the last day he ever worked for the company.

Mudd has always maintained that his anger at CBS was based not on being passed over as anchor, but on being given such short notice of the decision. ''I felt that CBS owed me something more than an hour and twenty minutes' notice and that based on the long years in which I substituted, the assumptions in the newsroom, the assumptions of eighteen to twenty million viewers, all those years I gave up my summers when my children were young, they owed me something more than that. To me, it was an unpardonable disregard for the sensitivity and pride of an employee who had brought the company nothing but credit.'' As soon as Mudd was released from his contract, he went to NBC to become chief Washington correspondent, with a promise of becoming anchor when John Chancellor stepped down.

There are two schools of thought about whether Mudd would have stayed at CBS under any circumstances once Rather got the anchor job. Some people think he would not and deliberately remained ignorant of what was going on in New York to build a case whereby his honor, not his wounded pride, left him no choice but to resign. Others, including Mudd's friends, say he would have stayed at CBS if Leonard had gone to him in advance of Rather's decision, offering to work out a face-saver, such as promoting him to chief Washington correspondent. "How could I have done that," protests Leonard, "when I didn't know what was happening from one day to the next myself? It was not until the day Dan signed that I could have told Roger what was going on. What was true one day would have been reversed the next. Also, we didn't want to lose Roger in the interim."

Publicly, CBS justified choosing Rather over Mudd for the job by citing Dan's versatility and breadth of experience; no one mentioned the dirty word *ratings*. It would be unduly cynical to suggest that their qualities as journalists and broadcasters played no part in the selection process; it was precisely because they fulfilled so many qualifications for the anchor job that Rather and Mudd made it to the final cut. Still, when it came down to choosing between them, the primary consideration was star quality — who would attract a larger audience.

As one CBS corporate source put it, "When it came to nut-cutting time, the feeling was you could get away with either man as your anchor, but that CBS could not afford to let Rather go across the street to ABC."

Bill Leonard summed it up a little more delicately: "All three nets came to the same conclusion I did. If Dan was not the ideal, he came close to being it. He was the right age, had the right credentials, he was well known, he was popular on one of the most popular programs on television. If you weren't on top, he could put you there. If you were on top, he could keep you there."

2

The Murrow Legacy

There is no argument about television as a news reporting medium. Compared with the press and radio, video is as backward as a country cousin.
— *Newsweek,* March 4, 1949

AS ASTOUNDING as the Rather contract seemed in 1980, it would have been totally unimaginable in the early days of television. Until the mid-fifties, the fifteen-minute evening news — virtually the only news on TV at the time — was treated as a light, harmless throwaway by the networks. The anchors were seen as little more than glorified announcers. The notion of promoting them into world authorities and superstars never occurred to anybody.

The story of television network news begins, for all practical purposes, at the political conventions in Philadelphia in 1948, the first major event to be televised on a national hookup. That was the year that TV finally started to take hold,* when Milton Berle captured the public's fancy with his "Texaco Star Theater" and Ed Sullivan launched the "Toast of the Town." A total of fourteen Eastern stations were hooked up to the coaxial cable that summer, and one estimate put the number of people who would watch at least part of the conventions, either at home or gathered in bars, as high as ten million.

For newsmen, however, television held little appeal: The action, the glory, and the money were still in radio. Certainly it was no honor for John Cameron Swayze to be asked to announce the conventions for TV by NBC. At the time, he was doing a none-too-successful radio show called "The World News Roundup," which a number of NBC affiliates refused

*The number of sets in existence jumped from 15,000 in 1947 to 190,000 in 1948.

to carry. His career on the ropes, Swayze had been looking forward to the increased exposure he would get by doing radio at the conventions. The ad people would be listening, and he was hoping someone would come up with a new show for him. "Jeez, what a lousy break," Swayze recalls thinking when he heard he was being assigned to TV. "Nobody in the world will see me or hear me now."

It was murderously hot that summer in Philadelphia, almost unbearable in Swayze's crowded, primitive little studio perched among the rafters of Convention Hall. Good trouper that he was, however, Swayze wound up enjoying himself. "Forty-eight was wonderful," he recalls. "Nobody knew what they were doing. We couldn't make a mistake because nobody knew what we were *supposed* to be doing. Our little studio had been thrown together so quickly that the wood was still raw, just some two-by-fours with the nails sticking out. It had a swinging door that must have come from a saloon, and you'd be interviewing somebody, and the first thing you knew, a new person would come through the door. Now it was up to you to recognize the person, introduce them, and then carry on a reasonably intelligent conversation."

In this helter-skelter operation, Swayze fell back on his extraordinary memory, and when that failed him, he was quick on his feet. Once, when a guest came through the swinging door, Swayze recognized him as a leading politician, but could not for the life of him remember the man's name. Suddenly, he got an inspiration. "As my guest came up, I shook hands with him and turned him toward the camera, and I said, 'How do you do, sir? Won't you introduce yourself to our audience?' So he turned, swept off his hat, and said, 'I am Mayor James Curley of Boston.' I reached out and grabbed his hand and said, 'Thank you, Mayor Curley. I'm sure our audience recognized you even before you spoke.'"

The amazing thing to Swayze was that the politicians were all so eager to get on TV. "Do you know, not a single politician ever turned down the chance to climb those stairs in that heat to get on this new medium. They sensed something here, even before we did. One of the political parties even passed around a sheet that said, 'Things to be careful about: Television is here,' telling the delegates not to reach in their pockets and take out a bottle for fear of getting caught by the camera, things like that."

Swayze was pleasantly surprised to find that the public also was responding to TV. He and his co-announcer, Ben Grauer, one of the most famous voices on radio, started receiving congratulatory telegrams from viewers. One incident, in particular, impressed Swayze. "One day I got in a cab in Philadelphia, and the driver said, 'Oh, saw you last night.' And I said, 'Oh, you have a TV?' Television sets were pretty expensive in those days, you know — nothing against taxi drivers, but I didn't have one in the home. 'Sure,' he says. 'It's a great thing for the kids.' And as I'm getting out of the car, he says, 'See you on the set tonight.' And I walked away thinking, 'Jeez, I guess I made a mistake. People are watching this thing.'"

CBS's choice to handle the conventions was Douglas Edwards, a junior member of the all-star CBS news team. He already had a fair amount of experience with TV, though, having anchored a newscast twice a week in New York City for CBS since 1946. Like Swayze, he found that little had been done to help him at the conventions. TV was so low in priority, in fact, that nobody even bothered to tell Edwards about his assignment until he arrived in Philadelphia. He was to do the play-by-play, and Edward R. Murrow and Quincy Howe would help out with analysis and interviews when they could be spared from radio.

Logistically, the job was a nightmare. There were no facilities to switch down to the floor, so the correspondents had to come dashing up to the stand in a sweat, dragging interviewees with them, in order to get on the air. Edwards was perched so high up in the hall he couldn't even see the blackboard where the votes were tallied, a problem he solved by borrowing his daughter's Girl Scout binoculars.

In spite of all the handicaps, Edwards acquitted himself well at the conventions; he had the ability, so crucial to success in television news, to handle himself smoothly on camera, no matter what went wrong. If Edwards was assigned to most of the TV chores at CBS at the time, however, it was partly by default; the senior radio correspondents — CBS's "A" team — wanted to have as little to do with this new medium as possible. The "A" team, a group of distinguished journalists originally assembled by Edward R. Murrow at the outbreak of World War II, thought TV was a toy, a joke, a poor instrument for the dissemination of information. They were busy with the serious medium: radio.

Radio was king. As Red Barber once observed, you had to be around in the twenties to realize the force with which it burst upon the American scene. Whole families used to gather round their sets to listen. They even *watched* their Atwater Kents and Philco consoles. Social workers in the thirties noted that poor people preferred to part with their iceboxes and bed springs before they would give up their radios. In part, this irrational, almost fanatical, attachment sprang from the times. With the Depression on, who had the money to go to the movies or a vaudeville show? People were forced to spend more time at home. But theater's loss was radio's gain. Entertainers such as Eddie Cantor, Fred Allen, and Jack Benny flocked to radio, where they found legions of new, adoring fans.

Radio created a long roster of new stars — singers like Kate Smith and Bing Crosby, character actors like Gertrude Berg, and quacks like "Doctor" John Brinkley, who claimed he could cure impotence with male goat glands. Radio spawned a new kind of performer, too — the commentator, who was part journalist and part showman. They were a varied lot, the commentators. A few, like Lowell Thomas, stuck mainly to straight newscasting — with a liberal dollop of human interest. But most commentators brought a personal slant to the issues of the day, either as analysts (H. V. Kaltenborn) or as out-and-out propagandists (Boake Carter, Fulton Lewis, Jr.). The most famous of them all, Walter Winchell, used to attract twenty-five million listeners a night with his unique blend of gossip, innuendo, and biased reporting.

Even so, prior to the onset of World War II, the networks allotted very little time to commentary. The news of the day received, if anything, even more cursory treatment. In 1936, for example, CBS — generally considered the leader in news — offered only one five-minute summary at noon, one at 4:30 P.M., and fifteen minutes at 11:00 P.M. News caused too many headaches as far as broadcasters were concerned — threats from politicians, retaliatory acts by newspaper publishers,* and complaints from affiliates. In addition, news seldom attracted many sponsors.

It was not until late in 1938, with war threatening in Europe, that the demand for timely, up-to-the-minute news suddenly became acute. The networks responded quickly, hiring reporters and editors, and, for the first time, setting up their own news-gathering organizations. For the duration of the war, the airwaves crackled with news.

Of all the new voices reporting from abroad, one in particular was idolized by the public: Edward R. Murrow. He had been sent to London by CBS in 1936 to arrange for the broadcasting of concerts, lectures, and other cultural fare. An educator by profession, he had no training in

*The development of news on radio was retarded to some extent by the newspaper industry, which had become alarmed over shrinking advertising revenues. During the so-called press-radio war of 1933, many publishers refused to print radio schedules, and the wire services stopped selling news to the networks. By the end of the year, NBC, CBS, and the National Association of Broadcasters signed an agreement promising to air no more than two five-minute newscasts a day, with no item to exceed thirty words. Commentators were not permitted to use news less than twelve hours old. The agreement was widely disregarded, however, and fell by the wayside before the end of 1934.

journalism, but the approach of war turned him into a reporter. His eyewitness account of the events leading up to Munich and the sellout of Czechoslovakia made him an overnight celebrity. Millions of people sat glued to their sets, fascinated, as H. V. Kaltenborn in New York repeated, "Calling Ed Murrow. Come in, Ed Murrow."

Egbert Roscoe Murrow was a country boy raised in modest but comfortable circumstances. His father was a farmer turned locomotive engineer. His mother, a Quaker and the great influence in his life, believed in discipline, Bible reading, and hard work; Murrow would later say his upbringing had not equipped him to have fun. All the same, he was a popular boy, excelling in sports, music, and public speaking at his high school on Puget Sound in Washington. He was such a spellbinder that a neighbor asked the youngster to preach at his funeral when he died, a request that Murrow fulfilled. In college, he pursued his interests in speech and drama, while immersing himself in outside activities like ROTC and student politics. He also shed his countrified ways, learning to dress stylishly and to move easily among people with money and position.

There was in Murrow a quality that moved people. As a broadcaster, he made a deep impact with his rich, resonant voice and his elegant but restrained prose. Above all, it was his ability to capture mood, feeling, and drama that made him such a hero to Americans during the conflict in Europe. He had a flair for those small details that make a scene come alive; once he illustrated the eerie silence between air raids by putting his microphone next to a pierced can of peaches, catching the sound of the syrup falling drop by drop onto the floor of a bombed-out shop. He also ushered in a peculiarly American phenomenon — presenting news as theater, with the reporter playing the part of the protagonist. Murrow often placed himself in appalling danger for his live broadcasts, standing on London rooftops while German bombs were falling, sailing on minesweepers in the North Sea, and so on. The first of his rooftop broadcasts, said to have been delivered in a hoarse, tremulous voice that broke into sobbing at one point, must have packed an enormous emotional impact:

> I'm standing on a rooftop looking out over London. At the moment everything is quiet. For reasons of national as well as personal security, I'm unable to tell you the exact location from which I'm speaking. Off to my left, far away in the distance, I can see just that faint red angry snap of antiaircraft bursts against the steel-blue sky, but the guns are so far away that it's impossible to hear them from this location.
> [The fighting gets closer.]

I think probably in a minute we shall have the sound of guns in the immediate vicinity. The lights are swinging over in this general direction now. You'll hear two explosions. There they are! That was the explosion overhead, not the guns themselves. I should think in a few minutes there may be a bit of shrapnel around here. Coming in, moving a little closer all the while . . . The searchlights now are feeling almost directly overhead. Now you'll hear two bursts a little nearer in a moment. There they are! That hard, stony sound.

Besides his gifts as a writer, reporter, and dramatist, Murrow was a superb judge of talent in others. Charged with hiring and deploying a staff to report from the various European capitals, he looked for university graduates with a good, solid, print background. He didn't care much what his recruits sounded like; they had to be able to think, and they had to be able to write. The cadre of scholar-journalists he assembled — Eric Sevareid, Charles Collingwood, Howard K. Smith, Larry LeSueur, Richard C. Hottelet, David Schoenbrun — was a remarkable, brilliant, cultured group of men, and they proceeded, quite literally, to invent the art of broadcast reporting.

They detailed the comings and goings of statesmen, went on bombing raids, huddled in air raid shelters, rode with the wounded in ambulances, and dodged their share of bombs and grenades. Often their counterparts from NBC rode along with them — NBC, too, made a heroic effort to cover the war. The principal difference was that NBC didn't have Murrow. It was he who made it all seem real to the American public. At the end of the war, he returned home, lionized by politicians, socialites, ordinary listeners, even the intelligentsia. He and his "boys" had given radio news that most precious commodity: legitimacy.

For a new branch of journalism, radio news was embraced by the American public with surprising speed. In a poll taken by the National Opinion Research Center at the University of Chicago in 1945, 61 percent of those queried said they got most of their news from radio, compared to 35 percent who said they relied more on newspapers.

After the war, though, when interest in news began to wane, and the need for speed and immediacy became less pressing, newspapers regained some of the favor they had lost. A poll taken by the same organization in 1947 found newspapers ahead of radio by 48 percent to 44 percent. The networks resumed their escapist ways after the war, too, once again relegating news to the fringe hours of the schedule. But the network foreign correspondent remainded a figure of glamor and prestige, particularly at CBS, where the exploits of the Murrow team had brought the company so much critical acclaim. In gratitude, William Paley, the chairman and founder of CBS (destined to become a legend himself), dined with his correspondents abroad and socialized with them at home. Murrow, Schoenbrun, and the others had ready access to him at work, too. Their intimacy with Paley, as well as their immense standing with the public and the press, combined to make the Murrow group untouchable at CBS. Certainly, no lowly editor in New York or Washington presumed to tell them what to say or how to say it.

So great was their prestige, in fact, that the standards they set and the attitudes they shared would affect the course of television news for years to come. It was Murrow, naturally, who cast the longest shadow. When he began making documentaries for TV, he gave the long form instant credibility and glamor. Likewise, his belief that television was an inferior medium for breaking news and his refusal, to the end, to have anything to do with daily newscasting, colored the view of the critics and others in the industry. It was fashionable, in fact, to sneer at the evening news and the pioneering efforts of TV's first anchormen, Douglas Edwards, John Cameron Swayze, and ABC's John Daly.

Yet, if the Murrowites disdained TV in the beginning, who could blame them? TV *was* inferior to radio as a news medium, lacking the ability to go anywhere quickly. Live coverage was a nightmare, requiring huge mobile vans, miles of cable, and days of advance planning. Satellites for international communications were still fifteen years away, so film of events from abroad might be delayed as much as a week. Even within the United States, the interconnections were so poor that film generally had to be flown to New York, there to be processed and edited, causing a lag of twenty-four hours or more. Not surprisingly, the predictable or staged event, filmed mainly in New York or Washington, became a staple of early TV news.

Beyond these problems, Murrow suspected that TV might never become a legitimate purveyor of news, because of an inherent problem: Many stories cannot be told on film. "What seemed to concern television isn't the horror of the atom bomb," he once remarked, "but the unique picture it makes."

Also, television seemed personally threatening to the Murrowites and their newly acquired membership in the journalistic fraternity. To them, television, with its directors and technicians, its huge cameras and blinding lights, seemed more like show business, Hollywood. Television also seemed a bit sissified, the idea of make-up repulsive. Murrow's boys were proud, and justly so, of their reputations as brave, adventurous types who dashed around in trench coats, risking their lives to cover wars. "We felt it was kind of unmanly to go on TV and perform," says Howard K. Smith, "just as it was in an earlier era somehow unmanly for a newspaperman to go on radio. When Ed went into it later, of course, he showed that real men could take part in it without damaging their masculinity."

In spite of the reservations on the part of its senior correspondents, the massive technical limitations, and the embryonic state of the CBS-TV network (it consisted of only three stations), CBS launched the first nightly news service on television on August 15, 1948. No sponsors signed up, but it was thought necessary to go ahead anyway because of the need to provide some sort of public service. The networks had never been licensed by the government (only the individual stations are licensed), and they wanted to keep it that way. News, even though it lost money and would continue to do so for almost three decades, was regarded as a handy tool for warding off governmental interference and safeguarding corporate profits.

To Frank Stanton, the president of CBS, the obvious choice for newscaster on the new program was Douglas Edwards, one of the few people in the news division he saw any hope of converting to TV. Stanton had been watching Edwards at the convention, and he had a notion that he projected the right kind of "chemistry" for television. "Doug had an attractive personality," he says. "I don't want to use the word *winning* exactly, but there was a warmth about him. Besides, he was an experienced newscaster and popular, too. Millions of people followed him on radio." Edwards took some convincing, though, especially since Stanton wanted him to give up radio and concentrate full-time on TV. Television might be tolerable as a sideline, but radio paid the bills. The correspondents used to get a share of the fees from all commercially sponsored broadcasts, and Edwards was earning a lot of money on radio.

Beyond the money, he was worried about what TV would do to his reputation as a serious newsman, something he had been working for years to establish. Stanton assured him that television, not radio, would soon be the pre-eminent news medium, and the people who scorned it would live to regret it. He also offered to double Edwards's salary and let him continue on one of his most popular radio programs, "Wendy Warren and the News," a soap opera set in a newsroom. Edwards would need the exposure; the television program would have only about 30,000 viewers when it got under way. He was still not entirely convinced, but sensing that he had no real alternative, he finally agreed.

From the start, the CBS-TV News, as it was first called, was built around Douglas Edwards to an extraordinary degree, just as NBC's "Camel News Caravan" would be built around John Cameron Swayze, and the ABC Evening News* around John Daly, who was best known as the moderator of "What's My Line?" Although all three men had news credentials, they were clearly chosen more on the basis of their presumed appeal to viewers. This emphasis on the personality of the newscaster, which had its antecedents in radio, is uniquely American. Other countries have taken deliberate steps to ensure that the newscaster doesn't become more prominent than the news. Using announcers or "newsreaders" who make no pretense of involvement with the material they read is one commonly used device for de-emphasizing personality. Having a series of individuals to read the news on different days is another. Even those systems, such as the BBC and German television, that have begun using journalists to read the news, generally rotate them. In the United States, however, broadcast news grew up as an offshoot of large entertainment corporations whose real business is promoting the sale of products, and personality turned out to be the greatest selling device ever discovered. Personality was the key to radio's phenomenal success, and no one saw any reason to change the formula on TV, whether the program format was comedy, variety, or news.†

Marshall McLuhan hadn't yet coined the expressions "hot" and "cool" as applied to the communications media, but Edwards, with his low-key, pleasant but earnest manner, was clearly a "cool" personality and therefore suited to the demands of a cool medium like TV. He was easy to look at, too. Not dashing by any means, but handsome in a boy-next-door mold. Newspaper writers of the day invariably referred to his "choirboy good looks."

At thirty-one, Edwards had already been a broadcaster for sixteen years. He got his start at the age of fifteen as a junior announcer at a small station in Troy, Alabama, earning $2.50 a week. Edwards was a certified radio nut. As a boy, his idols were radio commentators like Floyd Gibbons

---

*ABC was such a frail network, getting off to such a slow start in news, that a discussion of its anchors will be saved for a later chapter.

†In the early twenties, station owners attempted to enforce anonymity on announcers, fearing they might become ungovernable celebrities. But the public became so infatuated with the voices of men like Norman Brokenshire and Milton J. Cross, and so curious about their identities, that management was finally forced to relent.

and Lowell Thomas; his favorite game, playing "announcer." He exhibited a gift for extemporaneous speech at an early age, a talent his mother pushed him to develop. She was a schoolteacher, widowed shortly after Doug was born in Ada, Oklahoma, in 1917. Her son became the "little man" of the family, the repository of all her hopes and dreams. She entered him in oratorical contests, encouraged his interest in debating and dramatics. By the age of nineteen, Edwards was a full-fledged broadcaster, reading the news on Atlanta's WSB. Since the station was owned by the *Atlanta Journal,* he managed to pick up some print experience, too, writing for the radio page.

His next big break was Detroit, where he signed on as one of the "Cunningham News Aces" — so named in honor of the sponsor, Cunningham's drugstore. Edwards and fellow "Ace" Mike Wallace were essentially announcers who did everything from introducing dance bands to reading newscasts, commercials, and dramatic narrations.

In 1938, however, Edwards, like millions of other Americans, got caught up in the Murrow-Kaltenborn broadcasts on Munich, and he began to dream of being a *real* newsman. He returned to Atlanta two years later as news director of WSB with but one goal in mind — to move to New York and go to work for CBS News. He got his chance in 1943, but the only opening on the staff was for an announcer, which was something of a professional risk. Although the other networks and nearly all local stations used announcers to read the news, CBS had a rule that newscasters had to be able to write their own copy, even if they didn't always do so. As a result, staff announcers at CBS did not enjoy much prestige. For Edwards, though, it was a foot in the door, and he accepted the job. Within a matter of weeks, Edwards convinced his bosses that he could write his own material, and he was assigned to handle the "World Tonight," a fifteen-minute roundup that aired each evening at seven-forty-five.

With his proficiency as a reader, his dramatic abilities, and his pleasant voice, Edwards was soon given additional assignments. Dramatizations of actual events were common on radio in those days, and Edwards narrated a popular program called "Report to the Nation," a re-enactment of the events of the war. It was an elaborate production, using a full orchestra and a repertory company of actors. An unknown named Art Carney did a very good Roosevelt.

With so much on-air exposure, Edwards built up a considerable following with the public. He was popular with management, too, a workhorse who would accept any and every assignment, always with the utmost good humor. On or off the job, Edwards displayed a remarkably sunny, even temper, always the perfect gentleman, treating everyone with a grave, deliberate courtesy. The one place his stock was not high was with Murrow and his followers, who constituted virtually a separate organization within the news division. "Murrow and his crowd always regarded Doug as a total outsider," says Sig Mickelson, who headed the CBS news division from 1949 to 1960. "Once, when we did a year-end roundup [an annual occasion when all the correspondents came home from their various posts abroad to discuss the state of the world], I suggested to Murrow that Doug, who was our only TV correspondent at the time, could use the exposure from participating. Murrow flatly refused. He felt that Doug was unable to perform with the Hottelets and Collingwoods of this world."

One problem was that Edwards was a fairly pedestrian writer, and the Murrow group set great store by the ability to write stylish, elegant prose. Nor was he considered a profound thinker. The long, highly literate "think piece" was almost a signature of CBS News in those days, but it took insightful, philosophical, well-read individuals to turn out those highly polished gems. Edwards could write a news story, all right, but he was no philosopher. Edwards's efforts to be accepted by the "A" team were further hampered by his lack of education and limited print experience. After high school, he had taken night classes, but his work at WSB had absorbed him far more than his journalism courses at Emory University.

He also had the great misfortune of missing World War II. It wasn't his fault. He had pleaded with his bosses at CBS to send him to the battlefront, always to be told there were no openings. When he finally arrived in London in 1945, the war was almost over. The CBS plan was to rotate him from one war zone to the next, relieving the correspondents on duty for a few months, but as the fighting was nearly over, he wound up staying in London. He became so glum over this turn of events that Murrow finally tried to console him by saying, "Look, Doug, I know you're frustrated, but there's nothing in the least intellectual about getting shot at."

After the war, Edwards was assigned to the Paris bureau for several months and went on a two-month mission to cover the Middle East, but as Larry LeSueur points out, it wasn't like sharing the same foxhole. "Doug was never a part of our group. How could he be? Murrow, Collingwood, Sevareid, Bill Downs, myself, we shared tremendously indelible experiences. We shared in the making of *history* in World War Two; we knew what it was like to be scared together.''

It was Murrow and his followers who set the standards for admission into the broadcast news fraternity, not only at CBS but at the other networks as well. Experience as a foreign correspondent was vital, preferably under dangerous conditions. It was not a profession for the faint-hearted, the desk-bound — or women.

The intellectual qualities that the Murrowites prized — the broad, philosophical outlook, the ability to stand back and analyze a situation and set it down in finely honed phrases — were not a passport to success in television, however, no matter how desirable they were in radio. Murrow would not have made a good anchor even if he had wanted the job, primarily because he was not at ease on live television. Even in the anonymity of the radio booth, tension caused his feet to jiggle and sweat to pour down his face. His great successes on TV, ''See It Now,'' the documentary series, and ''Person to Person,'' a celebrity interview show, were neither live nor in any sense spontaneous; even the questions on ''Person to Person'' were scripted in advance.

Edwards, on the other hand, could ad lib: He didn't fluster easily, and he wasn't camera shy. He was also one of the best ''readers'' in the business, able to take a script cold and read it on the air without any fluffs. Those were considered the main qualifications for an anchorman in the early days, although the term *anchor* had yet to be coined. The requirement that the newsreader be a top journalist never occurred to anybody, since editorial control was in the hands of the producer.

In television, producers are both the principal editors and chief packagers of the news; it is their job to see that the visual and editorial elements of the stories are combined in a creative fashion. The producer on the Edwards show, Don Hewitt, was only a twenty-five-year-old director when he went to work for the program, but he would soon come to be known as one of the pioneering geniuses of television. As director, Hewitt's main responsibility was to get the program on the air smoothly, calling the shots in the control room. But technical and editorial aspects of television are so closely linked that before long, he assumed editorial control over the program as well. Because of his expanded role, he needed a new title, but nobody knew what to call him. Finally, somebody came up with the term *producer,* which was borrowed, rather inappropriately, from Broadway and Hollywood.

Hewitt was a man with a forceful, bubbling, almost manic personality. He expended so much energy and enthusiasm in the course of the day that his colleagues joked that he had to be put in a basket and shipped to Florida for a complete rest every few months. Paradoxically, he had no real passion for news itself, seldom reading a newspaper or looking at the wires. He depended on the writers to tell him what was going on. What did interest him was finding ways to translate the news, whatever it was, for television. He would spend much of the day clowning around — playing poker or Scrabble in his office with cronies, waving away people who tried to interrupt him on legitimate business. But once he got revved up with an idea for the Evening News, he could galvanize the entire staff with his excitement.

Although in many ways an original, Hewitt patterned his style to a considerable degree on that of Fred Friendly, Murrow's producer and a man who also left an indelible mark on CBS. Friendly, variously nicknamed "the big moose," and "the electric cattle prod," was a domineering, flamboyant character given to incredible temper tantrums. Hewitt, who directed "See It Now" for Friendly and Murrow, had plenty of time to observe Friendly's tirades in the control room and to notice how well they achieved results. So Hewitt, too, adopted a bulldozing style and delighted in putting on great loud displays in public, although he tended to be more amusing than Friendly. His most dazzling shows were reserved for the control room; it was worth the price of admission to see him leaping on tables, cursing, yelling, whooping it up. His audiences loved it.

Friendly and Hewitt both had well-developed egos, common enough among creative people, necessary even, but in their particular cases, it caused a certain amount of pain. Their job was to make somebody *else* look good, and both men burned to be recognized for their own considerable talents and originality. Hewitt was the driving force behind the Edwards show, and he wanted to make sure everybody else at CBS knew it.

He deliberately spread the idea that Edwards couldn't write, which was untrue. Most of the "tell" stories (the items read by the anchor on camera) are merely rewritten from the wires anyhow, something Edwards had been doing for years. Hewitt's derogatory remarks were readily believed, however, especially since the Murrow group had been singing the same tune for years. In any case, Edwards was not the first anchorman whose writing style was unimpressive. Walter Cronkite was never known as a great stylist and seldom wrote much copy. The key issue in television news is editorial input, and there was no doubt in anyone's mind that Hewitt ran the Edwards show. It was he who originated the ideas, experimented with new ways to capture events on film, dreamed up the graphics, and decided what did or didn't go on the air. Edwards attended the ''line-up'' meetings, which were held late in the day, but he rarely questioned Hewitt's decisions.

Gradually, Edwards, once known as the workhorse of the news department, began to disengage himself from the program. He took longer and longer lunches and drank more than he should have. He was always in good shape by air time, but his drinking increased the perception, widely held in the news department, that he was Hewitt's puppet.

Hewitt's zany quality was a decided asset in the early days of television, when news was considered an essentially frivolous undertaking. He loved to dream up stunts, like the time during a heat wave in July when he arranged to have a 100-pound block of ice delivered to the studio, somehow finding a way to make it steam. As the camera lingered on the shot, Edwards told the audience, ''Have a look. Maybe it will cool you off for a while.'' Afterward, though, when producer and anchorman were congratulating each other on how well their ruse had worked, Hewitt suddenly slapped himself on the forehead and said, ''I must be crazy. I didn't have to spend a hundred and fifty dollars for that block of ice. A tight shot of an ice cube would have worked just as well.'' ''Things were more madcap then,'' Edwards recalls. ''We had a lot more fun. One time, I interviewed Miss Health, 1950, on the set in her bathing suit. At bock beer time, we got a brewer and his billygoat to come in. We could take more leeway to make the show interesting in those days.''

Mostly, though, Hewitt and Edwards relied on interviews to fill up the program, which usually resembled a televised radio show. A 1951 Edwards program, for example, devoted eight minutes to a controversy concerning General Charles Willoughby, Douglas MacArthur's chief of intelligence, who accused the press of biased and inaccurate coverage of the Korean War. The general was interviewed on film for several minutes; then, one of his print critics — an AP reporter — was interviewed live in the studio by Edwards. The primitive level of production was also evident, as Edwards, shown from the shoulders up, struggled surreptitiously for several seconds with something out of range of the camera. The shot widened to reveal the only visual element of the segment — several newpapers and magazines containing the critical articles — which Edwards had been arranging in front of him on the desk.

The talky nature of these programs resulted partly from the fact that CBS television news was the offspring, however unloved, of CBS Radio, where the word, not the picture, was valued. The main reason, however, was the ludicrously inadequate budget. For years, the entire staff consisted of Edwards, Hewitt, two writers, a secretary, and a couple of film editors in New York who doubled as cameramen. CBS had no TV correspondents; on occasion the radio correspondents contributed reports or "think pieces." There were no film crews, either; staff photographers would not be hired until 1953. An inexpensive syndication service called Telenews supplied most of the film, but for the most part it was typical newsreel trivia — stories about bathing beauties, children, and dogs. Hewitt says it was so bad it couldn't be used to fill more than 15 or 20 percent of the program. The rest of the time was taken up by Edwards talking, either on camera, with an interviewee, or over still photos, maps, drawings, et cetera.

Things were a little different at NBC, where the "Camel News Caravan," crude and hokey as it was in the early days, is still recognizable as a TV newscast. It used such comparatively sophisticated techniques as film clips of a wide variety of world events, rear-screen projection of graphics, and switches to correspondents in other cities.

The Swayze show did not get under way until February 1949,* six months after Edwards made his debut, but from the start, the NBC news program was fully sponsored. This meant that the sponsor had the right to approve the "talent" for the program, a tradition established in radio. Swayze's audition went well; when it was over, the account executive for Reynolds Tobacco told him, "I like your puss. You've got the job." His salary: $110,000 a year.

Advertisers got a lot for their money in those days. Besides the commercials (which, of course, were light years ahead of the news in terms of production and are to this day), every Swayze show ended up with a long, lingering shot of a lighted Camel, smoke curling upward from an ashtray. Swayze, always eager to please a sponsor, offered to carry a

*In the year preceding Swayze's debut, NBC aired a nightly news show produced for Camel cigarettes by an advertising agency. The program, which was done like a theatrical newsreel, consisted entirely of film clips, with voice-over by an unseen narrator.

pack of Camels around with him, even though he didn't smoke, but the Camel people felt it wouldn't be necessary.

Swayze was in some respects more of a radio personality than Edwards, rolling his *R*'s and indulging in some of the theatrical flourishes of the famous commentators. With his breezy manner and penchant for catch phrases, he was often compared to Walter Winchell. "Let's go hopscotching the world for headlines," Swayze would say brightly toward the end of each broadcast, and he always closed with the words, "That's all for now, folks. Glad we could get together." Not quite as colorful as Winchell's "Good evening, Mr. and Mrs. North America and all the ships at sea," but reminiscent of Winchell, all the same.

Swayze's chipper style meshed well with NBC's newscasts, which took their inspiration from the movie newsreels, once described by Oscar Levant as a series of catastrophes ended by a fashion show. Few examples of the Swayze program still exist, but those that do are priceless. A 1949 program, for example, includes a feature on the unveiling of a newly delivered motorcycle fleet for New York's police. As the camera pans the long row of policemen, posing on their shiny new motorcycles, the unseen narrator brightly asked, "If you were speeding, how would you like to see *that* in your rearview mirror?"

In that same newscast, President Truman is shown paying a call on several senators on Capitol Hill, but why he's there or what was discussed is never explained. The narrator refers to the visit as a "pleasant interlude" for the President, who "always enjoys going back to the Senate, a place where he spent so much time."

People critical of TV news today would probably emerge with a different perspective if they could go back into the network archives and see how many years it took television to delve beneath the surface of events. With the exception of some reporting critical of U.S. involvement in Vietnam, television would remain an extremely tame, almost totally reactive medium until the 1970s. In the 1950s, the networks were so submissive toward the government that when John Foster Dulles was secretary of state, he used to prevent film of his press conferences from being used until he had a chance to examine the transcripts and order cuts.

Coziness between the networks and government was the order of the day. In 1955, when President Eisenhower asked RCA chief David Sarnoff to head up a recuitment drive for the military reserve corps, the latter saw no conflict in harnessing NBC to the task. According to John Tebbel, Sarnoff's biographer, "The promotion drive Sarnoff organized was a model of its kind, in which the entire resources of the National Broadcasting Company were used in the most lavish way possible. More than 6000 radio and TV programs with nearly $2,000,000 in air time were employed to boost the reserve program . . . Enlistments showed a phenomenal increase.''

However, these were not matters that concerned Swayze, who seldom got involved in editorial or policy decisions. Most of the day, he was busy with outside narration and emceeing jobs, for which he was in great demand. At the time, nobody saw any conflict between his dual image as newscaster and as genial master of ceremonies. Contrary to popular legend, however, he wrote most of his own material, including the ''hopscotching'' section. This was a grab bag of the day's top headlines, little more than a string of one-liners, such as the following item from a 1950 broadcast: ''Washington: General MacArthur says U.S. forces will utterly destroy the Korean Commies before they reach the thirty-eighth parallel.''

Swayze was an amiable fellow, energetic and dapper, regularly making the ''best dressed'' lists. He was always ready with a joke or a quotation, some of which he carried in his pockets on three-by-five cards for handy reference. He had all the attributes of a good salesman, which he became after he gave up the news business.

At heart, Swayze was a performer. He had wanted to go on the stage before he got into reporting. Born in Wichita, Kansas, in 1906, the son of a wholesale drug salesman, he was raised in a middle-class home. Like Edwards, he, too, had a mother who encouraged his talent for public speaking and acting. Swayze attended college for a while, but gave it up to try his luck on Broadway. When he arrived in New York in 1929, he enrolled in acting school and make the rounds of the talent agencies, but it was a tough time to be looking for work. Before long, he headed back to the Midwest, desperate to find work. Through a friend, he landed a job at the old *Kansas City Journal Post*.

Swayze's credentials as a newsman were often belittled within NBC, but in fact they were respectable enough. He worked for the *Journal Post* for ten years, where he covered everything from murders to local elections. During that time, he doubled as a radio announcer on Kansas City's KMBC, the CBS affiliate, which had a tie-in with the paper. For an extra $15 a week, Swayze used to read news bulletins over the air from a little cubbyhole in the corner of the newsroom.

He even pioneered a TV newscast of sorts for an experimental station in

1933. Every day at noon, he went to the top of the Kansas City Power and Light Company, then the tallest building in the state of Missouri, and read the newspaper into a camera. Down below, people gathered in front of a set in a lobby to watch the fuzzy outline of Swayze on some newfangled thing called a TV set. "I felt like some sort of space cadet, sitting up there," he says, "but they never sold any sets that I know of." The experiment folded after six months.

By 1944, Swayze was getting restless in Kansas City and anxious for a taste of the big time. ("Nothing wrong with Kansas City, mind you," he adds. Swayze never liked to offend anyone.) So he packed up his wife and two children and headed for Los Angeles to look for a job. With the help of a friend, he landed the post of director of news and special events for NBC's western division, a job with substantial responsibilities. But Swayze, who was used to doing air work, soon tired of lining up coverage of luncheon speeches, conventions, and other news events. In 1947, he heard about an opening for a newscaster at NBC in New York, sent them a record — audio tape was still unknown in this country — and was hired.

Swayze's career bloomed only after he became anchor of the "Camel News Caravan," where he was an immediate hit. He may, in fact, have been the first serious student of the audience for news. Management didn't care much about the ratings for news in those days; in the corporate sphere, news was regarded mainly as a sop to the Federal Communications Commission. But Swayze noticed almost immediately that he got many more letters from children when he switched from radio to TV. And he became convinced that the audience could take only so much bad news. "What's the use of playing up the murders, tragedies, and the sorry side of life? What the hell's the sense of going into the details of a suicide, unless of course, it's a prominent person. TV has so much emotional impact. I see no reason to play these things up. Why leave people in a dismal fashion if you can help it. People regard you as their *friend*."

The bond between audience and newscaster was an extraordinary phenomenon from the start. Viewers felt they knew the anchor personally, and that *he knew them*. Many seemed convinced that he was interested in the most mundane details of their lives. In part, the illusion of intimacy is fostered by the circumstances in which people watch TV — in their living rooms, bedrooms, and dens, places normally reserved for family members and friends. And the anchors themselves foster the illusion by talking directly to viewers. Swayze says he always imagined he was speaking to small groups of twos and threes, never to millions. He also memorized his scripts, so that he could look directly into the lens of the camera. His phenomenal, trained memory was a valuable asset in those days before TelePrompTers were perfected and it was considered bad form to be seen reading. In the fifties, he dazzled audiences on "Who Said That?" with his encyclopedic recall of current events. And he could commit all his lines on the "Caravan" to memory after two or three readings.

He figured a few other things out, too. "TV reception was so poor in those days that I discovered that unless the pattern on my suit was very bold, it didn't register on camera. So I figured there were two things I could do — change my ties and wear a flower. It made you a little different — made people remember you."

He was right. To this day, many people remember that John Cameron Swayze changed his tie every day and always wore a flower in his lapel. They were gimmicks, though, and they began to annoy his colleagues, as did his obsessive concern about his appearance. Should he wear his toupee, or shouldn't he? Was his carnation fresh? Had someone remembered to refrigerate it?

The crew deviled him endlessly about his toupee, sometimes to the point of cruelty. They would sneak it out of his drawer and hide it, watching him erupt in anger as air time drew near. Finally, with only fifteen or twenty seconds left, some relenting soul would toss him his hairpiece. The teasing got so bad he had to keep it clamped on his head all the time.

The way most of his colleagues saw it, Swayze was more of a performer than a newsman. "Didn't know his ass from his car about news" is the way one of them put it. But the public loved him. For the first four or five years, he piled up huge rating leads over his primary rival, Douglas Edwards. The short, wiry Swayze, known as "the mighty monarch of the air," was popular with everyone from bus drivers to senators. Eisenhower swore by him; he would do favors for Swayze that he wouldn't do for anyone else.

Part of Swayze's popularity, of course, was traceable to NBC's superior strength as a television network. In 1950, for example, when NBC had fifty-six TV affiliates, CBS had only twenty-seven. NBC owed its head start to the fact that it was a subsidiary of RCA, a huge, profitable manufacturing concern with TV sets for sale.* David Sarnoff, the presi-

*CBS made a brief foray into manufacturing TV sets and picture tubes in the fifties, but the venture was unsuccessful.

dent of RCA (always referred to as "the General"), had dreamed of introducing television into the American home as early as 1923, and he promoted TV at every opportunity. This visionary genius, an immigrant from the steppes of southern Russia, was also the first to foresee the possibility of radio as a "household utility," a prediction he made in 1916. Ten years later, he created NBC, the first national setup for the dissemination of programming; and in 1939, he personally launched the first commercial television service with a speech at the World's Fair in New York City.

World War II put a halt to the manufacture of TV sets, but as soon as production was resumed in 1945, Sarnoff pressed NBC's radio affiliates to apply for television licenses. His rival in the broadcasting world, William Paley, normally so astute in business matters, was less prescient about the timetable for TV's expansion, so he was forced to play catch-up in the affiliate race for a long time.

Nor was CBS in a position to match the sums NBC committed to programming for television. Although CBS would eventually become a wealthy, diversified conglomerate, it was a comparatively small company in the forties, almost wholly dependent on its earnings from radio. RCA was awash in profits from a variety of enterprises, including defense contracts with the government and the sale of phonographs. Sarnoff, who had seen how a comedy team called "Amos 'n' Andy" had caused a surge in the sale of radios, knew that programming was the key to the sale of TV sets. People wouldn't buy them unless there was something they wanted to see. So he was willing to let NBC lose the millions of dollars necessary to get television going. CBS would lose huge sums as well, but Paley was forced to proceed more cautiously.

When it came to news, NBC's resources were so superior that there was practically no contest between the two networks, a fact that has become obscured in the mists of time and myth. Partly this is because the daily news programs weren't taken seriously by anyone at the time, not even scholars or political scientists, so much of the early history went unrecorded. In addition, the literature of television news has concentrated so heavily on CBS News and those two great fascinators, Murrow and Paley, that NBC's early innovations and triumphs have been largely ignored.

Who remembers that NBC was the only network to provide regular coverage of the White House and the Pentagon under Truman, that it scored beat after beat on Capitol Hill, or that it sent its camera crews to cover the fighting in Korea, the *first* armchair war? All this was possible because NBC began hiring its own photographers in 1949 and earmarked more money for building a TV news operation.

A clear demonstration of NBC's superiority in those days is provided by the two networks' coverage of Dwight Eisenhower's 1953 inauguration, copies of which have somehow survived and can be seen at the National Archives in Washington. NBC's new portable cameras were able to get close-ups of Eisenhower and Truman, emerging from the White House, stopping to pose for photographers, riding in their open car, waving to the crowds. CBS never showed either man's face until they reached the Capitol. The audience saw only a distant, rear-view shot of a car riding down Pennsylvania Avenue, held on the screen for several minutes — an eternity on TV.

Robert McCormick, a newsman who contributed daily reports from Washington on the Swayze show in the early years, remembers how disadvantaged CBS was in that era. ''NBC was all alone in town. There was simply no competition.'' Whatever the Edwards show got out of Washington was filmed by the lone newsreel cameraman, and professionally, he led a rough life. ''I felt so sorry for the poor little bastard,'' McCormick says. ''We had two two-man crews in Washington, and after a while, we added a third cameraman, and the Telenews guy was up against our entire operation. When he was up on Capitol Hill, he used to walk around and see if he could find our cables and then follow them to where we were shooting. That way he could crawl in after us and cover himself.''

It was all so new and experimental in those days; McCormick and his cohorts would try anything to put news on the screen. When film wasn't available, they substituted still pictures, charts, even animated cartoons. ''We had a nut who specialized in paper animations,'' McCormick recalls, ''but they were always going haywire. He would put up an elaborate graph, which, through manipulation of strings would be supposed to change as I talked, but the strings would get tangled up, and the damned thing would wind up in a ball or something. That never stopped us from trying, though.''

Gradually, NBC began adding more professional newsmen to the staff — people like Reuven Frank, the creator of the ''Huntley-Brinkley Report,'' and John Chancellor, an up-and-coming newswriter from Chicago, who along with McCormick and others pioneered the difficult art of marrying words and pictures. They also began to concern themselves with upgrading NBC's journalistic standards, which meant that the cameramen had to be taken in hand. Nearly all of them had trained with the newsreels, where faking of events was common and doctoring of film routine. They knew all kinds of tricks, such as carrying around a jug of water in the car in case they came across an accident. Since the film was black and white, the water looked like blood when it was poured on the pavement. One by one, such ploys were eliminated.

NBC's superiority in news was mainly pictorial, however; it was CBS that always took the lead in setting journalistic standards for the rest of the industry, partly because of Murrow's influence, and partly because top-echelon executives like Paley and Stanton took a personal interest in news, wanting to put out a product they could be proud of.

The Swayze show was not high on the list of matters that concerned Sylvester "Pat" Weaver, a brilliant advertising executive who was brought in to run NBC in 1949. From his fertile imagination sprang such long-running commercial successes as the "Today" show, "Tonight," and the NBC "Monitor" series on radio. Weaver also created the TV special — lavish entertainment productions he called "spectaculars." He had the vision to see that TV news would one day be great, but to him, it hardly seemed worth bothering with in the fifties. "The technology was so primitive in those days; it was obvious it was going to be a nothing thing, an inferior service. We had radio for our great service. The way I looked at it, why not let John Cameron Swayze go hopscotching the world for headlines."

Weaver remembers Swayze as a good reader, someone who came in on time, never caused any trouble, and kept the sponsor happy. But he did not generate much praise from the critics. Weaver's solution was to try to hire Ed Murrow or Eric Sevareid away from CBS, but both men turned him down. "If we had been able to get them," he says, "we would have done more with the evening news. I was thinking of expanding it from fifteen to twenty-five minutes, for example, but as long as we only had Swayze, I figured why bother?"

In spite of Weaver's low opinion of Swayze, his tenure as anchor of the evening news was secure as long as the sponsors were happy with him. By 1952, however, he was no longer used as the key man for conventions, elections, and other major events. Similarly, Douglas Edwards was replaced as CBS's "leading man" at the 1952 conventions. Sig Mickelson, the head of Television News, was convinced that Walter Cronkite, the network's only other full-time TV correspondent, would do a better job.

Cronkite was a seasoned wire service reporter who had been anchoring the local news for the CBS-owned station in Washington since 1950. Mickelson had known Cronkite since the forties, and had always admired his work, especially after seeing him handle the news in Washington. Cronkite was more forceful than Edwards, on and off screen, and he was an Olympic-class ad libber.

Three stars emerged from the 1952 conventions: Dwight D. Eisenhower, Betty Furness (who had a marvelous way with refrigerator doors), and Walter Cronkite. Newspaper writers called Cronkite's performance that summer in Chicago "memorable" and "superb."

The conventions also marked the introduction into the language of a new term: *anchorman*. In one of their preconvention meetings, Mickelson and Hewitt discussed the need to have their strongest person in the booth, holding together the coverage from the floor. Hewitt compared the arrangement to a relay team, where the strongest runner, who runs the final leg of the race, is called the "anchorman." It was not a particularly elegant expression as applied to television, but it stuck.

The year 1952 also marked the first time television became an important force in the nation's political life. The coaxial cable linking the network and its affiliates now stretched from coast to coast, and 35 percent of America's households, including people the politicians viewed as "influentials," had TV sets. Eisenhower, reluctantly embracing the new medium, hired an advertising agency and consented to star in a series of thirty-minute paid political commercials that depicted him as both a hero and a regular guy. Stevenson, who refused to be "merchandized," was at a great disadvantage on TV; reading his formal, prepared speeches, he came across as distant and cold. That was the year, too, that Richard Nixon saved his political life on television with the "Checkers" speech, denying that he had ever misused campaign funds.

Overnight, it dawned on the CBS radio correspondents that the action was shifting to TV, and they wanted a piece of it. People like David Schoenbrun and Charles Collingwood clamored the loudest, but it did them no good; Edwards and Cronkite had the only two news positions on television sewed up.

The following year, CBS took a major step toward improving its daily news service, canceling its contract with Telenews and hiring its own cameramen. But the evening news, renamed "Douglas Edwards with the News," remained a humble one-man show, a stepchild within the network, even though it had been fully sponsored for several years and was beginning to cut in on John Cameron Swayze's lead in the ratings.

The physical conditions under which the program was produced were appalling. While the patricians of radio worked in modern offices at CBS headquarters on Madison Avenue, the Edwards crew occupied a cramped, dingy, airless space on Forty-second Street over Grand Central Station. One employee, seeing the place for the first time, likened it to Dante's Inferno. More serious was the location of the broadcast studio, a converted German singing club called Liederkranz Hall, thirteen blocks away from Grand Central. Every night, at exactly seven-twenty, the staff would make a mad dash by taxi for Liederkranz, praying they would arrive with the film and script by seven-thirty, when Edwards had to go on.

The quality of the program began to improve after CBS hired its own film crews in 1953, but superhuman effort was still required to get the show on the air because the film was developed at a *third* location across town. Once, when film of Queen Elizabeth's visit to Bermuda was coming into Idlewild (now JFK) Airport, the film director realized there was no way the film could be transported to the lab and then to the studio in heavy traffic by seven-thirty. The solution he devised — setting up a portable processing machine at Liederkranz — seemed brilliant; but the machine failed, and the film rolled out dripping wet. The film editors, seeing their duty, stretched the Queen's arrival all over the men's room floor until it had dried, then rushed it onto the projector. Finally, in 1955, after repeated complaints from the sponsor, Pall Mall cigarettes, CBS built a broadcast studio on Forty-second Street.

By comparison, the company spent lavishly on Murrow's weekly series, "See It Now," which was launched in 1951. It had the best equipment money could buy and a permanent staff three times the size of the Edwards crew! In fact, the Murrow staff was larger and better paid than the entire CBS network television news operation, of which it was not really a part.

"See It Now" was never a great ratings success, but it was an enormous hit with the critics. Murrow garnered so much acclaim for CBS that the company saw little reason to spend more money on the Edwards show, the theory being, apparently, that one prestige vehicle was sufficient.

"See It Now" was a source of tremendous in-house pride, especially to those who worked on the show. Nobody thought of going to work on the Edwards show; that would have been tantamount to a demotion. As Joe

Wershba, one of the original field producers on "See It Now," explains, "Once you were with Murrow and Friendly, as far as I was concerned, you were on the top. After that, anything in a way would have been a comedown."

The early programs often focused on serious topics, such as mine safety, the Korean War, and economic recession, but the approach was not particularly controversial. Then, in 1953, Murrow decided to take on Senator Joseph R. McCarthy and the excesses of the anti-Communist movement. Murrow was not the first journalist to challenge McCarthy, but no other newspaper columnist or radio commentator had as powerful a pulpit or the same store of personal prestige. The first program, broadcast on October 20, 1953, examined the injustice committed against Milo Radulovich, a twenty-six-year-old college student who was stripped of his Air Force Reserve commission because his sister and father were accused of radical leanings. The program was a triumph for Murrow, but the reaction was pale compared to the uproar after his broadcast the following March when he attacked McCarthy head on. After refuting various McCarthy allegations point by point, Murrow concluded with these memorable words:

> We will not be driven by fear into an age of unreason, if we dig deep into our own history and our own doctrine and remember that we are not descended from fearful men, not from men who feared to write, to speak, to associate and to defend causes which were for the moment unpopular.
>
> This is no time for men who oppose Senator McCarthy's methods to keep silent. We can deny our heritage and our history, but we cannot escape responsibility for the results. There is no way for a citizen of a republic to abdicate his responsibilities.

The result was electrifying. The day after the broadcast, CBS received over 12,000 letters, the most ever for a single program, running fifteen to one in Murrow's favor. For weeks afterward, he was mobbed by people who wanted to shake his hand. A British friend of Murrow's who lunched with him two days after the broadcast was awed by the reaction: "After lunch, we walked up Fifth Avenue; it was a rash thing to have done. Of course, he was instantly recognized. First, our own pavement was jammed with people who were determined to give him the hero's treatment, and then Fifth Avenue traffic was brought practically to a standstill as the news of his presence spread, and men and women came rushing across the road in all directions. It was a most moving experience for him, and though he took it modestly, he clearly found great satisfaction in such a demonstration of support and approval.''*

The McCarthy broadcasts took considerable courage on Murrow's part, because he was knowingly violating CBS policy, which forbade newscasters to editorialize, or ''to further either side of any debatable issue.'' Tired of the commotion that arose every time a controversial opinion was voiced on the air, Paley laid down the edict in 1937, hoping to confine all expressions of political opinion to round-table discussions and other ''balanced'' forums.

Although Paley telephoned Murrow the day of the McCarthy broadcast to promise his support, the chairman clearly did not relish the furor he knew it would arouse. A measure of the company's ambivalence can be read into the fact that CBS would not pay to advertise the broadcast in the newspapers. Murrow and Friendly had to dig into their own pockets for $1500 to run an ad in the *New York Times*. As Murrow himself well knew, had it not been for his status as a great star, he would never have been permitted to defy established company policy.

Eventually, Murrow would pay a high price for his independence; in 1956, ''See It Now'' was cut back from a weekly half-hour to a one-hour program broadcast eight times a year. Two years later, it would be abolished altogether. But Murrow had established another tradition of American broadcasting — the crusading reporter. In his hands, of course, it was an honorable tradition, but it presented possibilities for misuse by less scrupulous, more self-serving individuals.

In 1955, however, Murrow was still at the height of his fame and public prestige. To the liberal press, he was everything that was good about television, virtually canonized by a *Time* cover story that began, ''Amid the trite and untrue that shed a honky-tonk glare from the nation's TV sets come moments that pierce reality and live up to television's magic gift for thrusting millions of spectators into the lap of history in the making. As television moved into its second decade, chances were that some of the best of such moments would come from a dark, high-domed man with a hangdog look, an apocalyptic voice and a cachet as plain as his inevitable cigarettes.''

Murrow's phenomenal prestige began to haunt the executives at NBC, which had nobody on the staff who came close to him in terms of

*Quoted in *Prime Time: The Life of Edward R. Murrow,* by Alexander Kendrick (Boston and Toronto: Little, Brown, 1969).

reputation. Every time they picked up a newspaper or magazine and read another ode to him, it was like having salt rubbed into an open wound. By comparison, NBC's best-known newsman, John Cameron Swayze, began to seem an embarrassment, a relic of an earlier era. His standing among executives plummeted even lower when Douglas Edwards overtook him in the ratings in 1955.

The NBC chieftains were determined to hire their own attractive, in-house intellectual, not to anchor — after all, Murrow did not anchor TV newscasts — but to tackle issues as a commentator on radio and as narrator of a public affairs series on TV. It was especially urgent, they felt, to find someone in time for the 1956 conventions — again, not necessarily to anchor, but to add luster to NBC's lineup of talent. "The reason the conventions were so important to us then," explains Reuven Frank, who was already a senior producer at the network, "is that news never got on the air — no bulletins, no pre-emptions, no late-night specials, nothing except the fifteen-minute evening news. So the conventions gave you the first real whack at the audience. If they liked you, maybe they would come back."

A clutch of candidates were considered — novelist John Hersey, columnist Stewart Alsop, Henry Cabot Lodge, Jimmy Stewart. The name Chet Huntley came up, too. An anchorman for the ABC station in Los Angeles, he was said to resemble Murrow physically, and he, too, had a reputation for championing left-wing causes.

Sylvester Weaver, the president of NBC, says the first time he saw Huntley was at a luncheon in New York in 1955, where he made a "brief but very intelligent speech. I turned to Davidson Taylor [the vice president in charge of public affairs] and said, 'Get him.' Some people were afraid we might have some problems with him because of his reputation as a free-thinker, but I said, 'Everybody can be controlled. Get him.' " NBC was prepared to live with a fearless liberal if that's what it took to get good write-ups from the critics.

3
Chet and David:
The First Superstars

*Huntley and Brinkley . . . long ago ceased to
be mere newsmen and became personalities,
taking their place in American popular culture beside such immortal duos as Blanchard
and Davis, Abbott and Costello, Roy Rogers
and Trigger, and Fibber McGee and Molly.*
— William Whitworth
The New Yorker, August 3, 1968

THE 1956 political conventions did not make for great theater. Even before the Republicans met to nominate Dwight Eisenhower for a second term, the movement to dump Richard Nixon as Vice President had fizzled, thereby removing the only possible element of suspense. The Democrats, who were more boisterous, as usual, struck a few sparks when Adlai Stevenson threw the vice presidential nomination open to the floor. Estes Kefauver emerged as the winner, while the runner-up, John F. Kennedy, established himself as a national political figure. But the real stars of both conventions turned out to be a pair of relatively unknown newsmen, Chet Huntley and David Brinkley.

Their success came as a pleasant surprise to Davidson Taylor and the other NBC executives who had reluctantly approved the Huntley-Brinkley combination. Although Huntley was recruited to play a major role at the conventions, his lack of national political reporting experience led some to question the wisdom of letting him do the play-by-play. Reuven Frank, then a senior producer, was urging the selection of the Washington correspondent of the Swayze show — a twelve-year veteran of NBC named David Brinkley. Frank was impressed with Brinkley's instinct for television: He never told viewers what they could see for themselves ("The President is waving to the crowds now"); instead, he amplified the pictures with intelligent, often witty commentary. Brinkley also knew when to be quiet and let the pictures speak for themselves. But a number of executives thought he was impudent and lazy — he *was* known to oversleep on occasion.

As the NBC executives pondered the situation, all kinds of names were proposed, including a suggestion by Davidson Taylor to use a double bill: Ray Scherer, NBC's White House correspondent, and Bill Henry, a political columnist for the *Los Angeles Times,* who had anchored NBC's convention coverage in 1952. "As soon as he mentioned putting two people together," says Frank, "it was as if a light bulb was turned on." Everyone in the news department realized simultaneously that a Huntley-Brinkley combination might work. The proposal was coolly received by higher management, however. Even after an agreement was reached, there was so little faith in the arrangement that NBC did not release the news to the press for another six weeks. And while the two men were given their material and told to bone up, no fuss was made over their selection.

In Chicago, Huntley and Brinkley clicked as a team immediately, Brinkley's irreverent, offbeat sense of humor playing well against Huntley's air of settled authority. At forty-five, Huntley looked and sounded mature — the wise father figure in contrast to thirty-six-year-old Brinkley's slightly naughty younger brother. Together, they projected a tone of amused but reasonable skepticism that was not only novel at the time, but ideally suited to covering the conventions, where pomposity so often vied with silliness for attention. Whereas Cronkite in those days had a tendency to make everything sound terribly important, contrary to what the cameras showed, Brinkley, especially, had an eye for the phony, the deliciously absurd. His favorites were people like the delegate who wore a shirt with neon tubing across the front; every time the camera picked him out of the crowd, the delegate would press a button in his pocket and make the name of his candidate light up.

Brinkley also had the Southerner's gift for colorful speech, which flourished in the political milieu. Commenting on the platform committee, which was about to make its report, he predicted that "the two platforms will fearlessly commit both parties to favor mother love and the protection of the whooping crane, and to oppose the man-eating shark and the more unpopular forms of sin."

He had been discreetly but strenuously preparing for the conventions months ahead of getting the assignment, which did not hurt the quality of his ad libs. In a black leather notebook he had been writing down, with his small, meticulous lettering, facts and anecdotes about all the participants. Huntley was equally well-versed. A superb professional, he carried the bulk of the commentary, while Brinkley supplied the sidebars that made their coverage distinctive.

Some of the executives watching Huntley and Brinkley suspected that they might be on to a winning combination, but what guaranteed their future as a team were the good reviews they got in the print press, especially the *New York Times*. Jack Gould praised the two men for having "injected the much-needed note of humor in the commentary," adding that "the CBS news department needs to cheer up." Of Brinkley in particular, Gould wrote prophetically, "Mr. Brinkley quite possibly could be the forerunner of a new school of television commentator . . . He is not an earnest Voice of Authority . . . He contributes his observations with assurance but not insistence. But during the many long hours in Chicago, where at times it has seemed there has only been a national convention of commentators, Mr. Brinkley's extraordinary accomplishment has been not to talk too much. He has the knack for the succinct phrase that sums up the situation."

Brinkley, for one, believes that the importance of praise from critics like Gould at that stage of his career cannot be overstated. "The people running news in those days either had no background in journalism, or they came from print, and they were not inclined to rely on their own judgment about television. They were inclined to rely on the critics to tell them what was good and what was bad, and they never thought I was any good until the *New York Times* said so."

As the favorable notices poured in, another light bulb lit up at NBC. Why not have Huntley and Brinkley replace John Cameron Swayze? Using the same individuals to anchor the evening news and to handle special events would multiply the opportunities for exposure and help establish them as stars.

Although television was now a booming, highly profitable enterprise, watched in more than 70 percent of American homes, the network news divisions were still largely marking time in the midfifties, programming only two or two and a half hours a week of news and public affairs for TV. Staffing was minimal. Besides the Washington correspondent assigned to the Nightly News, NBC had only two full-time TV reporters — John

Chancellor, who traveled the South and Midwest, and Roy Neal, who was based in Los Angeles. CBS and ABC had no correspondents whatever outside the capital. What little domestic coverage the nets offered came mainly from the local staffs of their network-owned stations. Even in Washington, only a handful of beats existed — the White House, the Pentagon, and Congress — and even there the reporters concentrated on radio. TV was still primarily a picture show, for which photographers, not reporters, were the essential element.

Amazingly, CBS and NBC had more bureaus abroad than they did in the United States in the 1950s.* London, Paris, Tokyo, and Bonn were all staffed, but not Atlanta, Detroit, or San Francisco. This was in part an unthinking holdover of the pattern established in World War II, but no doubt it also reflected the public's lack of interest in domestic affairs, generally. People worried about Communist infiltration, but they didn't lock their doors at night. Happily unaware of the time bombs waiting to explode — crime, race relations, the deterioration of the cities, the failure of the schools, the energy shortage — Americans were confident that whatever problems came up would be taken care of by the self-correcting nature of their political and economic institutions.

There was also little incentive for the networks to build up their domestic operations so long as the only regular outlet for news was a slender fifteen minutes a night. The atmosphere of sleepy neglect surrounding network news was interrupted, however, by the success of Huntley and Brinkley, the first newscasters whose popularity was systematically exploited on behalf of higher commercial revenues for the network.

Not that Huntley and Brinkley created an overnight sensation when they made their debut on October 29, 1956. The ratings, which were already embarrassingly low under Swayze, dropped even lower. Many viewers were irate when he was taken off the air, including his biggest fan, President Eisenhower. Ike's press secretary, James Hagerty, called in NBC White House correspondent Ray Scherer to pass the word that the President was unhappy about the switch.

At first, the sponsors didn't think much of the change, either. In the summer of 1957, the program was completely "sustaining"; that is, not a single commercial was sold. "I was convinced I would be asked in some Friday and be told, 'Thank you very much, but your services won't be

*ABC did not establish foreign bureaus until the sixties.

needed any longer,' '' says Frank. "We all knew we were in trouble, and we would ask ourselves if we should do anything different. We decided that we wouldn't, but we were all prepared for the axe to fall.''

Davidson Taylor complained that Huntley was too dour. "Can't you get him to smile more?'' he asked Frank, suggesting that they write the word *Smile* at appropriate intervals on the TelePrompTer. Frank wisely ignored him. For one thing, Frank was afraid Huntley would try to oblige. When Huntley first came to NBC, he was acutely conscious of the fact that he had been hired to be "the new Murrow,'' and wondered if he should emphasize the similarity by smoking on camera, as Murrow did. Frank told him, "You've got a choice. You can either be the second Edward R. Murrow or the first Chester R. Huntley. Do it straight, and whatever personality you have will come out.''

The sign-off that Frank dreamed up for the "Huntley-Brinkley Report'' — "Good night, Chet.'' "Good night, David'' — was controversial at first. At the White House, Ray Scherer would cringe as his colleagues called after him, "Good night, Raymond,'' in their best limp-wristed manner. Huntley and Brinkley didn't like the ending, either. "I resisted it with every ounce of strength I had,'' says Brinkley, "but Reuven insisted on it. Finally, I agreed to try it for a week or two, but I really hated it. I thought it was irrational. I thought it was hokey. I don't know how I would phrase it now, but at the time I said it made us sound like two fags. Then, of course, it began entering into the language, appearing on billboards and what not, and we couldn't change it.''

Frank ran the show. Huntley and Brinkley had veto power, and Brinkley, in particular, played an important editorial role, but everyone took it for granted in the early days of television that the producer had the final say. TV news was such a complicated undertaking, requiring so much convoluted choreography to get the program on the air smoothly and on time, that power naturally tended to gravitate to the person who understood the mechanics of the operation and could manipulate it best. But Frank was an intellectual, too, widely admired for his intelligence and imagination. Under his guidance, the "Huntley-Brinkley Report'' evolved into a literate, well-written program, with an emphasis on good picture stories. "I laid down the principle that we were talking to the lawyer's wife in Dubuque, who was president of the PTA,'' he says. "When there was no news, we didn't pretend there was. One day, we led with the fact that James Gould Cozzens's book, *By Love Possessed*, didn't win the Pulitzer Prize — there had been a tremendous build-up over the whole thing; it made the cover of the news weeklies and so on. Also, we felt that not all news was serious. If it wasn't we wouldn't pretend that it was.''

Frank broke once and for all with the old newsreel clichés — the ship christenings, fashion shows, and baby parades. He hated verbal clichés, too, insisting on a care and accuracy in writing news that was previously unknown on television. The writers were instructed not to say "Chinese Reds," for example, but "Chinese Communists."

By today's standards, the program was fairly highbrow. Charlie Sieg, one of the first directors on the show, recalls the time that Frank scheduled eight minutes on the Middle East but was not planning to include the fact that Ingrid Bergman had twins that day. Sieg recalls that he said to Frank, "'Reuven, do you think it's going to hurt the American public to cut forty-five seconds out of the Middle East story so we can mention that Ingrid Bergman, somebody that millions of people know, had twins?' Reuven grunted — that's what he did when he was preoccupied — but later he came out and said, 'You're right.'"

If Frank set the editorial policy, Huntley and Brinkley set the tone for the program. In place of the cutesy, corny tone of the Swayze era, the humor was strictly adult. It was apparent to the audience that Huntley and Brinkley were not merely neutral conveyor belts for facts; they were real, live men who quite obviously possessed a set of values and opinions. In the early years of the show, they did a fair amount of editorializing, Huntley more than Brinkley. At the afternoon meeting, Frank used to ask if anyone had a "sermon" to give that day. Huntley, who was deeply interested in foreign affairs, used to do an opinion piece about once or twice a week. Brinkley was more apt to do ironic little essays, which, though not overtly political, conveyed his fundamental populism — his distaste for big government, taxes, bloated and inefficient bureaucracy, and the idle rich. They were moralists. And, after the shock of Sputnik, when Americans exhibited a new willingness to criticize themselves and their government, their gently chiding tone fit the mood of the country.

Even in later years, when the power of television had been grasped more fully and there was less freedom to editorialize, viewers thought they could detect opinions lurking beneath the surface. "We're quite used to Mr. Huntley's eyebrows taking positions," wrote James J. Kilpatrick, the conservative columnist. Others thought Brinkley's eyebrows said it all.

The "Huntley-Brinkley Report" *looked* like a news program for grownups. For the first time, TV newscasters were trying to provide a bit of context with the news. An admiring critic, writing about the two men in the *Saturday Review* in 1957, noted ''their propensity to introduce, every now and then, a revelatory footnote to the mere facts.'' The program was primarily a triumph of style, not substance, however. Television news was still almost entirely dependent on ''pseudo events'' — presidential press conferences, airport arrival scenes, and other events staged for the benefit of the cameras, as well as pictures of floods, train wrecks, and other filmable catastrophes. Still, the show caught the public's fancy. By 1958, Huntley and Brinkley pulled even with Douglas Edwards in the ratings, and in the fall of 1959 they acquired the full-time sponsorship of Texaco, two enormous boosts.

The title of the program was changed to the ''Texaco Huntley-Brinkley Report,'' but from all indications, Texaco did not attempt to interfere with the program; advertiser influence over television news had substantially weakened by this time. In 1961 Reuven Frank told an interviewer for the now-defunct *Television* magazine, ''To my knowledge, Texaco has never gotten into the news aspects. When they get a letter of criticism — and with television as the only truly national news medium, you cannot avoid regional criticism — they don't buck it to us, but ask for the script and reply themselves. They don't call us with their own ideas of stories. When Castro confiscated their refinery, we got no instructions on how to handle the story. In fact, they called us for news of the situation.'' Things had come a long way from the time that the R. J. Reynolds Tobacco Company forbade anyone to be shown smoking cigars on its programs except for Winston Churchill.

The one person who did as much as, if not more than, Huntley and Brinkley to glamorize news at NBC was Robert Kintner, who became president of the network in 1957. A former president of ABC who started his career as a newspaper reporter, Kintner took over NBC at a time when it was firmly mired in second place, trailing CBS in programming, profits, and revenues. For more than twenty-five years after its founding in the 1920s, NBC had been the dominant network, CBS the upstart. By the early fifties, however, William Paley reversed the situation by stealing away almost all of NBC's great entertainment stars. (Told it would take at least $250,000 to keep Jack Benny from going to CBS, David Sarnoff was unmoved; unlike Paley, he had no feel for or interest in programming. ''I won't pay it,'' he said. ''Why, that's more money than I make.'' Apparently, it didn't occur to him that people didn't turn on their sets to watch the president of RCA.)

Kintner knew it would be a long time before he could turn NBC's entertainment picture around; in the meantime, he thought he could achieve quick, dramatic results in the area of news, especially with the dynamic combination of Huntley and Brinkley spearheading the operation. Supremacy in news, he believed, would help the network regain its dominance in programming and thus restore its image as the leader of broadcasting.

Kintner made sure the news division received two things it never had before: more money and more air time. Under his patronage, news executives had carte blanche to break into scheduled programming — something the networks almost never did up to that time — whenever major news breaks occurred. A man of great audacity, when he heard President Kennedy had been shot, Kintner ordered all commercials off the air and scheduled twenty-four hours of news presentation. (The other networks were shocked, but they were forced to follow suit.) The Kintner formula — plenty of sex and violence in the entertainment shows and the best, most aggressive news department money could buy — worked like magic. NBC's revenues rose to an all-time high.

A short, stocky, forbidding-looking man with thick spectacles and a gruff manner, Kintner frightened most of his employees, especially since he was known to get drunk at times and browbeat people. At the end of his tenure at NBC, when he was sipping vodka steadily from a large tumbler, he would summon executives into his office and harangue them for hours. But morale in the news division soared in the Kintner era. Unlike other network executives, who like to surround themselves with show business celebrities, Kintner had a genuine passion for news, and preferred the company of his correspondents, inviting them to his home in Westport, Connecticut, or to his apartment on Fifth Avenue. Not only did he promote Huntley and Brinkley, he also set out to make stars of his other reporters, such people as John Chancellor, Ray Scherer, and Edwin Newman. He would bring them to New York for a week, put them up in hotel rooms, and instruct the NBC publicity people to arrange for interviews with the leading TV critics.

Kintner used every means at his disposal to create an aura of excitement and momentum at NBC News. At the beginning of every Huntley-Brinkley broadcast, an announcer informed the audience that the program had been "assembled for television every weekday night by the world's largest and most comprehensive broadcast news organization: the news department of the National Broadcasting Company." After Huntley and Brinkley pulled ahead of Douglas Edwards in April 1960, a tag line was added, reminding people that the program had more listeners than any other newscast in the world. A barrage of press releases streamed from the publicity department, trumpeting each new feat.

While all this attention to news proved to be a boon to the public, spurring the other networks to increase *their* output of news and public affairs, Kintner also stands accused as the man who precipitated the ferocious, almost juvenile rivalry among network news divisions — a contest that shows no sign of abating. Kintner had a rule, "CBS plus thirty," meaning that no matter how late CBS stayed on the air during elections, space shots, et cetera, NBC would not go off until at least thirty minutes later. "He pushed the news department simply outrageously," says David Brinkley. "He insisted, *demanded* that we be the first on the air, sometimes behaving quite brutally. He would call people at 4:00 A.M. — he was one of those half-crazy people who never slept — but we didn't object to his tactics. We liked it because it was paying off beautifully."

Before national political conventions, Kintner would gather the news staff together and exhort everybody to get out and beat the opposition. He was not particularly gracious in victory, however. After the Democratic convention in Atlantic City in 1964, when NBC demolished CBS in the ratings (at one point, more than 80 percent of the audience was tuned to NBC), Brinkley recalls being asked to stop in Kintner's office. "This was one of the greatest ratings victories in the history of television, but when I went into his office, all he did was offer me a warm glass of whiskey — no ice — a damp handshake, and a gruff word of thanks."

Kintner's personal idiosyncrasies aside, his determination to promote news was a huge success. By 1960, the NBC News team was so popular it attracted a 51 percent share of the audience at the conventions, an almost unheard of share, as opposed to 36 percent for CBS and 13 percent for ABC. Brinkley, as usual, was in good form. "The Republicans should have an honest-to-goodness convention this year," he quipped. "Last time it was a coronation." The mood in NBC's control room was jubilant, especially after CBS put Eric Sevareid and Ed Murrow into the anchor booth with Cronkite. Ostensibly they had been brought in to provide additional commentary and analysis, but everyone knew they were there to shore up Cronkite, who was thought to be no match for Huntley and

Brinkley. At one point Murrow loosened his tie on camera because of the sweltering heat, and Reuven Frank, who was directing NBC's convention coverage, cracked, "If Sevareid takes off his coat, Huntley and Brinkley are going to their undershirts." The reporters and producers standing there laughed uproariously; they felt invincible. A note of smugness was creeping in, too. "We thought we were so good," says Frank, "that we didn't even watch CBS. *Our* competition was the 'Today' show."

Huntley and Brinkley became so enshrined in the popular culture that, at JFK's inaugural gala, Frank Sinatra and Milton Berle sang a parody in their honor: "Huntley, Brinkley/Huntley, Brinkley/One is glum/The other twinkly . . ." to the tune of "Love and Marriage." Throughout the first half of the sixties, they consistently outdrew their rivals on the evening news, although the margin of victory over CBS was never as wide as it was for special events.

Over the years, TV writers have remarked on the mysterious "chemistry" that made the team so successful, but their appeal is not all that puzzling. Huntley was an exceptionally gifted and attractive broadcaster — it was he who carried about two thirds of the show. Brinkley was the highly stylized, individualistic writer who left viewers with a thought or a phrase they could relish — something that made them feel a little cleverer at the end of the program. An illusory feeling, perhaps, but a pleasant one nonetheless.

Huntley's great strength was his ability on the air. He had a magnificent, resonant voice, and a presence that made him admired and believed. He was also one of the great readers. Like Douglas Edwards, he could take a script, absolutely cold, and give it a polished reading. In the fifties and sixties, anchors often had to read film narrations live, a rather delicate and dangerous operation since they rarely saw the film before it rolled on the air. The script would contain instructions, such as "Pause for five seconds to let sound of locomotive come up," and a writer would stand behind Chet and tap him on the shoulder, cuing him to begin reading again. "He was just beautiful," says Pat Trese, a long-time writer on the show, "absolutely unflappable. He was one of those guys who made everything you wrote sound better."

Huntley's professionalism made him easy to write for, too. He read two words per foot of film, or three words a second, as steady as a metronome, unless somebody died. Then he would slow down to his death mode, which was two words per second.

Of the two men, Huntley undoubtedly had the broader audience appeal.

Not everyone realized it at the time, though some producers noticed that when David was off, Chet would carry the show alone with ease. Brinkley alone did not wear as well. Despite the simplicity of his language, his sophisticated ideas demanded the viewer's full attention. And, even in the early days, he had a certain detachment verging on boredom that did not appeal to everyone. It was Brinkley's light touch, however, combined with his unique way of looking at things, that gave the program its distinctive feeling, that made it talked about, sometimes even memorable. Connoisseurs used to collect his pithy gems, known as "Brinkleyisms" — like the comment he made about the starlings that were making a nuisance of themselves in Washington. "The proper name of the starling is *Sturnis vulgaris*. Well, they may not be so sturnis, but they certainly have proved themselves vulgaris." Or the time he said, absolutely deadpan, that the translation of the Arabic writing on Washington's new mosque meant "Bingo every Thursday night."

His stock in trade, of course, was bungled bureaucracy, the perfect target for his dry, understated style. On the subject of aid to Peru one evening, he told the audience, "Some time ago, word came to Washington that the Indians in Peru, thousands of men, women, and children, were starving. So the U.S. government shipped off a hundred thousand tons of food to Peru and unloaded it on a dock. The rest of the story is this. A lot of food was stolen, the Peruvian government sold some of it and spent the money on houses for its officials, the Peruvian cavalry fed some to its horses. More of it decayed on the dock in the weather until it spoiled. The Indians were, and are, hungry still . . ."

Brinkley mastered the art of writing for the air in a way that no one had ever done before. He had a knack for reducing the most complex stories to their barest essentials, writing with a clarity that may be unequaled to this day. In part, he wrote clearly because he thought clearly; he is one of the most brilliant and original people ever to have worked in broadcast news. He also understood that the ear is a poor conductor of information, so he kept his phrases short, simple, and direct. His individuality was further enhanced by his speaking style — those famous clipped cadences that were themselves an aid to understanding. Soon, a throng of young broadcasters began imitating his speech patterns, whether consciously or unconsciously. (Walter Cronkite says he used to avoid watching Brinkley for fear he would pick up his mannerisms.) Once, an ad appeared in *Variety* offering $1500 to the person who could do the best imitation of

David Brinkley. But his imitators, by definition, lacked his authenticity and originality, and none of them succeeded in making the same impact on an audience.

David the imp and Chet the statesman — they made a terrific combination. They had sex appeal, too, the secret ingredient that made them so much more exciting than other newscasters. Both were manly, so men liked them, but women went wild over them. Huntley was six feet two inches tall, weighed 195 pounds, and had light brown, wavy hair, classic features, and thick blond eyebrows. Although his style of delivery was grave, when he flashed his radiant smile at the end of the program, he evidently convinced a lot of women he was smiling just for them. The mail was often torrid; his secretary could spot the regulars — Inez, Hazel, Dorothy, to name just a few — without even opening the envelopes.

Brinkley, too, was tall and attractive. His height, almost six feet two, never ceased to amaze people who saw him in person for the first time, his impressive physical size being somehow at variance with the pixie-like quality he conveyed on the screen. He, too, was constantly besieged by female admirers, sometimes to the point of harassment. Once, a woman camped outside the Brinkley home with two suitcases and a portable radio, refusing to leave until she was dragged off by police.

The appeal of Huntley and Brinkley was magnified by the era in which they burst onto the scene. They seemed like a tonic when pitted against the blandness and complacency of the Eisenhower years. But they became even more popular during the Kennedy era. Kennedy, the first President to understand how to manipulate television for his own purposes, made government a form of home entertainment. Because he was glamorous, he made the news seem more glamorous, giving added glamor and sophistication to the two most popular newscasters of their day.

The early sixties saw a dramatic increase in both the quality and quantity of news and issue-oriented programs on television. In part, this was an attempt by the networks to placate the Federal Communications Commission after the quiz show scandals erupted in 1959. The election of John Kennedy and his appointment of Newton Minow as chairman of the Federal Communications Commission acted as a further spur. Minow, a strong proponent of public television, made it plain to the networks that he considered it a matter of necessity, not choice, for them to engage in public service programming. In his now-famous address before the National Association of Broadcasters in 1961, Minow called TV "a vast wasteland,'' citing the endless ''procession of game shows, violence, audience participation shows, formula comedies about totally unbelievable families, blood and thunder, mayhem, violence, sadism, murder, western bad men, western good men, private eyes, gangsters, more violence, and cartoons.'' Warning broadcasters that they would be held to account for this mindless drivel, he told them that in the future, the license renewal process would no longer be a mere formality. The FCC could not, of course, dictate what the networks programmed, since they are not regulated by the government. But the FCC *could* take action against the profitable network-owned TV stations, which *are* licensed by the FCC. (Each network is allowed to own a maximum of five VHF stations.) That year, the networks found it expedient to double the number of hours devoted to news, documentaries, and other informational programs on TV. The following year, NBC and CBS laid plans to expand their early-evening newscasts from fifteen minutes to half an hour.

Improvements in technology also played a part in this sudden explosion of news. The introduction of videotape, which permitted prerecording and instant playback, was a major advance. Producers now had the option of recording a report from a correspondent in a distant city *before* the newscast, eliminating the need for risky, on-air switches. The launching of Telstar, the first communications satellite, was another breakthrough. It made same-day transmission from abroad possible, although the cost was so high that the use of satellites did not become routine until the 1970s. Even so, NBC's slogan on the old ''Camel News Caravan'' — ''Today's News Today'' — was coming very close to being a reality.

Advertisers began showing a new interest in news and public affairs about this time, although most maintained their traditional reluctance to be associated with controversial issues and downbeat subjects. Gulf Oil's decision in 1960 to sponsor all of NBC's instant specials was a landmark, winning much favorable press attention for the company. In 1961, Nationwide Insurance agreed to sponsor Howard K. Smith's weekly program of news and analysis, and the following year the Metropolitan Life Insurance Company signed on to sponsor CBS's breaking news reports. *Business Week* predicted more ''prestige advertisers'' would follow suit, attracted by the cut-rate prices being offered and the chance to reach an up-scale audience: ''As the networks improve their programs, the audiences will increase, and they will be heavily weighted toward the high end of the socioeconomic spectrum. If the experience of current sponsors is any guide, the public relations benefits of association with such shows are significant.''

News had clearly entered a new era, one that emphasized, above all, prestige. It had dawned on the business world that public affairs programs could impart a glossier image to both the network and the advertiser. At the same time, the networks could ingratiate themselves with the FCC and the TV critics. In the dualistic world of the networks, the critics did not carry much weight in the entertainment sphere, since most TV executives did not believe the critics had much effect on the size of the audience. But good reviews were avidly courted for news. Opinion-makers read what the *New York Times*'s Jack Gould and his fellow critics, John Crosby of the *New York Herald Tribune,* Harriet Van Horne of the *New York World-Telegram,* and syndicated columnist Steven Scheuer had to say; their pronouncements had a way of winding up as dogma among the intelligentsia and others the networks wanted to impress.

With prestige as the new watchword, it was desirable for the anchors also to promote an image of substance and seriousness. Advertisers were willing to pay more to be ''next to'' credible, admired journalists. It was not entirely coincidental that Douglas Edwards, still popular with the public but ignored by the critics, was replaced in 1962 by Walter Cronkite, an altogether weightier figure. An anchor still had to have a certain amount of mass appeal, but he had to be able to impress the critics and attract the educated, affluent viewer as well.

Not having to aim for the lowest common denominator, news divisions were encouraged to pursue excellence, to be innovative, to be significant. Documentaries thrived in this era — probing efforts like David Brinkley's ''The Great Highway Robbery,'' an exposé of graft in federal road projects, and CBS's ''Biography of a Bookie Joint,'' which resulted in the firing of the Boston police commissioner and several policemen. For broadcast journalists, it was a glorious moment; staffs were expanding, interference from the corporate sphere was minimal, and airtime was increasing. NBC, which spent more than $20 million on news in 1962, lost $12 million; CBS said it lost $5 million; but nobody seemed to worry about going over budget. News employees were deliberately insulated from the more mercenary aspects of broadcasting — demographics, cost-per-thousand, share points, profits, et cetera. It was important to have the top-rated show — being in first place is infinitely more prestigious than being in second or third — but news professionals did not discuss ratings. Few of them knew how to read a Nielsen rating book, no easy task for the uninitiated.

Within the network, a double system of values evolved, one for the news department, and one for the rest of the corporation. This dual mentality was aptly summed up by a remark CBS-TV president, James Aubrey, made to Fred Friendly, the head of the news division. As Friendly has recounted elsewhere, Aubrey told him, "They say to me, 'Take your soiled little hands, get the ratings, and make as much money as you can.' They say to you, 'Take your lily-white hands, do your best, go the high road, and bring us prestige.'"

Double standard or not, the networks created — no doubt unintentionally — an ideal environment for a fledgling profession to master its art and forge a set of high-minded traditions. As time went by, dedicated news professionals would fight to preserve these traditions, coming to represent a countervailing force against the commercial desires of higher management.

For television news, everything started coming together in the early sixties, including the realization that television could have a profound impact on the political process. One of the most convincing demonstrations of this was provided by the "Great Debates" of 1960; political observers generally agreed that Richard Nixon had lost the election in no small part because of his poor performance — his humorlessness, the dark shadow on his chin, the little beads of sweat on his upper lip. It also became apparent that, as President, John Kennedy had turned the televised press conference into an instrument of government; his bravura performances helped him solidify his narrow political base.

And during the Cuban missile crisis, television was exploited for the first time as an instrument of international diplomacy. On October 22, 1962, at 7:00 P.M., President Kennedy went on the air to demand that the Soviet Union remove its missiles from Cuba and to warn that all Russian vessels headed for Cuba would be stopped and searched. This was brinksmanship at its most extreme. By delivering the ultimatum on television instead of relying on normal diplomatic channels, Kennedy magnified the impact of his action many times over, signaling to the world that there could be no retreat. The American public anxiously waited during a tense two-week period, but the Russians finally backed down: Their ships stopped in midcourse and headed for home. The networks, now used to breaking into scheduled programming in time of crisis, played the drama to the hilt, especially NBC, which broadcast ninety-four bulletins and thirteen specials between October 22 and 28. (The situation may have warranted it in 1962, but NBC under Kintner often went overboard with bulletins. When Lyndon Johnson came down with a bad cold in 1964, for example, it was blown entirely out of proportion by NBC's constant updates.)

The other great drama being played out in the nation's living rooms during those years was the civil rights movement. Most historians, political scientists, and journalists agree that without the television cameras to show Police Commissioner "Bull" Connor and his police dogs in Birmingham, without the sight of Sheriff Jim Clark and his posse using cattle prods and clubs on blacks in Selma, there would have been no Civil Rights Act in 1964, no Voting Rights Act in 1965. The leaders of the movement became masterful at manipulating television, conscious of the way certain images could be used to move the electorate. Martin Luther King specifically chose Selma as the place to kick off his voting rights campaign because he knew Sheriff Clark could be counted on to lose control at the sight of marching blacks, with an audience of millions watching.

King and his fellow leaders were not the only ones who were beginning to understand that the real medium for galvanizing public attention was no longer newspapers — it was now television. Television had begun to scoop its print rivals with increasing frequency, but more important, it was proving to be a better medium than print for *certain kinds of stories.* There was no beating the experience of watching Alan Shepard blasting off in his space capsule *as it was happening,* or to see Khrushchev banging his shoe at the United Nations. Even the Associated Press recommended that its correspondents and editors monitor TV during major events like space shots and conventions to make sure they didn't miss anything.

The contempt with which most newspapermen viewed their brethren in TV was compounded by new emotions in the sixties: envy and resentment. The print press realized that they had become mere "extras" at JFK's press conferences — shows so obviously staged for television. Yet every newspaperman believed as an article of faith that his was the more serious, more legitimate medium for news.

It was a view widely shared by TV newspeople themselves in the sixties, and the feeling was not entirely unjustified. Examples of original reporting on TV were rare then, and the medium was still essentially derivative. Reliance on the wires and newspapers — especially the *New York Times* — was so complete that it sometimes became ludicrous. Once, when Tom Pettit was in Tuscaloosa, Alabama, covering George Wallace's attempt to block the integration of the University of Alabama, an NBC editor in New York called Pettit to ask him to do a story about how the president of the school was performing heroically. "Okay," said Pettit, "I'll check that out." "Oh," said the editor, "you don't have to bother. Everything you need to know is on the AP." "You don't understand," Pettit told him. "I'm sitting here in a crummy hotel room in Tuscaloosa, and I don't have the AP." "Well," replied the editor, "you could use the UP version, although it's not as good." Pettit told him he didn't have the UP, either. At that, the man said, "Good Lord. Well, go out and get a copy of the *New York Times*. The story's on page twenty-three," whereupon Pettit informed him the *New York Times* was banned in Tuscaloosa. After a pause, the man in New York said, in disbelief, "You don't have the AP? You don't have the UP? You don't have the *New York Times*? How in the hell do you know what's going on down there?"

This attitude was so prevalent that enterprising television reporters who got an original angle on a story would often feed it to a wire service correspondent; they knew that if "New York" saw the story on the wires, their chances of doing it for the evening news were greatly enhanced.

TV journalists were also sensitive to the charge of "show business" levied against them by the print press, because they knew it contained at least a grain of truth. TV newspeople do have to worry about the need for eye-catching pictures, proper lighting conditions, the cut of their suits, and so on, which seem to have little to do with the conventional journalistic concern, however necessary they are to the end result.

The broadcast news fraternity had also become uneasy about the use of "readers" — who seemed more akin to performers — to deliver the news, so it was a matter of considerable pride at NBC that their anchors were such experienced journalists. The presence of professional newsmen "up front" seemed to legitimize the entire operation.

Brinkley played a pivotal role in this regard. If Huntley was Mr. Outside, the public's favorite, Brinkley was the one with more appeal for the intelligentisia, who were longing for a breath of sophistication on TV. He was a particular favorite with the newspaper crowd, partly because he had once been one of them and has remained, throughout his long career in television, a wordsmith at heart. Huntley had no print experience to speak of, a lack that was long regarded as evidence of unworthiness in a TV newsman. Worse, he came from Hollywood, where he had played occasional bit parts in the movies and supplied the voice for scores of movie trailers.

It was also well known within the profession that Brinkley wrote all of his own material, while Huntley often read prepared scripts. In Washington, where journalistic reputations are certified, the perception grew that Brinkley had all the brains while Huntley was some kind of wool hat from the West. It was a view that did not do justice to Huntley, who was an intelligent man with a deep knowledge of and concern for world issues. As is often the case with legendary figures, both he and Brinkley were more — and less — than they seemed.

In part, the notion of Huntley as a mere front man stemmed from his role on the program, which differed from Brinkley's. Huntley was the conventional anchorman — the one who read domestic and international news and introduced reports from far-flung locations with no pretense of having been involved in the coverage. Brinkley functioned as the Washington *reporter,* covering the White House, Congress, the Supreme Court, et cetera — though he seldom left his office; in addition, he often gave his own interpretative slant.

Huntley's assigned area was much larger, and most of the stories he read — student rioting in Japan, fruit freezes in Florida, and so on — did not lend themselves to analysis or interpretation. So Huntley, who was always more interested in commentary than in straight, breaking news, was content to let the writers handle the routine writing chores of the program while he concentrated on his think pieces.

Those he always wrote. He spent most of his time preparing for his daily radio commentary, "Chet Huntley Reporting," which he did by consuming stacks of reading matter — books, magazines, newspapers, and scholarly journals. The fact is, Huntley's heart always belonged to radio, the medium where he first gained prominence and one that lent itself more readily to his specialties: opinion and analysis. The last day of his life, when he was dying of cancer, he put a sheet of paper into the typewriter and tried to finish a piece for his syndicated radio series.

Contrary to the myth that circulated within the news fraternity, Huntley was actually a proficient writer, at times even an eloquent one, who could turn out page after page of good, readable copy with relatively little effort. ("He could write like a streak when he felt like it," says Gilbert Millstein, Huntley's television writer from 1965 on.) If Huntley's style was not as original or trenchant as Brinkley's, the same could be said of almost everyone else who worked in television. Yet Huntley's reputation suffered by comparison with his partner's. The fact that Brinkley wrote all his own material, both for radio and television, had a certain novelty in those days, making him appear morally and intellectually superior to Huntley in the eyes of many people in the industry. It was a view that Brinkley and his partisans encouraged. Although the two men worked together for fourteen years in relative harmony, which must be some kind of record in a field known for its fierce, destructive rivalries, they were never close and seldom saw each other except on television. "They never liked each other very much," says one producer who worked with them for a long time. "Huntley respected Brinkley, but Brinkley did not respect Huntley. He would go around bad-mouthing him. He didn't feel that Huntley was very intelligent, and David is very intelligent. But they never had any arguments, because they both understood that they needed each other."

Brinkley's followers were not entirely responsible for the belief that Huntley was an intellectual lightweight, however. Huntley brought some of it on himself because of his penchant for getting involved in unwise business ventures and conflict-of-interest situations. He was so different from most of his colleagues at NBC, too; they had a hard time taking a happy-go-lucky, transplanted farmer like Huntley seriously — someone who got such a kick out of imitating the sound of a train whistle or a turkey gobble, or whose favorite program on TV was the Perry Como show.

He was, above all, a down-to-earth Westerner who never ceased to believe in the values of his frontier upbringing, qualities such as frugality, neighborliness, and manliness. Stubborn and individualistic, he also enjoyed playing the part of the maverick, which sometimes got him into trouble.

Huntley was born in 1911 in Cardwell, Montana, population 60, and raised in circumstances that were much closer to the nineteenth than the twentieth century. Shortly after his birth, his father, Percy (Pat) Huntley, gave up his job as a telegraph operator on the railroad to try his hand at ranching and farming. Chet's boyhood was spent on a 640-acre spread near the town of Saco, Montana, not far from the Canadian border.

It was harsh land, not really suitable for farming. It was prone to drought, hailstorms, fires, rattlesnakes, and a variety of plagues, among them wheat rust, locusts, and the dreaded Russian thistle (a weed that kills off grain). In his book, *The Generous Years*, Huntley describes the family's "brutal, soul-crushing struggle for survival. We came to know the stark face of poverty and avoided dire want only by unceasing toil and the fierce pride of my parents and grandparents. Several of the prairie families had gone on relief, and I can remember some talk about it in tones to indicate that it was the supreme disaster which could overtake an individual or a family.''

Amazingly, Huntley looked back on those days with nostalgia. A dutiful child with a streak of exuberance, he basked in the affection of his parents, grandparents, and three sisters. He also developed a lifelong attachment to the land and growing things. In his book he extols pleasures like the coming of spring with a sometimes moving lyricism: ''I stood on the hilltops and sang — sang words which came to me on the spur of the moment — sang what I was desperately trying to say . . . The world was renewing itself, and I wanted to seize upon it and hold it there, for fear it might not occur again.''

The idol of his youth was his maternal grandfather, Grandpa Tathum, a hell-raiser who couldn't resist whiskey or women, and who won and lost several fortunes speculating in commodities. But he also modeled himself on his father, a practical, industrious man who read ceaselessly and took a great interest in the outside world. By the time Chet was ten, his father gave up trying to eke out a living from the ranch and moved the family back to town, where he resumed his old occupation as a railroad telegrapher. Chet would never lose his romantic attachment to the land, though, telling an interviewer years later that he knew of no greater pleasure in life than seeing things grow.

Huntley matured into a physically powerful young man; with massive forearms developed from pitching hay, he was good at riding horses and roping steers but had a gentleness about him that he never lost. In his book he recounts the time he had to be goaded into fighting with a schoolmate who had been picking on him. He met his tormentor, Dale, on a snowy field, with his classmates looking on: ''Perhaps it was that day in that empty lot that I made a discovery about myself: I was stronger, and immune to physical pain if I was concerned or angry. In the dozen or so fights I had had with Dale, I could never get sufficiently aroused. I was invariably embarrassed, chagrined, humiliated, but I always had the feeling that it did not make much sense — that it was really rather silly.''

That day, however, he worked up a real surge of adrenaline and beat the other boy, who wound up lying on the ground, bleeding: ''I stood there for a moment, mildly aware of the cheers and congratulations — utterly consumed by a bitter inundation of remorse and sympathy. I wanted desperately to put my arm around him, help him up and tell him that I was sorry, but the rules did not permit that.''

Most of Huntley's career in school went smoothly. A straight-A student who excelled at public speaking, track, and football, he won a pre-med scholarship to Montana State College. After winning a national oratorical contest, he switched to the Corning School of the Arts in Seattle, where he flirted with the possibility of pursuing a career on the stage. In 1934, he got a BA in fine arts from the University of Seattle, making him one of the few network anchors, up until the eighties, to finish college. While still at Seattle, he met Ingrid Rollin, a breathtakingly beautiful girl from Sweden, whom he married in 1936.

By that time, he had already discovered his true vocation — broadcasting. In 1934, Huntley began working at a 100-watt station in Seattle, where he did everything from spinning records to sweeping out the station. Better jobs followed until, in 1939, he was hired by KNX, the CBS station in Los Angeles, as a commentator, news analyst, and reporter.

Like almost everyone who started out in radio in the thirties, he did his share of announcing. Even after he got to KNX, he used to put on a tuxedo at nights to announce the dance bands from Earl Carroll's restaurant for an extra $30 a week. He needed the money; KNX paid him only $75 a week, which wasn't enough after his two daughters were born.

In the forties, Huntley became known as a battling liberal, siding with the underdog and embracing the cause of individual liberty. In 1942, he won a Peabody award for a radio series he did attempting to combat prejudice against Mexican Americans. In the postwar era, he denounced the excesses of anticommunism and the cold war. Eventually, his outspoken views got him into trouble with the station management, culminating in his refusal to sign a loyalty oath. He quit before the head of KNX, Merle Jones, could fire him. Already a big-time radio newscaster, Huntley was earning $750 a week, and he soon joined the ABC station in Los Angeles, appearing on both radio and TV. At KABC he kept up his campaign against Joseph McCarthy and the witch-hunts of the fifties. This time, he ran into bigger trouble, as several pressure groups tried to drive him off the air. Although he lost most of his sponsors, Huntley never backed down or softened his rhetoric. He even fought his persecutors in court, winning a $10,000 judgment against a woman who called him a Communist.

Sam Zelman, Huntley's boss at the time at ABC, remembers him as hard-working and conscientious, a voracious reader but not really an original thinker. "I always thought he sounded very learned," says Zelman, "and then I found he was taking his information out of such publications as *The Economist* and *Foreign Affairs Quarterly.* He was smart enough to realize that if you took your material from obscure journals, nobody would be the wiser. I don't mean to imply that he was a phony or a cynic, because he wasn't. He may have started out as a radio announcer, but he grew into a journalist because he cared about news."

After Huntley joined NBC and came East, he remained basically a Westerner. His small, cozy office was cluttered with reminders of his days on the frontier — a brass spittoon in the corner, a Winchester rifle hanging above his father's old roll-top desk. A man with a monumentally powerful physique, Huntley always seemed a trifle out of place on the streets of Manhattan, as if the sidewalks weren't quite big enough for him. He was more at home in the outdoors in rough clothes, picnicking or hiking.

Like the good Westerner he was, Huntley remained open, friendly, and unspoiled, no matter how famous and sought-after he became, a genuinely nice guy. "Sometimes he was too nice for his own good," says David Brinkley. "Long after we both became, shall I say, household words, he kept his phone listed. And on a Sunday afternoon, the phone would ring and somebody he had never heard of would say, 'Chet, this is Sam Williams. My wife and I are here from Tulsa. You know my cousin, so-and-so, and he told us to look you up.' So Chet would end up going to some restaurant with this couple from Tulsa or wherever they came from. I wouldn't do that for anything in the world. It's just a recipe for wasting your time."

Huntley may have suffered fewer psychological effects from being famous than any other person in his position; he seemed to come through the experience totally unscathed. Colleagues who lunched with him would watch in amazement as he signed autograph after autograph with the utmost good humor. He really liked people; it was no act.

On the job, he was much easier to get along with than most star performers. "He was a real pussycat," says Charlie Sieg, who directed the "Huntley-Brinkley Report" for many years and who was a personal friend of Huntley's. "Today you hear constant bitching. 'Can't you get that damned monitor fixed? It's been two days now . . .' But Chet never blamed anyone. God knows, we used to shuffle him around, change pages in the middle of the show, or the film or the TelePrompTer would fail. He never said a word. After we had a disaster, which happened often enough, he would quote some poet and say, 'Let us drag ourselves away to bleed awhile and fight another day.'"

Besides the land, Huntley's other great passions were money and women. "Chet had an earthiness about him," Sieg says. "After a couple of martinis, he would get this mischievous look in his eye. He loved a pretty girl." Ralph Mann, Huntley's agent, remembers how he and Huntley used to get on a plane together, and by the time they got off, Huntley had a stewardess on each arm. Huntley also loved to drink and kick up his heels. Once, during a poolside party during a space shot in Clear Lake, Texas, he was horsing around with some girls who were perched on a piano that was sitting dangerously close to the swimming pool. He got carried away and pushed the piano, girls and all, into the pool, an incident that made the local papers.

Huntley's first marriage, which was already in trouble by the time he got to New York, ended in 1959. That same year, he married Tipton Stringer, a former vocalist and weather girl in Washington, on whom he doted. His drinking, which was never severe enough to interfere with his work, moderated after their marriage.

His zeal for making money never abated, though. He would take on as many jobs, inside and outside the company, as he could handle, and then some. Under the old fee system at the networks, he was paid extra for every commercially sponsored program he narrated for NBC, and he never passed up a fee if he could help it. When he went on vacation, he used to write and record ten or twelve "Emphasis" spots for radio before he left so he wouldn't lose the money. Once, during a convention, people started to notice how tired he looked. Later they found out that he had been getting up at 5:00 A.M. every day to write his radio pieces, even though he was seldom getting to bed until long after midnight.

Huntley, who was always a bit puzzled by his success, never thought it would last. He had a theory that people got tired of TV anchors after about five years. The way he looked at it, Swayze had his five years on top, after which Edwards was the public's favorite for five years. He figured that he and David had just about that long to enjoy the fruits of their fame, so he had better make his fortune while he could.

Brinkley, who lacked the same entrepreneurial spirit, came across as more dedicated, less crass than Huntley. Certainly, Huntley was not one to agonize over the more commercial aspects of television news. Once, he and his writer, Gilbert Millstein, were watching a particularly obnoxious commercial featuring a cure for warts. "Jesus, what a lot of shit," Millstein commented. Huntley replied, "Listen, don't knock it. That shit is your bread and butter, and it's mine, too."

For all of his devotion to the dollar, Huntley was not a particularly astute businessman. He was either too nice or too naive, depending on your point of view. Huntley's agent, Marvin Josephson, who represented him in tandem with Ralph Mann, says part of Huntley's problem was that he couldn't say no to anyone. "He had a friend who made industrial films that he did a lot of narrations for. We didn't take all the deals we were offered, of course, because we would get a higher price if we didn't. I would have long talks with him, explaining how we could make more if he did four programs a year instead of twenty, and how it was necessary to maintain your price. He would say yes, and the next thing you know I'd call his office and he'd be off doing a film for some friend of his."

Huntley invested in a number of business ventures, most of which turned out to be unprofitable. He bought a farm in New Jersey that he hoped to turn into a model cattle-raising venture, but it lost so much money he had to sell it; he confided to friends that an employee had been stealing him blind.

If some of his business involvements made him look like a sucker, others made him look slightly venal. He ought to have known better than to editorialize against the government's meat inspection standards while he owned shares (about 2 percent) in a livestock business, but he spoke out on the subject on his radio program not once but twice. The incident aroused so much controversy that the Federal Communications Commission finally issued a rebuke to NBC for failing to disclose Huntley's financial interests. Reuven Frank, who knew him about as well as anyone, maintains that Huntley's stand had nothing to do with his own financial interest. "He grew up on a farm and had the same attitude the farmers did. He felt as strongly as any farmer that the federal standards were wrong." If Huntley wasn't being greedy, however, it was certainly naive of him to risk such an obvious conflict-of-interest situation.

On another occasion, he got in trouble for lending his name to a new line of meat called "Chet Huntley's Nature Fed Beef." To add to NBC's embarrassment, Huntley editorialized against the beef industry's price structure on radio the same day his meat line was introduced in the stores.

After a lot of bad publicity and pressure from his bosses, he withdrew his name from the product.

Huntley was a stubborn man who seemed to enjoy going against the prevailing ideological tide. Although he never lost his commitment to civil rights and individual liberties, he became increasingly conservative and satisfied with the status quo as the years went by. On Vietnam, he stood apart from most of his colleagues, who were growing progressively more disenchanted with the war. In 1967, he told an interviewer for *TV Guide*, "I was there in 1955 and I saw the stupidity and selfishness of the French. We inherited this problem from them, and God, it's irritating to hear De Gaulle acting holier-than-thou about it. I'm not for escalation, but I'm not for pulling out. The big cliché has become, 'Stop the bombing.' Well, we've stopped the bombing five times now; why the hell isn't the onus on the other side?"

Brinkley had by then become an out-and-out dove. "We should stop the bombing," he told the same interviewer. "There is not much evidence that it has ever been as effective as the Air Force thinks it is, in this or any war, and I think we should take the first settlement that is even remotely decent and get out without insisting on any kind of victory. It was a mistake to get committed in there in the first place, but this country is big enough to survive it and go on to something else."

Significantly, the differing views of the two anchors were expressed in the press, not on NBC-TV. By the late sixties, commentary on NBC had become very muted as the realization of TV's impact sank in. Politicians, businessmen, blacks, labor leaders, *everyone* became sensitive to their portrayal on TV, so network executives found it easier to encourage newscasters to avoid taking positions that would alienate anyone. (CBS's commentators had been muzzled earlier; the exception was ABC, which instituted provocative commentary on its evening news in 1967 in an effort to offer something different from its competitors.) Vietnam was an especially sensitive issue, arousing strong, polarizing emotions. And the networks were wary of criticizing the government's actions, not only because it seemed unpatriotic, but also because the government might retaliate. It was still possible, however, to be fairly outspoken on radio, because the audience had shrunk to the point that it was no longer considered significant. Radio listeners, therefore, had a much better idea of where Huntley and Brinkley stood on the war.

Another ideological difference between the two men was revealed by the AFTRA strike of 1967. It resulted in an open rift for a time. Huntley was one of the few newsmen at NBC (Frank McGee was another) who refused to honor the picket lines set up by their union, the American Federation of Television and Radio Artists. Huntley said it was inappropriate for newsmen to belong to a union of performers, and he attacked AFTRA for its black-listing practices during the McCarthy days. By crossing the picket line, however, he created considerable ill feeling; a group of writers on the "Huntley-Brinkley Report" even refused to work with him when the strike was over, preferring to transfer to other units.

Privately, Brinkley used to criticize Huntley's politics, but philosophically the two were not so far apart as they seemed. Both were very pro-American, and both believed in the old verities, the values of honesty, hard work, and self-reliance. The greatest contrast between them was in temperament; Brinkley was as closed-off and reclusive as Huntley was open and gregarious.

Brinkley lacked Huntley's zest for life, his rapport with people; he seemed completely at ease and confident about one thing only in his life: his work. Where Huntley was expansive, impulsive, and high-spirited, there was a quality of spareness and economy to everything Brinkley said and did. He never wasted time or energy. His writing style was the very model of economy, pared of all superfluous words. When he sat down at the typewriter, he turned out his copy fast and clean, with no false starts and scarcely a correction. He was economical in conversation, too, refusing to engage in small talk or idle conversation, shunning bull sessions with colleagues. On the job, he was all business, impatient with stalling, delays, or fooling around. He even seemed to parcel out his emotions, reserving any outward display of warmth and humor for a select few, avoiding almost everyone else.

If Huntley was the product of a close-knit, loving family, Brinkley, from all accounts, had a lonely, unhappy childhood. Born in 1920 in Wilmington, North Carolina, and raised there, he was the son of a railroad clerk who died when Brinkley was eight. His mother had to go to work then, leaving him alone a good deal of the time. His brothers and sisters did not provide much company, either, because they were much older; the youngest was ten years older than David. At about the age of ten, however, he discovered what were to become his lifelong companions — books. He became a semipermanent fixture at the Wilmington public library, checking out books five or six times a week. Once, after he took out Oswald Spengler's *Decline of the West,* the librarian said he could keep it, because he was the first person who had ever asked for it.

Brinkley seems to have come by his reserve naturally. He was raised in a strict Southern Episcopalian milieu, in a family that produced several ministers and a sprinkling of doctors. Brinkley's mother, a staunch prohibitionist, was a stern, cold person who tolerated no foolishness. Of her Brinkley once said, "My mother was very ungiving in terms of affection. I have always liked to write all my life, and I remember writing a story which I think I thought was funny. I took it to her, and she read it and handed it back and said, 'Why are you wasting your time with that kind of nonsense?' And it was a long time afterwards before I understood the cruelty of it, so I might in fact have spent all these years trying to prove her wrong. It's quite possible."*

At school, Brinkley showed many of the traits that would mark his professional life. A quiet boy who never had much to say in a crowd, he stayed away from school a lot and made an effort only in those subjects that interested him — English, history, and shop. High school records show that he attended school intermittently from 1933 to 1939, but there is no record of his graduating. (Brinkley says he *did* graduate, that he simply never stopped by to pick up his diploma.)

Some of his teachers, recognizing his extraordinary intellect, arranged for him to work, with no pay, for the *Wilmington Star News,* while he was still enrolled in school. Watching him, his newspaper editor, Al Dickson, called him a "natural newspaperman." Within six weeks Brinkley had learned the ropes, turning out the cleanest copy anyone there ever remembered seeing. Two years later, Dickson put him on the payroll for $18.50 a week. While working at the paper, Brinkley also took some courses at the University of North Carolina in Chapel Hill, majoring in English. After a brief stint as an Army infantryman in 1940, he got a job with the UP, moving around the South in one-man bureaus in Montgomery, Nashville, and Charlotte. He was also one of the few to volunteer to write for UP's radio wire, so he already knew how to write for the ear when NBC hired him in Washington in 1943. He was twenty-two years of age.

When television came along after the war, Brinkley, who was still considered very junior, was one of the first people to go into it. He and Robert McCormick did a nightly half-hour for the NBC local station for a while, putting on anything that came into their heads, the theory being that

*Quoted in *TV Guide,* April 8, 1972.

nobody much was watching anyway. Once they brought a mechanical owl on the set. Another time they brought in a live horse, which had to be jammed into the elevator to get it upstairs to the studio.

When McCormick was assigned to go to Europe for NBC in 1951, he suggested Brinkley as his replacement for the nightly Washington segments on the "Camel News Caravan," but several executives needed convincing because Brinkley had a reputation for laziness. Everyone agreed he was good on the air, but they didn't like his attitude.

Brinkley acquired his reputation for laziness in part because he expended so much less energy on the job than most other people did. While others would plod through two or three hours' worth of film from a congressional hearing, trying to find exactly the right sound bite, Brinkley would quickly settle on something — anything — that sounded representative. "I was one of those who used to search right up to the last minute," says McCormick, "but now I think his approach was right, because he knew it wouldn't make any lasting impression on people. Maybe lazy isn't the right word, but he used to take shortcuts, and as I say, I think he was right and I was wrong."

McCormick remembers Brinkley as being more convivial in those days, always ready for a laugh or a joke. "I think he originated the gag about putting cigarette butts in the urinal," he says. "I remember that somebody at NBC put a sign up in the men's room which said, 'Please do not throw cigarette butts in the urinals,' and David printed under it in his precise handwriting, 'It makes them soggy and hard to light.' "

There seemed to be two David Brinkleys — one playful and mischievous, the other remote, dour, even forbidding. The fun-loving Brinkley had a fondness for running gags and practical jokes, usually conducted in his low-key, private way. One time he came across a story on the wires about a convict down South named Buster Lee Blivens, who got out of jail one day and stole the sheriff's dog before disappearing. Every two or three months, Brinkley would call the sheriff to find out if Buster Lee had been recaptured, or if his dog had ever come back, until the sheriff was ready to explode with rage.

Another running gag took the form of a fake correspondence between Brinkley and his friend Joe Derby, long-time head of public affairs for NBC News. Brinkley and Derby wrote to each other for over a year, posing as two rascally Catholic priests, Father Shakehands Muldoon and Father Vincent Cacciatore, who twitted each other about drinking in the rectory, stealing from the collection plate, and other lapses of priestly conduct. Staff members who knew about the correspondence, which Brinkley did not advertise, loved it. They relished those moments when he let down his guard and clowned around for their benefit. Once he bet somebody five dollars he could stuff himself into a foot-and-a-half-long film shipment bag; he lost.

The fun-loving Brinkley loved to eat well, and bet large sums on poker and the horses. He and Julian Goodman, a news executive who became president of NBC, and their wives often made the round of the racetracks in the Washington area. Brinkley's poker-playing pals included a number of Washington's elite — cabinet officials, politicians, and people like columnist Art Buchwald and *Washington Post* executive editor Ben Bradlee. (Brinkley never enjoyed being a celebrity himself, but he enjoyed being around them.)

More often, though, he liked to be alone — closed away in his study reading or writing, or building furniture in his woodworking shop. A master carpenter and a fine amateur architect, Brinkley designed and built his own cabin in the woods in Virginia and made the dining room furniture in his suburban Washington home. Some people say he preferred tools to people. "A tool is only designed to do one thing," he once said in admiration, "and it does it."

Brinkley's love of solitude sometimes ran counter to the desires of his first wife, the former Ann Fisher, who liked the Washington party scene and was fond of giving big parties herself. They were married in 1946 and had three sons, Alan, Joel, and John, but by the sixties, the marriage was undergoing severe strains. After they separated in 1968, Brinkley was linked romantically with several well-known women, including Lauren Bacall, but in 1971, he met a stunning young woman named Susan Adolph, twenty-three years his junior; within a year they were married. They have one child, a daughter named Alexis. Colleagues all say Brinkley is much happier these days and considerably more approachable on the job than he used to be.

Back in the days when he and Huntley were anchoring the evening news, Brinkley was extremely remote from the staff. His door was always open, but people seldom ventured in; they found him too intimidating. It was not that Brinkley ever yelled; on the contrary he has impeccable Southern manners. But he had a silence about him that seemed almost impenetrable. He was also given to making sardonic comments and harsh judgments that most people preferred not to expose themselves to. Even people who were on friendly terms with him approached him with a certain caution, knowing there were times when he did not want his privacy invaded. Other staff members, younger producers like Ray Farkas, say they held him in too much awe to risk familiarity. "This was David Brinkley, after all. I mean, would you walk in and make a joke with the President of the United States when he was working? If you did, of course, David enjoyed it. The way we felt, I guess, was here was the guy who founded the business. You didn't want to bother him."

Farkas and others concede that Brinkley's remoteness did not lead to a free flow of ideas among the Washington staff. If Farkas got an idea for a story, he was more likely to take it to the senior producer in Washington, who might then discuss it privately with Brinkley. The casual collaboration, the brainstorming, that marks so much of the decision-making in most television newsrooms was unknown in Brinkley's operation.

An unusually arbitrary — even ornery — human being once he took a position, Brinkley was almost impossible to turn around. If someone spotted a mistake on his script, a worried conference would follow, as the producers tried to figure out how they were going to get him to change it. If the mistake was minor enough, they might even let it pass.

Brinkley never took part in meetings or conferences, so producers used to proceed by cautious indirection to find out if something suited him or not. NBC correspondent John Palmer remembers a time when, as a new man on the staff, he was picked to share the studio duties with Brinkley for a space shot. Although Brinkley had met Palmer when he worked for the NBC affiliate in Atlanta, the producers were concerned whether Brinkley would accept Palmer as co-anchor on a space shot. "I remember they told me rather hesitantly that I ought to go in and have a talk with David," Palmer says. "It seems they were not quite sure where I would be seated, how close to Brinkley I would sit, or if David would even consent to share the podium with me at all, and evidently the matter wouldn't be decided until after our chat. As it turned out, David was extremely cordial. He said he remembered meeting me in Atlanta and that he was pleased that I would be taking part in the coverage. I guess the meeting went well, because I ended up sitting, not next to him, but not far from him either, perhaps about eight or ten feet away."

Brinkley's natural habit of withdrawing became more pronounced as his fame increased; he couldn't handle people fawning over him and making a fuss in public. Although Brinkley was basically an "inside man" by training and preference — he hated traveling and hotel rooms —

he did go out in the field to cover stories occasionally. But his celebrity status made it increasingly difficult. On the campaign trail with Hubert Humphrey in 1960, he was mortified by the huge crowds that followed him everywhere he went, ignoring the candidate and his outstretched hand.

Sometimes he ran into people who got nasty. During the 1968 primary campaign, Brinkley and his producer, Shad Northshield, went into the bar of the hotel where they were staying to have a drink. "There was a convention of something like optometrists — one of those borderline, dubious medical groups like chiropodists," Brinkley recalls. "They began shouting at me. I don't like that. I'm not a freak or a sideshow attraction. Then they began throwing peanuts, which was more than I could stand, so I left."

Brinkley's partisans at NBC claim incidents like this drove him into being a recluse, but in fact, he was moody and taciturn as a boy. Some Brinkley intimates think he retreated into a protective shell to cover up for feelings of inferiority stemming from his peculiar childhood and lack of formal education. Once, he agreed to give a lecture at the Cosmos Club, at the time a bastion for Washington's intellectual elite (to belong, it was necessary to have published a book), and to his astonishment, so many members wanted to hear him that he had to give the talk twice. "He couldn't believe that all those intelligent people were so anxious to hear him talk," one friend recalls. "He considered himself self-taught, and he was never quite sure he had done the right thing."

As an anchor, though, Brinkley was blessed with uncommon self-confidence. He made no secret of his opinion (and he may have been right) that no one in the business could match his ability to write or his editorial judgments. Nor did he have any trouble accepting the star system; he understood that people tuned in as much to see him and Huntley as they did to get the news.

The "Huntley-Brinkley Report" was the epitome of the star system, in fact — the program tailored to showcase its stars to best advantage. As time went by, however, an overly heavy reliance on their drawing power contributed to a decline in the organization's strength. The formula adopted by Reuven Frank and his successors was simple: 60 percent Huntley and 40 percent Brinkley. That way, Frank felt, the audience would be left wanting more of Brinkley. But it was important not to wind up with too much Brinkley, either. Naturally, considerations like these sometimes interfered with normal news judgments. For example, Frank had a rule that Brinkley had to do a minimum of two stories a day, whether or not anything important was going on in Washington. Brinkley, who was no air hog and who hated to report anything trivial or boring, often protested he had nothing worthwhile for that night, but Frank would insist. "Get up two or three stories," he would tell Brinkley, "and we'll pick the best two."

Playing up the role of the stars of the program also meant playing down the role of the reporter at NBC, which sometimes resulted in inaccurate or superficial coverage. (Later, the cult of the reporter, in which news sometimes degenerated into a mere vehicle for starring personalities, would lead to distortions of another kind.)

In the early years of the program, viewers saw a lot of Huntley and Brinkley out of necessity: There were few television reporters. But even in the early sixties, when more reporters had been added to the staff, their faces were seldom seen on the screen. Only their voices were used; "standuppers" were frowned on by Frank. He generally preferred to avoid using reporters because they got in the way of the kind of picture stories he wanted to do. "I had Huntley and Brinkley; I didn't need those other clowns. All I wanted was the pictures. Reporters inhibit film. With the reporter, the script, the words come first. With us, the script came last. We tried to let the pictures tell the story with as little interference as possible."

Frank believed that television ought to stick to what it does best — the transmission of experience — and that as a medium, it is not well suited to presenting facts. He is right, of course. The trouble is that not many news stories tell themselves on film. Most stories cry out for interpretation, which usually can best be provided by a reporter on the scene.

Even pure picture stories turn out to be more interesting if an editorial person — either a field producer or a reporter — accompanies the camera crew. It's not that editorial people are any smarter than photographers or sound men — often the reverse is true — but the cameraman's job is to get the pictures, not to ferret out additional facts or come up with an interesting or unanticipated angle. CBS never sent its film crews to do stories on their own, even in the early days of television, before reporters were used. "Contact men," who functioned like off-screen reporters, went along to make sure the facts were accurately noted. NBC had film crews operating on their own as late as 1970. It's the way things were done in the heyday of

Huntley and Brinkley, and nobody saw any reason to change a formula that had been so successful.

As the sixties progressed, NBC began to feature more reporters on the "Huntley-Brinkley Report," even their faces, but only a select handful of correspondents ever appeared in Washington. David Brinkley remained the principal reporter, "covering" the Justice Department, Congress, the State Department, et cetera. What started as necessity was perpetuated by the star system, with most of NBC's beat reporters systematically by-passed by the "Huntley-Brinkley Report." Carl Stern, who joined NBC in 1967 to cover the Justice Department and the Supreme Court, was on the staff for two years before he ever appeared on the evening news; he spent almost all his time reporting for radio. James Robinson, who covered the State Department, Peter Hackes at Defense, and Robert McCormick, who covered Congress, virtually never got on "Huntley-Brinkley," either.

Sometimes the beat reporters called Brinkley to feed him detailed information, but more often, he wrote his scripts on the basis of wire copy, just as he had done in the fifties. Brinkley's system worked as well as it did because he had an unusually good feel for Washington and a good network of private contacts, particularly in the political arena. But reliance on the wires had its limitations. At times the wire services would overplay stories or get them wrong, so Brinkley's version might have the wrong slant, too.

CBS, although believing in the star system as devoutly as NBC, nonetheless had made the decision to build up its reporting staff in Washington; and its strategy of emphasizing original reporting began to pay off. A bill-signing at the White House that might end up as a routine fifteen-second picture story voiced over by Brinkley could turn out to be a two-minute report by a CBS correspondent, offering a different interpretation or a vital piece of background information not available on the wires. The print press began writing about the extra dimension in the reporting done by CBS, criticizing NBC for favoring style over substance.

As usual, CBS News was taking what looked like the high road, but as is almost always the case with the networks (or any other profit-making enterprise, for that matter), commercial considerations were also at work. In addition to building up the role of the reporter, CBS decided to promote the identities of certain "star" correspondents — Dan Rather, Roger Mudd, Marvin Kalb, and others — because stars built audiences. It was a group of star reporters who made CBS News great during World War II, and nobody ever forgot it. In addition, nobody believed that Walter Cronkite could possibly compete on his own with Huntley-Brinkley in terms of personality; he would need a strong "supporting cast."

The CBS executives seriously underestimated their man. As the decade of the sixties and its shattering events unfolded, it was Cronkite, not NBC's "Gold Dust Twins," as one media writer called them, who seemed more in tune with the nation's mood — offering reassurance rather than flippancy, concern rather than world-weariness and detachment.

4
The Age of Cronkite

When I wanted to make a point, Cronkite was
one of the first people I would call.
— Henry Kissinger

ON NOVEMBER 22, 1963, at 1:40 P.M., Eastern Standard Time, Walter Cronkite's trembling voice broke into the CBS broadcast of "As the World Turns" to announce that President John Kennedy had been gravely wounded after shots were fired at his motorcade in Dallas. Cronkite's was the first announcement on television; ABC came on with the news two minutes later, and NBC followed at 1:45.

Cronkite earned this footnote in history almost accidentally; nearly everyone else at CBS News was out to lunch. Harry Reasoner, who was usually pressed into service for bulletins, had gone to Lindy's that day. Correspondent Charles Collingwood, another likely candidate for the job, was dining at the Italian Pavilion with Blair Clark, the general manager and vice president of CBS News. But Cronkite, who usually ate at his desk, was just finishing a light lunch of cottage cheese and canned pineapple when an editor burst in, waving a piece of wire copy and shouting that the President had been shot. Cronkite grabbed the bulletin and said, "The hell with writing it. Just give me the air." It was one of those times when even seasoned professionals have difficulty reacting unemotionally. "I can't break up," Cronkite recalls thinking. "I must control myself." Although he seemed on the verge of breaking down a couple of times, his professionalism didn't desert him, providing as coherent an account of the situation in Dallas as the barrage of conflicting reports permitted. And, with the aid of an unusually large CBS contingent that chanced to be in Dallas that day, he kept CBS News out in front on the story.

In addition to White House correspondent Robert Pierpoint, who was traveling with Kennedy, Nelson Benton, the New Orleans bureau chief, and Dan Rather, who then worked out of Dallas, were on hand. So were three camera crews and a field producer. Thanks to Rather, CBS achieved another "first" — the news that Kennedy was dead. Cronkite kept reminding viewers that Rather's report was unofficial, that it had come by way of an unidentified doctor at Parkland Hospital, where Kennedy had been taken. But at 2:30 P.M., the terrible news was confirmed. As Cronkite relayed it to the audience, his voice broke with emotion, and he wiped a tear from his eye.

Millions of people would hold this memory of Walter Cronkite; his colleagues, too, are apt to recall the incident as an element in what would become the Cronkite legend. However, Cronkite's emotional state was a matter of some concern at CBS that day. Appearing a bit numb and shaken, he kept taking his glasses off and putting then back on in such an aimless fashion, that finally, at 3:00 P.M., Don Hewitt, who was directing the now-continuous coverage, called for Charles Collingwood to take over. A few years later, of course, no one would have *dared* to propose that Cronkite step aside, but in 1963, he was just another newscaster as far as his colleagues were concerned. That night, Harry Reasoner anchored CBS's prime-time coverage.

Cronkite was still reeling with shock and grief when he left the newsroom and stopped by his corner office to call home, but his mood changed abruptly when he picked up the phone and found an irate caller on the line. "Is this CBS News?" a woman asked. Cronkite told her it was. "Well, I just want to say that it's in the worst bad taste to have Walter Cronkite on the air when everybody knows he spent all his time trying to get the President." "Madam," Cronkite replied, "this *is* Walter Cronkite, and you're a God damn idiot."

Although thousands of calls were received by stations around the country in the next few days, protesting the interruption of regular programming, the networks discovered that most Americans couldn't get enough details about the assassination, even if it meant listening to the same facts over and over. For the millions of people who sat transfixed in front of their television sets, that four-day period was an experience like no other. People mourning in their homes saw people weeping in the streets, imparting a sense of shared, collective grief. "It was our first genuinely national funeral," David Brinkley wrote later, "a death in our national family attended by every one of us."

For many, certain images would never be erased — Jacqueline Kennedy, her suit still spattered with blood, standing next to Lyndon Johnson as he took the oath of office; Lee Harvey Oswald's face contorting in pain after being shot by Jack Ruby; French President Charles De Gaulle towering over Ethiopian Emperor Haile Selassie as they marched behind the funeral caisson; Caroline Kennedy reaching up to touch her father's flag-draped coffin.

Television had already proved its ability to cover large-scale events that were preplanned, but never before had it attempted to keep up with a fast-breaking, unanticipated story of this magnitude. Once the networks began deploying their armies of men and equipment, however, they demonstrated an efficiency so remarkable it began to seem routine. "We just settled down to apply our resources," remarked one executive at the time. "I think we were frightened when we saw our capability." In a medium not noted for its dignity or restraint, the commentators and reporters also performed admirably, conscious perhaps of their role in keeping the nation calm and unified. What the networks lost in commercial revenues during the four days (an estimated $40 million) was more than compensated for by the good will generated. Senators and members of the House took to the floor of Congress to laud the networks' performance. Even the print press was unstinting in its praise. Television news had come of age.

As it turned out, 1963 was a pivotal year for television in more ways than one. That year, for the first time, more people said they got their news from TV than from newspapers — a shift that would grow more pronounced year by year. By this time, the transformation of America from a collection of provincial entities to a mass society — a process hastened and in part caused by broadcasting — was nearly complete. Americans were now more familiar with the names and faces of anchors like Cronkite, Huntley, and Brinkley than they were with their senators, congressmen, city councilmen, and school board members. As the places of public assembly continued to diminish, and people began to divide their time almost exclusively between home and work, television news would become for many the most important link to the larger world.

The bond of familiarity and dependence between anchor and viewer was strengthened immeasurably by another development in 1963: the advent of the half-hour newscast. By going from fifteen minutes to half an hour, CBS and NBC* doubled the length and impact of what Daniel Schorr has called America's "nightly national séance."

Many factors had been pointing to the expanded newscast, but there is no doubt that one of the precipitating incidents was the ratings upset of 1960, in which NBC established itself as the undisputed leader of television news. Shortly after the national political conventions that year, Sig Mickelson, the long-time chief of CBS News, was summarily fired, along with his deputies. The following year, Richard Salant, a corporate lawyer and protégé of Frank Stanton, was brought in as president of network news and given a mandate to build up the operation posthaste. CBS had been coasting too long on the reputation of Edward R. Murrow and the excellence of its World War II radio team.

Salant and his deputies, Blair Clark and Ernie Leiser, decided one way to compete with the "Huntley-Brinkley Report" was to expand to a half-hour, offering *more* news and *better* news than NBC. But to do so, CBS would have to make drastic improvements in its domestic news-gathering capability.

Previously, pleas from the news department for more money or airtime had gotten short shrift from the president of the CBS Television Network, James Aubrey, a man with undisguised contempt for news programming. He considered it a drain on corporate profits and was so infuriated by the huge outlays of money at the 1964 Republican convention in San Francisco that he stormed out before Senator Barry Goldwater was even nominated. Yet strong forces were arrayed against Aubrey on the subject of the half-hour newscast. Not only were Stanton and Paley, Aubrey's superiors, convinced of the need to make a greater effort in news, but that gadfly at the FCC, Newton Minow, was still pressing the networks to demonstrate a greater public service commitment.

Salant would get his half-hour, but first, more reporters had to be hired and a system of domestic bureaus established to produce the additional material required. As late as 1961, all the effort, the prestige, and the romance at CBS News still lay in foreign reporting. "The emphasis on Paris as against Chicago in those days was awesome," Blair Clark recalls, "even though nobody gave a damn if the government of France fell every six months." But in 1962, four new domestic bureaus were created to supplement the existing bureaus in Chicago and Washington, and a drive was launched to recruit aggressive reporters with television potential.

*ABC did not go to a half-hour of news until 1968.

The other major step taken to shore up CBS's sagging prestige in 1962 was naming Walter Cronkite as anchor of the Evening News. It was a move that many regarded as long overdue. As early as 1954, Sig Mickelson wanted to replace Edwards with Cronkite, who had already become the network's key man for special events. "Doug was gentle and amiable," Mickelson says, "but he lacked that slight bit of abrasiveness in his personality that Walter had. He didn't make a strong impression on viewers — didn't rub them one way or the other. The viewer has to feel some electricity, something that commands his attention."

Interestingly, in the 1950s no consideration was given to the audience-building potential of having the same man do both special events and the Evening News. "It was probably an omission," Mickelson concedes, "but we never thought about it — the increased exposure, the cross-promotional aspects, and so on. The Evening News was handled as an entity on its own, and we were searching for the best possible person."

As far as Mickelson was concerned, Cronkite *was* the best possible person. But Mickelson didn't feel he could back him when he made his first move against Edwards in 1955, because Cronkite's stock was not much higher with the Murrow faction than Edwards's was. Even though Murrow personally recruited Cronkite in 1950, the Murrowites came to regard him as a kind of superannouncer, someone who was good at "eyewitnessing" and hamming it up on camera. They couldn't understand his fixation on breaking news — his apparent lack of interest in the deeper context of events. Temperamentally he was different, too — a *bon vivant* who would rather spend his time rubbing elbows with celebrities at Toots Shor's than worrying about the fate of Western civilization.

So Mickelson proposed Charles Collingwood, a gifted broadcaster who wanted the job and had the advantage of being a Murrow man. "At that point," Mickelson says, "the Ed Murrow influence was still very strong. He was on the board of directors and he had Paley's ear, so I figured I had a better chance with Collingwood. I had almost everyone convinced to make the switch, but the agency people for Pall Mall cigarettes objected, and management backed off. Besides, Doug was about to pull ahead of Swayze, and nobody wanted to touch a winner."

Three years later, in 1958, Mickelson openly backed Cronkite for the job, citing the national reputation he had gained for his coverage of politics and special events, but James Aubrey didn't think much of the idea. Aubrey wanted someone with more pizzazz, like Mike Wallace, the charismatic host of a New York interview show called "Night Beat," or

Clete Roberts, a popular anchorman in Los Angeles. Failing to get a consensus, CBS stuck with Edwards, who, despite his low standing among the executives, managed to run neck and neck in the ratings race with "Huntley-Brinkley" until 1960.

By 1962, all the momentum had shifted to NBC; Edwards had been anchoring for fourteen years, and it was clearly time for a change. Considering his long years of faithful service, however, Edwards was treated shabbily by the company after his fall from grace. He had hoped to get the Sunday evening network news or one of the more prestigious public affairs programs, but he was offered only the local, late-night newscast in New York. The next few years were rough for Edwards. He was even hospitalized briefly in 1966 for alcoholism. Yet he bounced back, again becoming a mainstay of the news division, assigned to three radio newscasts a day and a five-minute television round-up at midday — a schedule he still maintained into the 1980s. The executives responsible for taking Edwards off the Evening News — Salant, Clark, and Leiser — all say the action was necessary because his performance had deteriorated, that he was "flubbing his lines." But people working on the program at the time say they saw no evidence of this. Evidently, it would be inconsistent with the high-minded traditions of CBS News to state the true reasons for his removal — his declining audience popularity and the company's desire for an anchor with a stronger news image.

This time there was no question that Cronkite would get the job. "I almost can't remember any argument about it," Blair Clark says. Charles Collingwood was still interested, but he seemed a trifle too sophisticated, his manners a bit too fancy to appeal to Middle America. Closer to the Murrow mold, Collingwood was regarded as better educated and more intelligent than Cronkite, but the executives were not entirely persuaded that those qualities were an asset for the Evening News. They weren't looking for another Murrow. Murrow made too many waves. His controversial broadcasts gave Chairman Paley stomachaches, or so he told Murrow.

By 1962, Murrow had quit the company in disgust, his appetite for doing battle with the corporation finally dulled. His specialty, commentary, was on the decline at CBS; the more outspoken commentators had either been reined in, or, like Howard K. Smith, they had quit. But those of Murrow's followers who remained in broadcasting continued to regard reporting the day's news as a lower order of journalism. Eric Sevareid, for instance, says he would not have taken the anchor position, even if it had been offered to him. "I had done daily news on radio and found it to be a terrible grind. It's like shoveling gravel, retailing the hard news of the day. It doesn't call for any great writing talent, and I prefer to write. It's so much more satisfying to put your own ideas down and get them across."

Cronkite, who was no intellectual, was not a crusader by nature and had no interest in commentary. Nor was he the type to make waves. Yet he was no mere careerist, no empty "personality." A hard-driving perfectionist, he turned out to be exactly the individual needed to mold the Evening News into what it became in the sixties and seventies — a fair, generally accurate, if highly compressed, summary of the day's events. Under his leadership, the Evening News became an increasingly respectable and respected electronic front page.

Cronkite did not become a national institution overnight. As almost always happens when a network switches anchors, the ratings fell after Cronkite replaced Edwards in April 1962, and thousands of people wrote CBS protesting the change. It also took time before Cronkite controlled his own program, despite his insistence on the title of managing editor. The term comes from the newspaper world, but it conveyed exactly what Cronkite and his superiors wanted it to — that he was a working journalist, not a mere performer. He also wanted it known that when disputes arose, *he* would have the final say, not the producer he inherited from his predecessor — Don Hewitt, who stayed with the program for two more years. Even so, Cronkite's influence would remain relatively limited until he had his own team assembled — until all the producers and writers owed their complete allegiance to him — and until his value as an audience draw was no longer in dispute.

More than anything else, Cronkite's approach to the Evening News was shaped by his training as a wire service reporter, a special discipline that emphasizes each day's developing stories, as well as fast, accurate, unbiased reporting. Cronkite wanted the Evening News to reflect, as fully as time would permit, everything of importance that happened that day, in the same way the daily news "budget" of the AP or UPI would do. Just as the *New York Times* is regarded as the "paper of record," under Cronkite the CBS Evening News was considered the broadcast of record.

Like wire service reporters, Cronkite was also more attuned to breaking stories than to "enterprisers" — original reports that are not simply reactive to the day's events and that take far longer to prepare. And after a while, Cronkite's preferences began to affect the judgments made by co-workers. Assignment editors always felt a certain amount of risk in passing up a hearing on Capitol Hill that might yield some news, however predictable. If the wires carried a story on the hearing that afternoon, Cronkite was almost sure to demand an accounting of why CBS didn't have it. Eventually, it became easier for the assignment editor to say no to the reporter who asked to do an original report on race relations or factory conditions and send him to cover the hearing instead.

There was something almost Pavlovian about Cronkite's response to breaking news. CBS News correspondent Bob Schieffer recalls the time he and Cronkite were in London during a presidential trip and Cronkite offered him a ride back to their hotel late one night in his chauffeur-driven limousine. "Suddenly an ambulance passed us with its siren going, and Walter, smelling a possible scoop, said, 'Hey, maybe that's got something to do with the bombings they've been having here lately. Driver! Follow that ambulance!' Of course, it turned out to be nothing, but there we were in the middle of the night in *London,* chasing a God-damned ambulance. I hadn't chased any ambulances since I was a cub reporter back on the police beat in Fort Worth, Texas."

Cronkite learned the value of accuracy as a wire service reporter, and he demanded it of everyone who contributed to the Evening News. Staff writers, whose job traditionally was to rewrite stories taken from AP and UPI, were expected by Cronkite to check back with the original source of the wire story and, if possible, to turn up a fresh, new angle. (This may not sound unusual, but it is far from the norm in television news.) In looking over a piece of copy, Cronkite interrogated the writer like a drill sergeant. "How do you know this? Are you sure of that?" "We were all a little afraid of him," says Bill Overend, a former writer on the program. "He asked hard, fact-checking questions, and he expected you to have the answers. You didn't try to fake. You said, 'I don't know; I'll try to find out.' One time I had written a minor environmental story, which Cronkite looked at for the first time about two minutes before air. He turned to me and said, 'Bill, would you find out when life began?' You never questioned Walter, so I called the researcher, who called someone else, and we finally came up with a figure."

This desire to cover all bases was augmented by Cronkite's unquenchable, almost indiscriminate curiosity; he always wanted to know everything about everything. "I get fascinated when I'm in a shoe store," he says. "I'd like to know how they keep their inventory. I'd like to work in one for a week to see if I could find out. I never know how they know what are in those boxes and how they keep enough models on hand to get their work done.''

His need to know was compulsive, particularly concerning major events like space shots or elections. He demanded so much research that by the time it was all assembled, it filled a thick notebook. Eventually, somebody figured out that the data would be valuable to others as well, so copies of Cronkite's briefing books were distributed to all the editorial personnel working on the event. It was such a practical system that it was eventually adopted by the other networks and by the more ambitious local stations.

Many aspects of Cronkite's character and background left an imprint on CBS. He was, of course, immensely more complex and sophisticated than he appeared on the screen. According to the conventional wisdom, television exposes people for what they really are, but Cronkite was unusually adept at concealing certain facets of his personality. The benevolent persona that viewers saw was not a fabrication; he *had* a certain courtly, mellow quality about him, particularly in social situations. But viewers never saw the other side — the tough, Germanic stickler who was on the whole rather aloof, even forbidding — the Cronkite colleagues saw at work.

The most legendary aspect of his personality was his fanatical competitiveness. Walter Cronkite simply would not be beaten at anything, whether it was auto racing, obscure parlor games, or news. His zeal to win was so ferocious it could fuel an entire organization. In 1968, the race between Hubert Humphrey and Richard Nixon was so close that the election hinged on the results from California, but by 3:00 A.M., the returns had slowed down to a trickle; it was apparent the final tally wouldn't be known until the next day. The CBS election team was exhausted, and people were beginning to slip away for the night when Cronkite noticed the ranks of his support team were thinning. "God damn it,'' he yelled at the producer. "Where is everybody? This election isn't over yet.'' So, everybody trooped back to their positions and stuck it out a while longer.

When CBS got beaten on a story, Cronkite's outbursts were dreaded. "We used to sit around watching the opposition after our program was over,'' recalls Joel Bernstein, a former producer on the show, "and wait for him to come charging out of his office. If NBC came on with something really good, you felt it. You felt the breathing down the hall, and you looked at your watch, knowing that in five seconds, he would be there, demanding to know why *we* didn't have that.''

His drive to win propelled him to amazing feats of endurance. During Apollo XI, the lunar walk, CBS was on the air for thirty straight hours, and Cronkite stayed on for all but three of them. After wrapping up the live coverage at 6:00 P.M., he anchored the Evening News at 6:30 and came back to do the special at 11:30 that night when the astronauts were leaving lunar orbit.

Another facet of his personality that never appeared on the air was his star-sized ego. He loved being on camera, so much so that his colleagues considered him an air hog. During conventions, Cronkite often refused to give up the microphone, even when producers signaled that a reporter was standing by with a new piece of information. Sometimes, Cronkite talked so long, by the time he was ready to go to the correspondent the story was outdated. He bristled at being interrupted in midthought, too, so communicating with him required the utmost delicacy and intuition. Someone who was adept at reading him was posted in a kind of pit near his feet, handing him messages at a propitious moment. If Cronkite ignored a message once, the producers might send a second note, but if he ignored it again, it was considered unwise to press the point a third time.

People working closely with Cronkite often got the impression he thought he *was* the news. The Evening News, which totals about twenty-two minutes after commercials are subtracted, was divided into two portions: Cronkite's time — six or seven minutes of him talking on camera, known as "the magic" — and the time set aside for all other reports. "The magic" would be affected to some degree by the nature of the day's news, but only somewhat. Cronkite rarely had less than five and a half or six minutes on camera, no matter how heavy the news was or how many correspondents' reports were stacked up.

In time, "the magic" assumed a certain ritualistic character. Each day, the editor checked with the writers about the time they needed for their stories. Then the bargaining would start. "I need thirty seconds for this story," a writer would insist. "Can't you do it in twenty-five?" the editor would plead. Then the editor would total the amount of time Cronkite needed and inform the executive producer, who had the job of fitting in the film or tape reports accordingly. Many correspondents felt that Cronkite's urge to talk kept legitimate news — especially their own reports — off the program. They appreciated the fact that when Roger Mudd substituted for Cronkite, he let the flow of the day's news dictate "the magic," even if he wound up with as little as two minutes on the air.

Cronkite always seemed more focused on *his* portion of the program. Although he read the scripts submitted by the correspondents, he seldom ventured into a screening room to see their reports, and he usually didn't watch them on the air, either. During the program when he wasn't on camera, he stayed busy with his own script, editing and rewriting. After the program, he preferred to monitor the opposition rather than watch the CBS replay. Sometimes when he was berating the staff for missing a story he had seen on a competing network, the producers would mutter, "We *had* that, Walter, only ours was better."

Always more of a word man than a picture man, Cronkite showed a sort of imperial disdain for the technical limitations of the medium. He figured it was up to the producers and directors to keep up with *him*. He didn't care how late it was when he came out of his office to start ripping up the program, demanding all kinds of changes that jeopardized the smoothness of the production. In fact, he seemed to thrive on the chaos he created. The staff all noticed how much more he enjoyed himself when they were skirting the edge of disaster, when, for instance, writers crawled around on their hands and knees, out of range of the cameras, handing him scripts only seconds before he had to read them on the air. The tension seemed to keep his adrenaline up.

If Cronkite's method of operation seemed highhanded, it made the staff extremely flexible and able to cope with late-breaking news. At NBC, where the producers liked to get the program locked in early to ensure against technical slip-ups, the Nightly News area looked like a sedate gentleman's club. Back when film was used and more time was needed for transporting and developing it, people at NBC used to say that if Jesus Christ came back to earth and walked on the Potomac, it wouldn't be scheduled to run on the "Huntley-Brinkley Report" unless he did it before four o'clock in the afternoon. At CBS, the feeling was that no matter how late a story broke, it would make the air somehow. Cronkite demanded no less.

"The Star," they called him behind his back, and he was used to being treated like one. If top producers scurried to do his bidding like copy boys, Cronkite accepted it as his due. Yet he was an excellent leader who gave clear, consistent signals to his subordinates and was capable of inspiring great loyalty and affection. The people who worked with him felt privileged; like members of an elite military outfit, they knew they were the best.

For all of Cronkite's imperiousness, he was seldom capricious or arbitrary. Robert Wussler, now the executive vice president of TBS, Ted Turner's communications empire, who was for many years the producer in charge of special events at CBS, recalls how exacting Cronkite could be. "It was my job to set things up so that he was pleased, which I understood. His attitude was, 'Let's be prepared,' and his comfort was very important, because we would be on the air for a long time, and if your creature comforts aren't there, the fatigue factor increases. The phones had to be just at the right position so that he wouldn't have to bend over or strain his neck. The monitors had to be placed just so." If things weren't arranged to suit Cronkite exactly, even senior producers like Wussler could expect a tongue-lashing.

People traveling in the field with Cronkite were more apt to see his warm, human side, so little in evidence at the office. On the road, he was a charming companion, telling jokes and uproarious stories with relish. He could be considerate, too. Once, during a harried and fatiguing trip to China, he managed to find time to wire flowers to a CBS cameraman's wife who had just given birth to a baby. When producer Sandy Socolow, probably Cronkite's closest associate at CBS, had a heart attack, Cronkite insisted that Socolow move into his home while he recuperated.

Generally, though, Cronkite didn't invite intimacy on the part of staff members, most of whom didn't dare speak to him unless he spoke to them first. "It wasn't that people were afraid of him, exactly," says Lee Townsend, the news editor of the program, "but when you approached him, you measured your words. You said what you had to say and looked for a good time to say it, unless of course you had a joke. Cronkite always loved a good laugh."

Cronkite often used to say that he regretted not getting to know the people on his staff better, bemoaning the fact that he never seemed to find time to have lunch with the writers and producers the way Roger Mudd and Harry Reasoner did. Yet he seldom made time. It was as though he sensed that if people got to know him too well, he would seem a little less awesome, his word more prone to be challenged. A less charitable interpretation has it that Cronkite didn't like to go out for meals with the staff for fear of having to pay the bill. Always a careful man with a dollar, he was seldom known to pick up the check when dining with colleagues.

In many ways, of course, Cronkite was much the way he appeared to be on the screen, a rather conventional, down-to-earth Midwesterner who shared the same world view as most people his age from that part of the country. That is to say, he was mildly conservative, fervently pro-American, and on the whole, not too discontented with the status quo. He had his biases and blind spots, just like anyone else, but in general, they were not too pronounced. He did not like stories dealing with crime, gossip, murder trials, or movie stars, which meant the producers sometimes had to do a selling job to get them on the air. It was much easier to find room for a story about space, science, or the environment.

Producers complained that Cronkite was out of touch with popular culture — a common failing among people of his generation — resisting the inclusion of stories about the youth movement, drugs, or entertainers like Woody Guthrie or the Rolling Stones. Once he wanted to kill a story about Bob Dylan, not recognizing his name until a writer told him that Dylan had written "Blowin' in the Wind." "Oh," said Cronkite. "Did he write that? Let's use the story then." (The same generational criticism used to be made of John Chancellor. Producers said you could always air an obituary for a short story writer famous in the thirties, but it was useless to try to persuade him to mention a country-western singer, no matter how popular.)

Cronkite's moderate, "reasonable" values tended to conceal an important fact, however: When an anchor as powerful as Cronkite takes a special interest in a subject, he can become an important link in the chain of public opinion. Cronkite's interest in the environment, for example, led to a long-running series on the Evening News called "Can This World Be Saved?" that almost certainly helped create the climate for passage of the environmental legislation of the seventies. Ronn Bonn, the producer in charge of the series, remembers its genesis vividly. "It was New Year's Day, 1970, and Walter walked in and said, 'God damn it, we've *got* to get on this environment story.' When Walter said 'God damn it,' things happened." Bonn was detached from his regular duties for the next six weeks to plot an approach and produce some introductory reports. Over the next few years, dozens more were aired.

Although the environmental movement was gaining momentum by the time Cronkite got his brainstorm, the issue had not yet captured the attention of the press or the politicians. In the 1968 presidential campaign, for instance, none of the candidates — Nixon, Humphrey, or George Wallace — devoted a single speech to the topic. The turning point for the ecology movement, environmentalists agree, was Earth Day, April 22, 1970, a nationwide "environmental awareness day." It was an event with great appeal for the media in general and for Walter Cronkite in particular, who plugged it on the Evening News and in his radio commentaries. Earth Day was wildly successful; millions of mostly middle-class people turned out to sing and pray, haul garbage from rivers, and take part in teach-ins and seminars. Congress, awakened to the popularity of the issue, passed the Environmental Protection Act not long afterward — the start of a major drive to curb pollution. One of the organizers of Earth Day, Sam Love, thinks Cronkite's support was pivotal. "Whenever he mentioned it on the air, I noticed that the mail increased. I always thought CBS and Cronkite helped make the event, because they gave it validation."

Cronkite was the engine that drove the Evening News. And since that was the enterprise around which most of the news division's efforts revolved, in time he became one of the driving forces behind CBS News itself. First, though, he had to prove he was a winner, and wresting the lead from NBC did not prove easy.

The low point of his career as anchor came during the 1964 political conventions. He was still relatively new to the anchor seat, and "Huntley-Brinkley" was in full flower. It was a time of turmoil within the administrative ranks of CBS News, Richard Salant having been replaced as president that year by Fred Friendly. At the Republican convention in San Francisco, executives barged in and out of the control room, creating chaos and upsetting Cronkite, who talked more than ever and lacked his usual good-humored assurance on the air. The ratings were disastrous: NBC pulled 55 percent of the audience to 30 percent for CBS and 15 percent for ABC.

William Paley, who was by that time getting tired of losing to NBC, proposed replacing Cronkite at the Democratic convention with the team of Roger Mudd and Robert Trout, one of broadcasting's most respected elders. Fred Friendly opposed the idea, but Paley and Frank Stanton were adamant, so Friendly gave in.

Cronkite, naturally, was crushed, but discreet company man that he was, he said nothing in public. He even held a press conference at management's request to defend the right of CBS to name anyone it chose to anchor the convention. Cronkite went to Atlantic City to anchor the

Evening News, but at night, when his duties were finished, he would walk the boardwalk with friends, agonizing over whether to leave CBS. Predictably, Mudd and Trout did even more poorly in the ratings than Cronkite had the previous month, and although Friendly and others tried to reassure Cronkite that his position at CBS was solid, the incident left a bitter taste in his mouth.

In 1966, after a tumultuous if sometimes inspiring reign as president of CBS News, Fred Friendly resigned, and Richard Salant was reinstated, ushering in a long period of administrative stability that would prove immensely beneficial. Salant seldom interfered in editorial decisions, but he was skillful at fending off pressures from the corporate level, and he led the industry in promoting high standards of journalistic ethics. (He was such a purist in matters of production that he issued an edict banning the addition of music to filmed reports, even for feature stories.) Gradually, the CBS television news staff began to recover its pride, developing an esprit de corps to rival the Murrow era.

NBC News, on the other hand, began to founder without the energizing presence of Robert Kintner, who was ousted as president of the company in 1966. Although he was a gifted executive, he never succeeded in imposing the same managerial discipline on NBC that his counterpart, Frank Stanton, brought to CBS. NBC had a reputation as a sloppily run company, a place where people hired their relatives and abused their expense accounts. In the news division, favoritism was rampant and management systems tended to be ad hoc. Instead of hiring and training a corps of professional researchers, individual producers would hire research assistants, only to let them go after their projects were completed. Script files were poorly maintained, and the retrieval system for film and tape was in catastrophic shape. Shortly after John F. Kennedy was sworn in as President, the videotape of his inaugural address was recycled for other uses. After his assassination, producers searching for footage of his administration came up with so little that it was impossible to put together a decent obituary.

At CBS, proper support systems were set up in the news division, including a good library, an excellent filing system for film, and a crack staff of researchers. Much of this fastidiousness reflected the wishes of Stanton, who liked things to be orderly and efficient. An educator by profession, he took a special interest in the news division, making sure the financial resources to run a first-class operation were available.

CBS News had another advantage that went beyond personalities.

NBC News did not enjoy the full corporate support of RCA, its parent corporation. "RCA screwed this place up," says Reuven Frank, the current president of NBC News, who also served in that capacity in the late sixties and early seventies. "The fact that we don't have any archives, things like that, can be traced to RCA. They would decide periodically they wanted more money from NBC, so they would either cut the archives or close a bureau."

Throughout the sixties, CBS News was also building a strong corps of recognizable star reporters — Dan Rather, Roger Mudd, Marvin Kalb, Harry Reasoner, Charles Kuralt, Hughes Rudd. So Walter Cronkite was not only backed by a more tightly run, better disciplined operation, he was flanked by a strong "supporting cast" on the Evening News. NBC's reporters did not have the same high visibility night after night on the "Huntley-Brinkley Report."

In 1966, for the first time, the Cronkite show edged ahead in the ratings. But NBC quickly regained the lead. In 1967, after Cronkite pulled ahead again, NBC decided it was time to take countermeasures. Shad Northshield, who succeeded Reuven Frank as executive producer of "Huntley-Brinkley," introduced a system of "contributing editors," which was, in effect, a device to showcase *NBC's* star reporters. The format, which put John Chancellor, Sander Vanocur, Douglas Kiker, and Jack Perkins on the set for supposedly spontaneous chitchat with Huntley and Brinkley, worked well at conventions, but it was extremely awkward on the evening news. The arrangement also generated resentment among NBC's other reporters, who found it even more difficult to get on the air. The experiment did not last long. And it did not boost the ratings. From 1967 until he stepped down in 1981, Cronkite held on to the lead, although his margin was sometimes precariously slim.

But Cronkite never took his position as the nation's premier news personality for granted. As the years went by, he drove his subordinates as hard as ever, never letting the staff forget that their function was to make *him* look good. For if Cronkite never succumbed to the boredom that overtakes most anchors after a while, the truth is, he never thought he *could afford to relax*. Even when he was the grand old man of television news, he watched the ratings anxiously, and it was well known he was not displeased if the audience dropped when he went on vacation. One summer he came back to work ahead of schedule, prompting speculation he had cut his vacation short because the ratings started to go up.

It was anxiety that propelled his brilliant career as a reporter for United

Press, as Cronkite himself concedes. "It was literally 'the deadline every minute,' particularly in a one-man bureau. You have the responsibility for an entire area of coverage, and you're working twenty-four hours a day, scared to death something's going to happen while you're relaxing for a moment."

Cronkite's daughter, Kathy, provides a clue to her father's extraordinary drive to succeed in her book, *On the Edge of the Spotlight*, an account of what it's like to be the son or daughter of famous parents. Although Cronkite never finished college, Kathy writes that he often faulted other people for their lack of formal education. Her sister Nancy sounds the same theme: "I remember when I was living out in the country, and I was telling [Dad] how funny the farmers were, how intelligent and what a good sense of humor they had, and [he] seemed to take the attitude that if they weren't well educated, they couldn't possibly be interesting or intelligent."

Cronkite enrolled in the University of Texas, but he never spent much time in class because of his many extracurricular activities — stringing for the *Houston Post*, working on the campus newspaper, acting in the local Curtain Club, reporting for the old International News Service, a wire service that later merged with United Press to form UPI. At one point, he tried his hand at sports announcing, which led to a job in a bookie joint in Austin, calling the race results for $75 a week. By his junior year, he was working full-time for the Scripps-Howard bureau in Austin (for $15 a week) and flunking most of his classes, so he dropped out of school. He had become addicted to a life of action by then.

All his life, Cronkite kept running to stay ahead of the pack, showing the same intensity in his leisure pursuits that he did on the job. A marvelous dancer and a gifted mimic, he always claimed he would have been just as happy as a song-and-dance man in vaudeville as he was in journalism. He drove himself so hard as a young man, working all day and playing all night, that he developed a bad case of pleurisy from lack of food and sleep.

Although Cronkite seemed confident in his early newspaper career, he showed a certain overeagerness that sometimes landed him in trouble. In one instance, while he was working for the paper in Austin, he was sent to a murder victim's house to ask the widow for a photo. When nobody answered the door, he looked through a window, and seeing a picture of a man on the mantel, he broke the window and took the photo. After the picture was published, his editors learned that Cronkite inadvertently had burgled the wrong house, and they had printed a picture of the dead man's neighbor.

The same unfettered zeal also got him into trouble on radio. After establishing himself as a popular sportscaster at a small radio station in Kansas City, where he called the plays from inside a radio studio by using reports relayed by telegraph wire, he was offered a job with a big-time radio station in Oklahoma City. He was hired to announce Oklahoma University's football games, which would have been fine, except that he had never broadcast a *real* football game in his life. Setting to work with his customary thoroughness, he devised a system for calling the plays, using spotters who were to press buttons on an electric board, indicating who had the ball, what player made the play, and so on. It sounded good on paper, but the day of the game, the spotters fell down on the job, the board didn't work, and Cronkite, who didn't even have a program, gave what must have been one of the worst sportscasts of all time. Listening to the station manager moaning, "Jesus, Jesus," in the background, he was sure he would be fired. He was given a second chance, though, and this time he performed professionally, memorizing all the players' names, meeting with them personally, and so on. Never again would he be accused of not being properly prepared.

Although he was becoming a successful broadcaster, Cronkite still yearned for the world of print. His future bride, Mary Elizabeth Maxwell, known as Betsy, a woman's page editor for the *Kansas City Journal Post*, encouraged him to go back to newspapers, too, even if it meant making less money. In 1938, however, he strayed even further from journalism, working for Braniff Airlines as a regional traffic manager and public relations man. Cronkite learned a lot about aviation, but he hated public relations and wanted to return to news. He had worked for the United Press a couple of years earlier, and in 1939, he persuaded them to take him back. In 1940, he and Betsy were married.

The next nine years, spent working for UP, were happy ones. He loved the wire service with a devotion he never seems to have developed for broadcasting. Even now, when he talks about his days as a wire service reporter, his face lights up and his manner becomes more animated. It was a perfect job for someone with Cronkite's adrenaline level. In 1942, he was posted to London as a war correspondent. His boss, Harrison Salisbury, who later became an editor for the *New York Times,* considered him the best on the beat. That same year he made his first appearance on camera, narrating film for a Paramount newsreel. Billed as an "eyewitness report from Walter Cronkite, the first newspaperman back from Africa," the film gives a good idea of Cronkite's instinctive flair for the dramatic, while managing to look so natural. The shot opens on him, sitting on a desk, dressed in a trench coat, typing. He looks up from the typewriter, as if he didn't realize a camera was in the room, and launches into the narration. It ought to look phony, but it doesn't. Twenty-six years later, in his famous prime-time special on Vietnam, he showed the same intuitive grasp of how to use the camera. As the program opened, he rode up in a jeep, his flak-jacket unbuttoned at the neck, his helmet untied and slightly askew. He jumped out of the jeep and, sounding slightly breathless, started to talk. Those little touches are the mark of someone who understands visual symbolism and drama. They telegraph to the viewer, "I have been there." When Dan Rather tried a similar approach in Afghanistan, crouching on a hillside, dressed in native garb, the sound of guns going off in the distance, the critics dubbed him "Gunga Dan" and said his performance was theatrical. In fact, the scene was no more contrived than Cronkite's, but Rather is not as adroit as Cronkite at playing himself. With Rather, you notice the mechanics behind the performance. With Cronkite, it always seemed artless.

The marvel of Walter Cronkite was to seem so *ordinary,* the kind of person who invites admiration, rather than jealousy. In part it may have come from his background — from his having grown up in the heart of mid-America. The son of a dentist, Cronkite was born in St. Joseph, Missouri, in 1916, and grew up in Kansas City and Houston. If he inherited his love of things mechanical from his father, he must have inherited his zest for life from his mother, Helen, who lived an active life past the age of ninety and even then liked nothing better than an evening of dancing. Cronkite himself insists he had an "absolutely average" childhood. "I dug caves, built tree houses, took piano lessons, did all those things an average kid does."

It was as a man that his pursuits and exploits began to be anything but average. As a war correspondent, he was attracted to danger, continually putting his life at risk. A member of "the writing 69th," a group of elite war correspondents, including Homer Bigart of the *Herald Tribune,* Gladwin Hill of AP, and Andy Rooney of *Stars and Stripes* — all of whom graduated to bigger and better things — Cronkite flew every kind of mission from low-level B-26 bombing raids to a glider landing in the

Netherlands. On one mission, thirteen of sixty-five planes were shot down; he escaped unharmed, but one of his buddies, Bob Post of the *New York Times,* was killed.

This apparent fondness for danger found an outlet in peacetime in Cronkite's passion for auto racing. He was a serious amateur, skilled enough to drive in races like the Sebring as part of the Lancia team. Once, in a sports car rally, the car he was driving plunged over a 100-foot cliff in the Smoky Mountains, but he landed in a stream and emerged unhurt. Cronkite claims he is not a thrill-seeker, but danger obviously exerts a certain fascination for him. "I don't think I'm particularly brave. As a matter of fact, if anything, doing some of the things I've done, particularly automobile racing, was an effort to prove to myself that I *could* do something like that. What it does have is an exhilaration of having participated and survived, and there is definitely an adrenal flow of some kind that comes from having overcome one's own fears and trepidations, I think."

During World War II, his bravery and stamina brought him to the attention of Edward R. Murrow, who offered him $125 a week plus fees to come to work for CBS. It was a substantial increase over Cronkite's salary at UP, $67 a week, so he accepted, but his boss, Harrison Salisbury, counteroffered with $92, a huge raise by UP standards. Cronkite was immensely flattered, and since he didn't want to leave UP anyway, he was forced to tell Murrow he had changed his mind.

After the war, Cronkite remained in Europe as chief correspondent at the Nuremberg trials, going on to become UP bureau chief in Moscow. By 1948, he was earning $125 a week, making him the highest-paid reporter in the organization, but wire service wages no longer seemed enough. He decided to take a few months to think things over, and he and Betsy arrived back in Kansas City just in time for the birth of their first child, a daughter. When the general manager of the Kansas City radio station, KMBC, offered him $250 a week to go to Washington as a radio correspondent for a group of Midwestern stations, Cronkite was faced with a familiar dilemma: stay with his first love — print reporting — or earn a lot of money as a broadcaster. This time, he opted for the money.

In Washington, Cronkite quickly made a name for himself with his charm and energy, but he was beginning to get restless by the time the Korean War broke out in 1950. When Murrow called and asked him if he would like to cover it for CBS, he jumped at the chance.

He never made it to Korea. While he was waiting to complete the necessary paperwork to go overseas, the local CBS television station in Washington asked him to give a five-minute briefing on the Korean War on its six o'clock news. "Gosh, after World War Two, I could have done a war briefing blindfolded," Cronkite says. "I said, 'Get me a blackboard, and put the outline of Korea on it and the thirty-eighth parallel, and I'll do a chalk talk.' I did that two nights, and they said, 'Would you like to take over the whole six o'clock?' I said, 'Sure, I'm just waiting around to go to Korea.' I thought it was as temporary as that." Within about a week, Cronkite's broadcast acquired a sponsor (still a novelty in television news at that time), and a couple of weeks later, he was asked to take over the eleven o'clock news as well.

Cronkite was an autocratic character even in those days. His assistant, Neil Strawser, now a CBS correspondent, remembers him as an exceedingly demanding boss. Among Strawser's other tasks, he was supposed to call for the weather during Cronkite's newscast. "I only forgot to give him the weather once. You only forget once with Walter. He was a stern taskmaster, but he was also the best city editor in broadcasting. It was invigorating to work with him. You knew when you did well, if only because he didn't tell you you'd done badly." Cronkite may have been more stick than carrot, but his methods were effective.

He remained in Washington until 1954, when he was asked to move to New York to be master of ceremonies on a new CBS program, "The Morning Show," CBS's answer to the "Today" show. Like "Today," "Morning" was soft, relying mainly on cute features and comedy bits. In place of J. Fred Muggs, "Today's" irrepressible chimp, "Morning" used puppets named Charlemagne the Lion and Huckleberry Houn'. Cronkite even had a gag writer, but he wasn't at ease in the patently show business format, and within a year he was replaced by Jack Paar. Cronkite stayed on in New York, however, becoming the staff narrator of CBS News and public affairs, host of such programs as "You Are There," "The Twentieth Century," and "Eyewitness to History."

Manhattan suited the racy, sporting side of Cronkite; he loved the all-night jazz clubs and felt at home in café society. In 1958, he and Betsy bought a brownstone in the East Eighties, where they brought up their three children, Nancy, Kathleen, and young Walter, known as Chip.

Betsy Cronkite was devoted to her husband. She drove him back and forth to work and followed him around the racing circuit on weekends, concealing from him the fact that she got sick before every race. When he gave up racing and took up sailing, it wasn't much better for her; she got seasick easily and hated cooking in the cramped galley.

It was not easy being Walter Cronkite's children, either. The daughters, in particular, seem to have been overawed by him, constantly feeling they were disappointing him, wanting more of his attention than he could give. Yet Cronkite strove to be a conscientious father, teaching his children how to swim and play tennis and nagging them to do their homework. He even switched from auto racing to sailing so the family could spend more time together. A great effort was made to give the children a normal home life, shielding them from publicity, concealing from them the occasional kidnap threats.

The fact is, Walter Cronkite was already a famous man when his children were growing up in the fifties, thanks to his exposure at conventions, elections, and the numerous public affairs programs he narrated. Even so, nobody at CBS, least of all Cronkite himself, could have foreseen how phenomenal and enduring his success would be. Never believing it would last, Cronkite was not one to overplay his hand or make undue demands on the company. A master of survival tactics, he carefully nurtured his image for honesty and integrity and steered clear of controversy. When he did voice an opinion, he chose his time and his place carefully.

He had learned the hard way that he was only as good as his ratings and that no quarter could be expected if the numbers went down. (The corporate executives *did* pay attention to ratings, even if they encouraged their subordinates in the news division to ignore them.) Cronkite had had a taste of the ruthlessness of TV in 1955, when he found out he was being replaced as host of ''The Morning Show'' by reading it in the newspaper. And he never forgot the way he was thrown to the wolves after the 1964 Republican convention.

The other great lesson of Cronkite's career was the fate of Edward R. Murrow. In 1960, when the ''CBS Reports'' documentary unit was being formed, Fred Friendly was asked to take the job of producer, and Paley made it clear that Murrow — despite his towering stature — would be permitted to play only a limited role; he could appear occasionally, but Friendly had to use other correspondents as well. By 1961, Murrow had become so estranged from Paley that when John F. Kennedy offered him a job as director of the USIA, Murrow gratefully accepted. If a man of Murrow's stature, once an intimate of Paley's, could be discarded, virtually driven out of the company, what kind of consideration could a Walter Cronkite expect?

Unlike Murrow, Cronkite avoided confrontations with management and never spoke out against the sins of television, as Murrow had done. He stayed out of office politics, too. While he did not hesitate to get rid of people on his own staff who failed to do the job, he disliked being put in the position of championing anybody or getting embroiled in others' problems. When Gordon Manning, a vice president in the news division and a personal friend of his, was fired in a shakeup in 1976, Cronkite did not intervene. Paul Greenberg, who once produced Cronkite's show and who was a friend of Manning's, brought the subject up one day while he and Cronkite were playing tennis. "I told him I had heard a rumor that ABC was trying to fire Reasoner's producer, and Reasoner told them, 'If he goes, I go.' Walter said, 'Yeah, Harry is tough all right.' Which gave me an opening. I said, 'When they canned Gordon, you could have saved him. You could have said, "If he goes, I go." Gordon's a good friend of yours. You go sailing with him; you see each other socially.' Cronkite said, 'No, if I had intervened, they would have gotten rid of me eventually, too.'"

Cronkite's approach to the news seldom made waves either. Although he genuinely believed in the virtues of impartial reporting, his approach also shielded him from controversy throughout most of his long career. Those cases that fired his enthusiasm, such as cleaning up the environment and exploring outer space, were fairly popular and relatively noncontroversial.

The space story was a natural for him. He had always been interested in aviation, as far back as his brief career with Braniff in the thirties; for him, Cape Canaveral was like a giant toy store. He became so involved in the nuts and bolts of the space program that he would go down to the Cape on his own time before a space shot to ride in the simulators and spend time with the experts.

Space was instrinsically a wonderful television story, too. A magnificent pictorial display, overlaid with such appealing themes as human courage, American ingenuity, and the charting of the unknown, a space shot had a structure that worked well on television — a breathtaking opening, a suspenseful middle, and a dramatic conclusion. And everything occurred on a fixed schedule, so the cameras could be situated in the right place. Space was also one of the few positive stories of the tumultuous sixties, and Cronkite's close identification with it helped further boost his image as the nation's patron saint and guardian.

He was so enthusiastic about the program that he sometimes seemed more cheerleader than reporter. "The eighth astronaut" they called him. He frowned on stories that reflected poorly on the program, and it was widely believed that unless such reports were kept very short, they did not stand a good chance of getting on the Evening News. Once, during Apollo XI, he was listening to several minority representatives complaining that the space program was a waste of scarce resources and a means of diverting attention from the nation's more pressing problems. Looking puzzled, he turned to CBS correspondent David Schoumacher and said, "I'll never understand these people. Why can't they rejoice in this wonderful thing that is happening to our country?"

Cronkite was fortunate that his principal rivals in the sixties, Huntley and Brinkley, did not have the same enthusiasm for the space story. In fact, they were thoroughly bored by it. They would come on, introduce the coverage, then let Frank McGee or Jim Hartz take over. Jim Kitchell, who was in charge of NBC's space coverage, says Huntley and Brinkley were allowed to get away with minimum participation because "they had enough star quality and clout to do it. Brinkley felt it was too technical a subject for him. McGee, of course, did his homework, but I couldn't trust Huntley and Brinkley. I would provide them with all the research and information, and they just wouldn't read it. They'd read the summaries in the press kits." By not establishing themselves as experts on space, Huntley and Brinkley abdicated the screen at moments when millions of additional people were watching — potential converts to NBC who might tune in to Huntley and Brinkley on the evening news more often.

Cronkite also played Vietnam, the most divisive issue of his time, like a violin — an apparent supporter of the war effort so long as the public seemed to approve, turning critic only after large numbers of people became disaffected. In 1965, Cronkite made his first trip to Vietnam, returning with an upbeat account of the U.S. war effort. Yet, as early as 1965, he allowed the CBS correspondents in Vietnam — Morley Safer, John Lawrence, Peter Kallisher, and others — to file negative reports on the course of the war, night after night on his program.

The reporting from Vietnam marked a turning point in television's relationship to the government. Only a few years before, during the Cuban missile crisis, an attitude of cooperation with the government prevailed. Media critic Edwin Diamond, in a recent study of how the networks covered the Cuban crisis, found a startling unity — by today's standards at least — of press-government interest. Reporters referred to "the administration," "the government," and "we" (meaning "our side") interchangeably. Discussing aerial reconnaissance photos of Cuba, Walter Cronkite spoke of "our" intelligence reports. But a combination of factors in Vietnam undermined this consensus. One was the lack of a clear-cut rationale for U.S. involvement. Another was the presence of a group of young, iconoclastic reporters who were allowed to travel freely throughout the country, reporting what they saw and heard without censorship. In addition, the deception practiced by U.S. civilian and military authorities seemed to attain new heights as the war dragged on. Because the lies — the inflated body counts, the "progress" being made in pacification, and so on — came from official sources, they were duly reported on the evening news, but many television newsmen also told the public that the U.S. military adventure in Vietnam was not going well.

In 1968, after the Tet offensive demonstrated how strong the Vietcong remained, the climate of opinion supporting the war suddenly changed; Cronkite decided to return to Vietnam. He says he didn't go with any preconceived notions, but it seems clear that he knew he wasn't going on any ordinary fact-finding mission. "It was a studied decision; it wasn't done lightly," he told an interviewer for *Broadcasting* magazine. "Dick Salant and I discussed the purpose of very possibly doing just the kind of report I did. Not with the preconceived notion that I was going to come down hard against the war, but with the preconceived notion that I would come out with some positions, some personal look at it. The country was so confused and had been told the war's nearly over, light at the end of the tunnel, and all that sort of business. And then the Tet offensive proved that the Vietcong were stronger than ever . . . The thought was maybe I could be helpful in trying to put this into some sort of focus. And we thought at the time, when one does that, one certainly is stepping away from the role of impartiality. No question about that. And it's a calculated risk. And I suppose we must have lost some viewers, or at least we created some doubts in the minds of some — a considerable number — as to how impartial I really was."

For someone of Cronkite's innate caution and deeply held patriotism, it was a major departure to return and announce to his viewers, "It seems now more certain than ever that the bloody experience of Vietnam is to end in a stalemate . . . To say that we are closer to victory today is to believe, in the face of the evidence, the optimists who have been wrong in the past.'' His Vietnam reports, broadcast for four nights on the Evening News, ending each night with his personal observations, plus a special report aired in prime time, mark the only time in his entire career that he spoke out so personally and forcefully on a controversial subject on the air. It turned out to be an act of tremendous significance, of course, giving strength and legitimacy to the antiwar movement. Lyndon Johnson, listening to Cronkite on television, is said to have told his press secretary, George Christian, that if he had lost Walter Cronkite, he had lost the country.

Another demonstration of Cronkite's enormous impact was his primer on Watergate. Shortly before the 1972 election, Cronkite, who had been reading bits and pieces of the Watergate story every day, mainly in the *Washington Post,* complained that the whole story was very hard to connect. Producer Sandy Socolow recalls Cronkite saying, ''Why don't we do a simple narrative account of Watergate, starting with the begin- ning, going through the middle, to the end, stringing it into a narrative so that it will make sense to the audience?'' According to Socolow, the reports weren't necessarily intended to break any new ground but simply to make the story more comprehensible to the audience. ''Dummies that we were, we didn't know how controversial it was going to be,'' says Socolow, who believes that if the series had not had Cronkite's im- primatur, it probably wouldn't have run at all.

The Nixon administration was playing rough with the network at that time, causing nervousness in the executive suites. In one instance, a report from the White House Office of Telecommunications Policy noted that it would be relatively easy to establish dozens of new TV stations in the top 100 markets, and although the report didn't say so explicitly, it was plain that the new stations would not only compete with established network affiliates but also might be fashioned into a new network.

Nevertheless, the Cronkite unit went ahead with plans for a two-part series that would try to tie together all the loose strands of the Watergate story. As it turned out, they were not able to break any new ground. The story still belonged to the *Washington Post,* although several other publi- cations, including the *New York Times, Newsweek, Time,* and the *Los Angeles Times,* had been able to break off pieces of it. Part one of the series was an incredible fourteen minutes in length, a simple recounting of the facts as they were known, mainly from the *Post*. Outraged, the Nixon administration attempted to put pressure on CBS to cancel the second part, but although it was shortened — to six minutes — it did run.

Benjamin Bradlee, the executive editor of the *Washington Post*, says the CBS series was a turning point. "Aside from a handful of journalists in Washington, the story had not captured the national attention in any sense of the word. The editors all thought it was some kind of weird crusade on our part, but after Cronkite's reports, they covered it out their ass. It came off page A-27 among the truss ads, up to the front pages overnight, and it was Walter Cronkite who did it. It was as if the story had been blessed by the Great White Father."

His decision to spotlight the Watergate story and to take a stand on the Vietnam War represent aberrations in Cronkite's career; good television politician that he was, he usually hewed to the middle ground on controversial issues. Taking sides very often, he felt, would undermine his long-term credibility with the public, and he was probably right. In the sixties, when Fred Friendly suggested he do a regular two-minute commentary slot, he turned it down, arguing that he was no good at punditry, and that furthermore, the commentator's role and the anchor position are basically incompatible — that viewers would begin to think his own personal judgments were coloring his accounts of the news. The one subject he spoke out on frequently in speeches and in public appearances was the need for a strong, free press. He was in the forefront of those who challenged Spiro Agnew and the Nixon administration after they launched their assault against the press, a position he did not feel was inconsistent with his role as impartial newscaster. "My attitude about freedom of press issues is if we don't protect that right, who is going to do it for us; speaking out against Agnew was a necessity. I don't think we're betraying anyone in doing that, either, because that's not a case where people would suspect we don't have any prejudices. They ought to know that we do."

Cronkite also took care to maintain his image as the kindly, avuncular type, seldom asking tough questions in an interview. One time he was preparing to interview the astronauts who were embarking on a joint space venture with the Russians, and a young producer, Barry Jagoda, tried to prime him to ask tougher questions. Cronkite did not seem to be paying much attention, so Jagoda persisted. Finally, Cronkite said quietly, "Barry, you've got to remember. I'm not Mike Wallace. I was trained as a wire service reporter, and the way I like to do it is to ask the questions, get

the answers, and come back later and write the story. It's not a performance." But, of course, it *was* a performance; TV interviewers can't go
back and write the story.

Cronkite was criticized for his failure to be tougher when he interviewed Chicago Mayor Richard Daley at the 1968 Democratic convention. Not only had Dan Rather been roughed up by Daley's security
forces, but other reporters were beaten, and the police were using night-
sticks and clubs on demonstrators outside the hall. Cronkite himself called
Daley's men thugs on the air, but face to face, he was exceedingly polite to
Daley — some people even thought he was obsequious. Cronkite himself
considers this interview as one of the low points of his career. He meant to
be tougher, he says, but Daley barged into the studio unannounced, not
giving Cronkite a chance to collect his thoughts. "What I was planning to
do was say, 'Mayor Daley, we have all watched this terrible thing happen
this week, and you have obviously been the central figure, the one that's
ordered these repressive actions by your police. And I'm not even going to
ask you any questions about it. We've all seen it take place in front of our
eyes. [Said in a firm tone.] So, I'll just give you the microphone and give
you five minutes to give people an explanation.' But I never delivered that
introduction. It was a soft interview, and I never put his feet to the fire."

Somehow, it is difficult to imagine Cronkite confronting Daley in that
manner; it would have been entirely out of character with his mild,
fatherly persona. He was well aware that his audience expected him to
behave in a certain way and would have been disappointed by such a show
of truculence.

Cronkite was also careful to promote a spotless personal and professional image, tolerating no loose talk or disloyalty from subordinates or
friends. When the author mentioned to Cronkite that she had not yet
interviewed his long-time agent, Tom Stix, Cronkite replied, "Well, you
can talk to him, but he won't tell you anything. That's why I've kept him
all these years."

Concerned with being tagged as a "reader" or a performer, Cronkite
did not advertise the fact that he seldom wrote his own copy. New writers
were warned to be discreet about the exact nature of their work. While this
was undoubtedly a shrewd tactic, Cronkite knew full well that rewriting
wire copy is not necessarily the best use of an anchor's time, unless of
course he or she is a superb stylist. Nor is writing one's own copy any real
measure of editorial input. The anchor's writers function as the President's

speechwriters do: They write what he wants them to write. And if Cronkite didn't like a piece of copy, he handed it back to be redone. Occasionally, he even rewrote it himself — a move dreaded by the offending writer.

But Cronkite didn't earn his reputation as the most trusted man in America solely through clever manipulation of his own myth. The turbulent times fostered it, too. By the end of the sixties, the American public had suffered so many traumatic events — riots, assassinations, an unpopular war, the disaffection of the young, the burgeoning drug culture — that many people experienced a profound loss of confidence in the society's institutions and leaders. Cronkite, so obviously decent and trustworthy, held a special appeal for people who had lost faith in the more traditional authority figures — business leaders, politicians, presidents, and priests. As a constant, someone who was thoroughly professional, believable, and honest for so many years, he filled a deeply felt need. There was also something peculiarly soothing about him that seemed to make the bad news on television a little more palatable.

He was fortunate that his principal rivals on the evening news were tiring of their nightly rendezvous with the public. The critics felt that Huntley and Brinkley had lost their sparkle, and both men talked publicly of wanting to do other things. Huntley always said he would quit when he had a million dollars, and one day in the fall of 1969, he took his friend and producer Wallace Westfeldt aside and showed him a check for that amount. It was given to him by a group of developers who were starting a resort in Montana — his ticket out of television. Huntley's decision to leave threw the NBC hierarchy into turmoil; amazingly, no arrangements for replacing either man had been made, in spite of the fact they had been doing the program for almost fourteen years and were plainly tired of it. When Huntley left in July 1970, a so-called troika was set up — a rotating three-man team consisting of Brinkley, John Chancellor, and Frank McGee; but the arrangement seemed confusing to the audience, who never knew which two men would appear on any given night, and the ratings dropped sharply.

Brinkley was by then looking so bored and detached that he was sidelined to a nightly commentary role; Frank McGee was assigned to the "Today" show, and veteran correspondent John Chancellor, who looked like the best answer to Cronkite, was made sole anchor of the NBC Nightly News.

By that time, Cronkite had been on the job for almost ten years, but he showed no sign whatever of letting up. He was no longer as involved in the day-to-day decision-making as he had once been, sometimes coming in as late as 5:00 P.M., but from the moment he came charging out of his office late in the afternoon to take the reins, there was no relaxation of his fervor. "Get Marvin at the State Department," he would bark. "Get Paris on the phone." "Find out what Dan knows about this tax bill." As Paul Greenberg, at one time the executive producer on the program, remarked, "Another person would say, 'Screw it,' once in a while. Not Walter. Every day he got made up, put on the high heels and the fucking girdle and went to war."

Like Huntley, Cronkite seemed to enjoy the adulation of his fans, politely chatting with people who interrupted him in restaurants or on airplanes. After a while, though, it became genuinely difficult for him to move through a public place, like an airport, without being mobbed. Nelson Rockefeller gave him a helpful piece of advice: Always keep moving. "Chat, wave, or shake hands," Rockefeller told him, "but never stop, even for a second, or you've had it."

It wasn't a bad life, though. Cronkite came and went as he pleased, exempt from the rules that applied to everyone else at CBS. If he stayed out partying at night and came in late the next day, nobody had the audacity to question him about it. His vacation time was ideal, too — three months a year off, much of it spent on his yacht, the *Wintje*, named for a seventeenth-century Dutch ancestor. By this time, his status as the dedicated guardian of the news was so secure that even those television critics who knew he was sloughing off on the Evening News never wrote about it. Cronkite had done such a good job of building and preserving his own image it became virtually unshakable.

Yet, if Cronkite himself had consciously nurtured parts of his own myth, he also became many of those things in reality — he *was* honest, fair, and impartial — never tilting the news, seldom seeking to advance his own views, at least not deliberately. He used his influence sparingly and did not seek to make the anchor post any more powerful than it already was. Once in a great while, he stepped out of his role of objective observer, as he did when he telephoned Egyptian President Anwar Sadat to ask what his terms were for meeting with the Israelis. This initiative, coming just before Sadat's historic trip to Jerusalem, produced a stunning result, but Cronkite appears to have been uneasy over his foray into world affairs and did not seek any further opportunities to engage in "TV diplomacy." A lesser man, with less self-restraint, might have developed a messianic complex and designed his own remedies for saving the world.

Arthur Taylor, at one time the corporate president of CBS, is acutely aware of what might have happened if Cronkite had taken greater advantage of his personal prestige. "I think Walter will go down in history for having the character not to exploit the power that was his. Had he not had the character to do that, he might have provoked an enormous change in the rules. Because I doubt very much whether the government — by that I mean the politicians — would have easily permitted anyone to achieve the kind of influence he had the potential to achieve. If, for example, he had used his enormous acclaim and tremendous popularity to mobilize American public opinion — not on the air, but off the air — for some particular cause, I'm not sure exactly what would have happened, but I think life would have been difficult. There would have been people who would have said, 'We're creating a monster, an emperor, a molder of public opinion.' And I think life would have become very difficult for the broadcast community. After all, these are the public airwaves. They are licensees of the government, and they have to be used in the public interest. I think you could have provoked a situation where you had license renewal every year . . . there are all kinds of wonderful ways that the Congress of the United States could interfere without getting involved in First Amendment rights."

Certainly, the temptation for Cronkite to try to influence the course of national and world events must have been enormous. That he did not was perhaps attributable to his instinct for survival — a realization that he would become a target for criticism if he stepped out of his role as the impartial observer more often — but it also demonstrated a great deal of wisdom. The genius of Cronkite — a cautious man in a cautious enterprise — was always to know exactly how far he could go.

5
Harry Reasoner:
A Booster Shot for ABC

*At ABC-TV, everyone knows that his is an
organization devoted to making a profit. No
one, it seems, allows higher pretensions to
interface with efficiency.*
— Thomas Morgan
TV Guide, December 8, 1962

ON A CHILL AFTERNOON late in November 1970, an unaccustomed
silence fell over the CBS newsroom on West Fifty-seventh Street in New
York. Harry Reasoner was departing for ABC, and as word of his decision
spread, people stood looking at each other with shock and dismay. *Harry
Reasoner,* the man once touted as Walter Cronkite's successor, the sage of
"60 Minutes," was leaving *CBS*? One by one, his friends drifted back to
the "60 Minutes" compound to wish him well, but the impromptu party
in Reasoner's office did not spread much cheer. Along with the realization
that CBS was losing one of its most talented writers and broadcasters,
Reasoner's colleagues had trouble assimilating the notion that anyone
would voluntarily leave CBS for ABC. By 1970, CBS had regained the
corner on smugness. "Our attitude was, 'We are Athens. Our news is
engraved on stone tablets,'" Hughes Rudd recalls. To people at CBS
News, joining ABC was the equivalent of voluntarily moving to a leper
colony.

It's true that Reasoner was leaving to become the co-anchor of the ABC
Evening News at what was then regarded as a very handsome salary —
$200,000 a year. But how prestigious was it to be associated with a
struggling organization like ABC News? For years it had operated on
budgets only a fraction as large as those of CBS and NBC; ABC did not
even hire its own camera crews until 1963, depending before that on film

supplied by newsreel companies. It was not until 1968 that a half-hour of news was scheduled, almost five years after the other networks had abandoned the fifteen-minute format. ABC's unwillingness to pre-empt commercially sponsored programs for news breaks made it the laughing stock of the news world. (As recently as 1973, when Archibald Cox was fired as the Watergate special prosecutor, the attorney general resigned, and his deputy was fired in the so-called Saturday Night Massacre, ABC presented no special programming.)

The ratings for its evening news lagged far behind those of NBC and CBS, too. When Reasoner joined ABC News, its evening program attracted a mere 15 percent of the audience. But the team of Reasoner and Howard K. Smith worked wonders; within two years, the broadcast's share shot up to 22 percent. It was still in third place, but after more than two decades, ABC had finally become a serious contender in the network news sweepstakes.

To appreciate Reasoner's feat and to understand why, ultimately, he was unable to sustain his success at ABC, one has to go back to the origins of the network and examine its historically weak commitment to news.

To begin with, ABC was born as a castoff of NBC, and for years it remained at a staggering disadvantage with its competitors in terms of size and profits. In 1942, the Justice Department ordered NBC to sell off one of its two radio networks, which were known as the NBC-Red and NBC-Blue. The Blue, traditionally NBC's dumping ground for unsponsored programming, was sold the following year to millionaire industrialist Edward J. Noble, the Life Saver magnate, and was renamed the American Broadcasting Company. Although ABC acquired a strong line-up of company-owned television stations in the late forties — each network is allowed to own a maximum of five VHF stations — it remained an embryo TV network for some time. In 1955, for example, when 411 television stations were operating in the United States, NBC had 189 affiliates, CBS had 139, and ABC had only 46. ABC's affiliate picture improved steadily as television's reach expanded, but the truth is that in the 1950s and 1960s, advertisers did not spend enough money to support a third network. It was not until the 1970s, when the broadcasting industry entered an incredible boom cycle, that the economics for three strong, viable networks finally existed. Before that, the people who ran ABC, knowing they were in a fight to survive, watched the bottom line attentively and discouraged any dreams of glory on the part of their news division.

Within this context, no problem confronting ABC News over the years had been more vexing than its inability to come up with a dominant, durable anchor for its evening news program. Ironically, this was true even though ABC's *first* anchorman possessed more impressive news credentials than either of his rivals, Douglas Edwards and John Cameron Swayze. John Charles Daly was a senior correspondent for CBS during World War II and was considered one of the two best ad libbers in the business, the other being Robert Trout, who had become famous in the thirties for announcing conventions, state visits, and presidential news conferences for CBS.

Daly succeeded Trout as CBS's "special events man" at the White House in 1937 — his first job in broadcasting. Five years later, he joined Murrow's team in London, serving with distinction in London, Africa, the Middle East, and Italy. His real claim to fame, however, was "What's My Line?" — an enormously successful panel show that he moderated for seventeen years on CBS, even after he went to work as a newsman on a rival network.

When Daly joined ABC in 1949, the news division consisted mostly of radio commmentators; at one time, ABC had dozens of them, including Walter Winchell, Drew Pearson, Elmer Davis, Paul Harvey, and Raymond Gram Swing. Announcers handled news on the hour, which was of the "rip and read" variety. Daly, one of the biggest names in the ABC stable and the most telegenic of the lot, was a natural to anchor the nightly TV news strip when it got under way — in typical ABC fashion, much later than NBC and CBS started theirs. There is some doubt about when the program actually made its debut; Daly and a number of executives of the era believe it was 1951, but a company history — based on admittedly sketchy data — gives the starting date as 1953.

If the other networks were struggling against mighty odds to put on their newscasts, Daly and his tiny staff performed nightly magic tricks. The film used to arrive so late that half the time he was forced to go on without a script. There was no money for decent graphics or artwork, and buying a hookup from AT&T to insert a report from the West Coast, which cost about $3000, could shoot the budget for a month.

Daly was magnificent when things went wrong on the air, which they did almost every night. Bill McSherry, Daly's writer, remembers how adept the chief was at saving them when the projector broke down or a live switch to another city failed. "Daly would make sure he had some wire copy," McSherry says, "and he would tell the story we had just blown. We really couldn't go on to the next story, which might be a live switch to Washington, because we learned from experience that Washington was probably still running down the hall with *its* film, trying to get it on the air for the time we had slotted. So, the best thing was to let John fill. Some nights we had four failures in a row; everyone had an ulcer sooner or later. But Daly was marvelous. When the shows were going to pot, he was just ideal'' (This kind of aplomb can't be learned. Just as great violinists and great center fielders are born with something that sets them apart from other musicians or athletes, only individuals who can function well in a crisis — be they anchors, producers, directors, or cameramen — are able to survive and thrive the high-wire tension of network news. Most people, deciding there must be an easier way to make a living, leave the field by the time they are thirty-five or forty, especially if they work in local news, where life is even more chaotic than at the networks.)

Daly was an exceptionally busy anchor. In 1953, he was appointed vice president for news, special events, and public affairs, a post that also put him in charge of sports. He was thus far more powerful than either Douglas Edwards or John Cameron Swayze. "It *was* a little hard to say no to me," Daly admits. ABC was not the kind of place to inspire delusions of grandeur, however. Daly recalls the time he went down to the newsroom and discovered all the new typewriters had disappeared. "There was my staff, mad as wet hens, because somebody from the entertainment side had taken our brand-new typewriters and substituted their broken-down wrecks. I got madder than they got and issued an ultimatum: 'Either get those God-damned typewriters back here for my people, or there will be no program tonight.' *That* was the kind of continuous struggle we faced.''

Daly's post as combined anchor and administrator created a certain amount of strain in the news department, especially among the correspondents, some of whom felt they were being shut out by the ubiquitous Daly. "He was a one-man TV news operation," recalls Bill Shadel, a CBS newsman who joined ABC in 1957 and anchored briefly after Daly left. "He was a delightful guy, of course, but nobody else really got a chance. He did all the conventions, elections, the six o'clock news — everything. Come election night, he would call in a few others. It wasn't that he feared rivalry; it was more a matter of economics. He was a very big figure, and the budget was so low, so lousy, that by the time he took his money out of it, there wasn't anything left for anybody else. That's why he could never build a news department.''

Daly was so popular with the public, moreover, that the news department was under orders to use him more, not less. He was thought to be ABC's "secret weapon"; the network couldn't compete in terms of newsfilm or coverage, so it tried to make the most of Daly. In addition to narrating most of the film, Daly did a commentary each night, which ran anywhere from a minute and a half to four minutes, depending on how much time had to be filled. (Commentary was never so popular with television as it was in the early days, when it afforded the least expensive way of filling a news program.)

Daly's influence was at its peak while Robert Kintner — the only man to be president of two networks — was head of ABC. It was Kintner who hired Daly and made him a vice president. Kintner used to tell people that the Daly name paid for the entire cost of running the news department. Together, Kintner and Daly were responsible for one of the most significant televised events in the fifties: live coverage of the Army-McCarthy hearings.

The hearings, which began on April 22, 1954, and lasted for more than a month, grew out of charges by the Army that McCarthy had improperly tried to obtain favors for a protégé of his, G. David Schine, who had been inducted into the Army. When Daly heard that NBC and CBS were not going to televise the proceedings, he immediately proposed to Kintner that ABC pick them up. ABC had virtually no daytime programming at the time, so it didn't face the same loss of advertising revenues as CBS and NBC, but carrying the hearings live day after day would nevertheless be an expensive proposition; Daly told Kintner he thought it might cost as much as a half-million dollars. "We discussed it for a while," says Daly, "what we could do with it, why it should be done, why we *ought* to do it, because it was something that sorely needed to be done. Finally, Kintner said, 'Let me think about it, and I'll call you before five o'clock tonight.' And he called before five that same day and said, 'Go.'" The move turned out to be a brilliant stroke for ABC, focusing national attention on the network and winning high ratings. When the hearings were over, even ABC's daytime sales began to pick up.

More important, 30 million Americans had the opportunity to watch McCarthy and his malevolent tactics in merciless close-up, and the majority recoiled at the sight. Suddenly, nightclub comedians began imitating McCarthy's "Mr. Chairman, Mr. Chairman!" and "Point of order!" McCarthy was finished.

Even though Kintner and Daly saw eye to eye on most questions, there was only so much Kintner could do to help the news division in that era. Right after the Army-McCarthy hearings, for instance, ABC lost nearly $2 million (a huge sum at the time) on a deal to carry the NCAA football games. Daly remembers how Kintner called in all of his vice presidents one day and said, "You will cut your budget by twenty percent by the close of business Friday night. I don't care how you do it, but there will be no excuses." This sort of order was issued with grim regularity at ABC.

But Kintner did not last. He fell victim to the merger in 1953 between ABC and the Paramount picture chain. As part of the deal, Paramount agreed to let Kintner stay on as president, but in 1956, he was forced out by Leonard Goldenson, the head of the new company. NBC promptly hired Kintner, who wanted to take Daly with him, but Daly was unable to get out of his ten-year contract with ABC.

Daly found it difficult to deal with the Goldenson regime. Although Goldenson later became a convert to the value of a strong news department, he concentrated his energies initially on building a good entertainment and sports line-up — a necessary strategy to attract affiliates, he felt — and ignored the pleas of his struggling news department. In 1960, Daly threatened to quit one too many times, and Goldenson accepted his resignation.

Daly's successor as vice president of ABC News was Eisenhower's White House press secretary, James Hagerty. A former newspaperman, Hagerty made a concerted effort to attract some well-known newsmen to the staff in spite of his minuscule budget. Some of these recruits who brought a certain amount of distinction to the staff included: William Laurence, a political correspondent with the New York Times, John Scali, the AP diplomatic correspondent, and Howard K. Smith, who had resigned from CBS in a showdown over his commentaries, which management considered too opinionated. Although Hagerty made some progress in building a Washington bureau, his efforts to settle on an anchor for the Evening News were much less successful: He became entangled in what seemed like an endless try-out period. Among those who came and went, some within a matter of weeks, were Alex Dreier, a Chicago anchorman, John Secondari, who later became a documentary producer at ABC, Fendall Yerxa, at one time managing editor of the New York Herald Tribune, and Al Mann, an ABC correspondent.

Toward the end of 1961, Hagerty came up with what he hoped would be the final solution — a triumvirate consisting of John Cameron Swayze, who was still a big name, Bill Laurence, and Bill Sheehan, an experienced Detroit newsman who went on to become president of ABC News. Swayze played a limited role on the program, coming on at the top of the show to give the headlines and closing each night with a feature story. In between, Laurence and Sheehan delivered the news.

Around this time, ABC also started a fifteen-minute newscast at 11:00 P.M., which operated for a few months with *no* anchor; the correspondents simply handed the stories off to each other. This was Hagerty's idea; a confirmed print man, he thought that television overemphasized personalities at the expense of the news. But the experiment was quickly abandoned because of implacable resistance, from both the advertisers and ABC's own sales division. "How do you expect us to sell a show with nobody on it to sell?" the salespeople wailed. In their minds, news programs were no different from other television shows: People tuned in to see their favorite *personalities*. Subsequently, a number of people, including Bill Shadel, Murphy Martin (a Dallas newsman), and ABC correspondent Bob Young, took a shot at anchoring the late news before it was discontinued in 1964.

Given the transience of the anchors, the principle of producer control inevitably became well established at ABC during this period, and it was to remain in effect for a long time. It started under Daly. Although it was always understood that he had the last word, he was wearing too many hats to give much time to the Evening News on a regular basis. After he left and the game of musical anchors began, nobody had the prestige or stayed on long enough to establish his authority over the staff.

In the spring of 1962, Ron Cochran, a former CBS newsman who bore a remarkable physical resemblance to Walter Cronkite, took over as anchor of the early-evening news and had a comparatively long run — nearly three years. Cochran was free-lancing when he was hired by ABC — before that he anchored the six and eleven o'clock news for the local CBS station in New York — but even so, he was reluctant to take the job at ABC. "I didn't think it would do me much good. I was right. We had no audience to speak of. ABC was in the dark ages at that time, absolutely nowhere."

By almost every measure, ABC News was still at a fearful disadvantage as the decade of the sixties began. In 1963, when CBS and NBC were each spending about $30 million a year on news, ABC's budget was only about $3.5 million. ABC News had 250 employees worldwide (including stringers), compared to 500 each for the other two networks. And the affiliate situation was still discouraging. Whereas NBC had 203 affiliates, ABC had only 117, and a quarter of them could not be persuaded to carry the Evening News. It was the equivalent of a newspaper being shut out of more than half the newsstands in town.

That same year, however, Elmer Lower, a tough news executive who had previously worked for both CBS and NBC, was brought in to replace Hagerty as president of the news division and was given a mandate to bring ABC News up to par with its competitors. Lower's first task was to get rid of the newsreel service ("They used plumbers on the assignment desk on weekends," he says) and replace it with an in-house photo operation. His next job was to build an editorial staff. "It was difficult. Some people I wouldn't even try to persuade to come because I began to see the lack of speed with which ABC could go forward. I thought it was too much of a gamble for a family man, so I sought out younger people and bachelors. We did manage to hire some better people; you could always find writers and street reporters by raiding local stations."

Like his predecessors, however, Lower found that his biggest problem was in hiring a recognizable anchorman. "I inherited Ron Cochran, but I didn't think he was going to lead ABC out of the woods. He was a good deliverer of news, but if you were looking for someone with as strong a news image as Huntley's or Cronkite's, he didn't have it." The trouble was almost everybody with a name was tied up by long-term contracts, and Lower found that even with the most open purse, he was unable to hire any stars. So he was forced to stick with Cochran a while longer.

In November 1963, when President Kennedy was assassinated, Lower put Howard K. Smith and Edward P. Morgan together to anchor ABC's coverage. The combination impressed a lot of people, including the critics, leading Lower to wonder if he had latched on to a winning team. "Smith and Morgan did a great job," he recalls. "Very sensitive and perceptive. As a result, I put them in at the conventions in sixty-four. But neither man was very strong when it came to straight newscasting. Smith had never done it before, and Morgan didn't do it very well. He just didn't react fast enough. You would tell him to do something, but he would have to sit and think about it, by which time it would be too late. That's when we came up with Peter Jennings."

For all Lower did to build up ABC News and raise its professional standards, the decision to install Jennings, a handsome, twenty-six-year-old Canadian, as the anchor of the ABC Evening News was disastrous.

ABC had always tried to attract younger viewers, and Lower and his bosses thought that Jennings might appeal to a young audience. At least they thought it was worth a gamble. The critics thought differently. They branded Jennings as a "glamorcaster," criticizing him for being too young and inexperienced. "I still bear the scars of trying to sell him to the TV writers around the country," recalls Lower. "They just wouldn't accept him. I couldn't get anybody to write anything good about him."

Jennings pleads guilty to having been too green for the job. "It was a little ridiculous when you think about it," he says. "A twenty-six-year-old trying to compete with Cronkite, Huntley, and Brinkley. I was simply unqualified." Jennings, the son of the vice president of the Canadian Broadcasting Corporation, was already a rising reporter-anchor in Canada when he was approached by ABC. He signed on as a reporter in the fall of 1964, but after a few months, Lower pressed him to take the anchor job. Jennings declined at first; he was covering civil rights in the South and found the assignment exciting. He also wondered if he was ready. One of those who counseled him to take the job at the time was Howard K. Smith, who told him, "It's like being nominated for President. You can't turn it down."

As ABC's anchor, Jennings ran into a stone wall with his colleagues, who thought of him as a male model. One time on "Issues and Answers," ABC's Sunday talk show, Jennings sat and listened as the venerable Bill Laurence monopolized the guest. When Jennings finally spoke up, Laurence cut him to bits. "That question has been asked and answered, Peter. Next question, please."

Part of the trouble was that Jennings looked even younger than his twenty-six years. He once quipped that the make-up artist at ABC had to *draw* bags under his eyes to make him look his age. To his colleagues, anybody as young as Jennings, by definition, had not paid his dues. His acceptance was not helped by his manner; he came across as vain and conceited to many of his peers, too upper-class and too expensively tailored. "We didn't take him as seriously as we should have," one colleague from that era recalls. "Sometimes his suggestions were fine, but we didn't listen all that closely because we didn't respect him." Jennings himself claims not to remember how he was treated in those days. "I was probably too full of myself to recognize when people said nasty things, but I was terribly aware that on a whole range of issues I just didn't have the background for the job."

His Canadian speech patterns aroused enmity, too. Jennings said "bean" instead of "been" and "Leftenant" instead of "Lieutenant." He firmly refused to bend in his pronunciations — a decision he now regards as a mistake. His unfamiliarity with American culture also led him to make some embarrassing mistakes from time to time, mistakes that sometimes seemed compounded by nervousness. Confronted with the word *Appomattox* in his script, he practiced the correct pronunciation several times, but he managed to say it wrong on the air anyway. Even worse was a gaffe he committed during Lyndon Johnson's inauguration. Looking down Pennsylvania Avenue, he saw the Marine band approaching and was horrified to hear himself announce, "Here come the Marines playing 'Anchors Aweigh,'" when he knew full well the song was "The Marine Hymn." (Jennings's co-anchor for the occasion was Marlene Sanders, one of the first female anchors on network television. The combination gave rise to a joke in the industry that ABC stood for "All Broads and Canadians.")

Although the ratings showed a small increase under Jennings, Lower finally concluded they would never improve enough. In addition, Jennings had little standing with the affiliates, many of whom refused to air his program. "We could never improve his image," says Lower, "not as long as he looked that young." Toward the end of 1967, as ABC prepared to expand to a half-hour of news, Jennings and his bosses agreed that he ought to go back to reporting for a while and get some more seasoning. It was a good decision. Today, Jennings's colleagues agree that he has matured both personally and professionally, and many regard him as one of the best foreign correspondents on television. "He is now as good as he used to think he was," says Walter Porges, a long-time writer and editor on the ABC Evening News.

Returning Jennings to the ranks of reporters left ABC with a familiar problem: where to find a newsman who could not only do the job but who would appeal to the anchor's four key constituencies — the audience, the critics, the affiliates, and the advertisers. This time, Lower was searching for credibility. Surveying his own ranks, he concluded that John Scali, Bill Laurence, and Frank Reynolds had the most distinguished reputations, but Scali and Laurence, both somewhat crusty, former print men, were simply not candidates. Reynolds was the only one who could handle the job.

At forty-four, Reynolds was a seasoned pro, a pioneer in television news who had reported and anchored at both the CBS and ABC stations in Chicago. He had thrived on the rough-and-tumble of Chicago politics, but

The man who set the style. Edward R. Murrow in wartime London.
(CBS Photo Department)

Murrow attending Eisenhower's inauguration with Babe and Bill Paley in 1953. *(CBS Photo Department)*

Members of the CBS wartime team in New York. Seated from left to right: Eric Sevareid, Robert Trout, and Jesse Zousmer. Standing: Douglas Edwards and John Daly. *(CBS/George Herman)*

Murrow with Fred Friendly during the "See It Now" period. *(CBS Photo Department)*

John Cameron Swayze reading the news on an experimental newscast in Kansas City, 1933. *(Photo courtesy of John Cameron Swayze)*

The set of "The Camel News Caravan with John Cameron Swayze." *(Photo courtesy of NBC)*

John Daly on the floor of
the 1944 GOP convention.
*(Photo courtesy of CBS/
George Herman)*

John Daly anchoring ABC's coverage of the 1956 political conventions.
At right is commentator Quincy Howe. *(Photo courtesy of ABC)*

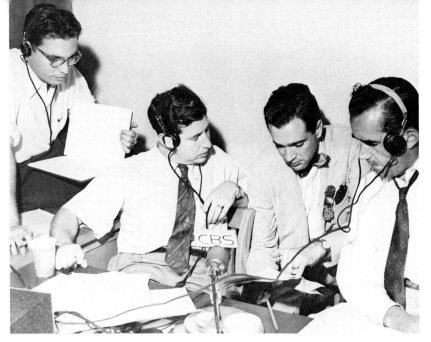

Douglas Edwards as "key man" for CBS at the 1948 conventions. Left to right, editor George Herman, Edwards, director Robert Bendick, and Edward R. Murrow. *(CBS/George Herman)*

Douglas Edwards in 1955, when newspaper writers were fond of noting his "choirboy good looks." *(CBS News Photo)*

Douglas Edwards today. *(CBS News Photo)*

Harry Reasoner anchoring "Eyewitness to History" in 1959. *(Photo courtesy of Harry Reasoner)*

Reasoner in 1976 as sole custodian of the ABC Evening News. *(Photo courtesy of Harry Reasoner)*

By October 1976, Reasoner was joined on ABC by Barbara Walters in a much touted but ill-fated anchor match. *(Wide World Photos)*

Life after ABC—Reasoner on the convention floor in 1980, this time for CBS. *(Photo courtesy of Harry Reasoner)*

Barbara Walters — the only woman to anchor a major network evening newscast. *(Photo courtesy of ABC)*

Walters and the 1971 "Today" team. Left to right: Barbara Walters, Joe Garagiola, Frank Blair, and Frank McGee. *(Photo courtesy of NBC)*

Walters with Mamie Eisenhower.
(Photo courtesy of Barbara Walters)

Walters at a party arranged by her at the Cuban Mission in New York during Castro's trip to the UN in 1979. *(Photo courtesy of Barbara Walters)*

Walters interviewing Dean Rusk in 1968. *(Photo courtesy of NBC)*

A major coup for Walters was the first joint interview with Anwar Sadat and Menachem Begin on Sadat's historic trip to Israel. *(Photo courtesy of* The Israel Sun/ *Barbara Walters)*

Floor reporter John Chancellor at the 1956 convention in Chicago. *(Photo courtesy of NBC)*

A rakish John Chancellor in Leipzig, Germany, in 1963. *(Photo courtesy of John Chancellor)*

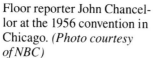

Chancellor reporting from Peking in 1975. *(Photo courtesy of John Chancellor)*

A producer confers with Chancellor on a last-minute script change. *(Photo courtesy of NBC)*

Howard K. Smith in high form as captain of the Tulane track team in 1936. *(Photo courtesy of Howard K. Smith)*

Smith collaborating with Murrow during a simulated bombing raid on "See It Now." *(Photo courtesy of Howard K. Smith)*

Howard K. Smith as a war correspondent in London. *(Photo courtesy of Howard K. Smith)*

Anchorman Howard K. Smith. *(Photo courtesy of Howard K. Smith)*

Roger Mudd covering the 1964 Democratic convention
with Robert Trout (far left) and Eric Sevareid (right).
(Photo courtesy of Roger Mudd)

Mudd sharing a light moment with Ronald Reagan at the
White House. *(Photo courtesy of Roger Mudd)*

Roger Mudd,
co-anchor
of the NBC
Nightly News.
*(Photo cour-
tesy of Roger
Mudd)*

Chet Huntley and David Brinkley with a pensive Richard Nixon during the 1960 presidential campaign. *(Photo courtesy of NBC)*

Brinkley and Huntley posing with their Emmys in 1961. *(UPI Photo)*

David Brinkley and Chet Huntley interviewing John F. Kennedy in the Oval Office. *(Photo by Ernie Newhouse)*

Huntley and Brinkley making their debut at the 1956 convention. *(Photo courtesy of NBC)*

Chet Huntley on his farm in Fleming-
ton, N.J., in 1963. *(Photo courtesy of
NBC)*

Huntley in 1963.
(Photo courtesy of NBC)

Huntley with his wife, Tippy, in 1963.
(Photo courtesy of NBC)

Chet Huntley as he appeared on his last broadcast, on July 31, 1970. *(Photo courtesy of NBC)*

David Brinkley at work in his office in 1957. *(Photo courtesy of NBC)*

David Brinkley in 1979 with the dollhouse he built for his daughter, Alexis. *(Photo by Rhoda Baer/* People *weekly/©1979 Time Inc.)*

David Brinkley in 1960. *(Photo courtesy of NBC)*

David Brinkley joined ABC in 1981. He told friends it was a "tragedy" for him to have to leave NBC. *(Photo by Joe McNally/ABC News)*

Chicago anchorman Frank Reynolds in 1955. *(Photo courtesy of Frank Reynolds)*

Reynolds making his debut as anchor of the ABC Evening News in 1968. *(Photo courtesy of ABC/Frank Reynolds)*

Frank Reynolds, co-anchor of the "World News Tonight." *(Photo by Henry F. Marx)*

Walter Cronkite as a war correspondent for UP—one of the first newsmen to fly a B-17 bombing raid over Germany. Others not identified. *(CBS News Photo/UPI)*

Cronkite interviewing Harry Truman in 1952. *(UPI Photo)*

Cronkite as host of the CBS Morning Show in 1954, with his sidekick Charlemagne. Left to right: James Farley, Averill Harriman, Cronkite, and Bernard Gimbel. *(CBS News Photo)*

Walter Cronkite and the CBS election team in 1962. Left to right: Harry Reasoner, Bill Leonard, Walter Cronkite, Eric Sevareid, Robert Trout, Dallas Townsend, Douglas Edwards, Ned Calmer. *(CBS News Photo)*

Cronkite in Vietnam in 1968. *(CBS News Photo)*

Cronkite conferring with Sandy Socolow, executive producer of the CBS Evening News with Walter Cronkite, 1979. *(CBS News Photo)*

Cronkite celebrating his twenty-fifth anniversary at CBS with William Paley. *(CBS News Photo)*

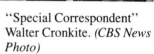

"Special Correspondent" Walter Cronkite. *(CBS News Photo)*

Cronkite and his wife, Betsy, on the *Wintje*. *(CBS News Photo)*

Barbara Walters, John Chancellor, and Walter Cronkite were honored by the Anti-Defamation League of B'nai B'rith for their interviews with Anwar Sadat and Menachem Begin in 1977. ADL Honorary Chairman Dore Schary said the three had "done more for the peace process than all politicians during the past thirty years." *(AP Photo)*

Tom Brokaw in 1961 at KTIV in Sioux City, Iowa.
(Photo courtesy of Tom Brokaw)

NBC White House correspondent Tom Brokaw announcing the resignation of Richard Nixon, August 9, 1974.
(Photo courtesy of Tom Brokaw)

Tom Brokaw and Jane Pauley on the set of the
"Today" show in 1979. *(Photo courtesy of NBC)*

Tom and Meredith Brokaw in 1976. *(Photo by
Arthur Schatz/*People *weekly/©1976 Time Inc.)*

On July 1, 1981, NBC announced that co-anchors Tom Brokaw and Roger
Mudd would replace John Chancellor. *(Photo courtesy of UPI)*

Roone Arledge, the man who put ABC News on the map. *(Photo courtesy of ABC)*

Roone Arledge directing coverage of the 1976 Olympics in Innsbruck. *(Photo courtesy of ABC)*

Roone Arledge presents the anchor team of Max Robinson, Frank Reynolds, and Peter Jennings to the press in 1978. *(UPI Photo)*

Max Robinson, the first black to anchor a major network evening newscast. *(Photo courtesy of ABC)*

Peter Jennings's colleagues no longer think of him as "a male model" after the many years he has spent as a foreign correspondent for ABC. *(Photo by Joe McNally/ABC)*

Dan Rather at the beginning of his career, broadcasting for KTRH, in Houston. *(Photo courtesy
of* Newsweek/*KTRH)*

Dan Rather being attacked by security agents at the 1968 Democratic
convention. *(UPI Photo)*

Dan Rather in Vietnam in 1966. His willingness to take tough, dirty assignments and his breadth of experience were cited as reasons why he was chosen for Cronkite's job over Roger Mudd, who seldom left Washington. *(CBS News Photo)*

Dan Rather squaring off with President Nixon at a press conference. *(UPI Photo)*

Dan Rather disguised in native dress in Afghanistan. *(Wide World Photo)*

At a press conference on February 14, 1980, Bill Leonard announces that Dan Rather is to succeed Walter Cronkite. *(CBS News Photo)*

Dan Rather and executive producer Howard Stringer (to the right of Rather in the photograph) and other members of the new production team.
(CBS News Photo)

Dan Rather in his famous sweater. Ratings for the CBS Evening News began to climb about eight months after Rather took over—just about the same time he took to wearing a sweater on the air. *(CBS News Photo)*

Bill Moyers, Van Gordon Sauter, and Dan Rather at a party at Harvey's Chelsea Restaurant, celebrating Rather's first anniversary as managing editor. *(CBS News Photo)*

Dan Rather. *(CBS News Photo)*

in 1965, he decided to take a 50 percent pay cut in search of greater glory as a network correspondent for ABC. His first assignment was the Johnson White House, a job he found so exciting that he resisted the invitation to go to New York to anchor. "It was such a fascinating time at the White House," he says, "not always pleasant, but fascinating. There was Vietnam, the turmoil in the streets. I felt that what I was doing was far more important and personally satisfying than anchoring would be. I felt they could find someone else to sit there and read the news."

Lower and his deputy, Bill Sheehan, reluctantly agreed to let Reynolds stay in Washington, falling back on Bob Young, an ABC correspondent who had previously anchored the network's eleven o'clock news, to replace Jennings. Young didn't last long, however, partly because the affiliates viewed him as retread; many stations refused to air the program, or "clear" it, as they say in the industry. In April 1968, Lower and Sheehan went back to Reynolds to urge him to change his mind; this time he could not resist the pressure.

Reynolds's fears about the job were borne out; he felt isolated and useless in New York. "I used to go to the office every day and read the 'situationer' [the outlook for the day, listing the assignments and the movements of all the correspondents and camera crews] and sit there, feeling very sorry for myself — and, frankly, bored."

One of the great paradoxes of the anchor position is that for all the money, the fame, the power, and the glory, it can be a stiflingly dull job on a day-to-day basis. Only major news events, which do not happen very often, break the monotony. Many anchors get so tired of the routine after a while that they start to withdraw from an active role in the broadcast — a condition that some producers call "anchoritis."

From a purely professional standpoint, the anchor position is far less glamorous than one would suppose. The post is usually awarded to experienced reporters, yet anchors spend very little time in the field. Most of the time, they are chained to their desks, performing what is, essentially, an editor's job, taking part in deciding what will go on the air and how much emphasis each story should receive. Typically, the anchor stays busy keeping informed, which he does primarily by reading the wires and newspapers. Otherwise, he is occupied in going over correspondents' scripts, writing his own copy (in some cases, at least), and in shaping the coverage that others will carry out.

The tradition of selecting anchors from the ranks of the reporting staff almost guarantees they will get bored and restless. Reporters tend to be action junkies — a study of the Washington press corps by Stephen Hess of the Brookings Institution showed that reporting attracts individuals who need excitement in their daily lives — and once reporters become anchors, they miss the close daily contact they used to have with stimulating events and the people who make news. The situation is doubly hard when the anchor is based in New York, as most of them are, because very little national news originates there. Although Reynolds was miserable on his first tour as anchor, he was happier the second time around when Roone Arledge tapped him in 1978. This time he was based in Washington, where he found it easier to keep up with his sources.

It was also a greater honor to anchor the ABC Evening News in the late seventies than it had been before because ABC News was starting to come on strong. In the late sixties, when Reynolds anchored for the first time, ABC News still had a terrible image problem, and the network as a whole remained on shaky ground financially, kept afloat mainly by the profits from its five owned-and-operated television stations. After an attempted merger with ITT fell through at the end of 1967, a drastic blow for the capital-starved network, Elmer Lower was called in on New Year's Day, 1968, and told to cut $8 million from his already bare-bones news budget of $40 million. (NBC and CBS were spending between $60 and $70 million a year at that point.) Lower figured his only option was to cut back on convention coverage, ending up with ninety minutes of excerpts each night, a move for which ABC was roasted by the critics.

At one point, the existence of the Evening News itself was in jeopardy. Shortly after Reynolds took over as anchor, some of the larger affiliates proposed eliminating the network newscast entirely, replacing it with a daily syndication service to supply material from which they could produce their own programs. It was a drastic approach, but Lower's boss, Leonard Goldenson, did not turn it down out of hand; he took the suggestion seriously enough, in fact, to summon Lower back from a worldwide tour of ABC's foreign bureaus. Lower recalls his meeting with Goldenson and Si Siegel [the financial vice president of ABC] well. "I told them I didn't want any part of it. I thought it would not pay economically at all, that none of the affiliates would be willing to pay for the kind of service we would have to provide . . . For Leonard Goldenson not to be able to go to Washington and say 'We did such and such on news' was unthinkable. Anyway, I told them I would resign if they did it, and I never heard any more about it.''

Although Goldenson respected Lower and gave him more support than either of his predecessors, it would be almost a decade before the corporation made a really determined effort to challenge NBC and CBS for leadership in news. "Goldenson was a bottom-line man," Lower maintains. "He really didn't care about news. It wasn't only a lack of money, but also a lack of time on the air. If you can't do any spot news specials, you are tremendously handicapped in building audience." Lower used to fight constantly with his superiors, who didn't even want to interrupt programming for presidential news conferences. Once, he went to Tom Moore, president of the ABC-TV network in the sixties, to ask for time to run a press conference scheduled by President Johnson, and Moore, a Mississippian, drawled disgustedly, "Why that Lyndon Johnson is just stealing money right out of our pockets."

Because of its weak programming line-up, ABC had very little power to influence the affiliates. If stations declined to carry the Evening News, the network lacked the clout to make them do otherwise. Many of the affiliates didn't like Reynolds as an anchor. Some complained that he was too stern and serious; others faulted him for being too liberal. After a year, with the ratings going nowhere, Howard K. Smith was brought in to co-anchor.

The Smith-Reynolds team was well balanced editorially. Smith, who had a reputation as a fiery liberal in his early days in broadcasting, had become quite conservative, especially on the subject of the Vietnam War. He editorialized so frequently on behalf of Nixon's policies that ABC acquired a new nickname: "The Administration Broadcasting Company."

Smith was a patrician man, a Rhodes scholar and collegiate athletic champion who wrote books and lived a genteel life on his estate outside Washington, surrounded by antiques and art. The successor to Edward R. Murrow as CBS's bureau chief in London after World War II, Smith was the epitome of a Murrow man — cultivated, well-educated, and interested in ideas, especially his own. In his first book, a best-seller written in 1942 called *Last Train from Berlin,* Smith offered his own plan for ending World War II. In 1949, in a book called *The State of Europe,* he suggested that advanced industrial nations might have to abandon the profit motive in favor of a planned economy.

Smith's career as a foreign correspondent for CBS progressed smoothly enough, but after he returned to the United States in 1957, he ran into continuous trouble with the CBS hierarchy over his outspoken commentaries. Matters came to a head in William Paley's dining room in 1961, and Smith, who refused to temper his views on the air, had no choice but to resign.

The other networks were not particularly eager to hire him, but he found his own sponsor, Nationwide Insurance, and joined ABC to do a weekly half-hour program of news and analysis. The contract between ABC and Nationwide contained a clause restraining both companies from interfering with Smith's "independence of mind and spirit." But ABC said Smith would have to assume liability for any lawsuits.

When Nationwide dropped the program a year and a half later, Smith had no regular outlet for his talents at ABC, other than his role anchoring special events, at which he was a master. "I have been wasted at ABC for three years," he wrote in a letter of complaint in 1966. "I am walking around with nothing to do and no particular function. I am in limbo and I am tired of it . . . It has become almost a cliché that 'we want to use Howard more.' " Smith wanted a regular commentary slot on the Evening News, but this was not considered feasible while ABC was limited to a fifteen-minute broadcast.

After the broadcast expanded to a half-hour in 1968, with Frank Reynolds as the anchor, Smith got an occasional chance to present his views, along with a large stable of outside commentators, including Bill Moyers, Marya Mannes, James J. Kilpatrick, Gore Vidal, and Medgar Evers. ABC's executives regarded the commentators as an inexpensive way to help them fill the program — still a serious problem given ABC's limited financial resources — as well as a device to give the broadcast some special identity in the minds of viewers. The mail in 1968 showed that viewers *were* interested in opinion, but a survey revealed that none of the commentators was on often enough to gain much recognition. The solution: Have the anchor do regular commentary. Better yet, have two anchors, one fairly liberal, the other conservative, give their views regularly. Thus, the team of Smith and Reynolds was born.

When Agnew blasted the press in his 1969 Des Moines speech, accusing it of negativism, elitism, and an Eastern bias, Smith and Reynolds came down on opposite sides of the fence. Smith, almost alone among newsmen, agreed with Agnew that the press was biased and vindictive, and that it was constantly emphasizing the negative. Reynolds hammered away at the dangers of muzzling the press, winning a Peabody award for one of his commentaries.

Interestingly, Agnew seemed to go out of his way to criticize ABC, perhaps because he thought it might be more vulnerable to government pressure than either of the other networks. He also singled out Frank Reynolds, accusing him of slanting the news. (Although Agnew did not use Reynolds's name, he made reference to two specific incidents in which Reynolds was the broadcaster.)

Agnew's speech cast a pall over all three networks. At NBC, everyone was sure that his remark about the raised eyebrow of the anchorman was a reference to Brinkley. At ABC, people were sure he was talking about Reynolds. It was not only the content of Agnew's speech that worried the network executives, but also the fact that he had so much support from the public. ABC got 40,000 letters in the month after the speech; they ran nine to one in favor of Agnew.

If the Nixon administration's unworthy aim of suppressing dissent against its policies in Vietnam had prompted the Agnew speech, the responsive chord it struck with the public suggests it contained more than a grain of truth. Indeed, network news *did* carry too many items aimed over the heads of the average person, and it concentrated on the doings of the well-known and powerful to an extraordinary degree. Sociologist Herbert Gans, analyzing the evening news in the seventies in his book, *Deciding What's News,* found that 75 percent of the coverage of the CBS and NBC evening news dealt with "knowns," principally incumbent presidents, leading federal officials, and state and local office holders. (Stories featuring "unknowns" were also peculiarly skewed, concentrating on rioters and strikers, victims of one kind or another, violators of the law, and "participants in unusual activities.") Looking at the evening news, ordinary viewers saw a world far removed from their own, more mundane concerns, such as rising food prices or the decline of downtown shopping areas.

Agnew's charges of an Eastern bias to the news had some foundation as well. The *New York Times,* the *Washington Post,* and the two wire services, AP and UPI, which were headquartered in New York, still set the tone for the evening news on television. Producers and anchors routinely checked the *Times* in the morning to see if they had led with the "right" story the evening before. The *Post* and the *Times* also set the agenda for the questions asked during the daily press briefings at the White House and the State Department — questions that would form the basis for reports that night on the evening news. In addition, a disproportionate number of stories came out of Washington, partly because it was *easy* to fill a television news program that way. News conferences, presidential photo opportunities, and the like were populated by recognizable individuals engaged in seemingly important activities, and the events were carefully scheduled to meet television's deadlines.

At ABC, Elmer Lower was more concerned about Agnew's charges of bias than he was about Eastern elitism. The heavy volume of pro-Agnew mail made Lower and his superiors so uneasy that they commissioned a set of studies on the overall fairness and balance of the ABC Evening News. The results were reassuring, according to both Lower and Av Westin, the executive producer of the Reynolds-Smith news. "We found that, by and large, the reportage on the Evening News was very fair and balanced," Westin says. "Smith was on the broadcast, and his commentaries, as well as his presence, were regarded as a balancing situation. There was a problem with Reynolds, though — his demeanor on the air. His facial expressions then and now are often quite revealing. Nothing was said to him that I know of, however, because we found that the broadcast itself was essentially fair."

Reynolds, however, says he was asked to curb his commentaries. "I was told that I was being a bit rough, not balanced enough. So I asked them, 'What should I do? Should I seek out Hubert Humphrey and get his opinion when I'm talking about Agnew?'" Reynolds believes he was penalized for his views. "I paid a price for it. Instead of doing three commentaries a week, I was cut down to once a week. It was not a very proud time in the history of television. Ultimately, I was taken off the air. I believe it [Agnew's attack] was definitely a factor. I think there were other factors, too, but Howard K. Smith was retained, and he endorsed Agnew's views."

In retrospect, it seems that Reynolds was penalized as much for his lack of box office as for his political views. ABC had commissioned a survey around that time by the consulting firm of McHugh and Hoffman that showed viewer opinion on Reynolds was sharply divided. While some people liked him, others found him too serious, acting as if he carried the weight of the world on his shoulders.

Still, the continuing perception by the affiliates that Reynolds was a left-winger contributed to ABC's lack of success in the ratings. "A lot of affiliate owners are very conservative," says Lower. "I can't prove that they didn't carry the program because of his politics, but I surmise that it was a factor."

Even so, according to Lower, ABC would most likely have continued with the Reynolds-Smith duo a while longer, had it not been for the sudden, unexpected availability of Harry Reasoner. In those days, it was still extremely rare for a big-name newsman to switch networks, and Reasoner was too good a catch to pass up. Lower and Sheehan knew from various personality surveys that he was extremely popular, scoring right behind Huntley and Cronkite in likability and credibility.

Reasoner's decision to leave CBS was not made lightly, but by 1970, his career was at a crossroads. A talented writer and the regular stand-in for Walter Cronkite on the Evening News, Reasoner was nevertheless in disfavor with his bosses because of his confessed aversion to hard work.

The son of a teacher, Reasoner was born in Dakota City, Iowa, in 1923. By the time he joined CBS in 1956, he had a published novel and several years' experience as a newspaperman to his credit, plus a stint in the Army, a career as an information officer for the United States Information Agency in the Far East, and some training in television news at Minneapolis station KEYD. (Equally prolific in his family life, Reasoner fathered seven children, five girls and two boys.) At CBS, Reasoner quickly distinguished himself for his highly individual style of writing and reporting, and in 1957, he became the first full-time CBS television correspondent. By 1960, however, his star seemed to be fading, signaled by the fact that he was passed over for various anchoring assignments. "It was quite clear that I could go on being a CBS News correspondent all my life and get the comfortable pension when I retired," he wrote in his book *Before the Colors Fade,* "but that I was tabbed as a journeyman, as one of the men who didn't quite make it."

Things did not turn out that way. Reasoner was another of those people in television news who was "discovered" by Jack Gould of the *New York Times.* In 1960, Reasoner was assigned to do two hourly newscasts a day on radio. To keep from sounding repetitive, as well as to stave off boredom, he started injecting a little more personality into his writing than was customary in radio newscasts. Once, after a Portuguese ocean liner was hijacked and the story continued for days, he started writing it like a soap opera. When Ernest Hemingway died, Reasoner delivered an obituary written in Hemingway's style. After a few months, Gould, among others, realized that Reasoner was doing something a bit different and devoted a whole column to praising him. "Mr. Reasoner's chief contribution," Gould wrote, "is to take the curse off the lifeless wire service prose of hourly newscasts. To items that already may have been broadcast several times, he imparts a turn of phrase that catches a listener's attention, and he is not hesitant in using a touch of his own dry humor when circumstances warrant.''

After that, Reasoner's career took off again. He quickly got many of the network's plum assignments, including host of ''Calendar,'' the forerunner of the CBS Morning News, and the designation as regular substitute for Walter Cronkite on the Evening News. But CBS News was not the kind of place where a newsman could afford to rest on his laurels, not even after earning such fulsome praise from Jack Gould. In 1966, Reasoner muffed his election assignment by appearing unprepared. Nothing was said to him at the time, but in the summer of 1968, when all of the choice assignments were being handed out in preparation for the election in November, Reasoner was not assigned to anything. Bill Leonard, then vice president in charge of special events and documentaries, let Reasoner know that his performance in 1966, as well as the general perception that he was lazy, had damaged his prospects at CBS. It was a terrible blow to Reasoner's pride; like most people who toiled in the vineyards at CBS News, he had a deep, almost mystical attachment to the organization. Nevertheless, he began entertaining thoughts of going somewhere else, somewhere, as he says in his book, ''where Cronkite, Sevareid, and Kuralt and all those people didn't cut holes in my penumbra.''

The last blow fell in 1970, when his contract was about to expire. CBS offered to sign him again, but for the same amount of money he was already earning. Reasoner's agent, Ralph Mann, contacted Lower and Lower's deputy, Bill Sheehan, at ABC, and a deal was quickly struck. It was a spectacular gain for ABC.

Reasoner was the kind of newscaster who made an impression on audiences. Like Brinkley, he captured the public's fancy because he made viewers *smile,* a rarity in a television newscast. People could identify with his experiences, so drolly recounted, like the difficulty of registering a complaint with the telephone company: ''They've got that defense in depth, whereby the first three people you talk to know only one phrase each, like a chimp trained to press a lever for a banana-flavored pellet.'' Although he touched on serious subjects, too, his essays were, in essence, exercises in wit and personality and had a way of going over better on television than editorial opinion or analysis.

Reasoner's on-air persona was attractive, too; he was the kind of newscaster the average viewer could imagine chatting with at a bar, or more to the point, inviting into the living room every night. Like Cronkite, Reasoner projected a homey, comfortable quality that wore well and endeared him to people. As *Newsweek* wrote of him in 1969, "Everything about his face — the grey-white shock of hair, shaggy temples, rugged chin, deep smile lines flanking a spreading nose — seems square, safe, and reassuring in a chaotic world. His manner brings viewers a message that middle-class values and Midwest calm still endure."

This was the kind of talk advertisers, concerned about the "environment" in which their products appeared, liked to hear. The ABC salespeople could sell ads on a Reasoner program with enthusiasm; commercial sales on the Evening News began to pick up almost immediately.

But the big problem, in terms of ratings, remained affiliate clearances. In 1971, when ABC had 168 affiliates, more than a third of them declined to carry the Evening News; even some of those that did air the program carried it at off-hours, such as four-thirty in the afternoon. The turning point came in May 1971, about six months after Reasoner began anchoring, when he flew out to Los Angeles to address a meeting of the ABC affiliates in Century City. "They asked me to speak briefly," he recalls, "and nobody said I couldn't be honest. I said I thought any station that didn't carry the Evening News was a disgrace, that we were living in important times, and that they were defaulting on their responsibilities not to carry us. I said I'd been convinced by Rule [Elton Rule, president of ABC] and Elmer Lower that ABC was serious about fulfilling its responsibilities in news, and it was up to the stations to do the same." Reasoner had the kind of popularity and credibility to persuade the affiliates to listen. Within weeks after the speech, twenty-five additional affiliates began carrying the program; within a year and a half, clearances had risen to almost 100 percent. At last, the ABC Evening News was available on almost as many "newsstands" as the CBS and NBC programs.

As the ratings increased, advertising revenues shot up. "We finally started making money," recalls Lower. "In the beginning, we were giving our commercials away. I remember they sold for $7000 a minute. With Reasoner and Smith, we got $38,000 a minute. Multiply that by 1560 minutes a year — six commercial minutes a night, five nights a week, fifty-two weeks a year — and you can see what I mean."

For all the progress in the ratings on the Evening News and the luster Reasoner imparted to the network as a whole, ABC News was still very much a stepchild within the industry, short of funds and unwilling to pre-empt regular programming for news specials. ABC correspondent

Sam Donaldson remembers the "Saturday Night Massacre" with bitterness. "I had exclusive film of [Deputy Attorney General William] Ruckelshaus resigning that never got on the air. I had to use the audio portion on radio. People realized there was no point in staying around because they would never get on the air with their information, so they went home." During Watergate, when NBC and CBS aired dozens of specials, ABC News almost counted itself out of the race, scheduling only a handful of special programs. To keep abreast of fast-breaking news during that frenzied period, the interested viewer knew better than to tune in to ABC.

Yet, ABC's reputation for being "the last with the least" was not entirely justified. All through the low-budget years, while the other networks were spending freely, ABC News was building a lean but skilled corps of professionals who put on a product that, in time, was not noticeably inferior to its competitors. Old-timers maintain that ABC News was actually much better than people gave it credit for. Bob Siegenthaler, one of the network's top producers since the sixties, thinks the stories of ABC's inferiority have been overblown, although he admits that lack of staff did hurt at times. "Our problem came in covering unanticipated events," he says. "I personally did not feel I was hampered in covering a convention or an election. For example, if I said I needed two cameras, I got them. The difficulty came in staffing. Some years ago, Howard Smith said we were only one deep. On any given day on a predictable event, our first team was competitive. But if the event ran long or it wasn't predictable, or the story broke out at two different places, we had trouble."

Ted Koppel, who joined ABC in 1963, says he never had the sense that he was working for a third-rate outfit. "It's like the story of the kid who says he didn't know he was poor until after he grew up. That's kind of the way we were at ABC in the early days. We didn't really know we were poor. We knew that we always had one or two crews fewer than the other guys did. And in Vietnam, we couldn't afford to send our film by satellite as often as the others, but this was already a first-class operation in the early seventies. The trouble was, nobody perceived us as a first-class operation, which is one of the things Roone Arledge has done for us. He's changed the perception."

Not until the arrival of Arledge in 1977, however, was the news division's budget entirely safe from the corporate bookkeepers. As late as 1974, for example, after ABC's record division had a bad quarter, seventeen people were laid off in the "Close-Up" unit, a documentary team that was winning awards by the handful and bringing ABC News a measure of much-needed critical praise. The following year, Bill Sheehan, who succeeded Lower as vice president of the news division, was called in and asked what the ramifications of shutting down all of ABC's foreign bureaus would be. Sheehan said it would be a terrible idea, and ultimately, no bureaus were closed, but the incident illustrates how long things remained precarious at ABC News.

By 1975, the Reasoner-Smith team, which had engendered so much optimism, had peaked, and the ratings started to decline. Reasoner was looking bored, and Smith was sounding more and more like a curmudgeon. Internally, they were not a happy combination; both men possessed outsized egos and were prone to flare-ups of jealousy. It infuriated Smith that Reasoner received all the credit for the improvement in the ratings and all the press attention. The way he read the Nielsens, *he,* not Reasoner, was the real draw. (Ratings are a little like tea leaves; they can prove anything the reader wants them to.) And Smith felt the producers favored Reasoner. "I confess to being damned mad that the Evening News was planning to pre-empt my commentary again in favor of one by Harry, and I think it would be a mistake to be silent about it," he wrote in one of his frequent letters bemoaning his treatment. In that same letter, he complained that ABC had all but ignored the fact that he was invited to a rare, small dinner at the White House the night before Nixon left for China. "It would be fascinating to see what CBS and NBC would have done had Cronkite or Chancellor been the only television reporter to spend three hours with the President on the eve of his departure on the biggest event of his term in office." He also complained that he was the only network anchorman not to go on the China trip, although he maintained he had no objection to Reasoner's going. "I am not a jealous or envious individual. I acquiesced in and wholeheartedly cooperated with Harry being sent to China."

For his part, Reasoner did not enjoy sharing the limelight with Smith. The one thing he wanted was the chance to take on Walter Cronkite head to head, and in 1975, when his contract came up for renewal, he demanded the opportunity to anchor the broadcast alone. Since Reasoner was regarded as the more valuable of the two, Smith was sidelined to a nightly commentary role.

The move did not help the ratings; ABC's share of the evening news audience slipped to 19 percent. While the news division was losing ground, however, the rest of the network was making a near-miraculous turnaround. ABC's sports and daytime programming had already become highly profitable by the midseventies, but the ratings during prime time (8:00 P.M. to 11:00 P.M.) were sluggish. Then, in 1975, Fred Silverman, a programming wizard known in the industry as "the man with the golden gut," was hired away from CBS to become president of ABC's entertainment division. (When word of Silverman's switch got out, ABC's stock immediately rose two points.) With him massaging the schedule, ABC's nighttime audience started to grow in record numbers; in just one season, ABC-TV's pre-tax profits rose 186 percent — from $29 million to $83 million. Flushed with success, the network decided it was time to fix its one remaining weak link: news. It was no longer simply a matter of corporate pride. The relationship between a popular evening news program and strong prime-time ratings had been noted for some time; ABC could not afford to let the Reasoner show drag down the rest of the schedule.

At this stage in the history of the networks, news was still regarded as more of a competitive tool than as a potential moneymaker in its own right, even though news divisions were finally breaking into the black. The evening news programs had been making money for years, of course. After the "Huntley-Brinkley Report" went to a half-hour, it became the network's single largest source of revenue — bigger than "Laugh-In" or "Saturday Night at the Movies." In 1970, for example, the NBC evening news generated approximately $34 million in revenues against a budget of $7.2 million. But news divisions still lost money at the end of the year because of the cost of producing documentaries and covering unscheduled disasters. As audiences for news grew steadily in the seventies, however, and advertisers overcame their traditional distaste for sponsoring news programs, the gap between revenues and expenditures steadily narrowed. According to *Variety*, news rose from "a 15 percent loss position in 1972" to contribute one percent of the profits for the three networks in 1975 and 1976.

Interestingly, the networks were not anxious to own up to the fact that news was becoming profitable, however modestly. "Making money from news was thought to be a very *bad* idea," maintains Arthur Taylor, who was president of CBS, Inc., from 1972 to 1976. "The thinking was if you are a broadcaster and charged with performing a public service, it was a good idea to be able to tell the FCC, 'Well, I *do* make all this money, but on the other hand, I have to be able to support our big loss leader, the news division.' And if your big loss leader, to which you are making large, financial contributions to serve the public, is making money, it doesn't look like you're doing all that much of a public service, does it?''

At the local level, where news had become a *prodigious* moneymaker, representing by far the largest source of revenue for most stations, any traces of self-consciousness about profitability had long since vanished. So had the goal, in most cases, of trying to win prestige. As a consequence, by the midseventies, network and local news had become two very different animals, a phenomenon worth examining in some detail. A kind of carnival atmosphere had taken over many local newscasts by then, and competition to become the number-one-rated news operation had become so fierce as to make the turn-of-the-century print wars look almost tame by comparison. In San Francisco, rival stations took out full-page ads featuring their reporters dressed, respectively, in dog masks and cowboy costumes.

Local newsrooms, once reasonably well-insulated from interference by higher management, were suddenly invaded by emissaries from the sales and promotion departments. Along with them came an army of outsiders — speech therapists, drama coaches, and others bearing prescriptions to enliven local newscasts, patterned closely as they had always been on the stolid atmosphere of network news. Most conspicuous among the invaders was a new breed of expert who began to surface in the late sixties and early seventies — the news consultant — who advised stations on everything from sets, graphics, and personalities, to the kinds of news stories they should cover; anything, in short, that would boost ratings. As *Broadcasting* noted in a 1976 report on consultants: ''It was the swiftness of some of those ratings turnarounds that dazzled the industry and elevated the news consultants to reigning lords of local news.'' In 1970, for instance, WFIL-TV (later renamed WPVI) went from fourth to first place in news in Philadelphia within one year of retaining Frank Magid, one of the industry's best-known ''news doctors.''

Within a few years, almost every station in the country either had retained its own consultant or was copying the stations that *had* consultants. Although each ''doctor'' offered his own panaceas for increasing the audience, certain consultant-sponsored features became virtually standard across the country. Among them:

- *A faster-paced newscast,* including more items and shorter items. Magid, for example, recommended that stories read on camera be no longer than fifteen seconds, while film reports not exceed ninety seconds.

- *More emphasis on local news.*
- *More sensationalism,* including a heavier diet of such tabloid-style items as fires, crime, sex, accidents, and the occult. San Francisco's KGO, another Magid client, whose call letters were jokingly referred to as "kickers, guts, and orgasms," employed the formula so successfully in the early seventies that it was able to charge three times as much for commercial time on its newscasts as either of its competitors.
- *Greater emotional content.* Consultants generally advised that coverage of local politics and city hall be de-emphasized, along with institutional stories in general, focusing instead on the kind of human interest story shown to hold a viewer's interest.
- *A consumer ombudsman.* Sometimes known as "action reporters" or "on-your-side reporters," they took the case of a person who had been victimized, often by a local business or government entity, and solved his or her problem. This feature not only gave viewers the opportunity to identify with (or perhaps feel superior to) the victim but also afforded the satisfaction of seeing a wrong righted. As a bonus, the feature helped establish that the news team and the station "cared" about the community and its viewers.
- *Advice on coping.* Service-oriented features by people such as "The Greengrocer," who dispensed advice on how to shop for fresh produce, financial experts with tips on how to manage money, psychologists, lawyers, and doctors all proliferated. (Television was actually a little late discovering "news you can use." "How to" articles and books had long been a staple of the publishing industry.)
- *Reporter involvement.* News directors urged reporters to be seen on camera as often as possible, preferably in an active mode — getting down underneath the chassis of an automobile with the mechanic, walking down the aisle of a supermarket with a shopping cart, playing ball with the neighborhood kids.
- *More humor.* Most stations acquired a resident "zany," a man usually, who specialized in the outrageous, pushing participatory journalism to its limits. Around the country these new video comics could be found swimming with polar bears, thrashing around in the mud with lady wrestlers, or ogling scantily clad girls at the beach. Producers often had standing orders to use their humorists every night, whether or not they had filmed anything interesting that day, let alone amusing. The weathermen injected another note of often

dubious humor into many newscasts. In Idaho Falls, Idaho, the weatherman once delivered his entire forecast standing on his head. Another time, he did his act outside the studio, dressed only in bathing trunks, in the midst of a snowstorm.

- *Longer newscasts.* Stations in small markets were going from a half-hour to an hour of news, while big-city stations were embarking on two-hour newscasts. In part, the expansion was fueled by the increasing profitability of news, but the longer format lent itself more readily to the inclusion of the additional feature material that audiences liked.
- *The friendly anchor team.* This was perhaps the crux of the new approach. The jolly cast of characters — usually consisting of two anchors, often a male and a female, plus a sportscaster and a weather person — was meant to take the edge off the unpleasantness inherent in news. The team approach also afforded a better opportunity for the individual members to "warm up" and let their individual personalities emerge. On a more subliminal level, the news team served as a surrogate family for many viewers. One well-known consultant, Willis Duff, says he heard viewers, especially older ones, say over and over how much better they knew and liked a certain anchor team than they liked their own families. These "pseudo families" were carefully constructed, with each member playing a designated role — father figure, sassy younger sister, and so on. "We would have long discussions about who would play the part of the father," recalls Howard Glassroth, a former consultant. Motherly types were not in demand, however. "I'm not sure you'd look for a mother figure," says Glassroth. "But you might want to convey the idea of a husband-and-wife team, or maybe lovers." The station, naturally, was not advised to promote these relationships openly, but to get them across in a subtle fashion in their promotional campaigns.

The consultants placed tremendous importance on the "chemistry" among the members of the team, who had to be seen as enjoying one another. But it was the personality of the news anchor that was considered absolutely crucial to the success of a broadcast. "If you took all the factors that go into making up a news program," says consultant and former news director Al Primo, "and assigned each a weight so that the total added up to ten, the anchor would get eight and all the other factors together would add up to two. Why do you think they pay these people so much money?" In station after station, the authoritative, often middle-aged anchor was replaced by a good-looking, carefully coiffed young person who was better at "communication" — the industry's new buzz word. Other qualifications for the new-style anchors included warmth, energy, and likability. It was considered a definite plus if the job went to a qualified journalist who knew how to write, but it was infinitely more important that he or she *appear* knowledgeable.

Surveying the advice the consultants dispensed, certain constants could be discerned: (1) a greater emphasis on personality; (2) a cast of characters that made viewers feel comfortable; (3) more material that appeared relevant to viewers' lives; (4) an attempt to counter the average person's growing feelings of helplessness and alienation from society; (5) relief from the steady recital of bad news, which had reached such a pitch by the seventies that many people felt overwhelmed and depressed when they turned on the news; and (6) a more entertaining presentation. The American public, conditioned to a diet of fun-filled fantasy on television, wanted something a little sweet to help the castor oil go down. In support of these findings, the consultants came armed with an impressive set of facts and figures, based on apparently exhaustive research.

Market research has long been a fundamental tool of American industry, but no business, perhaps, is more reliant on numbers than television. In one sense, this reliance is unavoidable; since the public doesn't *buy* television programs, research is the only way to measure their acceptance of the network's products. The basic unit of measurement, of course, is the ratings. The A. C. Nielsen Company, the most widely quoted service, estimates the size of the audience through a mechanical contrivance called the audimeter — a small black box wired to the TV sets in 1200 scientifically selected homes. The other principal rating service, Arbitron, pays viewers a small sum of money to record their viewing habits in a diary. Because people's viewing patterns are relatively fixed, the networks, armed with data from Nielsen and Arbitron, can promise to "deliver" a certain number of viewers to an advertiser at a certain hour; generally speaking, the more viewers, the more the network can charge. In addition, the ratings services supply data on age, sex, income, and other factors that help to set rates. A program that attracts a higher-than-average percentage of men or one that appeals to young adults can charge higher rates.

But the ratings only tell broadcasters how many people watch a certain program; they don't tell them *why* viewers watch, or what they might prefer to see instead. The news consultants, using greatly refined techniques for measuring audience preferences, were able to pre-test news formats, on-air personalities, even subject matter. Among the techniques used is the large-scale survey; the consulting firm interviews as many as 1000 residents in an area to find out what people do and do not like about a particular station's newscast. Another widely used technique is the focus group. The consultant brings together a small group, composed of ten to fifteen people, and shows them a series of videotaped excerpts. In trying to determine the appeal of a particular personality, for example, the interviewer first shows a tape and then tries to draw out such information as how likable or believable the personality appears, and to what degree he or she commands the group's attention. The results of these sessions, which last from one to three hours, depending on the firm, are tabulated and boiled down into a narrative.

Some firms try to probe viewers' attitudes with other devices, such as one called Real Time Conscious Opinion Measurement, a tool used by the Audience Research and Development Company of Dallas. During this particular test, viewers push four different-colored buttons while they watch tapes, indicating their level of interest. The green button signals intense interest; as company president Willis Duff puts it, "Your wife calls you to come to dinner, and you say, 'Wait a minute. I want to see the rest of this.'" The blue button signifies moderate interest, the yellow, moderate boredom, and the red button signals a total lack of interest. ("You leave the room to get a beer even though you're not thirsty.") Duff attained a certain measure of notoriety for his work with another device, called the galvanic skin response — GSR — originally used to predict rock 'n' roll hits. The subjects' palms are hooked to electrodes to record their unconscious responses, because, as one of Duff's colleagues told an interviewer, people may *say* they hate something, "but their belly-buttons tell the tale."* Recently, however, Duff's company stopped using GSR for news clients because the tests became so controversial. "It creates wonderful data for news," he maintains. "It basically measures degrees of attentiveness, which correlates very well with how well people understand and remember what they see. But for political reasons, we've stopped using it." Instead, the firm now relies primarily on focus groups, polling-by-button, and large-scale surveys.

The consultants' methods raised a furor among professional journalists, however, because the researchers were submitting news to the

---

* For a fascinating account of the development of GSR, see Ron Powers's book, *The Newscasters* (New York: St. Martin's Press, 1978).

same rule of arithmetic that had created such disastrous artistic results elsewhere on television — at least from the point of view of the educated, upper-middle-class viewer. As Frank Magid advised one of his clients in a report, "Ratings rise when a broadcaster is successful in exposing the listener to what he wants to hear, in the very personal way he wants to hear it. In terms of news, this means ratings are improved not when listeners are told what they should know, but what they want to hear."

To traditional journalists, the idea of letting an outsider, *particularly* one armed with research, decide what should be shown on the news was anathema. CBS News president Richard Salant summed up this attitude well in a speech before a group of CBS affiliates in 1974:

> It is a harsh but inevitable fact that news judgments just must be unilateral, can't be shared, can't be delegated outside the news organization, and can't be put to a committee vote. Sound journalism does not permit substituting a head count for news judgment. In fact, the whole business of journalism is a great deal more than, and is inconsistent with, providing only those stories which most people want to hear, giving those stories the treatment most agreeable to a majority of people.

The people at CBS News, in particular, were confident that they *knew what news was;* the idea of tampering with it to broaden its appeal was abhorrent. Hughes Rudd, who anchored the CBS Morning News from 1973 to 1977, recalls the time in the early seventies when the ratings for the Cronkite show were dipping, and he suggested to the executive producer, Les Midgley, that they ought to take a survey to find out what the audience wanted. "Midgley said he thought that was the worst possible thing we could do, that it would be pandering, that that was how we got 'I Love Lucy.' He was afraid you might find out what people wanted was cartoons, I suppose. News people in those days figured if they were interested in something, other people with brains would be interested, too. As for the people without brains, well, the hell with them."

The trouble with this approach was that it ignored the nature of the audience. While some studies showed that news attracts an above-average proportion of better-educated people, the bulk of the audience is composed of lower-middle- and lower-class people. McHugh and Hoffman, another well-known consulting firm, devised a chart for its sales presentations, shaped in the form of a diamond, to illustrate the distribution of society by education, profession, and income, along with data on who did and didn't watch television. The top 2 percent — the upper classes — watch almost no television. Just below them, the upper-middle class, the managers and professionals who constitute roughly 13 percent of the population, are light, very selective viewers. They watch news but do not depend heavily on television for information, since they have so many alternative sources. But the lower-middle class (white-collar workers, small-business owners, et cetera) and the upper-lower class (factory workers, retail clerks, et cetera), who between them constitute 70 percent of the population, watch a *lot* of television, and depend on it as their primary source of information. (The bottom 15 percent, the unemployed and unemployable, are the heaviest viewers of all, but are of little interest to the consultants and their clients.) The message this chart hammered home was that in order for a news program to be numerically successful, it had to be aimed at the lower-middle and upper-lower classes. Heeding this advice, news directors across the country began exhorting their staffs to avoid expressions like "double-digit inflation" or "nuclear nonproliferation." At the CBS affiliate in San Diego, a memo was posted in the newsroom to remind the staff about the nature of their viewers:

> Remember, the vast majority of our viewers hold blue-collar jobs. The vast majority of our viewers never went to college. The vast majority of our viewers have never been on an airplane. The vast majority of our viewers have never seen a copy of the *New York Times*. The vast majority of our viewers do not read the same books and magazines that you read . . . in fact, many of them never read anything. The vast majority of the viewers in this television market currently ignore TV news.

To encourage more of these people to watch, local newscasts took on a homier, more casual, purposely anti-intellectual atmosphere, in recognition of the fear with which the average American is thought to view anything even faintly smacking of intellectualism. The publishing industry has adopted some of the same tactics to sell "good" books, putting pictures of half-naked women on books that are not actually erotic in content, for example. Writing about this trend in the *Washington Post* recently, critic Jonathan Yardley asserted that publishers assume that ". . . the prospect of reading a 'genuine work of literature' is 'discouraging' and 'frightening' to most people. And behind the promotional campaigns for the paperback editions of such 'serious' novels as *The White Hotel, Sophie's Choice, The World According to Garp,* and *The French*

Lieutenant's Woman lurks a related assumption: that in order to sell these books in the mass market, the prospective buyer must be persuaded that they are *not* serious books.''

While a few literary critics have criticized the publishing industry for trying to sell books with low-class promotional campaigns, such complaints are minor compared to the furor that erupted over the attempt by broadcasters to widen the appeal of television news. Part of the outcry has rested on a legitimate basis; hucksterism and greed *have* led in many cases to the trivialization and debasement of local newscasts. But part of the vociferousness has arisen because of the consciously anti-intellectual atmosphere being projected. Apart from news, the occasional documentary, and certain sporting events, many educated Americans find very little that appeals to them on commercial television. Now, even the news was being "taken away" from them.

Even when local stations do a fairly good job of covering the news — and a sizable number do — the critics continue to vilify them for the forced joviality and chitchat on the set — in effect, an aesthetic objection. Local news, the critics have pronounced, is *tacky.* Well, so it is, as are shopping malls, fast-food chains, motels, and most of the other artifacts of mass society — at least from an upper-middlebrow point of view. The general public, however, seems reasonably well satisfied with them. But the uproar over local news raises an interesting question: For whom *should* the news be broadcast? The critics and the intelligentsia evidently think it ought to be aimed at them. A strong hint of this emerges in Ron Powers's book, *The Newscasters* — an examination of the influence that consultants have had on TV news. Among the solutions that Powers proposes for improving local news:

> A minority of citizens within the mass audiences — a minority that perhaps may not be persuasive on the scale of TV's competitive viewing requirements, but which nonetheless contributes leadership to neighborhoods, communities, cities, and the nation — could *assert its proprietorship over the airwaves* and demand reform. [Italics added]

What Powers seems to be suggesting is that TV news be "returned" to the educated, progressive members of the community — something that might not be wholly desirable, even if it were possible. It is the *least*-educated citizen who needs television news, not the better-educated one, who has so many other places to turn to for information. Making the same argument about network news in a slightly different way, political scientist James David Barber has written, "To the argument that the better-informed are also ill-informed, I would say let them go to the *New York Times* or the 'MacNeil-Lehrer Report.'"

In any case, studies have shown that people *like* local news, in spite of what the critics say. In 80 percent of the nation's television markets, local news outdraws network news, often by significant margins. Acceptability cannot be the only criterion for judging, of course. Local news would be less vulnerable to criticism if it did a better job of *informing* the people it tries to reach, rather than merely entertaining them. Although the pendulum has begun to swing back and many local newscasts are again placing more emphasis on good, solid reporting, most operations are still far more concerned with style than content. By some estimates, for every dollar spent gathering the news, two dollars are spent on "cosmetics" — expensive sets, helicopters and other gimmicks, promotional campaigns, grossly inflated anchor salaries, and so on. The challenge for local stations would be to take the best recommendations of the consultants, namely, making the news more interesting, understandable, and relevant to the lives of the average American, while not shirking their responsibilities to cover the legitimate news of their communities.

6
The Barbara Walters Fiasco

Participant reaction to Barbara Walters was consistently negative. There is virtually no aspect of her total presentation that does not come under attack.
— Excerpt from study conducted for ABC in 1978 by Frank Magid

In 1976, the year ABC hired Barbara Walters, executives at all three networks found themselves torn between the desire to maintain the prestigious aura of their evening news programs and the temptation to adopt some of the trendy techniques local stations were using to lure audiences and build ratings. Not surprisingly, the temptation was greatest at third-rated ABC News. In fact, certain minor changes recommended by consultant Frank Magid *had* already been instituted on the ABC Evening News, but it was a risky course to take because of the critics, who were keeping a vigilant eye out for signs of "creeping localism." In an article written in February 1976, Gary Deeb of the *Chicago Tribune* blasted the "comfy-cosy" set that had been built for Harry Reasoner, saying it looked like a basement "rec room." As further evidence of the debasement of the program, Deeb lamented "a pair of 'news windows' . . . built into the background set in which reporters would pop up to gab with Reasoner." According to Deeb, "This 'peeping Tom' effect triggered loads of belly laughs in the industry." There was also intense criticism of ABC News vice president Bill Sheehan for suggesting that the Evening News pay more attention to popular culture. In a memo to the staff, Sheehan said, "After the major stories of the day, we must go after the stories that grab people where they're involved . . . I want more stories about the 'pop people.' The fashionable people. The new fads. Bright ideas. Changing mores and moralities . . . The back of our show must be different from the competition's. Provocative. Funny. Interesting, because we're getting to the subjects that many people are interested in, and people are interested in many things that are not intrinsically important.''

Sheehan's memo was attacked as virtually demonic after it was leaked to *Chicago Sun-Times* critic Ron Powers. Yet such guidelines might easily have been issued to the staff of a national news weekly such as *Time* or *Newsweek* during that period without raising eyebrows in the news fraternity. Indeed, nearly every newspaper in the country was then in the process of adding ''soft news'' sections bearing such titles as ''Lifestyles,'' ''People,'' or ''Home'' — sections commonly shaped by just the sort of market research that broadcasting consultants used. In effect, the TV critics were holding the evening news to a higher standard of journalistic ''purity'' than newspapers like the *New York Times* or the *Boston Globe.*

While some of the attacks stemmed from elitism, the critics' concern for the future of network news was understandable. If local newscasts could make so much money using a combination of sin, sex, and packaged personalities, it was reasonable to wonder how long it would be until the networks — also dedicated to maximizing profits — followed suit. How long would it take, in other words, before the evening news gave up informing in favor of entertaining?

The critics thought the answer had become all too clear in the spring of 1976, when ABC hired Barbara Walters to co-anchor its Evening News with Harry Reasoner — at a salary of $1 million a year. In fact, the Walters contract did take television news a significant step closer to ''show biz,'' but not for the reasons usually cited.

Walters, one of the biggest names in television, had been toiling on the ''Today'' show for fifteen years. Two or three years earlier, she would not have given the anchor job a thought, but suddenly in 1976, the course of her personal career and the evolution of television news seemed to flow together. Weary from the ''Today'' show's pre-dawn routine, she was ready for a fresh challenge. And 1976 was a year in which female reporters and anchors were being hired in unprecedented numbers at the local level; even at the network level, where change comes more slowly, a number of women were being featured prominently on the air, including Lesley Stahl, Judy Woodruff, Ann Compton, and Cassie Mackin.

Moreover, at the time when Walters's agents, Lou Weiss and Lee Stevens, signaled her availability, it happened that ABC was already in the midst of an active search for a woman to co-anchor its weekend newscasts. Although Magid warned against using Walters as an anchor, Sheehan found the prospect of signing a star of her stature too tantalizing to pass up. "Hiring her, it seemed to me, would eliminate a step," he says, "in that you weren't trying to build a personality, which takes time. Here you had a ready-made personality who was recognizable and had some credentials."

To Walters, the anchor position looked like the answer to a lot of problems. All those years of getting up at 5:00 A.M. had taken their toll. So had the struggle to establish herself in the male-dominated world of news. "I was doing two five-day-a-week shows [the "Today" show and her syndicated program, "Not for Women Only"], and it was killing me. I don't know how I did it. I did 'Not for Women Only' because I wanted to prove that I could do my own show, that I didn't have to have a partner. It seems rather pathetic that I had to go out and prove that. A man wouldn't have had to. The other thing was that I would be able to lead a normal life. Being an anchor can be a very difficult job, but it can be the easiest job, too. Nobody's going to know how much you do except you, yourself, and your producers, and they're not telling. You have writers who write the material. You can take it and rewrite it, or you can decide to write the headline every night, or the opening story. Or you can walk in at 3:00 P.M. every day, pick up the script, make a few changes, and read it. You also don't have to travel, which appealed to me."

The anchor position, she reasoned, meant less work, better hours, more time to spend with her daughter, Jacqueline, and built-in prestige. "As the anchor, you are the automatic head. You are the one who does inaugurations. You are the one who does space flights. If the President goes on a trip, there's just no question of who is going to cover it." Because she had to scramble for good assignments for so many years at NBC, it's understandable that this aspect of the job would appeal to her.

Walters had worked her way up in television news against great odds. When she started out in the 1950s, so few women rose above the level of secretary or researcher that few even developed professional aspirations. But Walters was unusually tenacious and hard-working, and she was determined to be noticed. She was also fascinated by celebrities, having grown up around show business personalities as the daughter of Lou Walters, a well-known nightclub proprietor and founder of New York's Latin Quarter. After her graduation from Sarah Lawrence College in 1954, her first ambition was to be an actress, but too many disappointing auditions convinced her to turn elsewhere. Through her father's connections, she landed a job in the publicity department of NBC. That led to a training program in television production, followed by a succession of writing and producing jobs — interspersed with bouts of unemployment. Finally, in 1961, she found a secure berth as a writer-producer on the "Today" show.

"Today" had a format that devoured material, and Walters, who never lacked for ideas, contacts, or energy, soon progressed from writing for others to filming her own reports as "the 'Today' show reporter." She rarely appeared on the set with host Dave Garroway, however. That was an honor reserved for the " 'Today' girls," a succession of actresses and models, including Estelle Parsons, Betsy Palmer, Florence Henderson, and former Miss America Lee Ann Meriwether. Their function was to handle the lighter topics, such as food and fashions, and to add a decorative, feminine note to the proceedings. Evidently it was not an easy role to fill; a total of thirty young women came and went in the first thirteen years of the program. Many of them departed in tears, complaining of harsh treatment by Garroway or other members of the predominantly male staff.

Walters's big break came in 1964, when the " 'Today' girl" of the era, Maureen O'Sullivan, was fired. Coming in the midst of the Democratic national convention in Atlantic City, it left the producers with no time to find another "name," so they reluctantly agreed to give Walters a thirteen-week tryout. (She had applied for the job on two previous occasions but was turned down.) Walters had the support of host Hugh Downs; he quickly let it be known that she was a welcome addition to the cast — "the best thing that's happened to this show in a long time," he said. The audience liked her, too, in spite of the fact that she had a lisp and a sometimes abrasive manner. "I was very serious and didn't have an easy on-air manner," Walters recalls, "but the audience knew me as a reporter and accepted me, and so it worked well. I keep thinking of what Jack Benny once said, 'If they like you, nothing can stop them from liking you, and if they don't like you, nothing can make them like you.' And for whatever reason, the audience accepted me."

If Walters was less of a glamor girl than her predecessors, she was still expected to stick to the women's beat, which bored her. The only way she could do interesting things was to go out and film on her own. Thus it was that she developed her specialty, the celebrity interview. She discovered that, with hard work and perseverance, she could snare such elusive subjects as Princess Grace of Monaco, Britain's Prince Philip, Rose Kennedy, Ingrid Bergman, Fred Astaire, and Rex Harrison. She also discovered that it was helpful to know these people socially, that they were frequently willing to do her favors, celebrity to celebrity. As she became better known herself, her subjects became curious about *her,* so it grew easier to draw them out.

She proved as adept at handling serious subjects as she was at celebrity chitchat. An interview in 1968 with then–Secretary of State Dean Rusk (also a Barbara Walters fan) was deemed so impressive it ran as a series over five days. Not everyone liked Walters's style, of course, but many were fascinated with her unorthodox, sometimes daring approach, bringing up subjects that other interviewers wouldn't dream of broaching. Who but Barbara Walters would have asked Mamie Eisenhower if she was aware of the rumors that she drank, or probed Lady Bird Johnson's feelings about her late husband's reputation as a womanizer? Walters could put guests in their place occasionally, too. Once, after eliciting little more than bored grunts from Warren Beatty, she ended the interview by throwing up her hands and saying, "Oh, let's just forget the whole thing."

All in all, the Downs years were a boon to Walters. Though he held center stage on "Today," Downs gave her plenty of latitude. She was becoming one of the most sought-after speakers on the lecture circuit, and her book, *How to Talk to Practically Anybody About Practically Anything,* was a best-seller. NBC seemed to give no thought to elevating her to the role of co-host, but she and her agents were quietly laying their plans.

In 1971, after Hugh Downs left the "Today" show and Frank McGee took over as host, Walters was reminded of how precarious her professional situation still was, despite her rise as the pre-eminent woman in television news. McGee had been a member of the ill-fated troika experiment on the NBC Nightly News, and he regarded the shift to "Today" as a demotion. "He never really accepted the fact that he had to do the morning show," says Walters, "and he certainly didn't like sharing it with a woman, especially not one who did serious interviews." McGee arranged with the producers to pick his interviews; Walters was handed the leftovers. He also had the right to decide whether or not Barbara could participate in *his* interviews. It was understood that if she *was* allowed to join in, he asked the first question. Once again, the only way to assure herself a featured role on the program was to pursue big names and high government officials and film them outside the studio.

NBC had finally taken notice of her "star" quality, however, and she began receiving occasional prestige reporting assignments, such as President Ford's trip to China. One of only three female reporters on the trip, Walters impressed a number of NBC executives there with her dedication and professionalism. "Barbara was tops," says Lee Hanna, who was vice president of news programming at the time. "She worked about fifteen or sixteen hours a day in China, and she had marvelous contacts. Even if it wasn't her assignment and had nothing to do with her, you could count on her to get on the phone and check a story out."

Walters worked hard to cultivate her contacts, which she did in a highly personal fashion that differed from the way most reporters operate. Former White House press secretary Jody Powell says she uses the tactics of a skilled politician. "She remembers to ask about your children, and she has a habit of telephoning with little messages of congratulations or condolences, depending on whether something good or bad has happened." The day after Carter was defeated for re-election in 1980, for example, Walters called to wish Powell well, which impressed him. "These gestures, however sincere they are, can't help but make an impression over the long haul. I'd have to say they're effective."

But Walters did not rely solely on personal gestures and flattery to cultivate the powerful; she was resourceful, as well. At the Conference of Non-Aligned Nations in Cuba, she wanted to line up interviews with King Hussein of Jordan, Yasir Arafat, and Fidel Castro, but tight security kept her from getting near the principals. Her solution was to send them notes. To King Hussein she wrote, "Dear Your Majesty. Can we confirm our interview? I'm sitting in the press gallery in a pink blouse. Wave if you can see me. Barbara Walters." A messenger delivered the notes to the three leaders, who, upon receiving them, could be seen scanning the press box — and waving. She got her interviews.

If the definition of a journalist is someone who recognizes a news story, knows how to go after the facts and present them effectively, Walters certainly qualifies. But in television, reporters are not thought to have "paid their dues" unless they have spent long years in the field, trudging through rain and snow, covering natural disasters, or enduring endless "stakeouts" in front of courthouses or embassies. These are unpleasant, exhausting, dirty assignments — performed for years almost exclusively by men — and any reporter who has not done enough of them is unlikely to be regarded as a card-carrying journalist by other members of the profession. Surviving these rigors is no real proof of editorial ability, but the tradition persists. Walters had handled many field assignments throughout her career, but most of her experience in television was spent inside a studio, interviewing guests — generally deemed to be a lower order of journalism. Even within the NBC News hierarchy, a number of executives didn't take her seriously as a newswoman, in spite of her proven editorial abilities. Her colleague, Frank McGee, certainly did not accept her as an equal, treating her with icy condescension. He seldom spoke to her off camera, but if he did pay her a compliment after a particularly good effort, it was apt to be something cutting like, "We'll make a journalist out of you yet, Barbara." Walters and McGee were too professional to let their antagonism surface on the air, however; after McGee died of cancer in 1974, Walters even got letters expressing sympathy for her losing such a close friend. She was always careful not to seem too aggressive in relation to McGee and other male partners. "I was always a little reticent," she admits, "even a little subservient, because I felt that was the best way to be, that it was the most comfortable for the men, and I guess the most comfortable for the audience."

Despite the fact that McGee's illness was no secret, the network was unprepared to replace him when he died. Again, it did not seem to have occurred to anyone to give Walters a chance at the top spot on the program. But in her contract was a clause, forgotten by NBC, that stipulated that if Frank McGee ever left the show, she was to become a co-host. "Nobody expected Frank to leave the show, I guess, and maybe they figured he'd be there for ten years, and they'd worry about it later. Then he died, and I remember they put out all kinds of statements saying they were looking for a new host. And my agents and I very quietly said 'co-host.' NBC said, 'Co-host, co-host? What do you mean, co-host?' But it was in the contract, and that's how — quite literally, over Frank McGee's dead body — I became co-host of the 'Today' show."

Walters's hand was now immeasurably strengthened. Although she did not have veto power over her new partner, she was deeply involved in the selection process, a protracted affair that saw a long procession of NBC newsmen auditioning for the job — Garrick Utley, Tom Brokaw, Douglas Kiker, Bill Monroe, Edwin Newman, Jess Marlow, Floyd Kalber, Tom Snyder. In the end, Walters got the person she wanted: Jim Hartz, a lanky, laid-back, thirty-four-year-old from Oklahoma. A rising star in the NBC firmament in those days, Hartz was also an aviation buff, replacing McGee as the network's premier space expert. With Hartz co-anchoring on "Today," the tension on the set disappeared, much to the relief of the staff. The executive producer, Stuart Schulberg, told a reporter that Hartz brought a "warm, sane, stable quietude to 'Today.'" But "quietude" may not have been what viewers were looking for at that hour; the program lost a sizable number of viewers during the Walters-Hartz era — some of them lured away by ABC's new morning program, "Good Morning America," and its folksy host, David Hartman.

Walters, who had wanted to move on to other things for some time, now felt a certain urgency about leaving "Today," before her reputation as a major box office attraction became seriously damaged.

The one job she wanted at NBC, however — co-anchor of the evening news — was closed to her. Chancellor would not agree to it, and a number of executives did not think it was a good idea in any case. Yet NBC was desperately anxious to keep her, eventually offering her as much money as ABC and a promise that she would receive "first consideration" if the network decided to pair Chancellor with someone else.

ABC had no such reservations about using Walters as a co-anchor on the ABC Evening News, but it took a good deal of arm-twisting before Harry Reasoner agreed. He had gained sole custody of the program only a few months earlier and made no secret of the fact that he was hoping to become the next Walter Cronkite. Nor was Walters willing to be harnessed to someone who did not want to work with her; she insisted there could be no deal unless Reasoner gave his wholehearted acceptance. The ABC executives hovered over them like old-fashioned matchmakers, arranging lunches, dinners, and other occasions where the two could become better acquainted. Sheehan also had a series of separate meetings with Reasoner to extol the benefits of the dual anchor arrangement. Reasoner finally agreed, reluctantly and conditionally. If, after eighteen months of trying in good faith to make the arrangement work, he still was unhappy, Sheehan promised to let him out of his contract.

Walters knew that Reasoner's acceptance was grudging, but she was optimistic. "I thought, I've been able to work with anybody, and I'll be able to work with Harry. I liked Harry, and I admired his work. And I sort of liked the combination. He was sort of gruff and amusing, and I was a little harder as a personality. I thought we could work together, and I really had high hopes about it." Mindful of her experiences with Frank McGee, however, she insisted on contractual guarantees that all assignments be split evenly between her and Reasoner.

The one issue that didn't prove troublesome was the money, in spite of the fact that her salary demand — an unnegotiable $1 million — was almost twice the going rate. ABC-TV president Fred Pierce was so eager to sign her that he devised a plan for splitting the cost of her salary between the entertainment and news divisions; she would be paid $500,000 for anchoring, and another $500,000 for producing and hosting four entertainment specials a year. (ABC also agreed to increase Harry Reasoner's salary from $400,000 to $500,000 so that both stars would be paid equally for their duties as newscasters.)

It was Walters's other demands, which were so lengthy, complicated, and in some cases unprecedented, that took weeks to resolve. The last week, when negotiating sessions continued around the clock, three suites were rented on the sixteenth floor of the Essex House in Manhattan — one for the ABC team, one for Walters's agents, and one that could be used by either side as a place to caucus.

It was not that Walters was so much greedier than other TV news personalities; it was more a question of the kind of advice she was getting from her agents, Lou Weiss and Lee Stevens. They were show business agents — at that time still a novelty in the corridors of network news — and their Hollywood orientation was evident in the contracts they negotiated for Walters over the years. Having plotted her rise to stardom, Weiss and Stevens meant to see that her standing was not jeopardized by the move to ABC, drawing up a document fit for a movie queen. The billing provisions, for example, could have come straight out of Hollywood:

> So long as Artist [Barbara Walters] and Harry Reasoner are co-anchorpersons of the evening news programs and so long as the name of any such anchorperson is included in the title of any evening news program, such title shall include the name of both Harry Reasoner and Artist in equal-size type (if type is used) and in any case, equal prominence with Harry Reasoner's name preceding Artist's name.

The contract also contained a long list of perks, many of them reminiscent of the kinds of "extras" that Hollywood studios throw in for big stars:

> — A researcher to be employed by ABC and designated by Artist, who, if Artist so elects, shall accompany Artist to any location . . . and shall be furnished with appropriate hotel accommodations and reimbursed for all other reasonable expenses.

— An additional secretary, to be employed by ABC and acceptable to Artist.

— A makeup consultant, to be employed by ABC and acceptable to Artist.

— A wardrobe person to be employed by ABC and acceptable to Artist.

— A private office at Artist's base of operations, which is acceptable to Artist and shall be of such size and contain such appropriate decorations as shall be mutually agreeable to ABC and Artist, and which shall include at least one outside direct telephone line.

— At such times as Artist performs any of the agreed-upon services at any location other than at Artist's base of operations, Artist shall be furnished with first-class hotel accommodations (suite if available), the services of Artist's regular hairdresser or a local hairdresser, which, in the reasonable opinion of ABC possesses comparable skills, and shall be reimbursed for all other reasonable expenses in connection with such travel.

ABC could not accommodate some of her demands, such as paying for baby-sitters for her daughter when she was away on assignment or reimbursing her for the cost of entertaining ABC officials in her apartment, because they violated the company's accounting procedures. So an extra lump sum was tacked on as a "buy-out," upping her salary to one million four thousand dollars. But the company held firm on some of the more substantive issues, such as editorial control. For example, she did not get the right to control the guest selection on "Issues and Answers," which she was to moderate once a month, although one concession *was* made:

The person who regularly serves as the principal moderator on those "Issues and Answers" programs on which Artist does not appear shall not appear on any "Issues and Answers" programs on which Artist appears.

Another provision successfully fought by ABC News was the inclusion of a regular "Barbara Walters" segment on the Evening News. Weiss and Stevens, realizing that Walters probably would not set the world on fire as a news reader, asked for a segment of the program that would bear her personal imprint — a regularly scheduled feature such as "What the News

Means to Me'' or ''People in the News.'' The news executives resisted on grounds that they would be giving up too much editorial control if they subcontracted a portion of the program to Walters on a regular basis. They did sign a letter of understanding, promising to include a ''Barbara Walters segment'' on the Evening News ''from time to time.''

Walters's agents had better luck in negotiating with the entertainment division of ABC for control over the content of her specials. The specials were essentially a device that enabled the entertainment division to pick up half her salary; at the time nobody recognized how popular they would prove with viewers. Walters had almost complete control over their content; nobody at ABC saw them until they were ready for air. Under the terms of her contract, they were produced by her company, Barwall Productions, Inc., but all expenses were paid by ABC. She also obtained the residual rights to these programs, meaning that they belonged to her once they were aired by the network.

Network entertainment divisions were accustomed to making such concessions. Stars like Carroll O'Connor, Henry Winkler, and Larry Hagman, who bring in millions of dollars, have enough leverage to negotiate an incredible array of concessions. When Johnny Carson was at the height of his popularity, he got a commitment from NBC to buy three half-hour series of twenty-two episodes each from his production company, although no ideas for these programs even existed on paper at the time. NBC also promised to buy three TV movies to be produced by him, on top of his reported salary of $5 million a year, plus fifteen weeks' vacation, twenty-five three-day workweeks, and twelve four-day workweeks. Carson had so much clout he even got the right of approval over the program scheduled to run *after* the ''Tonight'' show. By comparison, the Walters deal was peanuts. Yet it raised some disturbing problems, particularly the attempt by her and her agents to gain control over part of the Evening News — to use it, in effect, as a vehicle to further her stardom. Although ABC insisted on retaining editorial control, such contractual inhibitions would gradually disappear over the next few years, as the network news race heated up and the competition for the services of star-quality journalists became more intense.

Fortunately for Walters, the critics were not privy to the provisions of her contract. As it was, the outcry that greeted her move to ABC was almost hysterical. The newspaper headlines conveyed the hostility: ''DOLL BARBIE TO LEARN HER ABC's'' [*New York Daily News*]; ''IS BARBARA WORTH A MILLION?'' [*Newsday*]; ''BARBARA LEAVES JIM FOR

HARRY" [*Christian Science Monitor*]; and so on. CBS News president Richard Salant responded by saying "Yecch," adding, "This isn't journalism. This is a minstrel show. Is Barbara Walters a journalist or is she Cher?" Cartoonists pictured her reading the news in low-cut gowns. Among columnists, Charles Seib, the *Washington Post* ombudsman, struck a common chord when he wrote of Walters's salary, "The line between the news business and show business has been erased forever . . . That's not journalism money. That's entertainment money — up there with the likes of Johnny Carson and the rock star of your choice." Yet with Walter Cronkite already earning more than $500,000 a year, it is difficult to see what forbidden line Walters had crossed. Not that the huge salaries were a matter of no consequence. Journalists, by tradition, are supposed to be inconspicuous seekers of truth, objective observers who note what is happening but who play no role in shaping events. Million-dollar men and women can't walk into a room without causing a commotion. Salaries of this order inevitably color an anchor's news judgments, too. "I don't think any journalist should earn that much dough," says Fred Friendly. "I think journalists ought to belong to the middle class. When you belong to the upper class, it changes your view of life. You look at taxes differently. I see it in the way my friends reacted to Ronald Reagan's tax proposals." Friendly raises another important issue that is seldom mentioned: "All that money for anchor salaries is spent at the expense of news coverage. When I think of how many cameras those salaries could buy, I could weep."

The commotion over Walters's salary masked a number of other objections to her as an anchor of the Evening News, some more legitimate than others. It was legitimate, for example, to fear that an attention-grabbing celebrity like Walters could overwhelm the content of the news by her mere presence. Cronkite and Reasoner were "personalities," too, which is why the networks paid them hundreds of thousands of dollars, but they were careful never to call that much attention to themselves, adopting a low-key approach to the news. Walters had taken the opposite route, deliberately building herself into a glittery celebrity, which was certainly her right. But it didn't make her welcome among her more traditional colleagues. At ABC, her new co-workers watched the celebrity treatment she was given with dismay: "There was much ado about decorating Barbara's office," one ABC executive recalls. "They brought in a set designer from NBC, who did it in French Provincial. They wanted a pink typewriter, or maybe it was a particular shade of red; anyway, they ended up spraying a typewriter. There was this huge effort to make her happy, to give her all the accouterments. It was the first time anybody was treated this way at ABC. It was such an obvious intrusion of make-up people, hairdressers, and so on. People just couldn't believe it.''

Walters's large support staff and general method of operation also added to the in-house hostility. Reporters like Don Farmer, who covered the Senate for ABC at that time — he is now an anchor on the Cable News Network — became incensed when she stepped on his and other reporters' beats. ''One time I had scheduled a senator for a piece I was doing,'' Farmer recalls, ''and I got a call from one of her researchers or somebody who said, 'We don't want you to interview him because we want him on as a guest for Barbara this evening.' I admit that there's some professional jealousy here, but she would glom on to your beat, and I really got tired of her messing with my territory. It really used to irritate me when one of her flunkies would call and ask me to do her research. For example, they'd say, 'We're going to interview Tip O'Neill tonight. What should we ask him?' One day I got so mad I said, 'Barbara's making enough money. I'm sure she can find out without my help.' ''

Out in the field, covering presidential trips and other major stories, she traveled with an entourage and she demanded — and usually received — special treatment. A White House aide in the Carter administration recalls an incident at the Nile Hilton, when he found two ABC photographers and a producer sleeping in the hall of the overcrowded hotel. After a word to the hotel manager, an empty three-bedroom suite was discovered and the aide went off, thinking the ABC party had been taken care of. A couple of hours later, however, he found them sleeping in the hall again; Walters had taken over the suite for her own use. ''She was always treated differently from the other reporters,'' the aide says. ''You always saw her with the Sadats and people like that. She never hung around with the rest of the press.''

The boys on the bus, as writer Tim Crouse dubbed the press corps in his book about reporters on the presidential campaign trail, observed the fuss surrounding Walters and despised her for it. Some were scandalized during a trip to India when she got into a shouting match with the prime minister's aide, demanding that an interview he had set up for her be switched from Sunday to Monday because she couldn't get any airtime on Sunday. ''I'm Number One,'' she shouted, pointing her finger at the Indian. ''In America, I'm Number One.'' The boys on the bus don't always behave like gentlemen themselves, but when a highly paid, highly visible, and not very welcome woman conducts herself that aggressively, she sets herself up to become an object of hatred.

Many newspeople also disliked her interviewing style, which became increasingly personal over the years. There was the time she implored Jimmy Carter at the end of an interview, "Be good to us, Mr. President, be kind." In trying to erase her image as an abrasive interviewer, she became almost abject at times. In a parody in *TV Guide* comparing the way a number of well-known television personalities would interview a Martian invader, the writer imagined Walters saying, "Tell us, Mr. 240X3 — May I call you Gkjrfc? — tell us, please — and forgive me for asking this, but I must — what makes a man, or whatever, like yourself — now please don't hate me for asking this, sir, or whatever, but . . ."

When interviewing men, she often let a seductive, even sexual tone creep into her voice. "I love to flirt and be flirted with," she wrote in her book. "One of my favorite interviews was with the actor, Oskar Werner. I began on the air by commenting that I had read that he was a very difficult person. He gazed at me with luxuriant sleepiness for a moment and then asked softly, 'But how do you know? We never even had an affair.' I forget how the rest of the interview went." It doesn't seem to have occurred to her that such an open use of her femininity might be unprofessional. "When she first meets politicians, she comes on with them," notes Gerald Rafshoon, who served as Jimmy Carter's media adviser. "Her manner says, 'Don't worry, I'm your friend.' They all fall for it." Politicians also felt they could trust her not to bear down too hard. During the 1980 campaign, when Carter was being charged with "meanness," Rafshoon decided it would be helpful to address the issue head-on by means of a television interview, preferably with Walters. "She's very good about fighting with the producers for time. And the other reason we decided on her was that she's more reflective, less prosecutorial. She would be willing to discuss the issue with us and give the President more of a chance to say what was on his mind. Besides, he felt comfortable with her."

While Walters's methods worked very well with presidents, it was her peers in the media, in both print and broadcasting, who would judge her and influence the public's perception of her. She never understood that she had to play to *them* as well as to the world leaders and others she hoped to interview.

It must be acknowledged, of course, that most of Walters's critics were men, none of whom would dare suggest that she was unqualified to become the anchor because she was a woman. Yet sexism was still a fact of life in network news in 1976; whatever gains women made until then had been accomplished over the strong objections of the majority of their male colleagues.

Stretching back at least to the nineteenth century, women had been unwelcome in the newsroom, partly because they spoiled the clubhouse atmosphere and partly because of paternalism. In the 1860s, for example, big-city editors complained of the need to provide escorts for female employees who worked late. By the turn of the century, only a few women had managed to make names for themselves, including Elizabeth Cochrane ("Nellie Bly"), who became famous for her stunt reporting for the *New York World*, and the great investigative reporter, Ida Tarbell.

Not until the 1930s, a decade in which the "independent female" had a certain vogue, did notable female journalists emerge in substantial numbers. Among them were Hearst reporter Dorothy Kilgallen, financial writer Sylvia Porter, *Life* magazine cover photographer Margaret Bourke White, famed columnist and radio commentator Dorothy Thompson, and the inimitable Mary Margaret McBride, whose radio interview show on NBC was a must-stop for book authors and politicians. Eleanor Roosevelt contributed to the advancement of women journalists in the thirties, too, by barring men from her regular Monday morning press briefings — a move that forced several major dailies and the wire services to hire females.

The acute shortage of manpower during World War II served to further lower resistance to hiring women reporters. A few were even permitted to serve as war correspondents. But the end of the war brought a reappearance of the old pattern of one woman to a newsroom, and the lone woman's job was usually to cover "the woman's angle." Editors used the same old reasons for excluding females, according to Marian Marzolf, whose book, *Up from the Footnote,* traces the history of women in journalism. She quotes editors as saying they preferred to hire men because "assignments would take them where I wouldn't want any lady relative of mine to go after nightfall." Other reasons given by editors included:

> Women get married and quit just about the time they're any good to you . . . women expect special consideration . . . women lack the all-round grasp of affairs it takes to operate on these jobs . . . women lack evenness of temperament, dependability, stability, quickness, range, understanding, knowledge, insight.

Women advanced even more slowly in broadcasting than in newspapers. After World War II, when the switch from radio to television was taking place, many women moved into good jobs as producers, writers, directors, and engineers, but *not in news*. After Pauline Frederick was hired by ABC in 1948, she remained the sole female hard news reporter on network news for the next twelve years. Editors didn't like to use her on the air, she had been told, because a woman's voice lacked authority, a belief that persisted for a long time. As late as 1971, NBC's Reuven Frank told a reporter, "I have the strong feeling that audiences are less prepared to accept news from a woman's voice than a man's." Yet the public accepted Frederick very well; she became famous for her coverage of the United Nations, first as a correspondent for ABC, then with NBC. In the 1960s, visitors to the U.N. invariably asked their guide two questions: "Where did Krushchev bang his shoe?" and "Do you ever see Pauline Frederick?"

As the sixties progressed, a handful of female newscasters achieved short bursts of prominence. Nancy Dickerson scored several "firsts" as a correspondent for NBC; in 1963, she anchored a daily five-minute newscast called "Nancy Dickerson with the News," and the following year, she became the first woman to serve as a floor reporter at the political conventions. Marlene Sanders, who joined ABC in 1964, also received some anchoring assignments, but she recalls facing a continuous struggle with editors who insisted on assigning her to "women's" stories. Still, the principle of one woman to a newsroom was disappearing, which represented progress. And off camera, more women were being hired as producers, researchers, and production assistants, setting the stage for their later rise.

It took the women's movement in the early 1970s, however, to force the networks to put more women on the air. Several successful antidiscrimination suits were filed against network-owned-and-operated stations, and in 1971, the Federal Communications Commission began requiring stations to file affirmative action plans for women as a condition for license renewal. By 1974, the three networks had added about a dozen women reporters, and all were actively trying to recruit more. Not many of these women were well known to the public yet, though. At CBS, it was still considered an event when one of the three women in the Washington bureau, Marya McLaughlin, Connie Chung, or Lesley Stahl, made an appearance on the Evening News. Only Stahl, nicknamed Brenda Starr by her CBS colleagues for her aggressiveness, was achieving anything close to real prominence at the time. Assigned to cover the Watergate break-in because most of the other Washington bureau reporters were out of town and the story was considered minor, she couldn't be removed later because she had become so expert. Yet it was Daniel Schorr who handled the story for the Evening News; Stahl's main outlet, besides radio, was the CBS Morning News.

A few women were already playing major roles at the other networks. Cassie Mackin covered Capitol Hill for NBC. Ann Compton of ABC became the first television newswoman to be named a full-time White House correspondent. While the networks seemed to be adjusting, albeit slowly, to the idea of women as on-air reporters, they remained leery about using them as anchors. One of the first to land a major slot was Sally Quinn, a *Washington Post* reporter who was chosen to co-anchor the CBS Morning News with Hughes Rudd in 1973. The experience did little to encourage network executives to put women in the anchor seats. A talented writer and reporter, Quinn nonetheless failed miserably as an anchor for reasons that reveal much about attitudes toward women among network executives in the early seventies. An attractive blonde, she was hired in part because the news division was under pressure to put a woman in a prominent on-air position, and in part because CBS executives thought she was the kind of sexy personality who could bring viewers to their low-rated Morning News. The fact that she had absolutely no experience in television didn't seem to worry anyone, although it is inconceivable that the network would have hired a man — any man — for such a visible job, with no previous experience on camera. As so many women and members of minorities were to discover when they were thrown into jobs for which they were unprepared, she was being programmed for failure.

A crash training program to teach Quinn at least the rudiments of television delivery might have helped. Instead of doing anything as useful as that, CBS devised a huge publicity build-up that ultimately added to her problems by raising the expectations of viewers and critics. Worse, the executives consciously tried to promote her as a kind of blonde bombshell who used sex to get her stories. Quinn was furious to learn that a remark she made as an in-house joke while filming a promotional spot — "A senator will tell you more over a martini at midnight than he will over a microphone at noon" — was actually used on the air with the full knowledge and approval of the executive who hired her, Gordon Manning. In her book, *We're Going to Make You a Star*, Quinn tells how her friend Warren Beatty tried to warn her: "You've been made out to be a smug, tough, competitive little cock-teaser, and people aren't going to like you for it. There is no way you're not going to be attacked." He was right, of course; hostile letters from viewers poured in by the carload, and the critics tore her apart.

If the publicity backfired, so did Quinn's lack of experience in front of the camera. She looked and sounded insignificant, a small, scared figure who either fluffed her lines or read them without conviction. Ad libbing was supposed to have been her strong suit. But nervousness sometimes caused her to make horrible gaffes, a few of which had a tendency to make her sound like Marie Antoinette. Reacting to a piece about the exploitation of migrant children, she recalled on the air how she used to resent being made to clean her room as a child. To add to her woes, she couldn't adjust to getting up at midnight and was sick a good deal of the time, developing an ulcer and a bad case of acne.

Within six months, she decided she had had enough and escaped back to the world of newspapers — with the blessing of CBS. But Quinn was only one of many women who would take some hard knocks before men in the industry learned to treat them as professionals first and as women second.

If Quinn was wounded by criticism, Walters was nearly crushed by the negative reviews her own performance received. "I couldn't bear to pick up a paper for a year," she told her old colleague from the "Today" show, Gene Shalit, in an interview for *Ladies' Home Journal*. "I felt as though I were drowning . . . Every day at three o'clock the papers would be delivered, and there would be another blast. Tears would come to my eyes and I would blot my eyes so the mascara wouldn't run, and go on the air." Her boss, Bill Sheehan, and other supporters tried to comfort her, but to no avail. "She was irrational to the point of hysteria about anything that appeared in the press," says Sheehan. "She couldn't handle it at all. There was no way to convince her to sit back and let it roll over."

There is no question that the negative stories hurt her with the public. Soon after ABC announced that Walters had been hired to co-anchor the Evening News, so many unfavorable letters arrived that a form letter had to be devised:

Dear _____ :

We feel that the new co-anchor format with Barbara Walters and Harry Reasoner will add a very exciting dimension to newscasting, and we hope you will decide to continue to be one of our viewers. In that connection, we do ask that you keep an open mind and tune in for a reasonable period before making your decision.

Sincerely yours.

Walters was also unprepared for the depth of Reasoner's hostility. Contrary to the stories that circulated, there were never any public scenes, no personal confrontations or childish behavior. It was more subtle than that. "Harry ignored her," says Sheehan, "and it made her tight. It really affected her performance." From the start, Reasoner viewed being teamed up with Walters as a no-win arrangement. If the ratings went up, *she* would get the credit. If they went down, he would share the blame. As the wave of negative press stories swelled, he realized that his own credibility could be damaged by association with her. Every night after the program, he and his pals — Reasoner's little band of merry men, as one correspondent tagged them — gathered at the bar of the Café des Artistes, a restaurant across the street from ABC News. There they would vie with one another in ridiculing her, a ritual of which she became aware.

As the animosity between the two increased, little remarks that might have been harmless were interpreted as hostile jabs. Once, evidently in an effort to appear a little warmer on the air, Walters remarked of Henry Kissinger, "You know, Harry, Kissinger didn't do too badly as a sex symbol in Washington." Reasoner, who prides himself for being quick on the uptake, replied, "Well, you would know more about that than I would." Regardless of how the remark was intended, it was widely interpreted as a putdown, both by the press and by insiders at ABC. Bob Siegenthaler, who produced the program during that era, remembers how things got blown out of proportion. "I remember the corrosive nature, not so much of the publicity, but of their friends. There was a constant procession of meddlers who would go in and say, 'She's doing this to you.' 'He's doing that to you.' 'How about that Kissinger remark?' They were just a bunch of tattletales, fanning the flames."

Reasoner denies he was ever cruel to Walters. "I wasn't opposed to Barbara as a person or Barbara as a woman. It seemed to me inevitable that hiring her would be perceived as a stunt and would be treated that way by the print press. I told her that three weeks before she joined. I also told her she would find problems with the way ABC was going. As I've said before, we were the least of each other's problems."

Nevertheless, a bitter contest for airtime developed between them. The "Barbara Walters segment," which reverted to her old standby, the big-name interview, put her in direct competition with Reasoner, who had a personal vehicle of his own called "The Reasoner Report" — film essays that ran from four to six minutes, covering everything from spring training to the price of real estate in Los Angeles. Considering that only twenty-two minutes are left for news after subtracting time for commercials, there was bound to be trouble. According to Siegenthaler, it was a constant tug of war. "Harry wanted to do second-line stories — something like the House Select Committee on Interstate Commerce, which you can handle a number of ways. You can cover it as a twenty-second 'reader' by the anchor or as a two-minute film report. Harry would tend to say, 'Let's put on Joe Smith, congressional correspondent.' Barbara would say, 'Let's save the time and use it for an interview.' " The unlucky Siegenthaler would get to break the ties.

Part of the trouble lay in the fact that both anchors and ABC expected the Evening News to be expanded to forty-five minutes — it was the assumption underlying all of the discussions before Walters joined ABC — but at the last minute, in fact, the day that Walters signed her contract, the affiliates reversed their decision to give up the needed time to the network. With a forty-five-minute newscast, the competition for airtime between the two anchors would have been less acute, and, as local stations discovered when they expanded their own local news broadcasts, there would have been more room for feature material. It was difficult for Walters to do the kind of lengthy, highly personalized interview she excelled at within the confines of the half-hour Evening News.

To make the competition for airtime even more intense, a number of "soft" features, including a wildlife expert and a psychologist, were added to the mix — features originally designed to help fill the forty-five-minute format but retained after the plan fell through. Inevitably, the time they took up, together with Walters's interviews and the occasional "Reasoner Reports," made ABC's other reporters feel their work was being crowded off the air. To the disgruntled correspondents, Walters symbolized a perversion of the news process, and in a sense they were right. It was not that she was unqualified for the job. Assuming that it takes a journalist to read the news — an arguable point — her news credentials were certainly good enough. But her interviews with famous people like Henry Kissinger and Anwar Sadat were often designed more as a showcase for her than as a vehicle to elicit information. Even so, there was nothing intrinsically harmful about such interviews, nor for that matter about the wildlife expert or the psychologist, so long as they did not displace legitimate news. But the staff thought they did just that, and loathed Walters for it.

If the reporters had had a chance to get acquainted with Walters, who is charming and thoughtful with intimates, they might not have objected to her presence on the program quite so strongly. But Walters, a surprisingly shy person for all her on-camera toughness, has never been one to fraternize much with the troops and is not given to easy camaraderie. She is also famous for not remembering people she has worked with. She once spent a week in Cuba with an ABC crew interviewing Castro — an experience that generated great esprit de corps among all those involved because they felt they were making history together. A few months later, however, when she bumped into the cameraman, Vinnie Gaito, in Washington, she responded to his greeting with a blank stare. Gaito, a popular veteran of the network, was furious when he heard her whisper to a nearby producer, "Who is that guy, anyway?"

Part of the trouble is that Walters gets so wrapped up in what she is doing that she seems oblivious of others. Yet many people who work with her long enough find her warm and endearing. "The only problem I ever had was that she was hard to get to," says John Miller, a writer who knew her on the "Today" show. "She would be busy with her other program or lunching with important people. However, she could be an extremely concerned human being. I was feeling down in the dumps at one point over my divorce, and she was very solicitous when she heard what I was going through. Basically, she is a good egg."

Unfortunately for Walters, it took a while for people at ABC to see that side of her. Initially, she spent a lot of time behind closed doors with ABC executives, alternately heartsick and angry about her situation.

Within the industry, ABC News once again became the butt of malicious jokes. Even the public began to mimic her, thanks in part to Gilda Radner's "Barbara Wa-Wa" act on "Saturday Night Live." At ABC, an air of defeatism hung over the enterprise, almost from the start. Bill Sheehan, the man who hired Walters, believes the Reasoner-Walters combination was never given a chance to succeed. "ABC made its decision to drop them much too fast," he says. "They went on the air in October and by January, everybody was saying it wouldn't work."

Strong ammunition for this negative view came from an audience study conducted for ABC the following year by the consulting firm of Frank Magid and Associates. The conclusions, based on discussions with the so-called focus groups, did not mince words. "Many viewers are not comfortable watching her deliver the news. Much of this discomfort has to do with the aura that surrounds Barbara Walters at the present time, an aura that was perpetuated by the press regarding her switch to ABC . . . Viewers often volunteered that she is not worth the money she is being paid, that she appears lofty, 'stuck-up,' extremely difficult to understand and follow, has a bad voice, is not able to effectively handle the anchor responsibilities, and quite simply, is not the type of personality that viewers can relate to as an individual. The only area in which Barbara Walters is thought to be efficient is interviewing, and many feel she excels in this capacity. Nevertheless, many questioned her function as a newscaster." The report added that viewer discontent with Walters as an anchor colored their acceptance of ABC News as a whole. "[Focus group] members' perceptions of her so overshadowed the entirety of ABC News, that in many instances, Walters and ABC [were] spoken of synonymously."

Reaction to Reasoner among the focus groups was much more positive. "Reasoner is liked, trusted, and viewers are comfortable watching him. As has been the case in prior research, he falls just short of making the kind of impact on viewers that Walter Cronkite does." The irony of these conclusions, as ABC's executives saw it, was that Walters had been doing everything in her power to make the dual anchor work, while Reasoner was doing his utmost to undermine it. She would have to be replaced, but nobody wanted to make *her* look like the scapegoat.

Reasoner *was* behaving badly. Never inclined to work too hard under any circumstances, he began to grow more distant from the operation, acting temperamental and uncooperative. He would generally arrive about eleven o'clock in the morning, look at the wires, then go out for a long, invariably liquid lunch with his old pals from CBS. Back at ABC, he would retire to his office for a nap. At about five o'clock, he would check the script that had been written for him, and at ten past five, three or four of his buddies would join him for a round of drinks known as "fivesies." He used to tell friends that having a drink before he went on the air made him talk better.

Despite all the gossip about his fondness for the bottle — some of the stories put out intentionally by ABC executives when it became apparent that Reasoner wanted out of his contract — his drinking never seemed apparent on the air. However, his lack of interest became more and more evident. Reasoner acknowledges that he was partly to blame for the debacle at ABC. "By 1975," he says, "the fun had gone out of it. I got fat and lazy, and between management and me, we screwed up. There was a lot of turmoil in my personal life at that time, and I was tired of anchoring. I didn't give it my full shot. I should have. In any case, it probably came across on the air."

Throughout 1977, the trials of ABC News kept the TV writers busy — Reasoner's obvious dissatisfaction at the network, the Walters fiasco, and then, in June, the shakeup in which Roone Arledge replaced Bill Sheehan as head of the news division. Meanwhile, a drama just as engrossing was being played out down the street at NBC — a drama bearing directly on the future course of the NBC Nightly News.

7
Intrigue at NBC

Tom Snyder and I are not in the same business.
— Reuven Frank
President, NBC News

BY 1977, after six yeoman years anchoring the NBC Nightly News, John Chancellor was in trouble, and he knew it. He had always been a strong second in the evening news race, running firmly ahead of ABC. But Chancellor had never been able to overtake Walter Cronkite, and being first has an almost mystical importance in television. The corridors of NBC were buzzing with rumors that he was going to be replaced by Tom Snyder or Tom Brokaw. Or both. And stories about such changes had begun to creep into the trade press and the TV columns. Chancellor gave no public indication that he was distressed by the stories or even that he knew of them. But he found it humiliating to be named as the cause of Nightly News's ratings problems. Worse yet was his suspicion that certain NBC executives might be deliberately floating the rumors to encourage him to step down.

A veteran political reporter and foreign correspondent, Chancellor had great credibility with the print media and a sizable following among the public. Within NBC's executive ranks, however, opinion was mixed. Some considered him a dedicated, versatile journalist who imparted a patina of class to the entire organization. Others found him dull, professorial, and short on the indefinable quality known as "anchor magic." On all sides, however, a feeling was growing that Chancellor did not have sufficient charisma to put NBC in front. As one executive expressed it, "If John Chancellor lived to be two thousand years old, he was never going to be Walter Cronkite."

Actually, Chancellor's shortcomings as a personality had been a matter of concern for several years. It had been hoped that adding David Brinkley as co-anchor in 1976 would add some sparkle to the program, but the ratings did not improve markedly. At that point, some within the company, including Herbert Schlosser, the president of NBC, wanted to replace both Chancellor *and* Brinkley.

Schlosser's candidate was Tom Snyder, the electric and unpredictable forty-year-old TV news superstar who was then anchoring the six o'clock news at NBC's local station in New York. Snyder had a history of boosting the ratings wherever he worked, and he had also developed a big following as host of "Tomorrow," the late-night talk show. The trouble, as other NBC News executives saw it, was that he came across as more of a showman than a journalist. He did not project a "network news" image.

The man most NBC officials saw as the alternative to Snyder was Tom Brokaw, then host of the "Today" show. Brokaw had first gained prominence in the same Southern California milieu as Snyder. Both, in fact, had anchored at KNBC, the NBC station in Los Angeles. Unlike Snyder, however, Brokaw had a strong image as a professional journalist — experienced, well respected by his peers in the press corps, untainted by "show business." Brokaw's problem was that at thirty-six he still looked a bit too young for the job of network news anchor and would have to be paired with someone else. In addition, it would not be easy to replace him as host of "Today," an important source of network revenue.

To complicate things further, not everyone whose opinion mattered was convinced that Chancellor should be discarded. A distinguished newsman and loyal employee for twenty-five years, he was, after all, the news division's best-known personality now that Barbara Walters had left. The problem with the ratings, according to this school, was not Chancellor, but the news organization itself, which could not seem to recapture the glitter and excitement of the Huntley-Brinkley era.

The Chancellor-Snyder-Brokaw debate mirrored the division within the company as a whole over the direction that NBC News ought to be taking. The anchor is, after all, the most visible symbol of what a news division represents. Essentially, there were three views of what NBC should do. Some people — a declining number, to be sure — thought the most important goal was to continue producing a solid, prestigious evening news program; advocates of this approach noted that CBS had managed to be first for the past ten years without changing its approach to news. A second group figured it was time to abandon the quest for prestige and go after the ratings, even if it meant taking a cue from some of the more slickly produced, personality-oriented local newscasts. The third view, undoubtedly the one held by a majority in the news division, was that NBC News ought to pick up the pace a bit without sacrificing its journalistic standards. The debate led to corporate intrigue worthy of the court of Catherine the Great. It also illustrated the increasing tendency of higher management to interfere in the affairs of the once relatively autonomous network news divisions. Television news had become too important to leave to mere journalists.

For NBC president Schlosser, the prospect of "fixing" the evening news held a special attraction. Beating CBS would help counter the widespread impression that, under his leadership, NBC had been slipping. ABC's sudden surge had pushed NBC into third place in the all-important prime-time sweepstakes. NBC's daytime ratings were falling off at an alarming rate, too. Although the network's earnings, $86 million in 1976, were nothing to sneeze at, they represented a mere 12 percent increase over the previous year, compared to 22 percent for CBS and the spectacular 186 percent gain registered by ABC.

Schlosser, a West Coast programming executive, had been named president and chief operating officer of NBC in 1974. He was a lawyer with a background in the motion picture end of television. He knew little about news, but he thought he knew how to improve the ratings with a single stroke — replace the anchor. He brought with him a coterie of Los Angeles–trained executives known as the "California Mafia," and together they were all very high on Tom Snyder and Tom Brokaw. In particular, they had seen what Snyder had done for the ratings at KNBC, taking the evening news from third to first place. They were impressed by the techniques that made local news popular — the flashy packaging, the telegenic young anchors, the friendly banter on the set, the heavy emphasis on crime, sex, consumer tips, and show business gossip.

To the Californians, Chancellor was a symbol of everything that was wrong with NBC News. They considered him stuffy and ponderous, lecturing viewers as if he were conducting a civics class. And they disliked his approach to news, his insistence on stories they thought were boring, insignificant, or too complicated for television. "All those items about NATO and SALT," they would snort contemptuously. And what about the time he led for five straight days with the news that Spain's Generalissimo Franco was dying? (This lead became such a standing joke at NBC that it was parodied for months on NBC's "Saturday Night Live.")

To NBC's younger producers, moreover, Chancellor seemed something of a fuddy-duddy, a bit prudish and out of touch with popular culture, as well as overprotective of those in authority. Often, for example, he would argue against running items dealing with the private lives of public figures. He once threatened to read a disclaimer if producers insisted on airing a piece suggesting that Billy Carter had a drinking problem — something the President's brother later admitted publicly. (The piece was not shown.)

Increasingly, however, producers on the Nightly News were trying to enliven the program, and while most of them felt as strongly as Chancellor about keeping it honest, the anchor and the producers more and more often did not see eye to eye on how to do things. Chancellor's partiality for foreign stories was a particular bone of contention. "John is an internationalist," explains one producer. "He believes in the benefits of diplomacy and of reasonable men coming together. He is very interested in things like the European Parliament. I'll bet Nightly News did more stories about the European Parliament than any other news organization in history. He is also deeply concerned about the threat of nuclear war. At the mention of SALT [Strategic Arms Limitations Talks], most of us would glaze over, but his eyes would actually light up."

Chancellor's views could not be dismissed lightly, however, even when producers disagreed. He is a man of deeply held principles, and from the beginning, he had a strong desire to lead.

To most of NBC's correspondents, Chancellor was a hero. As reporters, they were less concerned about razzle-dazzle and ratings than about the accuracy and integrity of the news. In their eyes, Chancellor was the conscience of the organization, the person they trusted most to make sure that stories were not hyped or otherwise manipulated to make them tidier or more compelling. As Tom Pettit, a long-time NBC correspondent who was promoted to executive vice president of news, put it, "John set a tone that resisted tampering with the purity of the news. Perhaps that made it dull and gray at times, but it helped keep it honest, a virtue that is getting rarer in the business these days. He would defend the integrity of the news as if it were his own."

When he first took over as anchor, Chancellor had argued for the title of managing editor — Cronkite's title at CBS. Tradition at NBC gave the producer the last word, so Chancellor had to be satisfied with the title of principal reporter (later changed to editor). Over time, however, he became increasingly influential in shaping the broadcast, outlasting a succession of producers until he had enough clout to pick his own man for the job. Equally important, he stayed involved in the flow of decision-making throughout the day, not delegating as many of the nuts-and-bolts editorial decisions as Cronkite did.

A man with an enormous appetite for work, Chancellor was often the first person on the staff to arrive in the morning. Instead of sequestering himself in his office, he would sit out in the newsroom most of the day, taking part in the meetings, conference calls, and informal discussions that determined what was used on the air each night. He also wrote about four fifths of everything he read on the air. Although he did not directly supervise reporters' scripts and generally did not intrude on the assignment process, the program came to bear his stamp in almost every respect — from the placement of items on the broadcast to the overall tone of the news presented.

As editor of the program, he weighed every story for its importance, often voting against "sexy" items, such as pictures of a bank shoot-out, or a fire, in favor of stories of more enduring significance. He did not believe mass appeal ought to play a role in story selection. "I think network news can be defined this way," he said in an interview before stepping down as anchor, "what you *must* tell people, plus what you'd like to tell them if you had the time. After all, most people get their news from TV, and they only have one shot, for the most part, at finding out what happened in the world that day."

Chancellor saw himself as the guardian of journalistic standards at NBC, urging reporters and editors against taking short cuts or using sloppy methods. He tried to clamp down on the practice of using unnamed sources, for instance, instructing reporters to stop relying on the catch-all phrase, "NBC News had learned." "I'd like to see more of the kind of thing that John Osborne of *The New Republic* used to do, you know, 'A tired, third-level official at the White House who doesn't like Richard Nixon told me . . .' I want to know *what* officials these reporters are referring to. Are they officials in Washington? Are they officials at the Justice Department, or what?"

Chancellor himself took great care not to let any of his biases creep into his writing. "You try for something I call value-free writing and value-free delivery. You know, as I like to say, it's all in the verbs. There are ways of writing things that change the emphasis entirely. For example, 'The President *insisted* inflation is coming down,' instead of 'said.' 'The

Republicans *whined* when the Democrats cast that vote.' There are ways of doing that kind of thing absolutely deadpan, and you don't have to use a raised eyebrow, as Spiro Agnew used to talk about, or a sneer or a smirk.''

In many ways, Chancellor was a reporter's reporter — one of the few network news anchors who managed to stay actively involved in *gathering* the news while also performing the anchor's usual function of evaluating incoming material. In part, he relied on his contacts in organizations like the Council on Foreign Relations and the Carnegie Endowment for International Peace. He also made a point of getting acquainted with key people in each new presidential administration, flying to Washington on his own time on weekends for briefings by cabinet officials, press secretaries, or specialists in areas like defense or economics. He thus had a wide network of people to call on when he thought he could help advance a story or eliminate a point of confusion on the wires.

On the campaign trail, Chancellor never traveled with an entourage and took great pains to remain inconspicuous. ''I tried wearing hats that were too big pulled down over my eyes, sunglasses, that sort of thing. I used to take a lot of ribbing from the guys. They said I looked like a narc.'' Instead of traveling on the press bus, which attracts celebrity-watchers, he would split off from the pack and travel by car with one or two print journalists, such as Walter Mears of the AP or Bob Healy of the *Boston Globe*.

Like Roger Mudd, Chancellor seems to have a greater affinity for the print press than for his colleagues in TV. On prominent display in his office is a picture of the late Peter Lisagor, a reporter and columnist for the *Chicago Daily News* and a hero to many Washington reporters — a reminder, Chancellor says, to keep him honest and to avoid the trappings of stardom.

Not surprisingly, the print press lionized him. As David Kraslow, a long-time Washington newsman who is now the publisher of the *Miami News,* says, ''For me to run into a Cronkite or a Barbara Walters at a news event, other than at a state dinner or an embassy party or some big social occasion, would shock me, but Chancellor was an active TV reporter before becoming anchor, and he never lost the smell of the hunt.''

While Chancellor's affinity for the print press was probably natural, there was also a certain practical value in cultivating the good opinion of leading newspapermen, since they play an important role in ''certifying'' television reporters, i.e., deciding who is and who is not a legitimate journalist. (There is a certain irony in this arrangement, of course, because of the natural antagonism between the two media. As Eric Sevareid once told a group of publishers, "Broadcast journalism is the only business in the country I can think of that has its chief competitor as its chief critic.")

In keeping with his insistence on being a serious working journalist, Chancellor resolutely refused to play the celebrity game while he was anchor, discouraging personality profiles and articles unrelated to his job. He differed in this respect from Cronkite who, although publicly disparaging celebrity journalism, often cooperated with magazines such as *Life* and *People,* spending hours being photographed at such pursuits as sailing, cooking, or being served breakfast in bed by his wife.

For all his stature within the profession, Chancellor never attained the standing with NBC that Cronkite came to enjoy at CBS. Primarily, this was a function of Chancellor's position in the ratings: Never in first place, he was not viewed as the key to the success of the entire organization as Cronkite was. It was also a case of two contrasting personalities. By nature, Chancellor is a much less autocratic person than Cronkite — more collegial in his style of leadership. On Chancellor's staff, editorial decisions were reached in a gentlemanly atmosphere of give and take; at CBS, people were expected to snap to when Cronkite gave an order. Finally, not enough people in the NBC organization shared Chancellor's views of what news ought to be. During the 1970s, the people he grew up with at NBC were gradually supplanted by writers, producers, and editors who saw no harm in giving the public a little bit more of what it was thought to want, so long as the important stories of the day were covered. They felt that Chancellor geared his news judgments too closely to the *New York Times,* when in fact the audience was comprised of people who were more likely to read *People* magazine, if they read anything at all.

Some colleagues thought the problem was that Chancellor moved in Establishment circles and lacked the common touch. When a producer questioned him about giving so much play to Franco's impending death, Chancellor replied, "But that's all anybody's talking about, isn't it?" Similarly, while charming in social situations, Chancellor sometimes seemed to the staff to be both pompous and overly inclined to show off his knowledge. His decision to change the pronunciation of his name from CHANCE-ler to CHANCE-uh-LORE in the late seventies was greeted by hoots of derision within NBC. Somebody suggested they call themselves

CHANCE-uh-LORE and BRINK-uh-LEE. (Chancellor claims he always pronounced his name with three syllables, but that staff announcers, when informed of this, began overemphasizing the last syllable.)

In spite of his accessibility in the newsroom, Chancellor rarely fraternized with the troops on the Nightly News staff, seldom becoming intimate with colleagues. At the end of the day, he almost never joined writers or producers for a drink, as even Brinkley occasionally did. Even when he was sitting out in the newsroom in a polo shirt reading wire copy just like one of the boys, he always seemed a little removed, as if he dwelt on a higher intellectual plane.

Part of this seeming distance comes from the fact that Chancellor is a man who hates to waste time. A voracious reader, he could often be seen lunching alone in restaurants near NBC, plowing his way through a stack of newspapers and magazines. He is not one who is fond of frivolity in any form. "I like a dinner party where people talk business, which they do in Washington. I think life should be a seamless mix. In Washington, there will always be somebody who can sit down and tell you about productivity or something important. In New York, all people talk about is plays, movies, media gossip, and what's on at the museums. All of which is perfectly fine, perfectly legitimate, but sometimes I wish there was someone who was *doing* something."

In person, Chancellor comes across as something of a good-humored Oxford don. Tall and well-built, he seems to have cultivated the look of an academic, with his horn-rimmed glasses, his tweed jackets, and his thoughtful way of puffing on a pipe. He is nevertheless exceedingly suave and witty, a Renaissance man who is expert on Mozart and urban architecture, who plays tennis and goes skin diving, and who records the sounds of birds and whales for recreation. About the only avocation he has that seems out of character is his passion for horror movies, which he sometimes indulges on Saturday afternoons.

A very private person, Chancellor generally concealed his innermost feelings from the staff, hiding the fact, for example, that he is a deeply compassionate man. Once, when he learned that a floor director who had been with the program for many years was in the hospital with kidney failure, Chancellor visited him every night for two weeks. But he never mentioned his visits or asked anyone else to go with him. Another time, he noticed that Joe, a famous character who shined shoes for years at the RCA Building in New York, had not stopped by his office to give him a shoeshine for some time. Others must have missed Joe, too, but it was

Chancellor who took the time to find out that the man had been hospitalized for surgery. At Chancellor's instigation, the staff sent a large cartoon drawing of themselves, all wearing scuffed, dirty shoes, with the caption, "Come back soon, Joe. We need you."

Born on the north side of Chicago, John William Chancellor was the son of a hotel keeper, Estil Chancellor, who lost his string of small hotels in the Depression, and of Mollie Barrett, a spirited, independent woman, who became the bulwark of the family. An Irish immigrant with a brogue, she stayed in the hotel business, rising to the rank of chief housekeeper at the Conrad Hilton Hotel. Chancellor, an only child, does not remember his childhood as particularly happy. His parents were divorced when he was twelve. He had trouble getting along with the priests who taught at his Catholic high school and dropped out at the age of fifteen. His mother wanted him to go into the hotel business, but he had more romantic notions: He wanted to be a novelist or — failing that — a journalist.

After leaving school, he embarked on a vagabond-like existence, working as a hospital orderly, a carpenter's assistant, a chemical tester, a parker of trailer trucks, a job agency interviewer, and a deckhand on an Illinois river boat, hoping to store up experiences he could use later in his writing. On his lunch hours and his breaks, he buried himself in the works of F. Scott Fitzgerald, Ernest Hemingway, Theodore Dreiser, and other twentieth-century American writers. After a stint in the Army, where he picked up a high school equivalency certificate, Chancellor enrolled in the University of Illinois, taking almost nothing except history courses. But he was impatient to find out if he had enough talent to write, so he quit the university to try his hand at the great American novel. For the next few months, he shut himself away in a small apartment, subsisting mainly on boiled potatoes, he recalls, and becoming more and more depressed with the results of his efforts. "It was so junky," he says, "that I finally tore it up."

Chancellor's other romantic vision — the world of newspapers — turned out to be a more practical avenue for him: He was a natural-born newsman. His first taste of the business had come at the age of fourteen, when he worked during the summer as a copy boy for the *Chicago Daily News*. "I loved it there. There was such a wonderful raffishness about newspaper people, such a colorful group of men and women who seemed to enjoy each other and to enjoy life more than anyone else I had ever seen." So it was only natural that when he abandoned his efforts to write fiction at the age of twenty-one, he applied for a job with a newspaper.

Starting as a copy boy, within two years he worked his way up to reporter on the *Chicago Sun-Times*, an occasion he describes as ''the happiest day of my life.'' A short time later, let go in a cutback at the *Sun-Times*, he went to work as a newswriter for WMAQ, the NBC station in Chicago.

The year was 1950, which makes Chancellor a pioneer in television, ''the youngest member of the old generation,'' he calls himself. ''When I went to work at NBC, the only programs I had seen were in saloons — wrestling and a program called 'Kukla, Fran, and Ollie.' The people in radio wouldn't touch TV, of course. Who would watch those flickering images when there was the majesty of radio? We were recruited almost exclusively from print, so we were unfettered by their ideas. And we invented TV as we went along. I was the first film editor for NBC in Chicago, because there was nobody else to do it.''

At the 1952 Democratic convention in Chicago, the youthful Chancellor caught the eye of some of the network people, which led to writing assignments for the ''Camel News Caravan.'' Not long afterward, he became one of NBC's first television news correspondents, covering the South and Midwest. A tireless, conscientious worker, he had a number of other assets common to great reporters — a healthy constitution, a willingness to face danger, and ''street smarts.'' While on ''loan'' from the network to the NBC radio station in Chicago in the midfifties, he became a local celebrity for his coverage of the capture of Richard Carpenter, a fugitive who killed six Chicago policemen — one a day for six days. His account, delivered while lying on his stomach, bullets whizzing overhead, was so dramatic that NBC later issued a recording of it.

A couple of years later, in 1957, he established a national reputation covering the crisis in Little Rock, Arkansas, for the ''Huntley-Brinkley Report.'' The Little Rock story was the opening chapter of the civil rights story on television; night after night viewers watched pictures of National Guardsmen, bayonets fixed to keep back the jeering mobs, escorting their young black charges into Central High School. The nearest affiliate from which Chancellor could feed his reports to the network was Oklahoma City, an hour away by chartered plane, requiring Chancellor to leave Little Rock each day at 3:00 P.M., but somehow he always managed to stay on top of the story. A ritual even developed at the Press Club in downtown Little Rock, which served as headquarters for the out-of-town press corps. Every night at six-thirty, conversation would cease so the reporters could watch Chancellor, who led the "Huntley-Brinkley Report" for weeks. One of those watching, Wallace Westfeldt, who later became a producr for NBC but was working at the time as a reporter for the *Nashville Tennessean*, recalls seeing other reporters slip out of the room some nights to update their dispatches on the basis of Chancellor's reports.

The other exploit for which Chancellor is best remembered is his exit from the 1964 Republican convention at the Cow Palace in San Francisco. The convention was a noisy, rancorous affair; Goldwater's followers, who had wrested control of the party from traditional conservatives, turned vindictive in their hour of victory, especially toward the press. Delegates could be seen wearing buttons that said, "Stamp out Huntley-Brinkley," and Goldwater's security forces tried to hamper the movement of the television reporters on the convention floor, leading to Chancellor's arrest on camera. "I'm being taken off the arena now by police," he announced with comic serenity. "I'll check in later. This is John Chancellor, reporting from somewhere in custody."

Chancellor's career with the network was exceptionally well rounded, including several years abroad as a foreign correspondent and one year as host of the "Today" show — an interlude that is not too fondly remembered. Despite his fine, dry wit, Chancellor did not have the same easy manner on the air as his predecessor, Dave Garroway. After Chancellor had been doing the program for about two months, he had dinner with NBC president Robert Kintner, regaling him with one funny anecdote after another. Kintner finally couldn't resist asking Chancellor why he wasn't that funny on the "Today" show, to which Chancellor confessed that he never realized that he said something funny until after people laughed. Chancellor also refused to read commercials, and ad revenues for the program began to fall off sharply. Before long, he was replaced by Hugh Downs, who was more in the Garroway mold.

In 1963, after the assassination of John F. Kennedy, Chancellor was assigned to cover the White House, where he became a great favorite of Lyndon Johnson. Two years later, Johnson asked Chancellor to serve as the director of the Voice of America, but Chancellor, who loved reporting, was not eager to take the assignment. He also worried that serving in the government might destroy his credibility as a newsman. He soon found himself under pressure from two presidents, however. One was Robert Kintner, who was anxious to do Johnson a favor. The other was

Johnson, who could be irresistible when he chose to be. Pouring on the charm, he invited Chancellor and his wife, Barbara, to Camp David for weekends two or three times while trying to persuade him to take the job. It worked, but Chancellor never saw Johnson again until the day he resigned two years later.

Back at NBC after his stint in government, Chancellor was faced with the classic dilemma of television news correspondents: what to do about their future. As satisfying and exciting as television reporting can be, it is a young person's game. Very few network correspondents go into management or switch to producers' jobs, and fewer still wind up as anchors. Most simply leave the profession, often for jobs in public relations. "I began to think that I didn't want to be an old guy, standing in the rain in front of the foreign ministry somewhere at two o'clock in the morning," Chancellor says. "The legs go after a while." So he approached management about the possibility of anchoring.

In July 1970, Chancellor was named one of three rotating anchors on the NBC Nightly News, but the so-called troika was disbanded a year later, and he was sent in to do battle alone against CBS and ABC.

In spite of the spurt put on by ABC News after Harry Reasoner joined, CBS remained the network to beat throughout most of the seventies. Cronkite was by now viewed as the Mount Rushmore of television; articles on TV news inevitably focused on him, just as articles about higher education were apt to center on Harvard. Yet, in spite of the perception that Cronkite was the runaway leader in the ratings, the margin between CBS and NBC was seldom all that wide. At times it was paper thin, and every so often, Chancellor even came in ahead of his venerable rival, such as the thirteen-week period in 1974 when the NBC Nightly News placed first for six weeks and tied CBS once. By the end of the year, however, Cronkite was still holding on to the lead — by a mere seven tenths of a ratings point.

That same year, a nationwide poll taken by the Sindlinger organization, which surveyed nearly 2000 people, found that although Cronkite was still the best-known television newsman, recognized by more than 98 percent of the respondents, Chancellor emerged as the best liked and most watched. Although the NBC publicity machine duly trumpeted the results to TV writers, executives knew from their own audience research that Chancellor elicited mixed feelings from the public.

It was unfortunate, but his warm, human side was not very apparent on the air. Nor was his considerable wit; he is not a man who reads a funny line well. According to news consultants, the audience looks for two things in an anchorman: One, does he know what he is talking about? And two, how does he come across as a human being? Does he communicate a sense of concern? Consultants like Peter Hoffman, of the firm of McHugh and Hoffman, say Chancellor did not score well on the second criteria. People found him knowledgeable and intelligent, but thought he came across as stiff and cold. ''John Chancellor would read the end of the world the same way he would read the telephone book,'' Hoffman says, adding that Chancellor appealed mainly to better-educated, upper-income viewers, whereas Cronkite, with his everyman quality, appealed to viewers from all walks of life.

By the midseventies, NBC news executives, like their counterparts at ABC, were studying the results of audience research before making decisions about on-air changes. The only holdout was CBS News, where Richard Salant adamantly refused to look at any ''numbers.'' (The five CBS-owned-and-operated stations did research, however, as did all the other network O-&-O's.) It was becoming increasingly difficult for network news executives to turn their backs on the tools used so successfully by local stations for increasing audiences — techniques like demographic studies, attitudinal studies, and high-powered promotional campaigns. They were, to be sure, tools developed by salesmen, not journalists, who have always preferred to rely on gut instinct to tell them what is important or interesting and do not believe it is their job to ''sell'' the news.

Chancellor naturally abhorred anything that in his view cheapened or commercialized the news, but executives found that he was not necessarily unreceptive to new ideas. In 1974, Lee Hanna, then vice president of news programs, came up with an idea for improving the promotability of the NBC Nightly News. Since it was so difficult to design a promotional campaign around breaking news, Hanna suggested preparing in-depth ''cover stories'' about trends and the like, which could be scheduled in advance and would thus lend themselves more easily to promotion. But the executive producer of the Nightly News at that time, Lester Crystal, was afraid that Chancellor would object to using four, five, or six minutes of the program for a segment not growing directly out of the day's news. So it was with considerable trepidation that Crystal began outlining the idea to Chancellor one day over lunch. Chancellor said nothing at first, but after a while began doodling on his napkin. ''Let's call it 'Special,' '' he said, ''and here's the kind of lettering it should have.'' Everyone heaved a sigh of relief.

"Special," later titled "Segment Three," featured well-produced reports on everything from the housing squeeze and homosexuality to the history of the SALT talks. It was not only promotable, as Hanna had predicted, but it was a hit with the critics, who cheered a network for finally attempting to probe beyond the surface of the news with stories providing background and perspective. How were they to realize that the impulse behind "Segment Three" was fundamentally commercial?

By some measures, NBC News was still a healthy organization in the midseventies; its evening news broadcast was a solid second, and revenues for the division as a whole were coming close to equaling expenditures. But signs of trouble were becoming increasingly apparent. Ratings for "Today" were sluggish. NBC had failed to mount a successful weekly prime-time magazine show to compete with "60 Minutes." And the news operations at NBC's O-&-O's were in a poor competitive position. Most worrisome of all, a lethargy had settled over the organization; the drive that had characterized it in the Kintner era seemed to have vanished. It was Kintner who ignited the fire under NBC News, but the effect of his departure in 1966 was not immediately noticed. The "Huntley-Brinkley Report" was still on top, and the esprit and sense of pride it engendered did not vanish overnight, even after the team split up. "The excellence of Huntley and Brinkley lingered as a mythical source of inspiration," says Tom Pettit, "but NBC was resting on their laurels. Without Chet, the magic was gone, but it took people a long while to realize it."

Paul Duke, who joined NBC News in 1963, when its competitive spirit was at its height, recalls how frustrated he felt by the organization's complacency in the seventies. During the 1972 presidential campaign, for example, Duke lost out on a major exclusive: He learned one hour in advance on unimpeachable authority that George McGovern was dropping Senator Thomas Eagleton as his vice presidential running mate — the biggest bombshell of the election campaign. As soon as he found out, Duke called the news desk, expecting to be put on the air with a bulletin, but "New York" decided against it. Later, he was told by news executives that since an announcement of some kind on Eagleton was scheduled to come down within an hour, it was deemed unnecessary to "bulletin" his scoop. For a reporter like Duke, who always believed that competition was the lifeblood of journalism, it was a mystifying and infuriating decision. Another time, during the Senate Watergate hearings, he and two other reporters, one from the *New York Times*, the other from the *New York Daily News*, were handed a great exclusive by Connecticut senator

Lowell Weicker — documentary evidence that FBI director L. Patrick Gray, acting under instructions from the White House, had destroyed documents taken from the safe of Watergate burglar E. Howard Hunt. Duke filmed a "standupper" for the Nightly News, expecting to lead the broadcast, but was astounded to learn later that afternoon that the producers in New York had dropped the story from the line-up. Christie Basham, the Washington producer for "Nightly" (as the program was called in-house), succeeded in getting the story reinstated, but ten minutes before air, New York reversed itself again and killed it. Basham told Duke the producers simply didn't understand its significance. They understood it the next day, however, after the *New York Times* ran the story on page one under an eight-column headline. The "Today" show asked Duke to come in that morning and do a report, but after completing it, he felt so heartsick and overwrought that he went home for the rest of the day. "We should have been first," he says. "We would have been way ahead of the *Times*. To me, the incident symbolized everything that was wrong with NBC at the time — the lack of the old fighting spirit, a feeling that we weren't 'out to beat their asses' anymore." Duke left NBC for PBS in 1974, becoming the moderator of "Washington Week in Review" and other public affairs programs.

Morale at NBC News, which was already flagging, began to plunge after Herb Schlosser became president of the network in 1974. NBC was never known as an organization where quick decisions were reached, but under Schlosser, indecision reached epidemic proportions. Just as bad was his tendency to meddle, to undercut subordinates by getting personally involved in matters like talent negotiations and program deals.

By 1975, Schlosser had not yet reached a decision to jettison Chancellor. Although a consensus existed for pairing him with another anchor, as usual, it took a while for anything to happen. The possibility of a Chancellor-Snyder combination was mentioned, but everyone realized it wouldn't work. The idea of putting Barbara Walters and Chancellor together came up, too — a suggestion more popular at the corporate level than in the news division, where some of the executives did not regard her as a serious newswoman. The most promising possibility from within the ranks of NBC seemed to be Tom Brokaw, who was making a good name for himself as the White House correspondent. In 1975, however, he had been with the network only two years, and the president of the news division, Richard Wald, did not want to rush his progress.

The two leading "outsiders" for the job were Dan Rather and Roger

Mudd of CBS, both of whom had contracts that were about to expire. NBC tried out several prospective combinations on focus groups — Chancellor and Rather, Chancellor and Mudd, Chancellor and Brokaw — by splicing tapes together into mock newscasts. All three combinations tested very well, and talks were begun with both Rather and Mudd. Mudd, in particular, seemed interested, but somehow, NBC never got around to making him an offer.

Once the presidential primary season got under way early in 1976, a new co-anchor possibility suggested itself: David Brinkley. Brinkley seemed newly energized by the political season, and he and Chancellor clicked so well covering the early primaries that by June, he was returned to co-anchor status. Some staff members and executives thought the addition of Brinkley made the program livelier, but to the California Mafia, he was just another retread. He was looking tired and starting to show his age; yet Brinkley, as independent and ornery as ever, refused to wear make-up.

The Chancellor-Brinkley combination did not prove to be as happy internally as people supposed. Chancellor thought Brinkley was careless with his facts, and Brinkley, whose style was more irreverent and folksy, thought Chancellor had become impossibly elitist in his story choices.

Brinkley took a rather casual approach to the editorial process and generally couldn't understand what all the fuss was about. "Why do you agonize so over what the lead story is?" he once asked a producer. "The people at home aren't going to know or care." Brinkley believed in giving people what they wanted, as opposed to what they needed, which naturally put him in conflict with Chancellor. "If the viewers are bored or disinterested," Brinkley would tell producers, "it isn't our job to get them interested."

The two men got along better while Brinkley was based in New York, where they could work out their differences face to face. Gentlemen and professionals both, they never disagreed with one another in public; only insiders were aware of the extent of their differences. Once Brinkley moved back to Washington, however, the distance between them grew, increasingly so, as Chancellor's control over the editorial content of the program increased. Brinkley, no longer viewed as indispensable to the success of the broadcast, learned an unpleasant lesson about what happens to an anchor when his star declines. Producers didn't jump quite so quickly when he spoke, and his suggestions for news coverage were often ignored. In the old days, he would have made sure that a producer who flouted his wishes too often was assigned to another program. The second time he anchored, he was powerless to do much about this. Sitting in his office in Washington, feeling neglected and unappreciated, he used to complain that the staff had more loyalty to Chancellor than to him. He would tell Washington staffers how well he and Huntley used to work together, how they always saw eye to eye on everything. The longer he co-anchored with Chancellor, the more saintly Huntley became in his eyes.

Indeed, by the late 1970s, Brinkley had become fed up with the news business altogether, though he knew he couldn't earn as much money doing anything else. He admits the monotony of the anchor job got to him. "It's such a grind. Rain or shine, Thanksgiving, Christmas, the Fourth of July, you have to be there. And it's particularly painful on nights when there's not much news, which happens fairly often. But mostly it's the physical grind that wears you down. It's like driving a bus. You have to leave Forty-ninth and Madison every night at exactly 6:00 P.M., and you're supposed to be somewhere by 6:30 P.M., which gets very repetitious. It's psychologically corrosive."

Although Herbert Schlosser approved the Chancellor-Brinkley arrangement, he showed little commitment to it. Brinkley had barely resumed his duties as co-anchor when Schlosser began to have second thoughts — daydreams really — about going into the 1976 nominating conventions with his two hottest young stars, Tom Snyder and Tom Brokaw, in the NBC anchor booth instead of Chancellor and Brinkley. The idea got a cool reception in the news division, however, and quickly died. For the moment at least, things would remain as they were.

Unhappily for Schlosser, that left NBC with a problem on its hands — a very impatient and angry Tom Snyder. It was only under protest that Snyder had come east at the end of 1974 to anchor at WNBC. He had been reporting and anchoring at local stations since the 1950s and was desperate for a crack at the network; he had no desire to "save" yet another local station. The success of "Newscenter 4" was so crucial to the financial health of the network, however, that Schlosser finally prevailed upon Snyder to do it. (One of NBC's most serious problems at this time was its local news operations. With the exception of KNBC in Los Angeles, they were in bad shape — not earning as much money as they should have and exerting a downward pull on the ratings for network broadcasts.)

Eventually, Schlosser, Snyder, and Snyder's agent, E. Gregory Hookstratten (familiarly known as "The Hook"), put together a package worth $600,000 to Snyder, making him the highest-paid local anchor in the country at that time. It also made Snyder the busiest; in addition to WNBC's "Newscenter 4," he anchored the network news on Sunday nights and did the "Tomorrow" show five nights a week. He also anchored a one-minute network "news break" at 9:00 P.M. on weeknights. The biggest carrot used to get Snyder to agree to all these chores was not money, though; it was the NBC Nightly News. In essence, Schlosser told Snyder, "You've proved yourself in Philadelphia, you've proved yourself in Atlanta and Los Angeles, but you've never proved you can crack New York City. Show us you can bring the ratings up here, and you'll get the Nightly News."

The news operation at WNBC, the network's flagship station, had been causing giant headaches for executives since the 1960s. Despite massive infusions of money and countless changes of news directors, sets, and anchors, it had resisted all attempts at resuscitation, capturing only a small portion of the audience. By the end of 1975, however, seventeen months after Snyder began anchoring the 6:00 to 7:00 P.M. portion of the newscast (Chuck Scarborough anchored from 5:00 to 6:00 P.M.), "Newscenter 4" more than doubled its viewership and was closing in on top-rated WCBS. It was an astonishingly fast turnaround, and as far as Snyder was concerned, he had proved himself in New York; it was time for Schlosser to make good on his promise to give him the NBC Nightly News.

Schlosser, however, did not feel he could simply wave his hand and order Snyder to take Chancellor's place. Besides, that was not Schlosser's style. He preferred to throw out ideas, hoping that someone else would volunteer to carry them out. Unfortunately, Dick Wald was not volunteering. Wald, like everyone else, was intrigued with Snyder, rating him as a qualified journalist and an excellent writer for television. But Wald thought that Snyder would be miscast as anchor of the NBC Nightly News. "It would really be a mistake to put him into a situation like that because you would not be using his strengths, which are his ability to ad lib and to interview. Putting Tom Snyder on the Nightly News would be like taking the battleship *Missouri* and using it to deliver mail between Martha's Vineyard and Hyannis Port. Now, it's feasible — you could deliver mail that way — but why would you want to? Similarly, you wouldn't want to ask John Chancellor to do the 'Tomorrow' show. He could do it, but it wouldn't be the best use of his talents." Also, there was the matter of Snyder's image. "He came across more as a show business personality, rather than a news personality," says Wald. "Even if you acknowledge that he is a journalist, he is not a journalist in the mold of John Chancellor. It is a question of appropriateness, and Snyder is more appropriate for anchoring a local newscast. He simply would not have fit in as anchorman for the NBC News at that time. NBC News was a different kind of animal from Tom Snyder, and unless the decision was made to change NBC and the kind of news it put on, Snyder wouldn't have made the grade.''

Wald was also exceedingly worried about Snyder's propensity for saying and doing outrageous things. ''I told him I could never trust him not to embarrass me — not on the air, but in civilian life. He has a loud-mouthed personality. He also has a tendency to say absolutely anything and everything to the press.''

A huge (six-feet-four), boisterous man with great animal vitality and an obsessive need for attention, Snyder has a history of causing problems for management. Always on stage, he can be extremely funny, unless you happen to be his boss. Once, when Snyder was an eager young reporter at KTLA, an independent station in Los Angeles, the infamous Madame Nhu had come to town on a visit from Vietnam and was staying at the Beverly Wilshire Hotel. Snyder was assigned to stake out the hotel and get a statement from her, but for two days she swept past the assembled reporters into her limousine. Snyder's boss, Sam Zelman, then news director of KTLA, was furious. He ordered Snyder to try again the next day, warning him not to come back without an interview.

The following day, as Madame Nhu again attempted to wade through the crush of reporters and cameramen, Snyder threw himself in her path, sank to his knees, and implored, ''Please, Madame Nhu. You've got to speak to me. If you don't, I'll be fired.'' Madame Nhu barely deigned to glance at the young man flailing away on the sidewalk in front of her, but every other station in town filmed the scene and showed it on the air that night.

Snyder could never resist getting a laugh, whatever the consequences. Once, while introducing Dr. Frank Field, WNBC's dignified weatherman, he said, ''Now, here's Dr. Frank Field, the weatherman, to take a leak — I mean a look — out the window'' — a slip he later admitted was intentional.

Producers who have worked with Snyder at NBC attest to his abilities as a journalist and his mastery of the live medium, but most agree that he rarely showed deep interest in the material he dealt with. Normally, he breezed in and read whatever was handed to him on ''Newscenter 4.'' He seldom read the books written by guests on "Tomorrow." On the Saturday network news, which he anchored for a year — from 1975 to 1976 — he used to write some of his own material, but he seemed to have trouble getting down to work. "He was always turned on, always making jokes," says Joe Angotti, a weekend producer at the time. "Once in a while he would drop the façade and show he cared. One time, we divided up the rundown, and I asked him what he wanted to write. He said, 'I'll write this, this, and this.' I made some kind of remark like, 'If you were any kind of a man, you'd write the whole show in two hours or less.' I told him he couldn't do it without the help of a writer. For the next forty-five minutes, he just sat there working; he didn't say a word. He wrote the whole show and casually tossed it at me and said, 'Here's your show.' It was only five-twenty, and normally, the show isn't completed until 6:00 P.M. I took it as a challenge and went through it carefully. I couldn't find a single mistake. He could do it easily when he wanted to. But being funny absorbed too much of his time. He could do anything anyone else could, but he was too busy clowning around."

In his personal life, too, Snyder made no effort to curb his antic behavior, shouting across crowded restaurants to catch a waiter's attention, telling crude jokes in the most inappropriate circumstances. Reared in a middle-class, Catholic home in Milwaukee, Wisconsin, Snyder discovered the joys of laughter and applause as an actor in high school theatrical productions. "It was like shooting heroin into my veins," he told a *Playboy* interviewer. "I loved it."

On camera he was a mesmerizing performer, projecting so much energy and volatility that it is almost impossible *not* to watch him. Yet he was a potentially dangerous choice for network anchor even though NBC executives and producers all agree that he had the editorial ability to handle the job. One problem was that, with Snyder as anchor, the NBC Nightly News would almost certainly have moved in the direction of an entertainment program because producers would inevitably have sought to tailor the format to fit his personality. In addition, the attention of the audience would have shifted from the news to Snyder; like Barbara Walters, he seemed bigger than most of the material he read. But Snyder, unlike the seasoned, professional Walters, was like an overgrown, undisciplined child. Given the degree of influence an anchor can exert over the selection and presentation of news, and his importance at moments of national crisis, the prospect of an unpredictable character like Snyder at the helm of the evening news was disturbing, to say the least.

Concerned especially about his lack of self-discipline, NBC executives decided against giving Snyder an assignment at the 1976 political conventions. Among other things, they concluded he probably would not bother to study the required volume of material. Predictably, Snyder was puzzled at being overlooked. Here he was, the apparent heir to John Chancellor, and he was not even making an appearance as a floor reporter at the conventions. The failure to get a convention assignment was only one of the things upsetting Snyder. He was also exhausted by his frenetic schedule. By the end of 1975, he had insisted on giving up the Sunday network news and voiced a desire to stop anchoring the New York local news as well. That was considered too dangerous for the ratings, so he stayed in harness. Yet, every time he asked Schlosser when he was going to get his crack at the Nightly News, Schlosser would reply, "Stay cool, Tom. Stay cool. Everything is going to work out fine." Snyder heard the refrain so often that he named his production company "Stay Cool."

If the future was imperceptibly darkening for Snyder, it was unquestionably brightening for Tom Brokaw. The departure of Barbara Walters for ABC left an opening on the "Today" show. And it was a revealing indication of things to come that Brokaw was the nearly unanimous choice of NBC executives to fill it. Snyder let it be known he wasn't interested, but he was never really a serious candidate, the general feeling being that he was too abrasive for early-morning viewers. In the larger context, though, Snyder's weaknesses were becoming all the more apparent by contrast with Brokaw.

Certainly, as far as "Today" was concerned, Brokaw had nearly all the right qualifications. He had an unassailable reputation as a journalist, he had a broad range of interests, he looked good on camera, and he could ad lib in any situation. His only drawback was a tendency to come across a bit cool, always playing the hard newsman when a dash of folksiness might have been helpful at times. No matter, though; he had the most prized attribute of all — star quality. Producers were confident they could get him to loosen up on the air.

It was inevitable that Brokaw and Snyder, the network's two most exciting news personalities, be compared. Both were "children of television" — members of the generation who had never worked for newspapers but had served their entire apprenticeship in broadcasting. Both were naturals on television, handsome and glib, with extensive experience working for NBC-owned or -affiliated stations around the country. As young men, both idolized the "Four Horsemen" — Chancellor, Edwin

Newman, Sander Vanocur, and Frank McGee — and dreamed of making good at the network themselves one day. And both had become celebrities in Los Angeles, a city that knows how to recognize a star. In their personal and professional lives, however, they could not have been more different. Where Snyder flouted convention at every turn, determined to succeed on his own terms, Brokaw was a smooth operator who almost never made a false step.

In 1973, when the network was looking for a reporter with enough charisma to counter the impact Dan Rather was making at the White House, Robert Mulholland, then executive producer of the Nightly News, suggested Brokaw. It was Mulholland who cautioned his bosses not to be put off by Brokaw's cute button nose — that he was a solid, hard-working newsman. Dick Wald, who was already intrigued by Brokaw, was pleasantly surprised when they met. "I remember he took me to a vegetarian restaurant in L.A. — it was called the Aware Inn. So this nice young man started talking California politics, the national economy, the environmental movement, and so on, and it was apparent that here was not just someone who was good on the air, but a fellow with a good head on his shoulders."

Wald says that Washington seemed like a good place to locate Brokaw, making light of the fact that in 1973 it was highly unconventional to take a local anchor, with no previous network experience, and assign him to the White House, the most prestigious reporting beat the network has to offer. Both Wald and Brokaw ran into a lot of static at first. To begin with, the news fraternity scorned local television anchors as blow-dried pretty boys. In fact, not all of them were as empty-headed as popular legend made them out to be; a considerable number, although probably not the majority, were experienced and reliable newspeople. But it remained true that local stations put a lower premium on anchor editorial expertise than on their personalities. The stations regard anchors as bait to lure audiences and are almost shameless about exploiting their "stars" for that purpose. Typically, the anchor is pressed to make frequent appearances at local high schools, civic clubs, churches, and the like, both as an introduction to potential viewers and as a way to demonstrate the station's concern for community affairs. When not out on speaking engagements, anchors are expected to shoot "promos" for the station or tape reports that can be promoted during rating periods. In addition, most anchors do both the early and late news, which means they can rarely be on hand for the crucial early-morning meetings when story assignments are made. Local anchors who are able to meet their heavy promotional schedules and still play an active role in shaping their broadcasts (other than rewriting the wires) have to be exceptionally dedicated and energetic.

In his years with local stations, Tom Brokaw was nothing if not energetic. In the anchor chair in Los Angeles, he managed to satisfy the promotional appetites of management and at the same time keep his credentials as a bona fide newsman. At KNBC, he was fortunate in having to anchor only one program, the eleven o'clock news, which left him free for reporting most of the day. During the political season in California, he usually got up about 5:00 A.M. to cover a candidate, spent all day in the field, then returned to the station to write and edit a report for the early-evening news. Afterward, he began work on his own newscast. His stamina became so legendary that Steve Friedman, a producer who worked with him in Los Angeles and later on the "Today" show, dubbed him "Duncan the Wonder Horse," a mysterious term that somehow stuck.

Brokaw also acquired a reputation as an excellent reporter. Ed Guthman, formerly national editor of the *Los Angeles Times* and now editor of the *Philadelphia Inquirer*, was one of those who watched Brokaw's progress in Los Angeles. "The thing that impressed me about Tom was his seriousness and his high standards. In print, we have certain ways of working, certain ethical standards, and Tom operated with the kind of thoroughness I would expect of a good print reporter. If Tom Brokaw told me something, I'd believe it."

In spite of Brokaw's stature among his colleagues in California, he got the cold shoulder on arriving in Washington. Part of the problem was that he looked a little too handsome to be taken seriously. Tall and slim, with light brown hair and brown eyes, he came across more as an Eagle Scout than a hard-bitten newsman. And the older correspondents at the NBC bureau in Washington resented the way he had been leapfrogged over them to the White House spot. Brokaw, of course, was acutely aware of their contempt. "I remember after the first presidential news conference I handled, everybody was watching me as I went back to the studio at NBC to introduce it. Nixon made a long statement, and I was able to summarize it quickly and succinctly, and to understand the issues being talked about. And Paul Duke walked up to me afterwards and said, 'That was a good job.' And I knew that what he was really saying was, 'I didn't quite understand that you could do that.'"

If Brokaw resembled the newer, more telegenic breed of TV reporter the networks began recruiting in the seventies, he had no trouble fitting the older NBC mold, which emphasized straight, factual, and dispassionate reporting. Indeed, he had emulated the style from the start in local news, hoping it would help him make the grade at the network one day. Nor did he change when pitted against Rather's flashier, more personal style at the White House — much to the delight of network producers like Joe Angotti. "Tom was every bit as aggressive as Rather at the White House, but he did not succumb to Rather's kind of personal involvement in the story during Watergate. Rather would stand there with so-called exclusives — stories that had been rampant in Washington all day. It would have been easy for Tom to say, 'Wait until you see what I have,' but he was always restrained. Rather had no qualms about showing his emotions and displaying intense kinds of feelings. Brokaw played it straight. He showed the discipline of a dedicated journalist."

Unlike Tom Snyder, who was outrageous in his personal life, Brokaw led an exemplary private life. He was married to his high school sweetheart, Meredith Auld, who had competed in the Miss America pageant as Miss South Dakota. And Meredith Brokaw had the looks, brains, and charm to match her husband's. A marathon runner, she also became a successful businesswoman, the owner of two prosperous toy shops in Manhattan. Friends credit her with helping Brokaw keep his feet on the ground when his career was climbing with potentially unsettling speed.

Socially adept, Brokaw not only says and does the right things, he knows the right people, counting many glamorous figures from the world of art, entertainment, sports, and politics among his intimate friends. In California, he ran with a rich, politically liberal crowd that sought out the company of prominent journalists. Norton Simon, the millionaire industrialist, was so taken with Brokaw that he installed him on the board of directors of his art museum in Pasadena. For a working-class boy from South Dakota (Brokaw's father was a construction foreman for the U.S. Army Corps of Engineers), he has had unusual exposure to wealth and power. A Brokaw conversation is invariably studded with a lot of famous names. In fact, the suspicion that Brokaw is a social climber is almost the only criticism ever voiced about him, though friends say the charge is unfair. Bob Abernethy, a long-time NBC correspondent who knows Brokaw well from California days, put it like this: "Social climbing implies buttering people up to get their friendship. Actually, the beautiful people seek Tom and Meredith out. There is a natural affinity. I don't think he is a name-dropper, either. Name-dropping implies the conscious use of famous names to impress people you're talking to. It's a fact that he has been playing tennis with Art Buchwald. It's a fact that he taught a seminar at Yale. His life, his world includes those people."

Brokaw intimates also point out that his circle of friends extends beyond the rich and famous. He is good at keeping up with family and old friends from school. Cokie Roberts, a correspondent for National Public Radio, says Tom is the kind of guy you can count on in a crunch. "When our house in California was threatened by a brush fire," she says, "Tom insisted that my husband, two babies, and my mother all come over to his house that night. You don't forget friends who come through for you at a time like that."

Brokaw has led such a charmed life that some friends worry he may be tempting fate. Bob Abernethy, himself a former anchor at KNBC, says, "There are so many influences in that job that can cause you to become very egocentric. Fame, fortune, people treating you well because you are well known. You can get to thinking that the rules might be a little different for you than for others. People are often attracted to you because of who you are, but it's easy to start thinking, 'Gee, I'm irresistible, aren't I?' It's such a phony, unnatural world. A man who gets into that world is very lucky if he has a strong, loving wife with a good sense of humor. Tom has one. My question is: Can the golden couple survive all that gold? As far as I can see, he is weathering all this very well, and if anybody can do it, Tom and Meredith can, but boy, do I have my fingers crossed. Not because I think Tom is weak; in fact, it's just the opposite. Because he is so strong, so talented, you want him to survive, and you know the pressures are tremendous."

Brokaw owes his rise to the top in television to a combination of talent, luck, and hard work, but he has also been unusually skillful in analyzing the rules of the game. He can run with the beautiful people and not get tagged as a social butterfly himself because he has carefully cultivated his image, and he understands the value of symbolism.

In his office, he, like John Chancellor, keeps a picture of the late Peter Lisagor prominently displayed, a nice touch to reinforce his news image. He is also smart enough not to travel with an entourage on the road or fall into the trap of limousines and press agents. And like other savvy television journalists, he courts the good opinion of the print press. "I have always been very protective of my image," he says. "Partly it was a necessity, because of the way I look. I have always been determined that people would realize there was more to me than just cosmetics. I have always been conscious of being taken seriously as a journalist.'' Thus, in 1974, when he was approached about reading commercials on the ''Today'' show, he realized it could tarnish his professional image, so he turned it down. He seemed to know that success would come to him eventually; there was no need to rush things. As it turned out, he was right. When he was asked to do ''Today'' in 1976, he was able to set his own terms.

He is, say veteran Brokaw-watchers, one of the slickest political operators around. Having the ability to mask his ambition better than Rather, he does not excite the same kind of envy and backbiting from colleagues and the television critics. As his friend Dick Wald described him in a newspaper interview: ''Tom fits the British aristocracy's definition of 'amateur.' He's like the guy at Oxford who finishes first in his class and doesn't seem to try. In fact, he's studied the whole night and just hasn't told anyone. It's the laid-back style of Tom's success that leads you to think of him as perfect.''

Gradually, Brokaw began to emerge as the compromise candidate for Chancellor's job. He was in the NBC mold, yet he was young and glamorous; and he was so much more level-headed and disciplined than Snyder. There remained a serious obstacle, however. Schlosser continued to look toward Snyder as the kind of dynamo needed to shake up the Nightly News. He was not alone in this view, either. Wald's chief deputies, Bob Mulholland, Dick Fisher, and Joe Bartelme, all of whom had worked with Snyder in California, felt the same way. They thought Snyder was the most dynamic broadcaster they had ever seen, although they worried about his lack of discipline. ''We discussed the kinds of problems it would cause using him at conventions,'' says one of Snyder's executive-level admirers. ''We knew he wouldn't have the drive to do his homework, but we thought we could make up for it. It's possible to prop a guy up. It needs a lot of work, but it can be done.''

NBC producers who had worked with Snyder began receiving peculiar telephone calls, both from Wald and Schlosser, asking, ''Has Tom Snyder ever done anything to embarrass NBC News?'' It was obvious that a change was pending. Behind the scenes, though, the struggle between Schlosser and Wald continued. As usual, Schlosser was unable to persuade Wald to ''volunteer'' to make the change.

John Chancellor, meanwhile, was growing increasingly unhappy with the situation. He was tired of executives repeating, almost like an incantation, "In every market where Tom Snyder has ever anchored, there has been an increase in the ratings." And he was getting even more irritated with the rumors that Snyder and/or Brokaw were in line for his job. Chancellor was particularly upset by the prospect of Snyder taking his place. In his view, Snyder was only in it for the money and the ego, using journalism purely to promote himself as a celebrity.

If Chancellor was in trouble, he was no neophyte to office politics; he had not been around all those years without picking up a few tricks. He also had a smart agent, Ralph Mann. So in the spring of 1977, Mann contacted CBS and suggested his client might be willing to change networks. CBS executives were interested. They offered to make him host of "CBS Reports," the documentary series. Although it would have meant a pay cut and less visibility, Chancellor said yes, provided NBC would let him out of his contract, which still had one year to run.

Schlosser was dumbstruck when he learned about the offer. Still shaken by the loss of Barbara Walters, he recoiled at the sudden realization of how it would look if NBC News lost another star just then. He refused to let Chancellor go. More than that, he agreed to negotiate a new seven-year contract for Chancellor. It contained both a salary increase and a promise that when Chancellor stepped down as anchor, he would be given a regular commentary slot on the Nightly News. All in all, it was a much better deal than Chancellor was able to obtain from CBS. Schlosser also made a verbal promise that Chancellor would be consulted on the choice of his successor and the timing of any change, although as Chancellor and his agent knew, there was little he could do if management made up its mind to replace him. Chancellor's power play had not derailed the Snyder locomotive, but it had certainly delayed its progress.

By early fall, however, Schlosser had a new plan: Brokaw and Snyder as co-anchors. Brokaw had been getting excellent notices as host of the "Today" show, and he would obviously provide an element of respectability and solidity to the combination. Schlosser had also been looking at the research on Brokaw, who showed considerably more strength than he had suspected. Schlosser took the co-anchor proposal to Wald, but again, Wald demurred. According to one party close to the situation, Wald said he would only do it on condition that Schlosser order him to, a circumstance that would enable Wald to tell John Chancellor and David Brinkley the plan wasn't *his* idea. Whatever transpired in that conversation, the result was the same; no action was taken.

Wald's ability to act as roadblock was diminishing, however, because his own position was becoming dangerously eroded. Not only had he thwarted Schlosser on Snyder, but he had also criticized his boss for deals Schlosser made with former President Gerald Ford and former Secretary of State Henry Kissinger. Schlosser, who liked to hobnob with important people, personally negotiated the special deals himself, promising Kissinger $1.5 million for a five-year "consultancy." Ford and his wife Betty were reportedly paid an equal amount "to take part in newscasts and documentaries." In the process, Schlosser agreed NBC would not question Ford on the most crucial act of his presidency: the pardoning of Richard Nixon. As far as Wald was concerned, they were bad deals. In essence, he told Schlosser, "Okay, now you've got Jerry Ford. What are you going to do with him?"

In October 1977, Schlosser fired Wald, replacing him with Les Crystal, a long-time NBC News producer, and the way now appeared clear to go ahead with the Brokaw-Snyder plan. The only task remaining was to find a replacement for Brokaw on the "Today" show. Accordingly, executives and producers hurled themselves into meeting after meeting to decide on a successor — a decision not easily arrived at.

The choice of host was critical because ABC's "Good Morning America" had begun giving "Today" a run for its money, the first serious challenge to the venerable program in twenty-five years. Both Alan Alda and Phil Donahue were approached for the "Today" job; neither was interested, so the meetings at NBC continued.

Schlosser's plan for putting Snyder on the Nightly News was also running into resistance from above. Julian Goodman, then chairman of the board of NBC, opposed Snyder. "Schlosser used to think by putting Snyder on it would improve the ratings," Goodman says. "But ratings aren't the only standard. You have to maintain the objective cast to your news that you have worked so many years to maintain. You can't put on Paul Newman and Robert Redford to do the news, for example. They would get the ratings, all right, but you would lose your trust factor. Basically, the main reason to keep Chancellor was that he had built up the kind of trust Cronkite had by virtue of his having been there so long and showing the audience that he was reliable and believable. Tom Snyder, as good a record as he had in California and in the New York local station, had become a split personality. He was a little dichotomous when it came to show business and the news business. I know that Tom blames me for casting the negative vote against him, but the truth of the matter is I voted to keep Chancellor.'' Snyder's agent, Ed Hookstratten, has a blunter assessment. ''Julian was afraid Tom would say 'shit' on the air.''

Others in the news division approached Schlosser and urged him not to make Snyder the anchor, warning that Snyder would wreck NBC News. Apparently, Schlosser himself began having second thoughts. ''The anchor must be credible to his own organization as well as to the public,'' he acknowledges. ''To get the support he needs, he must be perceived as a man of credibility, experience — a man who has earned the job. There must be a belief in his character and stability. It is not just his appearance, but his whole history in TV. After all, the anchor is called on in time of national crisis. It's an important job, requiring literate, experienced journalists. They have to be perceived as the best you have.''

While Schlosser was delaying, rumors about an impending anchor change at NBC kept circulating. Although no time for Chancellor's departure had been set, he was anxious to make it look as if it was *his* idea, to avoid giving the impression that he was being forced aside. As a realist, he had already begun to contemplate the next phase of his career, and he believed the role of commentator would be compatible with his talents and interests. In December 1977, Chancellor announced to the staff and selected members of the press that he planned to step down as anchor, at a time still not specified, and that he was looking forward to assuming the role of commentator.

The next month, however, he got a reprieve. Edgar Griffiths, the chairman of the board of RCA, stunned the broadcasting world with the announcement that Herb Schlosser was being replaced as president of the network by none other than Fred Silverman, the man who had spearheaded ABC's drive from number three to number one. The day of the announcement, RCA's stock jumped $1.25 a share and ABC's lost $1.75.

Silverman's contract with ABC was not up until June 1978, so NBC rocked along without much leadership for the next four and a half months. Meanwhile, everyone wondered about Silverman's opinion of Tom Snyder. The betting was that the two men would regard each other as soul brothers. Snyder had given up ''Newscenter 4'' by mid-1977 and moved back to California, but he had not given up on his desire to become the network anchorman. As he told Silverman, ''Fred, if NBC had come to you when you were at ABC and said, 'Listen, we want to hire you as a programming executive vice president at NBC,' you would have told them to go fuck themselves. He said, 'That's right.' I said, 'Because you wanted to be president.' He said, 'That's right.' I said, 'Fred, in my own area, I want to be president, too. I want to be the single most important on-air talent at National Broadcasting Company.' ''*

As it turned out, Silverman was leery of Snyder and fearful of what the critics would do to him if he replaced Chancellor with Snyder. He was also afraid of upsetting the NBC affiliates, many of whom would not be pleased by the switch. In the months before he assumed the presidency of NBC, he became obsessed with improving his own image and deeply upset over articles portraying him as the man "who was driving the quality of television down." As Sally Bedell recounts in her book, *Up the Tube: Prime Time in the Silverman Years*, Silverman himself started to wonder if the accusations being made against him didn't contain a kernel of truth: "With his critics uppermost in his mind, Silverman plotted his strategy for reviving NBC. He buried himself in every book he could find on television news and resolved to strike a statesmanlike profile befitting his new job."

Clearly, replacing John Chancellor with Tom Snyder did not come under the heading of statesmanship. One of Silverman's first acts after taking over as president was to announce at the annual affiliates meeting that Chancellor had been persuaded to stay on as anchor, at least for another year, dispelling the notion that Snyder would be his successor. The news was greeted with resounding applause. In essence, the affiliates were applauding the decision to retain the NBC Nightly News as a prestige vehicle.

Chancellor's fortunes got another boost when Richard Salant was recruited to become vice chairman of the board of NBC in charge of news. Salant had always admired Chancellor and felt that NBC owed him a debt of gratitude. He was in no way disposed to hurry Chancellor's departure as anchor.

The following year, David Brinkley was again removed from the NBC Nightly News, leaving Chancellor as sole proprietor of the program. He stopped talking about stepping down. The ratings for the Nightly News were worrisome, though. It was not just that the gap between Chancellor and Cronkite was widening; it was the sudden spurt by ABC. Quite unexpectedly, ABC News with Roone Arledge in charge was threatening NBC's secure lock on second place.

---

*Quoted in *Playboy*, February 1981.

8
The Arledge Experiment

I see it this way. If all three networks delivered the same news in the same way, it would get down to which anchorman the viewer liked best. That's a contest Walter Cronkite would win.

— Roone Arledge

IN THE WAKE of the Reasoner-Walters fiasco, ABC became fired with a new determination to make its news operation competitive with NBC and CBS. The weakness of ABC News was more than an insult to corporate pride or a drain on quarterly earnings. The also-ran status of ABC's news operation was hindering one of the company's most cherished long-range goals — the strengthening of its affiliate line-up.

By 1977, ABC had 190 affiliates, putting it close to CBS, which had 199, and NBC with 208. But the ABC chain included too many losers — stations only marginally profitable. To compensate, ABC recruiters were intent not only on signing up new, unaffiliated stations, but also were going after established CBS and NBC affiliates. ABC's strength in prime time made the courtship possible, but station owners were still wary of switching because of the network's poor image in news. And the well-publicized troubles with Reasoner and Walters did not help. As the owner of a CBS affiliate that finally switched to ABC said, "The most serious question, and one we kept coming back to, was why drop Walter Cronkite for Harry Reasoner and Barbara Walters?"

In May 1977, ABC moved to do something about its problem. First, the news division got a 25 percent increase in its budget. Second, it got a new president — ABC Sports chief Roone Arledge. The size of the budget increase made it clear ABC was serious. The naming of Arledge meant it was also ready to take the kind of risk corporations normally shrink from.

An executive who had become something of a legend in television production but who had scant experience in news, Arledge would almost certainly embark on a radical departure from the conventional forms of network news, even if it meant incurring the wrath of the critics. What remained to be seen was whether the changes would affect the integrity of the news.

Traditionally, presidents of network news divisions have come from the ranks of journalists. The one exception had been Richard Salant, who began his career as a corporate lawyer. And Arledge's field — sports — and the history of his career made him particularly suspect to the news fraternity. Arledge's genius had been showmanship. He had pioneered the use of slow motion, stop action, the instant replay — new techniques that gave the fans at home a better view than they could get from the stands. He had also packaged sports in inventive ways, creating such programs as "Wide World of Sports," "Monday Night Football," and "The American Sportsman." By the age of thirty-six, Arledge had made ABC *the* network for sports.

Recognized as a big spender, Arledge was also a sharp businessman who made millions of dollars for ABC through his wheeling and dealing. Marvin Josephson, who founded ICM, the largest talent agency in the world and a pretty good horse trader himself, recalls the coup that Arledge pulled off in the competition with NBC and CBS for the rights to televise the 1976 Olympics in Montreal. "Roone locked it up before anyone else could get to it. After a number of meetings with the Montreal Committee, he took them all out to dinner and convinced them if they didn't sign that night, he would leave town. The committee was on the verge of asking us to represent them in their negotiations with the networks, but by the time we got into it, we had to deal with *his* piece of paper, promising the committee would go with ABC. He knew they had been talking to us, and he wanted to beat us to the punch, and the other two networks as well. The other nets couldn't believe it; they were absolutely convinced something funny was going on. But it was just Roone being faster on his feet than anyone else."

The son of an attorney, Arledge grew up in an affluent household on Long Island. Already ambitious for glory as a student of business administration at Columbia University, he became president of his class, president of his fraternity, editor of the school yearbook, and a member of the wrestling team. After serving in the Army during the Korean War, Arledge decided on a career in television, honing his skills as a producer and director at NBC. He was twenty-nine when he joined ABC Sports as a field producer in 1960, the start of a career that was both brilliant and highly publicized. Certainly, viewers were never allowed to forget that it was Roone Arledge who was the executive producer of ABC Sports: Among other things, the fact was frequently mentioned on the air.

Yet for all his awards (including twenty-five Emmys and four Peabodys), the acclaim he won for ABC's spectacular Olympics coverage, and his indisputable originality, Arledge was never very popular with the critics. Some called him "the master of hype," deriding the trash sports he introduced to TV, like the contests between men carrying refrigerators on their backs. Others wrote that he was destroying viewers' ability to concentrate over long periods of time by conditioning them to a diet of exciting "highlights." The charge most often raised was that he, along with TV in general, was distorting the true nature of sports, that he was changing game times to fit TV's needs, adjusting time-outs to create commercial breaks, and turning sports heroes into millionaire entrepreneurs. He was also branded as the man who foisted the abrasive Howard Cosell on an unsuspecting football public.

Cosell was not chosen as a commentator on "Monday Night Football" to explain the game, as Arledge has freely admitted. "We knew there was a large segment of the audience that didn't care about football. So we had to come up with an idea that would grab them. Hence, the trio of announcers [Cosell, Don Meredith, and Frank Gifford] was born, plus such things as Don Meredith singing and the rest that goes on in the broadcast booth. We brought an entertainment element to the game," Arledge said in 1973.

The fear that Arledge would bring an "entertainment element" to news, hyping or perhaps even tampering with events themselves, led to a chorus of protests when his appointment was announced. A headline in the *New York Times* read, "ARLEDGE WILL HEAD ABC NEWS: Disclaims Theatrical Flourishes." *Time* magazine compared the appointment to the scenario in *Network,* Paddy Chayevsky's chilling 1976 film in which the head of a TV entertainment division assumes control over news, with devastating results. Arledge himself was kept busy denying that he planned to name Jim McKay or Howard Cosell as anchors on the Evening News.

Nowhere was the announcement greeted with more skepticism than within ABC News, where employees took great pride in their professionalism, if not in their ratings. Although they were intrigued by the prospect of a news chief with so much corporate clout, they were fearful of how he would use it. Only a handful of staffers had ever met Roone Arledge, and for many, the first glimpse that May of the redheaded, flamboyant sports guru was not particularly reassuring. The occasion was the famous "Montauk meeting," a two-day get-acquainted session at the yacht club on Montauk, Long Island, to which all the major correspondents, producers, and directors were invited. In order to keep the group manageable, the participants were rotated in and out, delivered by limousine, seaplane, and chartered aircraft. To people used to being treated as second-class citizens, it was quite a show. A little too much of a show, some thought.

Present for the entire weekend were Arledge and Fred Pierce, the president of the ABC Television Network. So were members of the "old" regime, including Bill Sheehan, the outgoing head of the news division, and all of his vice presidents. Their presence cast a slightly surreal pall over the meeting. "It was clear to everyone that they were all going to be axed," says one ABC correspondent. "If Arledge was going to give us a 'new beginning,' as they promised, all of the people responsible for the past failures would have to be swept out." Arledge and Pierce sought to strike an upbeat note, expressing confidence in everybody. Yet the mood remained tense and wary. One of the vice presidents kept doodling "bull" on a piece of scratch paper. The person sitting next to him would write out the word *shit*. Arledge, dressed in a polka-dotted sport shirt, open at the neck, and wearing a medallion, listened more than he talked, but everything he said was studied intently for clues to his philosophy of news. "We were all alert for nuances of funny farm," says Sam Donaldson, one of the senior correspondents in attendance.

One thing that triggered alarm was Arledge's evident admiration for Geraldo Rivera, the flashy, eyewitness-style reporter who was then working for ABC's entertainment division. "Is this where we're headed?" people wondered, and some of them began asking themselves if they would be able to work with Arledge. At one point, the entire room seemed to bristle when he suggested that the Evening News could use a kind of Washington gossip column. "It was the word *gossip* that got us," says Donaldson. "He actually meant something like *Newsweek*'s 'Periscope' — inside stuff that doesn't warrant a full-blown report by a correspondent — but he didn't know the correct terminology at the time. He does now, of course. Roone is a fast learner. But given everyone's apprehensions, the worst was naturally assumed. Some of us got up and made speeches about the integrity of the news, and so on, until it became clear what he meant, and people calmed down."

Adding to everyone's discomfort, of course, was the feeling that Arledge was taking *their* measure as well. And this feeling was not confined to the Montauk soiree. An atmosphere of mutual distrust would mark relations between Arledge and his new subordinates for some time.

But the question of employee morale, however important, was not the highest item on Arledge's agenda just then. His most immediate problem was what to do about the incompatible team of Barbara Walters and Harry Reasoner. Arledge's initial move was to buy time by making format changes designed to minimize their impact on the Evening News while he worked on a replacement formula. "Two-shots" were eliminated, meaning that Walters and Reasoner were not shown together on the screen, and something called a "whip-around" was introduced — correspondents handing off their reports directly to each other instead of going back to the anchor for introductions. Subanchors also began to appear: Frank Reynolds was featured prominently in Washington, as was Peter Jennings from various European capitals. One critic wrote that "the new mode at ABC News might appear to be entitled 'the disintegration of the anchor-person.'" In reality Arledge had no intention of weakening the anchor role, although he hoped to alter it.

In part, Arledge's vision of a new role for the anchor was prompted by a technological development that was about to revolutionize news coverage: the Mini-Cam. A portable tape camera, the Mini-Cam eliminated the need for time-consuming laboratory processing of film. The new camera also made it possible to transmit pictures directly from the field to the television screen with much greater ease. The new technology, Arledge declared, made it unnecessary to have a man sitting in a studio reading "regurgitated wire copy" when he could be out reporting from the scene. In a presentation to the ABC affiliates in May 1977, he said, "I think the old concept of the anchor position is outdated and outmoded, and it can be changed. This doesn't mean we are going to eliminate anchor people, and it doesn't mean people are going to tune away from Walter Cronkite right away, because he's the best there is . . . But we can offer an alternative, and I think we will. I think we will offer more coverage and better coverage, and more lively and more interesting coverage."

In a sense, Arledge wanted to make presentation, rather than the anchor, the star of the show. It was one way to offer something different from the competition, and it was a solution that would relieve him from having to attract a new, big-name anchor, something he couldn't guarantee in any case. By focusing on production — his forte — he was choosing an approach he could most easily control. As an extra bonus, if it succeeded, *he* would get the credit. Still, the unrestrained way in which Arledge pursued first Dan Rather and then Tom Brokaw makes it clear he never doubted the value of a certifiable star in the anchor slot. Getting a star anchor into the field would increase the anchor's importance — not diminish it — because of the heightened immediacy and drama of the settings.

Perhaps more important than what he ultimately did to the format, Arledge sought to shift the sights of ABC's news program — targeting another segment of the population. He made it clear from the start that he was going after a different audience — young people and blacks, for instance, and others who don't watch much network news. In spite of the often-quoted statistic that almost two thirds of the American public gets most of its news from television, a number of studies show that the average person pays little attention to the network evening newscasts. According to some studies, only one American in 50 watches network news every night, and only one in 100 gives these programs "full attention." To attract the non–news junkie, Arledge believed, the news had to become easier to understand and more broadly appealing.

Although the primary motivation behind his approach was certainly commercial, i.e., a desire for higher ratings, some serious students of network news agreed with Arledge's approach. In a 1979 article for the *Washington Monthly* entitled "Not the *New York Times*: What Network News Should Be," political scientist James David Barber wrote, "The trouble with television news is that it is too good, too intellectual, too balanced. It passes right over the heads of the great 'lower half' of the American electorate who need it most." Surveying the CBS Evening News on May 16, 1979, Barber compiled a list of thirty-one words and expressions he guessed would turn off the less well-educated (and therefore average) viewer: allocation formula, collusion, improprieties, consumption levels, political conspiracy, political ironies, alleviating, surcharges, most-favored-nation trade status, trade credits, tariff concessions, strategic arms, cold shutdown, performed an analysis, wage-price guidelines, assets, dividends, capital gains, honoraria, Republican conference leader, cottage industry, secluded, confiscate, legalize, pork-barrel legislation, all deliberate speed, long-range facility plan, racially imbalanced, litigation, enrollment, and vanguard.

"There is no way that vocabulary can catch and hold the average high school graduate who happens to tune in on his way to 'The Jeffersons,'" Barber wrote. "In addition to the strange language, he is asked to take an interest in events far away, largely among the rich and powerful who are foreigners to him. There is little (though some) attempt to connect the news to his concerns and values and images, to begin or end where he is. He is asked to take it on faith that somehow, someday, he will be glad that he got the message. Educationally, that rarely works. To avoid intellectual strain, all he has to do is switch off; Roger Mudd will never know."

While most of the old hands at ABC realized the value of trying to make the news more accessible and more relevant to viewers' lives, they took a dim view of Arledge's early attempts at popularizing the Evening News. In particular, they were appalled at his handling of the capture of David Berkowitz, the suspect in New York's "Son of Sam" killings; it was an incident that seemed to confirm everyone's worst suspicions.

At 3:00 A.M. on August 10, 1977, a few hours after Berkowitz's arrest, Arledge himself went down to police headquarters in Manhattan, dressed, according to the *Los Angeles Times,* "as if for a touch football game, a glass of scotch in one hand, a portable two-way radio in the other, directing his network's 'feeds to the Coast.'" That night, nineteen and one-half minutes out of the twenty-two-minute evening newscast were devoted to "Son of Sam," featuring Geraldo Rivera, wearing jeans and a T-shirt, as a subanchor. Giving an emotional performance, Rivera dispensed with the legal niceties, such as "alleged" and "confessed," and called the not-yet-convicted Berkowitz a "fiend" and a "murderer." Rivera's theatrics and the lurid nature of the program in general so offended a number of producers and correspondents in the Washington bureau that they wrote to Arledge to protest. "It was a very diplomatically worded letter," maintains one of the signers. "Geraldo's name wasn't even mentioned. We told him that we were concerned by the tone and content of some of the coverage and that we were worried that some of the traditional means of protecting people's rights were not present."

Arledge, who already knew and resented the fact that feeling against him ran highest in the Washington bureau, was infuriated by the letter, particularly after parts of it were leaked to a television columnist. Those who wrote the letter insist that none of them leaked it, that it had *not* been their intention to embarrass Arledge. As one of the drafters explained, "We were all together in one room, almost like conspirators, agonizing over every nuance. We didn't even make a copy of the letter because we didn't want the contents to become public. After we wrote it, we sealed it up in an envelope and sent it.'' When an account of the letter appeared in Frank Swertlow's TV column in the *Chicago Daily News*, the signers concluded that it had been leaked by somebody at ABC News in New York who didn't like Arledge, a deduction that left a large number of suspects.

In spite of the uproar over "Son of Sam," Arledge was beginning to win points for his willingness to spend money to cover the news and to break into regular programming with bulletins and specials. As he knew, when an important event occurs, people tend to flip the dial, searching for information. If they turned to ABC and liked what they saw, they might be disposed to come back on a regular basis. So he set about making ABC *the* network to watch when a big story broke. It was the same strategy Robert Kintner had employed successfully twenty years earlier at NBC. When a U.S. helicopter crew was shot down in Korea in July 1977, ABC interrupted its regular programming with a total of ten bulletins. A news special on the blackout in New York that summer actually aired in prime time. Under Arledge, ABC News could no longer be accused of being ''the last with the least.'' Correspondents were pushed to develop exclusive stories, to anticipate developments rather than react to planned events, and above all, to beat the competition. As a demonstration that he meant business, Arledge fired the correspondent in Johannesburg for doing a sluggish job on the story of Stephen Biko, the South African black leader who died in prison under mysterious circumstances.

Assessing the ABC Evening News a year after Arledge took the reins, a *Wall Street Journal* writer found the program had improved, even if it didn't always please journalistic purists, adding, ''Its correspondents are showing new aggressiveness and enterprise, and the program is livelier and more informative than in the past. Except for a few notable lapses, it bears little resemblance to the 'National Enquirer of the Air' that some had predicted.''

Arledge still made good copy, though, with his safari jackets, his foot-long cigars, and his chauffeur-driven silver-colored Jaguar. And he continued to invite criticism with some of his other programming efforts. Chief among these was ''20/20,'' with which he seemed to be exploring the limits of how far he could go to attract an audience and still label a program ''news.'' The premier of ''20/20'' was a disaster — a grab bag of interviews, sensational reports, including one by Geraldo Rivera on the maiming of jackrabbits and a less-than-convincing piece on nuclear terrorism, and assorted silly gimmicks, such as an animated segment featuring a Jimmy Carter doll singing "Georgia." Unanimously, the critics declared the program an abomination; John J. O'Connor of the *New York Times* called it "dizzyingly absurd." The following week, a new host, Hugh Downs, was brought in to replace the team of Harold Hayes and Robert Hughes, and the gimmicky features were eliminated. The program retained its tabloid flavor, however, and its correspondents continued to resort on occasion to shoddy journalistic practices.

Unhappy members of the old guard also continued to cause Arledge problems, sometimes by leaking damaging stories to the press and sometimes by attacking him publicly, as Howard K. Smith did when he gave a speech comparing the multiple anchor format to a "Punch and Judy" show.

Arledge was deeply wounded by the criticism. He felt misunderstood by the press and by his subordinates. For every critical poke taken at him as president of ABC Sports, he had received a barrel of commendations, awards, and articles praising his creativity and ingenuity. "One of the things that surprised me about some of the vehemence of the press when I took this job," Arledge says, "is that I thought I had a fairly good — maybe even distinguished — record in sports. We had set the standards for things, fought all the battles [against the owners] for control of our own product, for bringing some integrity to sports reporting. Years ago, sports was awful. Newspapers were worse than television; we were expected to be the cheerleaders, period. In addition, I had a number of personal offers, all of which would have made me very, very rich. One was at NBC — it was a combination of packaging sports and other entertainment programs. There were other offers, too. Marvin Josephson wanted to represent me personally. He said, 'I can make you millions of dollars.' But I gave it all up to do the toughest job around, a job everyone said was impossible. Anytime you buy something exclusively, as you do in sports or entertainment, you can turn things around, if you buy the right things. If you have 'Dallas,' then everyone who wants to see 'Dallas' has to watch CBS. But in news, you more or less have the same thing on all three networks, which makes building much harder. And building from the bottom, like we were at ABC, makes it a real bitch. What I've never been able to understand was, given the opportunities I had, and given the fact that I had a certain degree of recognition in the industry for excellence, why people would think I would want to take a job like this and do a schlock job or lower the standards."

At heart, Arledge was burning to be taken seriously, to be regarded as someone doing well at a job that *mattered.* Of all the Emmys he won as head of ABC Sports, the only one listed on his official biography was the one awarded for his handling of the terrorist attack on the Israeli compound at the 1972 Olympics in Munich — an award in the category of news and public affairs. ''We could put on a program tomorrow, a pop news program that would beat the other two,'' he says. ''If we hired Alan Alda and Gregory Peck, did celebrity interviews and so on, we could wipe out the competition. But you want to excel at things you consider important. I would much prefer to excel in news than come up with a successful sitcom series.''

Much as he desires legitimacy, Arledge is above all a man who wants to win. And initially he thought that could not be done with the crew he inherited at ABC News. He thought the staff shared a third-place mentality, and he believed most of them would never accept his leadership. So he concentrated on wooing staff people from the outside, not only because ABC needed to expand, but because the new employees would owe primary loyalty to him. Within a year, almost all of the members of the old executive cadre were either forced out or shunted aside, replaced by some tough customers, including David Burke, a former aide to Senator Edward Kennedy who was made chief of staff, and Dick Wald, the ex-president of NBC News, who also happened to have been a college classmate of Arledge's at Columbia. Av Westin, who had been fired in a power struggle with Bill Sheehan in 1975, was brought back and made part of the inner circle, too.

Spending freely, and upping the salary levels for the entire industry, Arledge set about hiring as many ''names'' as he could, landing such early prizes as NBC News correspondent Cassie Mackin and Sander Vanocur, who in times past was one of the biggest luminaries at NBC. Arledge's real sights, however, were set on CBS. David Burke, the chief recruiter, remembers how rough it was in the beginning. ''At first we went after all sorts of people. They would listen politely, but the response was 'no way.' Once you worked for CBS, you might consider going to NBC, but you never went to ABC. It was like a sign your career was over, a stigmata. Imagine our difficulties talking to someone like Fred Graham or one of the top producers in the business.

''I felt that, rather than go for anchors, we should go for the praetorian guard, the pillars — the reporters and producers. Our job, really, was to build an organization. We could hire an anchor, but he would be unhappy. The staff wouldn't measure up to what he was used to. There were a lot of good people here, but they didn't have the kind of support they needed from management and the corporation to show all their talents.''

Gradually, however, the job of recruitment became easier. "As time went by, there were come changes. One, there were a lot of unhappy people at CBS, plus the company was not very watchful. Their contracts weren't airtight. The other thing that happened was that we were doing a better job. The sign that we finally made it was the hiring of Rick Kaplan and John Armstrong [two young CBS producers] and Barry Serafin [a CBS News correspondent]. It was a signal that to come to work at ABC was allowable.''

Others from CBS migrated to ABC, including nearly a dozen directors and producers, and such highly regarded correspondents as John Lawrence, Sylvia Chase, Hal Walker, and a bit later, Hughes Rudd and Richard Threlkeld. At first, the newcomers were Arledge's darlings, getting lavish attention from him and the choice air assignments. ABC's veterans watched resentfully as they were frozen out, treated like expendable commodities. A few months after Arledge arrived, Ted Koppel, then anchor of the Saturday Evening News, returned from vacation to find that, in his absence, his regular producer had been taken off the program. Arledge, who wanted the weekend news as a showcase for one of his new acquisitions, had not even bothered to notify Koppel of the change. At that point, Koppel realized that he was being forced off the program, and he admits he was crushed. "It was my show,'' he says. "I had editorial input, and when you and your executive producer get along well, it's magic. You have access to millions of people who see *your* perception of how the news should be presented. As an anchor, you have what every politician, every business leader, every religious leader, every charitable organization wants: the opportunity to reach their fellow citizens.'' Koppel tried to contact Arledge several times, but when his calls weren't returned, he decided to hand in his resignation. Ultimately, Arledge talked him out of quitting, but almost two years passed before the breach between the two men was fully healed.

The old guard found Arledge's *modus operandi* puzzling, almost sinister. For one thing, the staff seldom saw him. If he was pleased with their contribution to a program, he let them know by telephone or telex. If he was displeased, he generally dispatched one of his deputies with the bad tidings. It was Dick Wald, for example, who had the unpleasant duty of flying to Washington to inform Howard K. Smith that his regular commentaries were being discontinued, a move that so enraged Smith he resigned.

Arledge's most maddening habit, and one that reached almost epic proportions, was his failure to return telephone calls. He was also notorious for breaking appointments or keeping people waiting for hours. He seemed to enjoy playing Peck's bad boy, keeping even top members of the corporation in suspense about his attendance at board meetings. Arledge is so elusive that when he was named president of ABC News, while retaining the title of president of ABC Sports, a publicity agent cracked, "Now he has two offices where he can't be found." He keeps odd hours, too, often not coming into the office until 5:00 P.M., then staying until midnight or later. ("He's like Dracula," jokes one admirer. "He only comes out at night.")

Sometimes, Arledge's failure to return telephone calls could be seen as a deliberate tactic to get rid of somebody. Marlene Sanders, who was vice president in charge of documentaries when Arledge arrived, kept a log of dozens of attempts to reach Arledge in the year before she left. After their initial meeting in Montauk, Sanders saw Arledge only twice, once to accept her resignation. "I would try to consult him about programs," she says, "or inform him when things were ready to screen. He never returned my calls." After months of being ignored, she went to ABC president Fred Pierce, who promised to remedy the situation. Sanders recalls that she heard from Arledge's secretary just before Labor Day weekend. "I had given everyone Thursday afternoon and Friday off. On Thursday, Arledge's secretary called and asked me if I was free that day. I said I was, and I hung up and waited. I never heard anything. I finally left for the weekend around noon on Friday. Later that afternoon, he called. When I got back to the office the next week, there was a memo from him saying, 'Communications work both ways. I called to see you today.' After that, I began to step up my efforts to leave ABC."

A master manipulator, Arledge plays the bureaucratic game with the same zeal he brings to everything else he does. At one point, when rumors were circulating that Arledge would be named president of ABC, he told a friend that he had absolutely no interest in the job, but he didn't mind if the story got around. "It doesn't hurt if the people you have to go to to ask for this or that think they might end up working for you one day," Arledge said.

Without even being physically present, Arledge managed to dominate ABC News completely. "He's like De Gaulle," says Hughes Rudd. "The invisible boss can be much more intimidating than the one standing over your shoulder. Roone understands that." His staff never knew what hour of the night or day Arledge might decide to call, but they knew he was never very far from his TV set; he watched *everything*. "I don't know when he sleeps," says Dorrance Smith, a news producer who started out in the ABC sports department as an assistant to Arledge. "He never takes a day off. The pressure is always on."

For all of his odd habits and Machievellian ways, Arledge is an able leader, adroit at motivating people; praise from him is considered high praise indeed. "He radiates energy and intensity like a powerful sun," says ABC correspondent Brit Hume. "When it's shining on you, you're warm. When it's not, you're in a meat locker."

Remarkably seductive in person, Arledge has a pleasant, soft-spoken manner, a golly-gee-whiz air that most people find disarming. An indefatigable conversationalist, he thinks nothing of extending a lunch or an interview session into a five- or six-hour nonstop talkathon. "The very things that make him so charming are precisely the characteristics that make him so frustrating," Ted Koppel says. "While you are with him, there are no interruptions. Margaret Thatcher could be on the phone, or Muhammad Ali. But he makes you feel that there is nothing more interesting or more captivating than answering your questions or listening to what you have to say. If you are on the outside, trying to get through, it's frustrating as hell. Once you are there, however, you are enveloped by his total interest, attention, and affection."

Arledge is never more charming than when he is out to make a new conquest. He seems to know the exact spot where most people like their egos to be stroked. Something of a celebrity hound, he is able to indulge his fascination for famous people as president of ABC News, inviting Henry Kissinger to watch a boxing match on closed circuit TV, hiring notables like George Will, Ben Bradlee, or Jody Powell as "contributing analysts." He seems to have a special fixation on the Kennedy family. Some of his early hires were people who either worked for one of the brothers or who had been close to them, including David Burke, who used to work for Senator Edward Kennedy, Pierre Salinger, John F. Kennedy's press secretary, and Sander Vanocur, a long-time Kennedy family friend.

If Arledge develops crushes on people, he is also capable of losing interest in them. Many of his prize acquisitions, including Serafin, Mackin, Vanocur, and former *Washington Post* reporter Carl Bernstein, found themselves playing less prominent roles than originally envisioned. "Roone collects scalps," says one Arledge-watcher. "He likes to put his scalps on a shelf and admire them. He may not use them very much, but once he has them, nobody else can get them. All of us correspondents have to put on the black negligee once in a while and parade in front of him saying, 'Hey, Roone, remember me?'"

In spite of the furious pace of new hires, Arledge was unable to attract any nationally known star-quality journalists to round out his anchor team. For several months, he negotiated with Robert MacNeil, one half of Public Television's prestigious "MacNeil-Lehrer Report," about anchoring the Evening News from New York. But MacNeil was unable to get a guarantee of the same kind of editorial control he enjoyed at PBS. "It's true that I wasn't making the kind of money you make on commercial television," he says, "but it was my feeling that Jim [Lehrer] and I had created such an ideal situation, and we had such a congenial working environment, that it was going to take a hell of a charge of dynamite to get me out of my present job." Talks dragged on even longer with Bill Moyers, another star of Public Television, who eventually decided to go to CBS instead. As a result of these and other failures, when Arledge finally unveiled his plans for the Evening News in the spring of 1978, the format had considerably more novelty than the cast. Avoiding the word *anchor*, Arledge explained there would be three principal desks, one in Washington for "national" news, one in London for "foreign" news, and one in Chicago for "domestic" news. "We want our news people as close to their stories as possible," Arledge said at a lavish news conference at Manhattan's "21" Club, "so that our viewers will benefit from a greater sense of immediacy." Two of the three principal personalities, Frank Reynolds and Peter Jennings, had anchored for ABC before. Only Max Robinson, a Washington, D.C., newscaster who became the first black to anchor any network's premier newscast, was new to ABC.

Robinson did not have the kind of credentials that have come to be expected of network anchors — all of his experience was in local news, most of it sitting behind an anchor desk — but he was a handsome, articulate man with great presence on the air and a huge following in Washington. He was so popular there that the day before he left to go to Chicago for ABC was declared "Max Robinson Day" by the D.C. City Council. Arledge had had his eye on Robinson almost from the start, and the research conducted for ABC by Frank Magid Associates confirmed his audience appeal. When the researchers played tapes of Robinson to selected groups in Philadelphia and Grand Rapids, Iowa, they found reaction to him to be "consistently and strongly positive." According to the report, "He was praised for being very easy to understand and follow, dynamic in his speech, and comfortable to watch. Furthermore, many said Robinson appears to be honest, very personable, and that he definitely has network anchor potential. There were very few substantive negative reactions to Max Robinson."

Although TV news executives like Arledge consult available research before making decisions, they do not necessarily follow the advice they are given. Virtually every consultant advises against heavy emphasis on foreign news, for example, but ABC News under Arledge plays foreign stories more prominently than any other broadcast news outlet. Nor was Robinson hired solely on the basis of a positive recommendation from Frank Magid. Before a decision was reached, the ABC bureau in Washington recorded Robinson's newscasts on WTOP, the CBS affiliate, for several weeks and shipped the tapes to Arledge and other executives in New York. They liked what they saw. They were also aware that attitudes were changing quickly and audiences were growing less resistant to black newscasters. As recently as 1970, viewers in Washington, a city with a black majority, had threatened to boycott WRC, the NBC-owned station, for taking a white man off the air and replacing him with a black. As the 1970s progressed, however, black reporters and anchors had gotten a foothold in the nearly all-white world of television news, but they were advancing faster at the local level. In part, this was true because local stations, which are licensed by the government, were forced to pay more attention than networks to federal affirmative action requirements. In addition, station executives in cities with large black populations discovered that putting blacks on the air could improve ratings.

At the network level, after a flurry to recruit and train blacks for on-air positions in the late 1960s and early 1970s, momentum had slowed. Even those minorities on staff were seldom prominently featured. During five randomly selected days in 1977, the U.S. Commission on Civil Rights found that of all correspondents appearing on the three network evening newscasts, 82 percent were white males, while minority males accounted for 8 percent of the appearances, and minority females did not appear at all. (White females accounted for the remaining 10 percent.) The only black anchoring at the network level in 1978 when Robinson was tapped was Ed Bradley, who had been appearing on the CBS Sunday Evening

News since 1976. (That same year, Bradley, a tough, seasoned correspondent, was voted the best electronic journalist covering Jimmy Carter's election campaign by fellow campaign reporters and Carter campaign staffers.)

By recruiting Max Robinson and giving him such high visibility five nights a week, Arledge was clearly hoping to attract more black viewers, perhaps even creating a new audience from among that sizable number of blacks who seldom watch network newscasts. As an economically depressed group, blacks might not be a prime target for advertisers, but black viewers could nonetheless help lift overall ratings. Besides, ABC officials reasoned, as long as Robinson was sandwiched between two whites, he was unlikely to turn away many white viewers. (At the local level, management is so concerned about the potentially "threatening" effect of black males on white audiences that they seldom assign a black man to anchor any of the station's major newscasts alone. The preferred combination is either two men — one white and one black — or a white male and a black female.)

Another old face on the new team was Barbara Walters, who was to report from a "special coverage" desk in New York, meaning that she would appear from time to time with big-name interviewees or would handle reporting assignments. This was, in effect, a device to ease her off the news program without making it look as if she was being dumped. Arledge had reason to try to spare Walters's feelings. A personal friend, she had been one of the few people to support him when he arrived, sympathizing with him and his troubles with the press. "Now you know what I went through," she told him. He had another reason to be grateful to her: Under the terms of her contract, she was entitled to remain on the air as co-anchor. "To her everlasting credit, she was very, very nice about not enforcing [the contract]," Arledge says. "She could have done anything she wanted. One of the reasons I used the term *desks,* in fact, was that Barbara's contract said she was entitled to be an anchor or a co-anchor, so we didn't have *any* anchors."

The one name conspicuously absent from the new line-up was Harry Reasoner's. He was already fed up with ABC by the time Arledge was named president of the news division. At their first meeting, Reasoner announced that he intended to return to CBS, citing the escape clause promised to him by Bill Sheehan. According to the understanding they reached, Reasoner was free to leave ABC in June 1978, two years before his contract expired, if he was still dissatisfied with the Walters co-anchor arrangement. Initially, Arledge did not want to lose him; he needed every star he could get, and he saw no reason to let CBS have one of the biggest plums in broadcasting. Yet he could not let Reasoner continue to anchor. "That way it would look like it was Barbara who was the failure," Arledge says, adding, "Contractually, I couldn't have done it, even if I had wanted to."

Arledge tried to interest Reasoner in a magazine show, but to no avail; Reasoner was determined to leave. For a time, Arledge refused, maintaining that Reasoner had forfeited his early out since he hadn't made a good faith effort to work with Walters. But Reasoner held the trump card; if he wasn't allowed to leave, he vowed he wouldn't show up for work. He said he didn't care if they paid him or not. That, and the prospect of his bad-mouthing the new management to every television critic in America, finally induced Arledge to give in. One of the terms of the agreement was that Reasoner was not to speak ill of his former employers to the press.

Reasoner, who had expected to take over as host of "CBS Reports," found when he returned to CBS that "60 Minutes" was preparing to add a fourth member to the team. According to Richard Salant, who was president of CBS News at the time, the new addition was supposed to be Ed Bradley, but when "60 Minutes" producer Don Hewitt heard that Reasoner was available, he wanted him back. "I gave in," says Salant, "but I always regretted it." Bradley would not get his chance to be part of "60 Minutes" until 1981, when Dan Rather left to anchor the Evening News.

When ABC's new broadcast, retitled the "World News Tonight," made its debut that summer, it was panned by most of the critics. They complained that the triple anchor arrangement was both confusing and hokey. Tom Shales, the *Washington Post* critic, wrote of the premier, "Within the first ten minutes there were at least seven shifts of location. Early in the newscast, Reynolds threw the ball to Jennings in London just so that Jennings could briefly introduce a report from Moscow. Then it was back to Washington, and time for a commercial. It should perhaps have been a commercial for Dramamine, but it wasn't." Critics also panned the look of the broadcast itself, finding it "junky" and crammed with too many gimmicky effects.

Although the techniques Arledge introduced were probably overused in the beginning, he did at least succeed in making ABC's presentation *look* different from other newscasts. A machine called a Chyron 4 generated charts, graphs, and symbols in dozens of shapes and colors, eliminating

the need for laboriously hand-painted artwork. Something called a QUAN-
TEL could suck the images in, widen them out, or move them around the
screen. Using the latest video technology, it became possible to illustrate
almost anything in a correspondent's script, eliminating the need for those
forty-five-second standuppers in front of the Treasury Department or the
Pentagon.

Arledge has always been interested in finding ways to allow the viewer
to "see" more. With "Monday Night Football," he realized that the guy
watching in a bar probably couldn't hear much, so Arledge started
plastering the screen with graphics telling the score, identifying the
players, and so on. "Roone plays the viewer very well," says producer
Dorrance Smith. "Say I have the Israeli defense minister being interviewed on the Sunday show. Roone will call me in the control room and
say, 'People don't recognize this guy. Make sure you keep matting
[visually identifying] him.' As far as he is concerned, you can't use too
many graphics."

In addition to the new graphic look, the whole pace of the broadcast was
speeded up. People were even encouraged to speak faster on the theory
that TV had conditioned viewers to absorb information faster.

While the changes Arledge introduced — the new graphic look in
particular — were mostly cosmetic, they were initially viewed by the
other networks and the TV critics as an intrusion into the almost sacred
character of television news. In fact, TV news production was behind the
times in terms of new equipment and new ways of doing things on
television, and it was only a matter of time before someone broke the
mold. The fact that the person who initiated the changes was Roone
Arledge undoubtedly made them more controversial than they needed to
be. Within a couple of years, everybody would be using the new visual
techniques, scarcely giving them a second thought. Furthermore, electronic graphics made it possible for television news to tackle certain
nonvisual subjects, such as economics, which had received short shrift in
the past. A producer or correspondent could now contemplate doing a
detailed report on interest rates or the money supply because the subject
could now be illustrated in a meaningful way.

More important than the cosmetic changes was the question of editorial
integrity — the overall fairness, accuracy, and balance of the stories
reported. Although Arledge got off to a rocky start, as exemplified by the
"Son of Sam" incident, he quickly made it clear that he recognized the

need to preserve the honesty and legitimacy of the Evening News. Once the old-timers working on the program realized this, the bad feeling many of them harbored toward him began to recede.

The triple anchor arrangement was more problematical. Inevitably, the arrangement distorted editorial decisions. The reason was simple. Most days, the news simply does not divide itself into three neat, equal bundles labeled "foreign," "domestic," and "Washington"; yet each anchor is supposed to get his "fair share." On nights when there is not much in the way of major stories from abroad, for example, Jennings may string together a series of brief film clips, reading one or two lines over pictures of minor events, such as the opening of the Bulgarian parliament. "It's true that more foreign news gets on under this arrangement," concedes one producer. "A major anchor presence is by definition an advocate for his own beat." But the result of the arrangement is that what gets precious airtime is not always what is most important on a given day.

At the outset, Arledge had intended all three anchors to be "equal": Whoever had the lead story on a particular day would open the program. But the arrangement didn't work because viewers seem to like to know who is in charge on a news program. Before long, Reynolds was made "more equal" than the others, as Arledge put it, opening and closing the program and introducing the other anchors. Reynolds was picked by Arledge for the same reason he had been chosen in 1968; of all the people working for ABC, he had the best combination of experience, credibility, and camera savvy. But there was no love lost between the two men. For one thing, Arledge regarded Reynolds as part of the diehard faction at ABC, one of those who mistrusted him. For another, he thought Reynolds came across as stern and pompous on the air.

For his part, Reynolds did not enjoy reading that his new boss thought ABC had no stars, a line Arledge often repeated to interviewers to explain the triple anchor arrangement. "I can't say I'm pleased to have read so many times over the past years that the reason we had to go to three anchors is that we didn't have anybody who could carry the thing by himself," Reynolds notes with an air of justifiable bitterness. "The rather strong implication is that we're not of comparable stature, and I disagree. I don't think it's necessarily a wise public relations gambit on the part of the network, if that's what it was. I think it was a putdown, frankly, of me, and I didn't like it. I don't want to be blowing my own horn, but I didn't come into this thing simply because of the way I part my hair or wear my suits. I spent years reporting, out on the campaigns and around the world. I have some knowledge of the news business. Nobody likes to be downgraded.''

For several years, Reynolds was forced to endure many such slights, some small, some large. In newspaper ads featuring the ABC News team, his face was seldom very prominent; sometimes it could barely be seen. And the fact that his job was shopped around so openly did little to make him feel appreciated. Arledge undercut him with producers by constantly making critical remarks about him — the way he didn't smile enough or the fact that he wore the wrong clothes for TV. It used to drive Arledge into a fury when Reynolds showed up night after night in light-colored suits, which, because of his white hair and general pallor, made him look washed out on TV. Arledge finally had ABC buy Reynolds some dark suits, but Reynolds would show up from time to time in his light suits, anyway. Some people thought it was Reynolds's way of saying, ''Up yours, Roone.''

Arledge maintains such matters as the color of one's suits *are* important. ''One of the things I've said is that if you're going to be an anchor, a lot of it has nothing to do with news altogether — your hair, how you dress, how you look. It's a shame, but if you're going to be in TV, that's the way it is. You have to take into consideration everything that's in the mix. People have certain expectations about how an anchor should conduct himself, and how he should look. Edward R. Murrow used to take guys to London tailors.''

But Reynolds was not a man to be intimidated. Soon after Dick Wald joined ABC News, he went down to Washington to meet the staff and made what Reynolds thought were condescending remarks about ABC News. The more Reynolds listened, the madder he got. Finally Reynolds rose to say that he and his colleagues had no apology for their work, and if Wald thought he was coming in as some kind of savior, he could forget it. ''Frank is a kind of James Cagney character,'' says Sander Vanocur. ''He's a tough little Irish Catholic mick. The important thing is that he comes out of the Chicago school of journalism, which gives you a certain attitude. It means you have paid your dues in one of the toughest journalistic towns in the world and you don't have to take any shit from anybody.''

Within ABC, two ''camps'' developed around Reynolds. The younger producers, who modeled themselves after Arledge — his mod squad — made fun of Reynolds's manner, which they found self-important, calling him ''the little king'' behind his back. To others, however, especially the older correspondents and producers, Reynolds was revered as one of the elder statesmen of the business — a position very much like that occupied by John Chancellor at NBC. "Frank is wonderful," says Brit Hume, ABC's Capitol Hill correspondent. "He is a jewel, a prince, the ideal Washington anchor. When I call on the briefing line, he gets on the telephone with the producers, and if I'm on to something hot, he relishes it. The guy is just so knowledgeable, it's a tremendous asset to have him there. He appreciates the quality of what we do. Sometimes you can see it on his face on the air when we've done something especially good. The correspondents get a lot of encouragement from him."

A strict Catholic and a highly moral man, Reynolds tends to see things in black and white. He is also prudish by newsroom standards, objecting to off-color language and dirty jokes. He has even asked that the soap operas be turned off in the newsroom "because all you see is people climbing into bed with each other." Reynolds is also a confirmed family man and the father of five boys. He spends most of his free time at home with Henrietta, his wife of thirty-five years. They are not great party-givers or party-goers. His one bow to conviviality is the open house he holds each night in his office when the program is over. But after one drink, he closes the bar and heads for the suburbs.

Although his deep religiosity and his height (five feet six) do not quite fit the pattern, Reynolds, like most network anchors, is a self-made man from the heartland of America. The only son (he has three sisters) of a midlevel steel industry executive, Reynolds was born in East Chicago, Indiana, in 1923. He attended Wabash College for a year but dropped out to go off and fight in World War II.

A man of strong views, Reynolds occasionally lets his opinions slip through on the air. For example, it wasn't difficult to detect what he thought about John Ehrlichman, President Nixon's domestic affairs assistant, when he said in a stern voice one night, "Ehrlichman, a convicted Watergate felon . . ." He also has a habit of tapping his fingers with annoyance at the conclusion of a report that offends him in some way. Reynolds makes no apology for the fact that he sometimes lets his true feelings show. "I'm not made of ice," he says. But to some colleagues he's a ham, trying to exercise a dramatic talent that he doesn't have.

In general, though, Reynolds belongs to the give-it-to-them-straight school and takes great pains to make sure stories are accurate and fair. "He really cares very much about the program," says one correspondent. "He cares almost too much. He really thinks he has messages for the country. I have heard him say many times, 'What are we going to say to the country about this?'"

Under the ABC system, final authority for decisions on the "World News Tonight" rests with the executive producer in New York, but Reynolds is still an influential voice in the mix. Like Chancellor, he arrives early and stays out in the newsroom most of the day, keeping up with the flow of news; he too prepares most of his own copy and is considered an excellent writer. He functions, in essence, like the Washington editor of the program, conferring throughout the day with reporters, pressing the producers in New York for more time for stories he considers important, and so on. Because his judgment is respected, he can get stories added to the line-up or dropped, or he might persuade a correspondent to alter the wording of his script. His influence on the non-Washington portion of the program is limited, however. When John Belushi died, for example, Reynolds opposed leading the broadcast with the story ("I didn't think it ranked up there with the death of Elvis Presley, or someone like Frank Sinatra"), but after expressing his opposition, he acquiesced in the executive producer's judgment. Had he felt more strongly about the subject — "I was afraid it might be a question of generation gap" — he might have gone to the mat on it, but like any sensible person in his position, he decided to save his ammunition for a story he cared more deeply about.

Peter Jennings plays a similar editorial role for international news, acting as an advocate for stories he thinks should be included in the line-up, advising producers on how such stories should be interpreted, et cetera. Jennings, an Arledge favorite, is widely respected within ABC for his command of foreign affairs. The relationship between the two men dates back to the 1972 Olympics, when Jennings, then a foreign correspondent, was asked by Arledge to handle the nonsports coverage at Munich. When the Arab commandos, identified as members of the Black September group, seized the Israeli compound, Jennings impressed everyone with his detailed knowledge of the organization and its aims. He also displayed considerable moxie as a reporter, hiding himself and a camera crew inside the grounds, close enough to the scene to obtain clear pictures of the guerrillas in their floppy hats and stockinged faces, darting in and out of the balcony of the Israeli building. It was among the most gripping episodes ever shown on live television.

Although Jennings occasionally takes up broadcast time with minor stories, he is often responsible for giving ABC the edge over its competitors in foreign coverage. Not only is he exposed to the European perspective from his base in London, he avoids getting caught up in the "Washington herd syndrome," in which reporters who all attend the same briefings and depend on the same administration sources tend to develop a common — but sometimes distorted — view of a story. When Egyptian President Anwar Sadat was murdered, for example, Jennings gave a far more penetrating analysis of the events surrounding the assassination and funeral than most other commentators. A hero in America, Sadat was less popular in Egypt after he signed the peace treaty with Israel. But most American correspondents either ignored the subdued reaction by Egyptians to his death or attributed the empty streets during his funeral to heavy security precautions. Recalling the panic and hysteria that gripped Egypt after Nasser's death in 1971, Jennings was one of the few who pointed out that the lack of public display for Sadat was a sign of how alienated he had become from his normally emotional countrymen.

But Jennings, like Reynolds, is forced to bow to the wishes of the New York producers at times. On the surface, then, it would seem that the executive producer of the "World News Tonight" is a very powerful person, and in many ways he is. But he is kept on a fairly short leash by the *real* power at ABC News, Roone Arledge. *He* is the person producers have to please if they want to keep their jobs. As Dorrance Smith, who produces the weekend news programs at ABC, explains, "Roone has a hands-on relationship with every program. *He* is the producer of the 'World News Tonight,' 'This Week with David Brinkley,' '20/20,' 'Nightline.' I work for him. There is nobody between him and me. If he doesn't like something, he changes it."

While the anchors at ABC are thus less influential than their counterparts at CBS and NBC, the situation could change. If ABC were to acquire an anchor with the stature and popularity of a Dan Rather — someone viewed as indispensable to the ratings — this individual would be in a position to extract significant editorial concessions from Arledge. Significantly, Arledge was prepared to give Dan Rather more editorial prerogatives than he would grant to Robert MacNeil, who for all his credibility has less mass appeal than Rather.

Jennings and Reynolds are not without audience appeal, of course, but they also derive influence over the editorial process because of their standing in the profession; they are regarded as experts in their areas. An anchor who is not respected as a journalist is apt to find his input limited, as the unhappy career of Max Robinson at ABC illustrates. Initially, producers say, he tried to make suggestions for the inclusion of stories, but after feeling rebuffed on several occasions, he began to take a less active role.

Coming straight to a network anchor slot from a local station, where his record as a reporter was considered unexceptional, Robinson was met with the condescending attitude that network veterans have toward anyone they suspect of failing to have paid proper dues; producers were not interested in his suggestions.

As Robinson saw it, he had *more* than paid his dues, fighting his way up to the top in an industry that had long shut its doors to blacks. Robinson was born in Richmond, Virginia, in 1939, the son of Maxie Robinson, a local legend and high school athletic coach for forty-four years. His mother, Doris, is a prominent community activist and professional public speaker. In 1958, after studying for a year and a half at Oberlin College, Robinson got a job as a TV announcer in Portsmouth, Virginia. One of his duties was to read the news, his face covered by a slide bearing the station's logo. One night, however, he decided to take the slide down so his relatives who lived in the area could see him. He was fired the next day. "The owner told me Portsmouth wasn't ready for color television," Robinson recalls.

Then came a stint in the Air Force, where he learned to speak Russian as a language specialist. Robinson has always been a man of broad interests, art being a special passion. He is an accomplished painter.

In 1965, he was taken on as a production trainee at WTOP-TV in Washington. The job normally paid $75 a week, but the station offered Robinson $50. "I was in no position to quibble," he says. When he was promoted to cameraman/reporter, a job that should have paid $160 a week, he received $100. The situation was even more difficult at WRC-TV, a Washington station that was almost lily-white when Robinson was hired as a reporter in 1966. "I would walk down the hall and speak, but people would look right through me. I had never encountered such hatred." Once, when the news director wanted to assign him to work on a documentary on life in the ghetto, Robinson was excited at the seeming breakthrough until he learned his assignment was to drive the truck. He refused.

Although Robinson turned in several outstanding reports at WRC — a series he did on life in an impoverished Washington neighborhood won several awards — people who knew him then say he was always more interested in "starring" than in reporting. He finally got his chance in

1969 back at WTOP (later renamed WDVM), becoming the first black anchorman in Washington and, in time, a local hero. But it was not easy in the beginning. "We used to get a lot of hate calls," says Jim Snyder, news director at the time. "People from some of the Virginia counties and parts of Maryland used to call and make these racist diatribes. I remember one of the studio cameramen used to peer around the camera and make faces at Max, trying to distract him." After a while, viewers became accustomed to black faces on the news, and Robinson, in tandem with his partner, Gordon Peterson, a white man, became the hottest anchor team in town. In 1974, they moved into first place in the local news race, staying there by impressively wide margins.

Robinson seldom went out on the street to report, however. Partly this was because he was so well known that his presence would practically cause a riot. In larger part, though, Robinson stayed inside because he liked it best there. As Snyder says, "He was always a studio creature. That's where he's most comfortable. He was never as effective on the street." Still, as an anchor, Robinson took an active role in shaping the station's coverage. In particular, he considered it his role to make sure that news of the black community was not neglected. "Max's question was always, were we giving the black community a fair shake?" says Snyder. "I remember he once called me an unconscious racist. I don't think I'm a racist at all, but it's fair to say that I made progress as time went by on my sensibility in those matters."

Robinson was especially popular in Washington's black community. He was always in demand for speeches and appearances. In the early 1970s, he often spoke in black churches, sometimes from the pulpit, making a lot of friends for himself and his station. Washington's blacks developed a tremendous loyalty to WTOP — it had twice as many black viewers as any other station in town. His contacts also led to one of his great coups — the first interview with Hamaas Abdul Khaalis, the Hanafi leader who masterminded the violent takeover of three buildings in downtown Washington in March 1977.

After nearly a decade in the same job, Robinson inevitably became restless; friends and family advised him that the time might be ripe for a black anchor at the national level, and in 1978, he got his chance with ABC. According to Robinson, it was a disillusioning experience from the start. The transition from Washington, where he was a roaring success, to Chicago was particularly painful. "Chicago is a town which has its racial problems, and I think it shocked people when I came to town. They

weren't ready for it. The things they printed — such as the local anchor
who said, 'I don't know how well he can relate to wheat fields in Kansas
as a black,' and the TV critic who wrote, 'When you come to Chicago, be
humble or Chicago will humiliate you.'* That's the kind of thing I had to
deal with, so the whole tone of my coming in terms of Chicago was badly
marred. It didn't exactly make me feel relaxed.''

Relations between Robinson and ABC headquarters in New York were
not much better. Producers complained that he was lazy and arrogant, that
he needed help with his writing, that he was not anxious to leave Chicago
to anchor from the field (a charge Robinson heatedly denies), and that he
couldn't memorize his ''standuppers.'' Executives say they were disappointed with his performance in the anchor booth during the 1978 elections, that despite intensive prepping, he couldn't assimilate enough
information to sound convincing. They say he also had to be ''pumped
up'' with a lot of help in the 1980 election. When the Iranian hostages
were released the day of Ronald Reagan's inauguration, Robinson had no
assignment at all, a slight that so infuriated him he offered to resign.

His bitterness spilled out not long afterward in a speech at Smith
College, in which he accused the networks in general and ABC in
particular of racism. ''They call me a journalist,'' he told the audience in
an address recorded by a student journalist. ''I work for ABC News, and
in the process of working for ABC News I have come to the fundamental
conclusion that I have very little to say about the mirror that is held up
every night on 'World News Tonight.' Very little at all. When I question
those things that are going on that are damaging, demeaning, insulting,
and dangerous to black people in this country, I meet with a stone wall. It
is not peculiar to ABC. It is peculiar to white America. I take an example
[from which] you may be able to see very clearly. When Ronald Reagan
was crowned and our hostages came home, there was an orgy of patriotism the likes of which I have never seen in my young life, and I'm
forty-one. I can never [forget] it. And as I watched — and I must tell you
that I watched from the sidelines because ABC elected not to include me

---

*Robinson is not the only newscaster to feel the sting of Chicago's television critics. When Jane
Pauley was hired by WMAQ in 1975, becoming the first woman to co-anchor a major nightly
newscast in Chicago, she, too, was subjected to a lengthy hazing in print. One critic wrote that
she had ''the I.Q. of a cantaloupe.'' Pauley, who pleads guilty to having been young and
relatively inexperienced at the time, says, ''I had no illusions of starting the second Chicago fire,
but I also didn't expect that I would be the second Chicago disaster.'' When she was offered a
spot on the ''Today'' show a year later, she jumped at the chance to leave town.

in the coverage of either event, even though I'm the national desk anchor responsible for a good deal of the ratings at ABC. They have admitted it publicly, and they have admitted it to me — so I had to ask the question. Why am I being excluded?''

Robinson maintained that he and all other black reporters suddenly disappeared from the screen that day because "in this patriotic fervor, black people would interfere with the process." While blacks are badly underrepresented on the air and in all other phases of network television, Robinson happened to pick a poor example. Two ABC reporters who are black, Royal Kennedy and Hal Walker, had been featured prominently throughout the hostage crisis.

Although Arledge and Robinson had an amicable four-hour meeting after the incident, the Smith speech left a bad taste in everyone's mouth; a number of people at ABC believe he may have done himself irreparable harm. Executives continued to downgrade him, not always in the most discreet fashion, sounding slightly defensive when asked why he was hired for such a high-visibility, demanding job in the first place. "I think we convinced ourselves his journalistic credentials weren't as thin as they turned out to be," says one executive. "After all, he was a pretty hot item in Washington. We turned to him, probably, as a result of the paucity of talent that was available." Ken Tiven, who was Robinson's producer in Chicago for two years (he is now news director at WPXI in Pittsburgh), has a slightly different view. "The question is, did they lose faith in Max because of something he did, or did they ever have any faith in him to begin with? As for Max, did he understand that he might not be entitled to play the game the same way he had played it as a local anchor in Washington?" At bottom, the answer seems to be that Robinson was a classic example of a minority candidate who is hired without the standard qualifications for the job — in the case of a network anchor, a long apprenticeship as a reporter, a reputation for credibility within the profession, and previous network experience — and who is then blamed for not living up to unrealistic expectations.

Whatever his shortcomings as a journalist may or may not be, measured purely in terms of his on-camera performance, Robinson is undeniably effective as an anchor on the "World News Tonight." He has a magnificent broadcast voice and an authoritative presence. He looks and sounds as convincing as the next anchor when he reads the news, which raises an interesting question: How good a journalist does a network anchor have to be? In fact, it depends on his duties. As Dick Wald put it, ''If all you ever did was a fixed program with a fixed set of requirements, you could probably get away with using a nonjournalist as your anchor. If I hired Gregory Peck to read the news, he would undoubtedly look full of integrity and credibility, and if all he was called on to do was read copy, he could wind up as a distinguished anchorperson. The minute you ask him to do something different, however, you get into trouble.''

In Europe, the news has traditionally been broadcast by ''readers'' or ''presenters,'' without any apparent harm to the population. In many countries, it is considered *desirable* to have a nonjournalist read the news. That way, the audience realizes it is listening to the collective news judgment of the organization, *not* the opinion of the individual who is speaking. Using nonjournalists also helps to ensure the anchor's subordination to the judgment of the producer, who is an experienced journalist in addition to being the representative of management.

In this country, however, journalists began replacing announcers in part because it seemed more ''honest'' to other broadcast news professionals, and in part because the networks realized that credibility translated into popularity, i.e., higher ratings. Then, in order to maximize the anchor's exposure and further build his popularity, he was given the dual function of reading the news each evening and acting as chief correspondent for important national events — duties that are divided in most other countries. In the United States, however, the evening news anchor has to step in at moments of national calamity, such as the shooting of a President, with no preparation and no filters between him and the audience, no writers or producers to save him from possible blunders or statements that might prove harmful. Given these varied and demanding duties, as well as the expectations and traditions that have developed within the profession, the job obviously calls for the most trusted and experienced journalists.

When Robinson was first hired, it was expected that he would be out on the road much of the time, covering stories from the field. Although he has proven effective on many of his reporting assignments, the notion of putting the anchor closer to the story has not worked out quite the way Arledge hoped it would. For one thing, when the anchor leaves the studio, a small army of producers, cameramen, and other support staff must accompany him. Beyond the logistical and technical problems is the question of money. ''It's as expensive as hell to move the anchor,'' says Jeff Gralnick, the executive producer of the ''World News Tonight.''

Gradually a philosophy evolved that the anchors would travel only in the event of a truly major story, and those, as it happens, do not occur every day. "When the story warrants," Gralnick insists, "we don't hesitate to send the anchors out," but the plan to recast anchors as "star reporters" has obviously been modified. On most nights, all three principals are sitting in studios that look virtually identical, despite their geographic distance, reading "regurgitated wire copy."

If Arledge was disappointed that his anchor scheme did not work entirely according to plan, he could take comfort in the fact that ratings for the "World News Tonight" were climbing steadily. By the middle of 1979, ABC had caught up to the "NBC Nightly News with John Chancellor," occasionally even beating it. Some of the increase in audience came from ABC's strengthened affiliate line-up; almost every month, it seemed, additional stations jumped from NBC or CBS to ABC. But ABC studies showed that the "World News Tonight" was also picking up viewers in cities where no such switches had occurred.

ABC's reputation as an aggressive news organization had to be helping, too. Certainly, the people on the other side of the camera — the newsmakers — were aware of how highly charged the organization had become. According to an informal survey of government officials and politicians by *TV Guide*,

> The award for the Most Aggressive News Operation goes to ABC. Roone Arledge's minions really do try harder. From the White House to Capitol Hill to overseas assignments, ABC employees are seen as real scramblers . . . ABC sets up more [special] screenings for Capitol Hill people than do the other two networks combined. And its promotion people are the most insistent in the flag-waving department. Arledge even sends his "World News Tonight" producers and desk people to meet with Capitol Hill press aides over wine and cheese, where they suggest that, when a story breaks, ABC be called first . . . When it comes to camera coverage, a White House source acknowledges that, "Nine out of ten requests for expanded coverage come from ABC. They're always pushing for more pictures."

Such hustle even began to make the aristocrats at CBS nervous, despite their continuing lead in the ratings. After all those years of viewing NBC as the competition, the real challenge now appeared to be coming from ABC.

When the Americans were taken prisoner in Iran in November 1979, Arledge regarded it as a golden opportunity to enhance ABC's image as the station to turn to for big, breaking events. Night after night, at 11:30 P.M., when the other network news operations had closed up shop, ABC aired a program called "The Iran Crisis: America Held Hostage." It attracted so many viewers that the following March, the program, retitled "Nightline" and devoted to the examination of a single issue, was made a permanent part of ABC's schedule.

"Nightline," the first significant increase in commercial network news programming since the Nightly News was expanded to a half-hour, not only brought ABC much critical acclaim, it also established a new star on the network news scene, Ted Koppel. Koppel, who was covering the State Department at the time, had been making regular appearances on the late-night specials, which were initially anchored by Frank Reynolds. After filling in a couple of times to give the overworked anchorman a break, Koppel was made a permanent host, quickly becoming a favorite with the press. "He's a smoothie, he's a rocket," wrote Tom Shales of the *Washington Post.* Howard Rosenberg, the TV critic for the *Los Angeles Times,* wrote that Koppel brought the show "instant credibility," exhibiting a "new dimension as a facile, pugnacious interviewer." All this attention astonished Koppel. He had been around for years — at ABC since 1963. With the creation of "Nightline," however, he suddenly zoomed into the national consciousness, a good example of how big events sometimes make big reputations in TV news.

The boost to Koppel's career was also indicative of a turning point within ABC News; Arledge was turning more and more to the old-timers as his mainstays, in front of the camera and behind it. Producers who "came with the place," like Jeff Gralnick, Bill Lord, and Bob Siegenthaler, were being given the top jobs, and most of the featured on-air anchors and correspondents — Reynolds, Jennings, Koppel, Steve Bell, Tom Jarriel, and Sam Donaldson — were also members of the "old guard." So were most of the prominent beat reporters like Ann Compton, Barrie Dunsmore, Brit Hume, Charles Gibson, Bettina Gregory, Dan Cordtz, and Roger Peterson. Arledge was learning that the old team contained more valuable players than he had first realized.

The veterans, in turn, were changing their opinions about Arledge. For many, the lingering reservations were dispelled by ABC's performance during the Iranian crisis. Former critics, like Steve Bell, who anchors the news portion of "Good Morning America," were now singing his praises. "Roone is one of those few geniuses that inhabit a business like ours," Bell says. "He has not only provided the corporate clout and the bucks, but he has literally infused a spirit in this place that we will absolutely not be anything except number one."

The critics, too, joined in the chorus of compliments prompted by ABC's handling of the Iran story. Although a few columnists continued to write negatively about Arledge, others were giving him what amounted to rave notices. "From the start of the hostage crisis," wrote William Henry III in the *New York Daily News,* "ABC dominated news coverage. Roone Arledge's organization sent the first correspondent and camera crew into Iran, even before the embassy takeover. It triumphed again at the end, with full details of the hapless secret negotiations. The prestige has spilled over into everything else ABC News does. In the eyes of the industry and the public, Roone Arledge, 'that man from sports,' and his staff, the former 'Almost Broadcasting Company,' have come of age."

Arledge complains, with some justification, that he wasn't taken seriously by the news fraternity, or the critics, until he increased the ratings. For all the critics' penchant for decrying the ratings race, they tend to accord a "winner" more respect. Ironically, television writers were actually fanning the competition for higher ratings by 1980, because they were giving the subject so much attention, printing the weekly figures for the evening news, the morning news, and even the Sunday panel shows. "Imagine the effect on a newspaper if its circulation figures were published every week," growls Walter Cronkite. "It adds tremendously to the pressures in television to have the whole world looking at your circulation figures." Eric Sevareid has also criticised the "breathless, relentless" way that newspapers report the ratings, almost as if they were a weekly national lottery.

If most members of the news fraternity had come to accept Arledge by 1980, he seemed to have gone at least halfway to meet them. Apart from "20/20," which continued to skirt the line between sensationalism and news, ABC was putting out a solid, credible product, breaking new ground with programs like "Nightline," and documentaries like the three-hour broadcast, "America Held Hostage: The Secret Negotiations" — a program Robert MacNeil calls "the single best piece of journalism on the subject done in any medium."

Arledge even began to dress differently, shedding his safari attire for navy blue pinstripe suits and conservative ties. (He still wears jewelry.) And although he took up the job proclaiming his determination not to be swayed by the opinion of the tastemakers in news, he obviously enjoyed his newfound respect. He must have realized also that success in network news was more than a question of ratings, that the news division as a whole — its programs, its anchors and reporters, even its executives — had to project an aura of prestige. Once Arledge had accomplished that, the only thing still needed to complete his triumph was supremacy in the evening news race.

For all his talk about making presentation the star of the show, of course, Arledge believed as devoutly in the drawing power of personality as any other network executive, which is why he was so intent on recruiting Dan Rather and Tom Brokaw. Ultimately, both men turned him down, but in the process, Arledge created a situation in which bidding wars flourished. However, even without Roone Arledge, a number of technological and economic developments in the world of network television were conspiring to confer previously unimaginable and far-reaching management prerogatives on star-caliber newsmen.

9
The Triumph of the Anchor

One of the basic troubles with radio and tele-
vision news is that both instruments have
grown up as an incompatible combination of
show business, advertising, and news. Each of
the three is a rather bizarre and demanding
profession, and when you get all three under
one roof, the dust never settles.
— Edward R. Murrow

FROM ITS helter-skelter origins three decades ago, when it was a clumsy stepchild scorned by its betters in radio, television news at the dawn of the 1980s had evolved into a national institution of awesome resources and power. Operating on budgets of nearly $150 million a year, each network news division employed more than 1000 employees, all of them laboring to produce the most compelling material mind and money could supply. For those who selected the material to be shown, the situation conferred enormous responsibilities; by what they ignored as well as what they emphasized, the editors of network news not only helped to shape the national agenda but also to color the average citizen's notions of reality. Without trying to overstate television's influence, it could safely be said that it had become one of the decisive elements in the formation of American public opinion — a statement to which government officials, business leaders, politicians, and presidents would all attest.

And increasingly, as the 1980s began to unfold, the anchors of the evening news were in a position to extend their control over these mighty institutions. Through a combination of circumstances that no one had really intended or controlled, the anchors had come to be seen as the single most crucial individuals in determining the success or failure of entire networks. The careers of correspondents and producers turned on the opinion held by the anchor; even the fortunes of senior executives were not immune to the displeasure of an unhappy anchor. Indeed, as history was to demonstrate, things had run so far beyond the old days that, if an anchor began to slip in the all-important ratings wars, it might very well turn out to be the senior executives — not the foundering anchor — who were sacrificed.

If all this raised disturbing questions about who and what shaped the news broadcasts that played so large a part in molding the issues of concern to the citizens, no one said much about it. As has often been the case in network news, important changes came about as the consequence of steps taken for other reasons. The rise of the anchors as superstars, for example, and the right they won to involve themselves in personnel decisions all up and down the line developed for an understandable reason: the anchors' desire to have a voice in matters that might influence their own success. An anchor working under a multimillion-dollar contract wanted to be certain he could do something about it if he was saddled with an incompatible producer or an unresponsive assignment editor. Yet the unintended consequences of the anchors' new power was the deterioration of the old system of checks and balances that earlier had limited the power of any single individual over what went on the air. Under the old system, the editorial product of network news emerged from consultations, or sometimes outright struggles, among anchors, producers, correspondents, and senior executives — a healthy state of affairs, since news judgments are seldom cut and dried. The relative power of the players waxed and waned, but almost always, a variety of viewpoints, ideas, and even personal backgrounds were involved in any major editorial decisions. Now, with fewer fiefdoms and independent power bases inside the news operations, there tended to be a greater premium on ''cooperation.''

As always in American journalism, the larger danger of concentrated power was not the rising up of a demagogue — a Joe McCarthy or a Father Coughlin in the anchor chair at NBC. The networks would not permit that to happen, if only in their own self-interest, no matter how popular the newscaster. The larger hazard was what might go *unreported* — a greater danger because it was more likely to occur. No anchor, nor any network, could ignore a major, breaking story. But what of the stories just below the level of major events? What of civil rights before Martin Luther King began to march? What of stories like the Soviet space program before Sputnik, or the onset of inflation before it reached double-digit levels?

Giving one man more and more power to decide what shall occupy those few minutes of precious news time is to increase the risk that important developments still in the making will be shunted aside, that important voices and points of view will go unheard, if only because they fall outside the experience of the anchor. In a society as diverse and tension-filled as this one, such a narrowing of antennae is too risky.

Part of the reason for the startling rise in the anchors' power had to do wth fundamental changes in the broadcasting industry. The changes had nothing to do with the evening news, but they had a great deal to do with creating a jumpy climate inside the networks that made executives almost desperate when it came to pleasing the superstars of the nightly news.

The problem was that the audience was shrinking. Cable television was finally beginning to take hold. Independent stations were steadily gaining strength. And new technologies, including direct-broadcast satellites, loomed on the horizon, promising to fragment the audience still further. Gone were the days when 95 percent of American viewers were tuned to one of the three networks during prime time. By 1981, their share of the audience had dropped to 84 percent and was falling so fast that some analysts were predicting it would hit 59 percent by 1990. The lone area in which ABC, CBS, and NBC could safely expect to remain dominant, it was thought, was in news and information. News was cheaper to produce than entertainment programming, and it was something the nets did better than any of their competitors. A conviction, in fact, was growing that news and information could one day become the backbone, perhaps even the principal product, of the three commercial, over-the-air television networks. With the Jeremiahs offering such grim visions, it was small wonder that network executives worried so incessantly over their news programs, and over the anchors on whom success appeared to depend.

But even in news, the networks could not take their traditional monopoly for granted, not after the establishment of CNN — Ted Turner's twenty-four-hour all-news cable network, begun in June 1980. Underfinanced, undermanned, and staffed for the most part by inexperienced unknowns, CNN nevertheless managed to out-report its rivals on occasion and to offer more live coverage of major news stories. One especially sweet victory was Turner's court suit forcing the ''Big Three'' to share their White House pool footage with CNN. Then Turner, sometimes called ''Captain Success,'' made a move that could be seen as a threat to the entire structure of the broadcasting industry: He began offering a round-the-clock headline service to non-cable TV outlets. As of June

1982, seventy-eight stations had signed up, and sixty-six of them were network affiliates. The networks were forced to counter by expanding their own news offerings into the late-night and early-morning hours, despite the small number of viewers available. Although some within the industry doubted the economic wisdom of this news explosion in off hours, the move demonstrated the overwhelming importance networks attached to news. It was not so much a question of profits, although news now made money, accounting for approximately 10 percent of network revenues. But a popular news operation was needed to buttress the ratings for entertainment programming, where the *real* money in television is made. Studies showed that if viewers think highly of a network or local news operation, they tend to have a higher opinion of the overall programming. A strong evening news was especially crucial; it meant that viewers were likely to give prime-time programming on that channel the first crack.

This combination of present-day economic reality and corporate anxiety about the future played a major role in conferring unprecedented new power on the anchors. The way in which Dan Rather took over from Walter Cronkite is a case in point, an unusually vivid microcosm in which to observe the forces that are reshaping television news. Most of all, the last chapter in the story of Rather's ascension to the CBS anchor desk illustrates how frenetically network executives have come to believe that everything rises or falls on the success of the anchor. And NBC's minuet with Tom Brokaw carried the trend a long step further.

Given the stakes, the corporate fathers at CBS felt they could not afford to be sentimental in choosing a successor to Walter Cronkite. Whoever followed Cronkite was likely to become the single most important employee in the entire organization, the linchpin holding the network and its nervous affiliates together. Thus Dan Rather could not be allowed to defect to ABC, even if it meant that CBS had to offer him more money and more influence than any other network news anchor in history.

Although Cronkite's word was law on his own program, he had almost always remained aloof from the overall running of the news division, preferring not to involve himself in the hiring, firing, or assigning of personnel. Rather was to take a much more activist approach. Using a clause in his contract that gave him the right of consultation on anything pertaining to the Evening News, he would eventually get deeply involved in the inner workings of CBS News. Today, as a result, when war erupts in the Middle East or a major trial is scheduled, Rather sits down with the executives in the front office and decides who will go. He is also heavily involved in longer-range assignments, such as who covers the Pentagon or the White House or who mans the CBS bureau in Chicago or Jerusalem.

But contractual guarantees alone, no matter how sweeping, do not automatically ensure the anchor's dominance, as any student of bureaucracy could guess. News divisions are, after all, large, entrenched bureaucracies, and like all such organizations, they are resistant to change. In order for the anchor to assume control, he must secure the loyalty of the key people in the chain of command. For Rather, the task was difficult, doubly so because of the circumstances surrounding his appointment and the reputation of the man he succeeded.

In the best of all possible worlds, Walter Cronkite would have stepped down at a time of his own choosing, probably some time in 1982 or 1983. A few weeks before he retired, his successor would have been named, leaving only a brief interregnum. Instead, thirteen months were allowed to elapse between the time Cronkite's retirement and Rather's appointment were announced in February 1980 and the day Rather finally took over. The long wait, agreed to by CBS executives in deference to Cronkite's wishes, turned out to be a nightmare for Rather. It subjected him to a prolonged siege of backbiting and hostility, coupled with a seemingly endless review of his shortcomings. As a result, CBS's desire not to offend a retiring godhead opened the door to a situation that almost destroyed the new deity.

Within CBS, no one disputed the fact that Rather was talented, charismatic, and hard-driving. Unlike Cronkite, however, he did not read the news in a reassuring manner. He seemed a little stagey and tense. Summing up his on-screen personality, a critic for the *New Republic* wrote, "We imagine, as he reads, that his knuckles are turning white." Fear that the public would reject Rather's high-voltage presence began to permeate CBS.

Some of the uneasiness was a purely natural reaction to change. Cronkite, after all, had been the anchor of the Evening News since the early 1960s, and he had won the ratings war for well over a decade. Beyond this, partisans of Roger Mudd were fanning the flames. A sizable number of people at CBS believed the wrong man had been chosen. Even those, such as Lesley Stahl, who agreed with the selection of Rather were saddened by the loss of Mudd. "The atmosphere was tainted from the start," she says. "It was hard to feel terrific about Dan at first because Roger was leaving."

Indisputably, Rather was in a difficult position. Anybody designated to replace so revered a figure as Cronkite would have had a difficult time. Yet something about Rather himself made people nervous. Though he had his share of partisans in the company, many people were not totally convinced of his sincerity and integrity; he was considered a little too nakedly ambitious to become the keeper of the flame. People wondered how he would react when he was in charge. What would he do if the ratings fell? Would he have the character to hold a steady course?

A man with finely tuned antennae, Rather picked up the nervousness eddying around him. It magnified his own feelings of self-doubt, compounded by his awe of Cronkite and the anchor position. He was well aware that his real strength was in the field as a reporter, not reading news from the studio.

As the year leading up to the changeover dragged on, everything seemed to conspire against him, including the press. When he went to Afghanistan for "60 Minutes" after the Russian invasion, almost every TV critic in America made fun of him. Tom Shales of the *Washington Post* said his peasant get-up "made him look like an extra out of *Dr. Zhivago*." At another time, he incautiously told an interviewer from the *Ladies' Home Journal* that he had tried heroin as a cub reporter in Texas. The admission was picked up by the AP and UPI and received widespread play in the newspapers. The most damaging incident, probably, was his argument with a cab driver in Chicago, who would not let Rather out of the cab, claiming he had refused to pay a $12.50 fare. Rather, who had to flag down police to stop the driver, said he would have been willing to pay fifty times that amount just to get out of the cab. The cabbie was eventually jailed, but Chicago columnist Mike Royko wrote a devastating piece on the incident — without talking to Rather — picturing him as an 800-pound big shot who didn't mind stepping on a little guy. The Royko version made headlines all over the country.

Then there was the Kuralt boomlet. Genial, plump, and rumpled, Charles Kuralt looked so avuncular that some at CBS began to suggest him as an alternative to Rather. Not only was Kuralt's manner similar to Cronkite's, but both men possessed a rich basso profundo. When Kuralt sat in for Cronkite at the end of the summer, Kuralt partisans floated stories to the press that the ratings rose. A close examination of the numbers for that summer shows they remained virtually static, give or take a share point or two, regardless of who was sitting in; in fact, the highest share of the audience for the CBS Evening News that summer — 29 percent — occurred during the last week in July, when Rather was anchoring. Nevertheless, the version favorable to Kuralt gained currency in the press, along with phony stories about a huge volume of pro-Kuralt mail. Before long, several critics were hinting, almost hopefully, that Kuralt was waiting in the wings should Rather fall on his face. Others stated flatly that Rather would soon be replaced by Kuralt. Kuralt, always a gentleman, was so distressd by the campaign that he went to Rather's office to assure him that he was not responsible for the stories. Still, it could not have been reassuring to Rather to see his successor being crowned before he himself had ever mounted the throne.

Cronkite was not helping his successor's state of mind, either. The closer his retirement came, the more ambivalent he grew, hinting to friends that he had been pushed into leaving. Rather grew so concerned about these reports that he went to management to offer to stay at "60 Minutes" a while longer if Cronkite was not yet ready to hand over the scepter.

In such a climate, it was perhaps inevitable that Rather should become haunted by the prospect that he might fail to win the loyalty of the troops at CBS — the producers, correspondents, and technicians whose support he needed in order to succeed. There were even those, he feared, who *wanted* him to fail. In an effort to rally support from the "Cronkites," as the Evening News production staff was called, he invited all of the producers and associate producers — about twelve or fourteen people — to his apartment that summer for an evening of fried chicken, beer, and morale-building. "It was a pep rally," says one producer who attended. "Rather was like the cheerleader showing her panties to the bleachers. Everything was all very upbeat." But the mood shifted at one point, when Rather told the group he knew a lot of people were predicting he would fail, reminding his guests that if he did, they would be out of a job before he was. "My ass will be the last ass to get waxed," he told them. "The remark was interpreted as a threat," says the producer, "possibly in an effort to show us he could be as tough as Cronkite. But it really jolted the audience, since we were all prepared to hump as hard for Rather as we had for Cronkite."

As the year wore on, Rather's spirits continued to sink. Reporters who interviewed him as the changeover grew closer noticed that he was not himself. He looked pale, haggard, and he seemed to have lost his sense of humor. He was no longer talking confidently about the changes he hoped to make in the broadcast; now he said he hoped to build on the great traditions of Cronkite.

Cronkite's funk was deepening, too, especially during his last weeks as anchor. He went around glowering, letting it be known that he felt left out, unappreciated. After reading a story in the papers about some alterations to be made in the program's format, he stormed into the office, demanding to know why *he* wasn't being consulted about such changes. The answer, of course, was that Cronkite was almost totally inaccessible to the staff those last weeks because he was so busy giving interviews and attending events staged in his honor. He was in the Evening News area so seldom, showing up just in time to check his script before going on the air, that the only way producers could communicate with him was by passing him notes.

He needn't have worried about the changes. A decision was reached, above the level of Bill Leonard, the president of CBS News, to retain the proven format. In fact Leonard, who was scheduled to retire that June, was persuaded to stay on an extra year in the interest of internal stability. The received wisdom at the corporate level was that Cronkite's stepping down would be so traumatic for the audience that any additional innovations or changes in the program would only be more upsetting. Proposals to showcase Rather differently from Cronkite were quietly dropped. Much was made in the press of the fact that the color of the screen behind Cronkite, a soft beige, was being changed to blue-gray, a color more flattering to Rather, but this was an absurdly inconsequential detail. For the sake of continuity, there would be no changes in the aging set, no newcomers added to the production staff, and no alterations in the way the news was presented. The retention of Sandy Socolow, the program's executive producer, was especially significant because of his extraordinarily close identification with Cronkite. Socolow was so adept at reading Cronkite and interpreting his wishes that he functioned almost as a surrogate for the anchorman — a situation that allowed Cronkite to disengage even further from the program, and one which made Socolow an exceptionally powerful person in the news division. When he said something, it had the same authority as if Cronkite himself had said it.

Keeping Socolow on was a clear signal that the traditions established under Walter Cronkite would not soon be abandoned.

When Rather finally made his debut on March 9, 1981, an air of defeatism hung over the enterprise. For the first few months, Rather looked ill at ease on screen, his manner almost tentative as he tried out various styles of delivery. Principally, he was trying to project more warmth, an effort that sometimes caused him to smile in the wrong places.

Off camera, Rather was much less tentative. He threw himself into his new job with abandon. Where Cronkite had been content to delegate most of the day-to-day decision-making, Rather was a hands-on anchorman, sitting in on the daily conference call with the domestic bureaus, staying in touch with the foreign bureaus, meeting with producers at the end of the broadcast to discuss the outlook for the next day. He seemed to be everywhere at once, in and out of screening rooms, calling correspondents with tips or leads. A man who knows news and who trusts his own editorial judgment, he seemed more at ease in his new role as managing editor than he did on the air.

He also continued the relentless pace that had marked his earlier career, arriving at the office before 9:00 A.M., not leaving until after 8:00 P.M. Lunch was often a quick sandwich at his desk. To prepare for the first space shuttle flight, he spent six hours a night for two weeks reading a stack of briefing books. He also read Tom Wolfe's *The Right Stuff* and studied tapes of previous Cronkite performances on space shots.

At the same time, he tried to put his own stamp on the Evening News by letting it be known that he wanted more original, hard-hitting pieces. Obviously influenced by the success of "60 Minutes," he urged the staff to come up with investigative pieces, exposés, and stories featuring heroes or villains. He wanted scoops, too, constantly exhorting everyone to work harder, to get out there and beat the competition.

Rather admits that he found the power of the anchor job exhilarating. "You do command a lot of resources," he says. "If I decide to swarm a story, I turn to the executive producer and say, 'Let's swarm all over this story,' and things start happening. People start moving. Crews start moving. That's quite a bit different from being a line reporter, where you're generally on the phone saying, 'God, can you just give me a hand-held camera? If you don't have a whole crew, I'll take a hand-held camera. This is really a big story.' And the guy says, 'Well, I don't know. I have a crew that will be wrapped up at the National Cathedral in fifteen minutes.' And I say, 'Jesus, fifteen minutes!' Well, that's quite a bit different from this end, when you just turn to somebody and say, 'Let's swarm it.' You push a button here and things happen.''

In spite of the ferocious pace he set for himself and those around him, the audience began to drop off shortly after Rather took over. By the end of the first three months, the ''CBS Evening News with Dan Rather'' had lost slightly more than one whole rating point, which translated to about 815,000 homes in 1981. Where Cronkite regularly drew a 27 share (27 percent of all TV sets turned on at that time), Rather was getting a 24 or 25 percent share of the audience. Coincidentally, viewership for network news as a whole was down in 1981, but CBS was by far the biggest loser.

For Rather, the strain of the ratings race that first year was much greater than he had imagined it would be. ''I was trained as a pressure player, and I had better be, coming in here to do this job, but I really had no idea, no idea at all. It's the pressure to do well for a lot of people. I do care about this place, and I do care about the people, and I'm acutely aware of how many people are throwing themselves into it to make this a good broadcast and to make me look good. And the pressure to deliver for them is the toughest pressure for me to deal with. When the scoreboard goes up, and if it doesn't light up in the right way, it doesn't bother me as much as I thought it would except that somehow it reflects badly on those people. It shouldn't, of course, and it makes me furious that it does.''

While a feeling of edginess pervaded the organization, nobody panicked, at least not at that point. The executives reminded each other that the ratings had fallen off when Cronkite succeeded Douglas Edwards, and besides, the CBS Evening News was still in first place, even if the race was much closer than it used to be.

Among the rank and file, Rather remained controversial. The production staff found him much more accessible than Cronkite, and they admired Rather's evenness of temper. In spite of the pressure he was under, it quickly became apparent that he was not a prima donna. At the same time, Rather instituted a change that provoked an enormous controversy throughout the organization: He insisted on getting more of the star correspondents on the Evening News. This policy was not entirely revolutionary. Producers had always favored the most talented reporters, which meant that they were generally assigned to the best beats and the best stories; that, in turn, meant they appeared on the air more frequently than less-favored correspondents. In the past, however, the policy existed in a more-or-less unspoken form. When Rather took over, those he wanted to appear as often as possible on the Evening News were placed on an explicit list.

On the so-called "A" list were many of the network's senior correspondents, including Lesley Stahl, Bill Plante, Bob Schieffer, Bruce Morton, Fred Graham, and Bob McNamara. And there were such favored newcomers as Susan Spencer, Steven Croft, and Lem Tucker. The "B" list included a large number of people, some of them quite senior within the organization, who were not deemed of "Evening News" quality. Assignment editors who made the mistake of putting a lesser light on what turned out to be an important story could expect to be sternly reprimanded by Rather. One day, for example, a "B" list reporter was assigned to cover an ERA rally in Washington that did not figure to be a very big story. (The networks cover many marginal stories "just in case." Some of them turn out to be good enough to make the evening news; others end up being fed to local stations for use on their own newscasts. Still others wind up on the morning or overnight news. The rest are simply junked.) Looking over the assignments that morning, Rather was furious that one of the preferred correspondents had not been assigned to a story he thought had Evening News potential, and he called to warn the Washington bureau chief, Jack Smith, that it better not happen again.

What galled staffers most was the practice of taking good stories away from those on the "B" list and feeding them to the favored correspondents. An incident that sowed particular bitterness was the way coverage was handled when an Air Florida jet crashed into a bridge in Washington during a blinding snowstorm in January 1982, killing all but four of the passengers. Jim McManus, a long-time CBS correspondent, happened to be at the Pentagon that afternoon, only minutes away from the crash site. One of the first reporters on the scene, he immediately began gathering information, filing radio spots, and thinking about how he would organize his material for the Evening News. To his chagrin, Bob Schieffer, who was off that day, was called in to handle the story on the Rather show. The idea of using a correspondent who never set foot near the story, when another reporter had actually covered it, was antithetical to most staffers' notions of fair play and sound journalistic practice.

Producers defend the creation of an "A" list by pointing out that when Cronkite was riding the crest of the wave, he had the full-time services of most of the organization's heavy hitters — Mudd at the Capitol, Rather at the White House, Marvin Kalb at the State Department, Schieffer at the Pentagon, et cetera. Now, the organization had grown so big that many of the major correspondents were off doing pieces for "60 Minutes," "Sunday Morning," the weekend news, the morning news, and even "CBS Reports." In fact, many of the organization's strongest and most creative reporters preferred to work for the other programs, where they had the opportunity to produce longer, more polished reports. The result was that the organization's premium newscast was gradually becoming a training ground for younger, less-experienced reporters. Rather wanted the front-rank correspondents working on *his* program, and he used the enlarged power of the anchor to see that they were available.

While the reasoning behind the "A" list was well understood, a widespread feeling persisted that it discriminated against older or less telegenic reporters, unless they happened to be exceptionally aggressive or talented. The fear was that CBS was becoming more and more like the local stations, where news often seemed to exist chiefly as a vehicle for putting attractive personalities on the screen.

The controversial "A" and "B" lists fueled the larger concern of many people at CBS over the extent to which Rather was getting involved in matters traditionally beyond the scope of the Evening News anchor. "The lines between management and talent have become blurred," says one CBS executive. "There's a great consultation now between the front office and Rather about personnel shifts. Walter always shied away from that; he didn't want to be the one who hired and fired. But Dan is deeply involved in all kinds of matters, from hiring and firing to story assignments."

The expanding power of anchors has stirred concern beyond the confines of the CBS Evening News staff, of course. "Producers are nothing more than chief operators today," complains NBC's Reuven Frank. "The way the system used to work, the producer was the principal editor, deciding what stories would be assigned, who would do them, what would get used on the broadcast, and so on. Huntley and Brinkley never gave me any trouble and management left me alone. Then in the seventies, management started to intervene. They would call the producer every day asking, 'What are you covering? What do you have for tonight?' The function of management should be to criticize afterwards, and if they're not satisfied with the producer's work, they should replace him. Then, management started giving away editorial control to the talent. The anchors are running things today."

In Rather's case, neither he nor the senior executives of CBS seemed to have realized just how much control was shifting to the anchor. Before the year was out, however, the new reality would be unmistakably clear to everyone. When he moved into the anchor slot in March 1981, Rather had several ideas for strengthening the Evening News operation. He presented his requests to CBS executives, but he found the response — or lack of it — frustrating. He found he was dealing with a quasi-feudal system that had developed time-honored ways for treating requests from its competing baronies. Just because Dan Rather wanted to add an extra producer in Washington or hire an investigative unit in New York did not mean that the money would be immediately forthcoming. In spite of CBS's reputation as the Cadillac of networks, CBS News was not an extravagant operation; by most estimates, it was at least three years behind ABC in terms of equipment when Rather took over as anchor, another situation he complained about. But CBS News president Bill Leonard and his assistants were not used to dealing with such an activist anchor. While lordly in guarding his personal prerogatives, Cronkite was not very aggressive about fighting for additional resources or complaining about intrusions on his turf. He preferred to leave such matters to his producers. Thus, when Rather first took his suggestions to the front office, he would be told, "Don't worry about that, Dan; we'll take care of that," or "That's a very interesting suggestion, Dan." Essentially, their attitude was "The way we've been doing things always worked well for Walter, and if we just give it a little time, it will probably work for you too."

Rather grew increasingly frustrated. Beyond the specific budget requests, he was coming to believe that the show needed a whole new look, and that he was ill-served trying to do the "CBS Evening News Without Walter Cronkite." But for the time being, he had no one in his corner who agreed that major changes were needed. Once, for example, he asked Sandy Socolow what he thought about telling viewers of upcoming stories before each commercial break, the way ABC did, instead of using the traditional CBS transition — a studio wide-shot with the teletype clacking in the background. Socolow said he thought it was a bad idea, that it would look like a blatant copy of ABC, and that it would eat up precious editorial seconds. To Socolow, the "tease bumpers," as they were called, were inconsistent with the policies established by Richard Salant, who had barred the addition of music, sound effects, and the like from news reports.

Had Rather insisted, Socolow might well have gone along — he was making every effort to support Rather and accommodate his suggestions. But Rather, still shaken by his thirteen months in limbo and perhaps reluctant to take full responsibility for the results, did not push for changes unless he could line up strong support in advance. As time went by, Rather came to feel that it would be easier to reshape the program with somebody who did not have the old Cronkite mindset, somebody who did not need to be prodded into trying new approaches. Quietly and informally, he began interviewing candidates for Socolow's job.

For the moment, the party line at CBS was that the slip in ratings was temporary, an expectable result of the transition from Cronkite to Rather. Beneath the surface, however, there was a sense of uneasiness, a feeling that all was not well. And the general uneasiness was not helped by ABC's steady advancement. In spite of the fact that the audience for network news was dropping in 1981, ABC's numbers held up. During one week in July, the "World News Tonight" actually wound up in first place! It was such a feat that it was celebrated with champagne, provided by an elated Roone Arledge.

ABC pulled off another coup in the fall, signing up David Brinkley. Brinkley had suffered a series of slights since Bill Small assumed the presidency of NBC News. His program, "NBC News Magazine with David Brinkley," a show he didn't want to do in the first place, was dropped into the schedule opposite "Dallas" on Friday nights. The magazine show thus had no chance to build an audience, sometimes winding up as the lowest-rated prime-time program of the week. Then Brinkley's executive producer was removed while Brinkley was on vacation. Deciding he had had enough, Brinkley asked Small to be let off the program. He assumed that something else would be found for him to do, but Small offered him nothing. Nor did Brinkley's supporters in higher management intervene in his behalf. At that point, Brinkley, who had a standing offer from ABC, felt he had no choice but to accept it. But friends say he was crushed at the prospect of leaving NBC, using words like *tragedy* to describe his situation.

Brinkley's departure so stunned and angered people at NBC News that it would eventually lead to the ouster of Small and the reinstatement of Reuven Frank, a man revered by NBC loyalists, as president of the news division.

ABC was jubilant about adding a man of Brinkley's stature to the staff. The move came just as Arledge was working on a plan to revamp ABC's old Sunday panel show, "Issues and Answers," so he made Brinkley the program's moderator, renaming the show "This Week with David Brinkley." Between the Brinkley triumph and the healthy ratings for the

"World News Tonight" and "Nightline," a feeling was spreading throughout the industry that Arledge was invincible, that it was only a matter of time before he accomplished his major goal — to be Number One in the evening news race.

At CBS, on the other hand, there was a growing fear that Rather was not cutting it as Cronkite's replacement; the audience kept slipping away. Rather looked like a man under strain, and it was obviously affecting his performance. Tensions between him and the front office continued to mount; he was not making much headway with his requests for an investigative unit or more producer help. Adding to his bitterness (some called it paranoia) was the feeling that "Sunday Morning" producer Shad Northshield could get anything he wanted. Rather resented it when top correspondents like Ed Rabel and Terry Drinkwater were not available to do pieces for the Evening News because they were working full time for "Sunday Morning."

Rather was also anxious to have his own executive producer installed, although he and Sandy Socolow continued to get along well. But Rather did not want to be seen as the heavy in getting rid of Socolow. He kept hoping Bill Leonard would step in and do it for him. Leonard seemed to be in no hurry, however. Replacing a long-time, valued employee like Socolow was a delicate business. Besides, Leonard had a lot of other matters on his mind at the time. On the drawing board was a new afternoon news program called "Up to the Minute." (It flopped almost immediately and was quickly withdrawn from the schedule.) Leonard was also working on the planned expansion of the Morning News from one hour to ninety minutes, and he was busy trying to sell the affiliates on an hour-long version of the Evening News. Dan Rather's problems were not at the top of his agenda; Leonard had not yet noticed the new world around him.

The last week of October 1981, the ratings fell apart. That week the Rather show placed second behind ABC's "World News Tonight." The following week, ABC won first place again, but for the first time in its entire existence, CBS wound up *last,* throwing the network into a panic. More than pride was at stake. The network was forced to lower the price of its commercials. Where the "CBS Evening News with Walter Cronkite" commanded an average price of $40,000 for a thirty-second commercial — $10,000 higher than either of the other two networks — ads on the Rather show were going for $30,000. The situation could no longer be ignored.

In mid-November, Bill Leonard was abruptly displaced by Van Gordon Sauter, a long-time CBS newsman turned executive, whose previous position (perhaps not coincidentally) was head of CBS Sports. One of several candidates in line to replace Leonard, Sauter was also a personal friend of Rather's. Although Leonard stayed on as president for a few more months, it was clear from the outset that his "deputy," Sauter, was in charge. The prospect of the Evening News's losing more viewers was considered too grave to wait six more months for Leonard to retire, whatever decency might dictate. Two weeks after Sauter's promotion, the announcement came that Sandy Socolow was being sent to London to take charge of the CBS News bureau there. His replacement, Howard Stringer, had previously worked with Rather as executive producer on "CBS Reports."

Sauter's mandate from the company made clear how much things had changed, how pivotal the anchor had become. One of his first priorities, Sauter says, was to make Dan Rather happy. "Dan had an agenda [of things he wanted done] that was adding to his sense of unease, and viewers could sense it. They were not getting the best Dan Rather. So my first task was to make him more comfortable, make him feel like he had the entire organization behind him. For me, as I've said, it's like being married to Dan Rather, that is, publicly declaring a total commitment to him." From then on, it was plain that Rather would not have to fight for money, turf, and resources like any other boy on the block. And henceforth there would be no shortage of willing help for the task of evicting the ghost of Walter Cronkite. If CBS had damaged its new anchor by clinging too compulsively to things that had worked for the old, it was now ready to give body and soul to Rather.

Some of the changes instituted were purely cosmetic, including the effort to get Rather to relax more on camera. Viewers wrote that "Dan was trying too hard," that they felt uncomfortable watching him. Stringer decided it would help to shoot Rather close up, instead of the standard three-quarter shot — that by bringing the camera closer, Rather wouldn't feel he had to strain or exaggerate to get his message across. Other stylistic changes included ABC-like bumpers, electronic theme music, and "two-ways" — live question-and-answer sessions with correspondents in the field. Correspondents were also exhorted to "dress up" their pieces with graphic effects, a change that met with considerable resistance. As the heirs to Edward R. Murrow, most CBS News staff members felt it was beneath their dignity to resort to gimmickry to increase ratings, and they had enjoyed poking fun at Roone Arledge and his "dancing graphics." The resistance had little effect. Reporters were also urged to behave more naturally on camera, not to be afraid to take a step forward to turn and look at their subject. "This was a rather delicate business," says Stringer. "People had a concern about hamming it up. Their attitude was, 'We're journalists, not actors,' which I sympathize with. The whole business can go too far, with reporter-participants running all over the place, like you get on local news. All I wanted them to do was to loosen up a bit more so they could communicate better with the audience. Staring straight ahead at the camera is not necessarily the best way of putting across what you're saying."

In concert with Stringer — with whom he had long discussions before deciding to bring him on as executive producer — Rather finally began to put his own editorial stamp on the program. Instead of treating the program like a headline service of the day's news, more time was allowed for original reports, feature stories, and backgrounders. It was no longer "the broadcast of record" as it had been under Cronkite. The important events of the day continued to dominate the top of the program, just as they had in the past, but ten or fifteen minutes into the show on a slow day, viewers might see a report comparing the relative strengths of the U.S. and Soviet nuclear arsenals or a piece illustrating how day-care cuts were affecting young children and their mothers.

Washington stories were downplayed, and the approach was changed. It was no longer assumed that viewers wanted to see all the routine comings and goings of the President or the secretary of state — those surface events that TV has tended to cover almost reflexively. Instead of sitting in a congressional hearing all day, reporters were urged to get out and dig up their own stories, an approach that required a great deal more time, effort, and creativity.

Commentary, which had been absent from the program since Eric Sevareid retired in 1976, was reinstated; Bill Moyers, who had worked with Stringer on "CBS Reports," was put on the set with Rather two or three days a week to provide commentary and analysis.

The overall presentation became more "people-oriented," less reliant on the word of officials. It was no longer good enough to find an expert or a politician who could talk about a problem; reporters were now required to show it, interviewing people who were actually affected. Also, the program was mildly sensationalized, with more time alloted to subjects like the singles scene and radio psychologists, or the occasional juicy murder trial.

With the changes in management and his own producer on board, Rather seemed to relax. Now Stringer and *his* deputies could argue with the correspondents and bureau chiefs, allowing Rather to take a more statesmanlike stance above the fray. About that time, too, his reading of the news improved. Some people asserted that the sweater he wore that winter (he had a bad cold for several weeks) encouraged the audience to warm up to him, but whatever the reason, the ratings picked up and CBS regained the lead.

Initially, the staff was suspicious about the direction of the program, fearing creeping "localism." In fact, the CBS Evening News had adopted fairly rigid ways of doing things under Cronkite and was due for an overhaul, but there is seldom much appetite for tinkering with a winner. Eventually, though, most staffers began to feel comfortable with the new format, finding it livelier and less predictable than the old one. The suspicions about Rather began to recede, too. Producers appreciated the fact that they could bounce ideas off him; many a story started out as a casual conversation with Rather. Correspondents were grateful for the supportive telephone calls and the attention they got from him when they handed in a superior piece of work. Most of all, staffers were reassured by his commitment to hard news and his respect for the integrity of the news-gathering process. "People realized that having Dan Rather as our anchor did not mean the end of civilization as we knew it," says Bill Plante, one of the ranking correspondents.

If Rather was no despot, preferring the safety of collective leadership, disturbing precedents were nevertheless being set. What happens if an anchor turns out to be an autocrat, surrounding himself with yes men? In the past, correspondents were always free to make loud, forceful representations to the producers, at times appealing decisions to the anchor or to management. But few reporters are likely to press an argument very far with an anchor who has what amounts to life or death power over their professional advancement.

An argument can be made that the editorial process is safer in the hands of experienced journalists like Rather, Mudd, and Brokaw than with the executives or producers who are answerable to the networks — organizations that have seldom demonstrated great courage or public-spiritedness. But a system that has to depend solely on the integrity of individuals, rather than on built-in checks and balances, is ultimately less secure.

If the past is any guide, furthermore, anchors will be able to extract even greater concessions from management in the future. Significantly, the contract Tom Brokaw signed with NBC in 1981 contained broader guarantees of editorial control than the agreement Rather signed with CBS in 1980. The Brokaw contract — an eye-opening document — gives a hint of things to come. Strangely enough, though, NBC almost let him get away.

Brokaw, an NBC loyalist, had no wish to leave his old network, but two people — John Chancellor and Roger Mudd — were standing in the way of the only job he wanted: anchor of the evening news. Nobody knew what Chancellor's plans were at the time that Brokaw's contract was set to expire in the summer of 1981, but Chancellor was clearly in no hurry to step down. In addition, Mudd had a contract that guaranteed him the anchor post in writing once Chancellor gave it up. Bill Small, then president of NBC News, no doubt wanted to keep Brokaw, but he had promised the spot to Mudd. To insiders, it appeared that Small was not pulling out all the stops to keep Brokaw.

Small's attitude stood in sharp contrast to that of Roone Arledge, who still had an anchor opening in New York, conveniently waiting for a superstar like Brokaw. Arledge and Brokaw, already personal friends, began to spend a great deal of time together, and it seemed inevitable to Brokaw's friends within NBC that he would end up taking the ABC offer. (CBS made a pitch, too, but negotiations with that network never got very serious.) One by one, the people he had worked with through the years began to approach Brokaw, pleading with him to stay at NBC. The company needed him, they argued; he couldn't abandon the ship.

The prospect of losing Brokaw added significantly to the despair gripping NBC News that summer. It was not only that "Nightly" was fighting to stay out of third place, but the rank and file felt alienated by the management style of Bill Small. A man with an abrasive, icy manner, he made it plain that he considered NBC News a second-rate organization and hoped to rebuild it in the image of CBS. Intent on recruiting personnel from his old organization, Small gave short shrift to many of NBC's long-time stalwarts, who came to understand that they no longer had much of a future with the company. It infuriated staffers when Richard Valeriani, who had covered the State Department for nine years, was shoved aside to make room for the Kalb brothers, Marvin and Bernard, whom Small had lured away from CBS. And it grieved NBC employees when Bob Abernethy was unceremoniously removed from his position as the "Today" show interviewer in Washington, receiving the news the same week his wife, Jean (also a long-time NBC News employee) died. NBC, with all its faults, had always been a place where management treated its staff with a certain decency and consideration. Small's abrupt, militaristic style repelled the staff.

In spite of Small's efforts to inject NBC News with a little more starch (as deficient as he was in the "people" department, he was an able administrator who knew how to make a fast decision), the operation continued to go downhill. According to *Variety,* the "Today" show, once a solid revenue-earner, was actually losing $18,000 a day, although the program was still holding its own in the ratings war with "Good Morning America." And by general reckoning, NBC bungled most of the big stories in the first six or eight months of 1981, including the attempted assassination of Ronald Reagan, the shooting of Pope John Paul II, and the flight of the first space shuttle. On the morning the shuttle was launched, for example, NBC went on the air at 6:00 A.M., but returned to its scheduled religious programming at 7:30 A.M., while the space story was still hot. Once the error was realized, the decision was reversed, but by then, it was too late; most of the audience had already switched to another channel and did not return to NBC. Again, when Reagan was shot, Edwin Newman was asked to anchor the coverage from New York, while John Chancellor was allowed to continue working on the upcoming evening news. Within the industry, people were incredulous. How could the network's chief anchor not be on the air while the President of the United States was undergoing surgery for a gunshot wound? (Chancellor felt he should have been on, but he did not want to be put in the awkward position of pushing aside a respected old friend. He thought it was a decision for management to make.)

All in all, NBC seemed to be running out of gas, and the prospect of letting Brokaw get away, in the view of many old-timers, was tantamount to admitting that NBC was no longer in the race to win. For Brokaw, whose youthful idols had been Huntley, Brinkley, Chancellor, and McGee, the thought of leaving NBC was painful. "I had been with NBC all my professional life, and although there had been a lot of changes within the character of NBC News in the last five to ten years, still, within the rank and file are the people I grew up with professionally. I think that the news business, journalism, has a lot more personal qualities to it than people think, and if I were to go across the street to either ABC or CBS, I would have to work up a real competitive edge about beating NBC, when I really didn't want to beat NBC. What I really wanted to do was to make NBC win.''

But negotiations with NBC did not appear to be going anywhere. Then, just as Brokaw was poised to sign a contract with ABC, a management shift at the top of RCA, NBC's parent corporation, changed everything. Thornton Bradshaw, formerly president of the Atlantic Richfield Company, was brought in as chairman, and it so happened that he was a personal friend of the well-connected Brokaw. Bradshaw also understood what a hot young star meant to his network and lost no time warning Small that he was not, under any circumstances, to let Brokaw get away.

Playing out a drama remarkably similar to the one that had been staged a year earlier at CBS, Small was forced to approach Chancellor and get his agreement to step down. (The date agreed on, April 6, 1982, was sooner than Chancellor wanted; he told friends he had hoped to remain until after the 1982 congressional elections.) As previously agreed, Chancellor would remain with the NBC Nightly News as ''resident commentator,'' appearing three or four times a week. Small also had to persuade Roger Mudd to agree to accept Brokaw as a co-anchor, something that turned out to be relatively easy. Mudd says he felt it was important for NBC to keep Brokaw, and the arrangement suited him personally by allowing him to remain in Washington.

The agreement with Mudd and Chancellor having been secured, the way was now clear for Small to offer Brokaw what he desired — co-anchor of the NBC Nightly News. In order to match the ABC offer, however, NBC had to come up with a hefty package, including a salary reportedly starting at $1.5 million a year, with annual increases bringing the total value to $18 million at the end of seven years. With his agent, Ed Hookstratten, hammering out the details, Brokaw was promised the key role, along with Mudd, in all live special events, plus the right to anchor three documentaries of his choosing per year. In addition, according to well-informed sources within the network, Brokaw won approval rights over the following items on the NBC Nightly News: the producer, the set, the director, the overall direction of the broadcast, and any new co-anchor should Mudd leave the program. Another clause in the contract promised Brokaw the right of consultation in matters pertaining to the running of the news division as a whole.

Agents like Hookstratten, Richard Leibner, Ralph Mann, Jim Griffin, and others had become major players in the increasingly high-stakes game of television news in the 1980s, intensifying the trend toward anchor control. Agents are nothing new in TV news — the top performers have been represented since the beginning — but the agent's role used to be limited. Essentially all he did was to negotiate raises for the few big names who earned enough money to make his services worthwhile. In the midseventies, however, with the scent of profit in the air, a new kind of agent, with roots in the entertainment industry, arrived on the scene, bringing with him a radically different perspective.

For one thing, the Hollywood-based agents figured out that anchors were underpaid vis-à-vis entertainers, since both are valued, in the final analysis, for their ability to attract audiences. The newcomers, also familiar with the art of building and protecting a client's star value, began to design contractual clauses to make sure an anchor's talents were properly showcased, as they would do with any other performer. "Agents today are doing a lot more creative thinking," says Jim Griffin, whose firm, William Morris, one of the world's largest talent agencies, established a separate division for television news in 1977. "This is not just the news business. It's the television business. When representing major players, we would look to broaden their horizons as well as cushioning any potential failures. A network has more than one division, and the news division is only one profit center within the corporation. For example, Barbara Walters benefited by making part of her deal with the news division and part with the entertainment division." The fine hand of Hollywood can also be seen in such devices as "status protection" (billing) clauses and guarantees of on-air appearances, whether it be on the prime-time magazine show, documentaries, special events, the Sunday talk shows, and even the evening news.

The influence of agents can be seen even more clearly at the local level, where station owners are less sensitive to charges of "show business" and less conscious, perhaps, of the dangers of giving away too many editorial prerogatives. Clothing allowances, transportation, limousines, dressing rooms, large support staffs, and other accouterments more appropriate to the world of entertainment have become commonplace. In a co-anchor situation, some agents are negotiating the percentage of on-air time the client is entitled to, the right to open and close the program, the right to choose which stories the client reads, and the conditions under which he or she will accept a field assignment. The contract might specify, for example, that the client cannot be called on to cover anything other than a "major" story after 8:00 P.M. The inevitable by-product of all this specificity is the agent's increasing intrusion into the editorial process. If an anchor or reporter has a disagreement with the news director over an assignment, the agent, who in all probability has no grounding in journalism, may be called in to mediate — to decide, for instance, whether or not the story qualifies as "major." "Talk to my agent" is an increasingly common refrain in local newsrooms.

The intrusion of agents has been more subtle in network news, in part because journalistic traditions are more firmly established, and in part because most top news personalities have learned to be wary of demanding the kind of perks that would hurt their image as news professionals. Agents agree that the trend toward limousines, press agents, wardrobe artists, and so on has peaked at the networks. Outwardly, in fact, network news operations look pretty much the same as they always did. An outsider who enters the evening news production area at any one of the three networks might be surprised at how unglamorous the setting is — no dressing rooms, mirrors, or lavishly decorated offices, no hairdressers or personal retainers standing around. All that greets the eye is a group, composed mainly of white men, engaged in such mundane pursuits as talking on the phone, typing scripts, or reading wire copy. These are working areas; a male anchor might take a couple of minutes at most to comb his hair and have some make-up applied before going on the air. Women, of course, take longer, partly because their make-up and hairdo requirements are more elaborate, and partly because more attention is paid to their appearance.*

Yet a dangerous erosion of traditional institutional safeguards is proceeding rapidly from within. Those in charge of running the television industry must examine the implication of giving up so much control to anchors and other star journalists and find ways to regain the old balance. Television news plays too central a role in this society to be permitted to dance to the tune of a small handful of individuals who have so much at stake personally.

Given the profound changes that have taken place in television news over the past few years — the rise of editorially powerful "stars," the multimillion-dollar contracts, the success of entertainment-oriented local news programs, and the increasingly feverish level of competition — it is

---

*As ABC's Lynn Sherr notes, "You hear from executives about your appearance, and heaven help you if you don't look good. But the general public is also more interested in how women look. You hear, 'My God, your hair looked fabulous,' or 'I loved what you were wearing' much more often than you hear remarks about the substance of your report."

also perhaps surprising that the three network evening newscasts have retained their traditional emphasis on hard news and solid, credible reporting. There have been some modifications, of course. All three programs have popularized their content slightly, giving a little more time to sports, show business, and "human interest" items. And personality is played up more than it used to be. Putting the anchor into the field is one example. There is no need for the anchor to "parachute in" to cover the outcome of the elections in El Salvador when the correspondent already assigned to the story is bound to have more expertise; sending the anchor in is mainly a device to reinforce his credibility and liven up the program. Similarly, the "two-way" conversation between the anchor in the studio and the reporter on the scene is designed primarily to show the anchor in a more relaxed, human light. And Tom Brokaw and Roger Mudd could easily be mistaken for a couple of happy-talking local anchors when they josh each other at the close of the NBC Nightly News. The networks have not overused any of these gimmicks, however, nor allowed such devices to interfere with the generally straightforward presentation of the day's news. In contrast to local news, where "reporter-participants" abound, the network correspondent still plays a subdued role, appearing briefly in "stand-up" openings or closings. In fact, the evening news on all three networks is, on the whole, more informative, understandable, and ambitious than it was five years ago, with more emphasis on original reporting and more time devoted to background analysis.

While the evening news and the Sunday talk shows have retained their dignified, serious-minded cast, the morning programs and the prime-time news magazines have all become "softer" and more personality-oriented — signs of a "split personality" within the news divisions themselves. The reason is not so hard to figure out: To break even or make a profit, a news division needs a highly rated morning show and/or a popular prime-time magazine program. Although Roone Arledge would no doubt be pleased if the critics said something nice about "20/20," the real function of this program is to make money. The same is true of "60 Minutes" and the morning programs; they have been designed to appeal to a mass audience. As with entertainment programming, the opinion of the critics has become more or less irrelevant.

The transformation of the CBS Morning News makes this plain. In spite of abysmally low ratings, little was done to change the hard-news flavor of the program for years, other than to change the anchor from time to time. When Charles Kuralt took over as anchor of the broadcast in

1980, he and his producer, Shad Northshield, felt so immune to the pressure for "numbers" that they put on a deliberately highbrow program. Called "Morning," it was patterned after "Sunday Morning," a low-key, literate, and leisurely affair, graced by unusually fine writing, editing, and photography. The critics and the intelligentsia loved "Morning," but unfortunately, it did not attract many viewers. In Los Angeles, the ratings were so low it was regularly beaten by the "700 Club," a religious program.

In the meantime, the "Today" show and "Good Morning America" were engaged in an all-out war to attract viewers. The ABC entry, which is produced by the entertainment division of the network, had begun to siphon off large numbers of viewers with its homier, more consumer-oriented approach. In response, "Today" began to popularize its content, too, putting on more celebrities, diet doctors, household hints, et cetera — a mix dubbed "info-tainment" by some within the industry. Information remains the basic commodity, but it is served up with a lot of sugar coating.

At CBS, these moves were viewed as pandering to the audience. Kuralt told an interviewer, "The competition isn't important to me. I go for weeks without even thinking about the 'Today' show or 'Good Morning America.' Oh, I suppose it would be neat if we could increase our audience, but that doesn't motivate me, or anything like that. I just want to keep putting on a good show each morning."

But Kuralt and other CBS-ers were about to be introduced to the real world of network news. Their attitude was a relic of the time when prestige, not ratings, was the watchword, when news was aimed at the intelligentsia. "Morning" itself was a relic that owed its existence mainly to CBS chairman William Paley, who liked the serious all-news format and did not exert any great pressure on his news executives to bring up the ratings. The jewels of CBS News — the Cronkite program and "60 Minutes" — were earning so much money that a classy trinket like "Morning" with Charles Kuralt could easily be afforded.

In 1981, however, a number of things happened to change the picture. One was the expansion of the program from one to two hours, a move that was supposed to improve the ratings but didn't. Another was the collapse of the ratings for the Evening News after Cronkite stepped down. Those two factors, coupled with the general nervousness gripping the industry just then, made CBS feel it could no longer tolerate a two-hour "loser" on the schedule. There was talk of putting the program under the auspices of the entertainment division, which would have fewer inhibitions about going after Mr. and Mrs. Average American. Shortly after Van Gordon Sauter took over, the morning news underwent wholesale changes in both format and personnel, much to the distress of most CBS News staff members. The biggest shock was the replacement of Charles Kuralt, a beloved figure, by Bill Kurtis, a Chicago anchor who had once been a CBS News correspondent. Ray Gandolf, a thinking-man's sportscaster, was replaced by a well-coiffed young man named Jim Kelly, and a chatty weatherman was brought in. The redoubtable producer of the show, Shad Northshield, was replaced by the former executive producer of "Good Morning America," no less. The only principal from the "old" program to survive was co-anchor Diane Sawyer, who was instructed to smile more.

Although the new program continued to tackle serious subjects, the mix was lightened; an entertainment reporter was added, and more news of interest to consumers was included. As disturbing as those changes were to traditionalists, the stylistic changes aroused even more controversy. The program had the look and feel of a local newscast, complete with local-style set and friendly chitchat among the principals — an effect intentionally created. "For better or worse," Sauter explained, "TV news today is being defined by local news. The audience likes local news more; it's news people can relate to because it takes place around the block, rather than around the globe." But he pointed out that there has been no relaxation of CBS standards on matters of content or reporting methods.

Predictably, the critics panned the new show. In-house, it was despised. Staff members thought it looked "tacky" — that is to say, local — lacking the kind of "classy" aura generally associated with CBS News. One producer summed up the general feeling by saying, "The outer package counts. A beautiful gift in a trashy wrapping cheapens the gift. In the same way, the outer package of a news show affects its credibility."

Apprised of the remark, Sauter took exception to it. "That's hogwash," he said. "That speaks to me of somebody who has been shopping at Bloomingdale's and Saks and not spending enough time in shopping malls, where the real people in this country spend their time. The broadcast was destined to be disliked by the traditionalists. It represents a significant departure from anything that's been done here before. But all those up-scale people who criticize it can't put together one tenth of one percentage of a rating point between them. A broadcast must have an audience.''

In spite of the steady increase in ratings for the CBS Morning News after its face-lift, Sauter maintains there are no plans to take the Evening News any further down the local route. Nor does ABC or NBC show any signs of charting new territory at the dinner hour. For the time being, at least, network evening news is to remain a ''prestige'' vehicle, helping to polish the corporate image and lend an aura of public service. Some tinkering with the format will continue, but no radical changes are being contemplated.

For the well-educated viewer, of course, this is good news. But how well is the high school dropout being served? For all the networks have done to popularize their evening newscasts, all three programs are still aimed too far over the head of the average, high school–educated viewer, who is presented with too much complicated information in too short a time to be able to absorb it. Studies show that few viewers recall much of what they've seen a short time after watching network news. Recall is better for interviews, where more time is allotted to a subject. It's also possible that people understand and retain information better when it is conveyed conversationally, rather than in the stylized, rapid-fire manner traditionally used by newscasters.

If the networks are doing a better job than they used to at supplying a background or context for the news, they still cannot claim to be fulfilling their responsibilities to informing the majority of citizens. For many people, the ''MacNeil-Lehrer Report'' on Public Television is a godsend. Devoted to exploring serious issues in a serious way, the program attracts almost five million people each evening. PBS's ''Washington Week in Review'' also has a large, loyal following. But both programs are unabashedly aimed at the well-informed viewer, which seems fair enough since television has so little to offer such people. ABC's ''Nightline'' — patterned after MacNeil-Lehrer but more broadly gauged — is another valuable addition to the schedule, but it comes on after half the audience is in bed. Viewers should not be forced to wait until eleven-thirty at night to find out why the economy is faltering or what is behind the latest outbreak of violence in the Middle East. The evening news broadcasts do a reasonably good job of covering these stories, but time is always too limited, given their responsibilities for covering the other major news stories of the day.

An hour of network news could help to fill the information gap, but not if the expanded format is used to copy "Today" or "Good Morning America." While the morning programs and talk shows like "Donahue" fill a need for many people, offering a wealth of information in a palatable form, there is no real need for more "info-tainment" on the schedule. Where the networks are failing viewers is in the lack of any in-depth examination of current issues, presented in a way that would attract a large number of viewers — shown during prime time, when people are not busy getting ready for work or preparing dinner. The networks like to blame the local stations for refusing to give up the necessary half-hour, but nothing is stopping the networks from putting on an hour of news between 8:00 and 11:00 P.M. The conventional wisdom has it that such a broadcast would fail against competing entertainment programs, but the Canadian Broadcasting Corporation is challenging that notion with its nightly one-hour mix of news and public affairs, presented from 10:00 to 11:00 P.M. The first twenty-two minutes, called The National, summarizes the news of the day. The remainder of the program, called The Journal, is a lively, unpredictable mix, sometimes described as a combination of "Nightline" and "60 Minutes." The Journal always features interviews on the top story of the day, plus one or more documentaries ranging in length from five to thirty minutes. The subject matter runs the gamut, from a report on Uganda after Idi Amin to a school in California that trains game show contestants. When the Canadian mountain climbers attempted to scale Mt. Everest in September 1982, The Journal conducted live interviews with team members in Katmandu. Another mountain climber was set up with a scale model of Everest in a studio in Canada to give nightly explanations of the team's location, the hazards they were facing, and so on. Begun in 1982, the two-program format has been a smashing success, attracting between 25 and 30 percent of the audience — a particularly impressive feat considering that most Canadians have a choice of six over-the-air channels, including the three commercial American networks and PBS.

For such a program to succeed in this country, the networks would have to keep in mind the primary responsibility of television news: to convey information and insights to a *mass* audience about events of demonstrable interest and relevance to that audience. The inspiration cannot come from the *Foreign Affairs Quarterly* or even the front page of the *New York Times*. Television and newspapers are such different media that they cannot be judged by the same yardstick. It is time for television to stop trying to be something it cannot achieve and forge its own authentic identity. This means that television news executives need to start putting more creative energy into improving the *content*, putting aside the near-hysterical pursuit of individual stars with all of its destructive potential. The success of local news may in fact spring less from the "happy-talking team" than its ability to communicate better with its audience and the willingness of local programmers to pay more attention to the needs and interests of viewers. Similarly, ABC News may have improved its ratings not because of any "show business" elements that Roone Arledge introduced, but because his graphics helped the audience understand the stories better.

Television news professionals and their colleagues, the critics, also need to start distinguishing between the "outer wrapping" and the content of a newscast. So long as the important stories of the day are being covered in a meaningful way, and the facts are presented as accurately and fairly as possible, what is the harm in putting the anchor in a setting that appears warmer and more relaxed, i.e., less threatening to the average viewer? The godlike authority and omniscience favored by network anchors is nothing but a pose, anyway. And the cries of "show business" that greet each modification of the evening news do little to raise the level of the debate about where TV news should be going; from its inception, broadcast news in this country has been an offshoot of the entertainment industry, which hasn't prevented it from achieving some very fine moments. The challenge facing the networks in this era of all-powerful anchors is to find a way to combine the elements of personality and style with the best traditions of journalism, to let people know what they need to know, and why they need to know it.

Selected Bibliography

Index

Selected Bibliography

Arledge, Roone, with Gilbert Rogin. "It's Sports, It's Money, It's TV." *Sports Illustrated* (April 25, 1966): 92–106.

Arlen, Michael J. *The View from Highway One.* New York: Farrar, Straus and Giroux, 1976.

Barber, James David. "Not the *New York Times:* What Network News Should Be." *Washington Monthly* (September 1979): 14–21.

Barnouw, Eric. *A Tower in Babel.* Vol. 1, *A History of Broadcasting in the United States to 1933.* New York: Oxford University Press, 1966.

————. *The Golden Web.* Vol. 2, *A History of Broadcasting in the United States 1933–1953.* New York: Oxford University Press, 1968.

————. *The Image Empire.* Vol. 3, *A History of Broadcasting in the United States from 1953.* New York: Oxford University Press, 1970.

————. *Tube of Plenty: The Evolution of American Television.* New York: Oxford University Press, 1975.

Barrett, Marvin. *Moments of Truth.* New York: Thomas Y. Crowell Co., 1975.

————. *Rich News, Poor News.* New York: Thomas Y. Crowell Co., 1978.

————, and Zachary Sklar. *Eye of the Storm.* New York: Lippincott and Crowell, 1980.

Barthel, Joan. "Huntley and Brinkley Ten Years Later." *TV Guide* (July 1, 1967): 15–19.

Bedell, Sally. "They Have a Nose for Newsmen." *TV Guide* (April 29, 1978): 11–14.

————. *Up the Tube: Prime-Time TV in the Silverman Years.* New York: The Viking Press, 1981.

————. "What Made ABC's Harry Reasoner Switch Back to CBS?" *TV Guide* (January 27, 1979): 25–28.

Beerman, Frank. "Nobody Really Hates a TV Critic: He Can't Make or Break a Show." *Variety* (November 15, 1971): 24, 64.

Bergreen, Laurence. *Look Now, Pay Later: The Rise and Fall of Network Broadcasting.* New York and Ontario: New American Library, 1980.

Bliss, Edward, Jr., ed. *In Search of Light: The Broadcasts of Edward R. Murrow 1938–1961.* New York: Alfred A. Knopf, 1967.

Bogart, Leo. "Television News as Entertainment." In *The Entertainment Functions of Television,* ed. Percy H. Tannenbaum. Hillsdale, New Jersey: Laurence Erlbaum Associates, 1980.

Brown, Les. "News Is Key to ABC Drive for Affiliates." *New York Times* (May 29, 1978): C22.

———. *Television: The Business Behind the Box.* New York: Harcourt Brace Jovanovitch, 1971.

Condon, Maurice. "Back Home in North Carolina They Remember David." *TV Guide* (January 1, 1966): 22–24.

Cronkite, Kathy. *On the Edge of the Spotlight.* New York: William Morrow and Company, 1981.

Diamond, Edwin. "From Patriotism to Skepticism: How TV Reporting Has Changed." *TV Guide* (August 7, 1982): 4–8.

———. *Good News, Bad News.* Cambridge, Massachusetts; and London: The MIT Press, 1978.

Efron, Edith. "David Brinkley." *TV Guide* (July 7, 1962): 7–9.

———. "David of the Devastating Quip." *TV Guide* (July 14, 1962): 23–25.

Fang, Irving E. *Those Radio Commentators.* Ames, Iowa: The Iowa State University Press, 1977.

Ferretti, Fred. "Chet Gets Ready to Say 'Good-by, David.' " *New York Times* (July 5, 1970): Section 2, p.13.

Fielding, Raymond. *The American Newsreel 1911–1967.* Norman, Oklahoma: University of Oklahoma Press, 1972.

"First Team" (profiles of Huntley and Brinkley). *Newsweek* (March 13, 1961): 52–57.

"Four Days, The." *Television* magazine (January 1964): 10–12, 27–33, 54–61.

Friendly, Fred. *Due to Circumstances Beyond Our Control.* New York: Random House, 1968.

Gans, Herbert. *Deciding What's News.* New York: Pantheon, 1979.

Gates, Gary Paul. *Air Time: The Inside Story of CBS News.* New York: Harper and Row, 1978.

Greenfield, Jeff. "The Showdown at ABC News." *New York Times* (February 13, 1977): Section 6, page 32.

Halberstam, David. *The Powers That Be.* New York: Alfred A. Knopf, 1979.

Head, Sydney. *Broadcasting in America: A Survey of Television and Radio.* Boston: Houghton Mifflin Co., 1972.

Hennessee, Judith. "The Press's Very Own Barbara Walters Show." *Columbia Journalism Review* (July/August 1976): 22–25.

————. "TV: Some News Is Good News." *Ms.* magazine (July 1974): 25–29.

Hess, Stephen. *The Washington Reporters.* Washington, D.C.: The Brookings Institution, 1981.

Hickey, Neil. "In This Corner: Peter Jennings." *TV Guide* (August 14, 1965): 6–9.

————. "Peace, It's Wonderful" (Jim Hartz portrait). *TV Guide* (January 25, 1975): 8–12.

Hilts, Philip J. "And That's the Way It Was." *Washington Post* magazine (March 15, 1981): 35–37.

————. "Howard K. Smith and the Rise of ABC News." *Washington Post/Potomac* (August 11, 1974): 28–36.

Huntley, Chet. *The Generous Years.* New York: Random House, 1968.

Kendrick, Alexander. *Prime Time: The Life of Edward R. Murrow.* Boston: Little, Brown and Co., 1969.

Knoll, Steve. "CBS 'Immoral,' Mudd Sez." *Variety* (January 21, 1981): 61, 88, 90.

Landry, Robert J. *This Fascinating Radio Business.* New York: The Bobbs-Merrill Co., 1946.

Lazarfeld, Paul. *The People Look at Radio.* Chapel Hill, North Carolina: The University of North Carolina Press, 1946.

————, and Patricia Kendall. *Radio Listening in America.* New York: Prentice-Hall, 1948.

"Local TV Journalism." *Broadcasting* (July 26, 1982): 37–52.

MacNeil, Robert. *The People Machine: The Influence of Television on American Politics.* New York: Harper and Row, 1968.

Mankiewicz, Frank. "The Great Certifier" (Cronkite profile). *Washington Post/Potomac* (October 31, 1976): 18–19, 24–25.

Marzolf, Marian. *Up from the Footnote: A History of Women Journalists.* New York: Hastings House, 1977.

Mayer, Martin. *About Television.* New York, San Francisco, Evanston, London: Harper and Row, 1972.

Metz, Robert. *The Today Show: An Inside Look at 25 Tumultuous Years.* Chicago: Playhouse Press, 1977.

Mickelson, Sig. Oral history interview, conducted by Elizabeth Heighton for the Broadcast Pioneers Library, Washington, D.C., March 13, 1979.

"Most Intimate Medium, The" (Cronkite cover story). *Time* (October 14, 1966): 56–62.

Murphy, Mary. "Tom Snyder: TV's Child Faces the Future." *Esquire* (March 28, 1978): 43–48.

"New Breed, The" (women in TV news). *Newsweek* (August 30, 1971): 62–63.

"News: The 'New Messiah' for Local TV as Content Gains Ground over Form." *Broadcasting* (August 23, 1976): 46–52.

Norton, Clark. "We'll Be Talking with Our Little Green Friend in Just a Moment." *TV Guide* (June 6, 1981): 14, 15.

Paley, William S. *As It Happened: A Memoir.* New York: Doubleday and Co., 1979.

"Playboy Interview: Tom Snyder." *Playboy* (February 1981): 63–82, 156, 168–174.

Powers, Ron. *The Newscasters.* New York: St. Martin's Press, 1978.

———. "When News Gets Lost in the Stars." *Channels* (June/July 1981): 32.

"Prime Time for TV Newswomen." *Time* (March 21, 1977): 85–86.

"Profile of Huntley and Brinkley, NBC's Double Threat in News Coverage." *Television* magazine (January 1961): 90–112.

Quigg, H. D. "Uncle Walter: Making of a Superanchor." *New York Daily News* (February 8, 1981): 5.

Quinlan, Sterling. *Inside ABC: American Broadcasting Company's Rise to Power.* New York: Hastings House, 1979.

Quinn, Sally. *We're Going to Make You a Star.* New York: Simon and Schuster, 1975.

Rather, Dan, with Mickey Herskowitz. *The Camera Never Blinks.* New York: Ballantine, 1977.

Reasoner, Harry. *Before the Colors Fade.* New York: Alfred A. Knopf, 1981.

Reel, A. Frank. *The Networks: How They Stole the Show.* New York: Charles Scribner's Sons, 1979.

Schecter, Leonard. "Roone Arledge Is a Major Reason Why It's Better to Watch the Game on TV." *New York Times* magazine (March 3, 1968): 32, 98–106.

Shales, Tom. "Gunga Dan." *Washington Post* (April 7, 1980): B1, B3.

Shaw, David. "Weather: Everyone's Number 1 Story." *Los Angeles Times* (March 1, 1981): 1, 3, 22–23.

Shayon, Robert Lewis. "Mileage in Morality" ("The Huntley-Brinkley Report"). *Saturday Review* (December 28, 1957): 24.

Smilgis, Martha. "What Makes Rather Run 110 Hours a Week?" *People* (September 5, 1977): 57–61.

Smith, Desmond. "Is This the Future of TV News?" *New York* magazine (February 22, 1982): 31.

———. "The Wide World of Roone Arledge." *New York Times* magazine (February 24, 1980): 37–39, 66–70.

Steinmetz, Johanna. " 'Mr. Magic' — The TV Newscast Doctor." *New York Times* (October 12, 1975): Section 2, pp.1, 25.

Sterling, Christopher, and Timothy Haight. *The Mass Media: Aspen Guide to Communication Industry Trend.* Aspen Institute Program on Communications and Society, 1978.

Stevenson, Robert L. "The Uses and Non-Uses of Television News." Prepared for the International Society of Political Psychology Meeting in New York, 1978.

Tebbel, John. *David Sarnoff.* Chicago: Encyclopaedia Britannica Press, 1963.

"This Is Murrow." *Time* (September 30, 1957): 48–54.

Trescott, Jacqueline. "Max Robinson Signs Off." *Washington Post* (June 1, 1978): B1, B13.

"TV Can't Cover Losses in Covering the News." *Business Week* (November 2, 1968): 64–66.

"Tycoon in the White House" (Kintner portrait). In Viorst, Milton. *Hustlers and Heroes: An American Political Panorama.* New York: Simon and Schuster, 1971.

Walters, Barbara. *How to Talk to Practically Anyone About Practically Anything.* New York: Doubleday and Co., 1970.

Weisman, John. "Drop In at Frank's Place — or Else" (Frank Reynolds portrait). *TV Guide* (September 1, 1979): 18–21.

———. "Washington Politicians Rate TV's Reporters." *TV Guide* (September 5, 1981): 6–10.

Wershba, Joseph. "Chet Huntley." *New York Post* (February 6, 1959): 24.

Westin, Av. *Newswatch: How Television Gathers and Delivers the News.* New York: Simon and Schuster, 1982.

White, Paul W. *News on the Air.* New York: Harcourt, Brace and Co., 1947.

Whitworth, William. "Huntley and Brinkley: An Accident of Casting." *The New Yorker* (August 3, 1968): 34–60.

"Window Dressing on the Set: Women and Minorities in Television." A report of the United States Commission on Civil Rights, August 1977.

Yurick, Sol. "That Wonderful Person Who Brought You Howard Cosell." *Esquire* (October 1974): 152–154, 244–248.

Index

65–66; political conventions handled by, 45, 64; replaced by Cronkite, 83, 108–9, 110, 260; rivalry between Swayze and, 61, 69

Ehrlichman, John, 32, 239

Eisenhower, Dwight D., 58, 63, 65, 70, 81, 140; and John Cameron Swayze, 61, 73

Eisenhower, Mamie, 170

Elizabeth II, queen of England, 66

Evers, Medgar, 148

Farkas, Ray, 99

Farmer, Don, 178

Federal Communications Commission (FCC), 60, 81–82, 83, 93, 156; and affirmative action plans for women, 181

Field, Frank, 207

Fisher, Dick, 31, 214

Ford, Betty, 216

Ford, Gerald, 11, 171, 216

Foreign Affairs Quarterly, 91, 278

Franco, Francisco, 191, 195

Frank, Reuven, 63, 69, 93, 189, 262; and Huntley-Brinkley combination, 70, 71, 73–75, 76, 79, 100–101; on RCA, 119; on women in journalism, 181

Frederick, Pauline, 181

Friedman, Steve, 211

Friendly, Fred, 16–17, 55, 68, 84, 125; and Walter Cronkite, 130; his presidency of CBS News, 117; resignation of, 118; on salaries of journalists, 177

Furness, Betty, 65

Gaito, Vinnie, 186

Galvanic skin response (GSR), 161

Gandolf, Ray, 276

Gans, Herbert, *Deciding What's News,* 149

Garroway, Dave, 169, 199

Gates, Gary Paul, *The Palace Guard* (with Dan Rather), 28

Germond, Jack, 30

Gibbons, Floyd, 51

Gibson, Charles, 248

Gifford, Frank, 221

Glassroth, Howard, 159

Goldenson, Leonard, 140, 146–47

Goldwater, Barry, 107, 199

Goodman, Julian, 98, 216

Gould, Jack, 72, 83, 151–52

Grace, Princess, of Monaco, 170

Graham, Fred, 32, 228, 261

Gralnick, Jeff, 246–47, 248

Grauer, Ben, 44

Gray, L. Patrick, 203

Greenberg, Paul, 24, 126, 133

Gregory, Bettina, 248

Griffin, Jim, 271, 272

Griffiths, Edgar, 217

Gulf Oil, 82

Guthman, Ed, 211

Hackes, Peter, 102

Hagerty, James, 73, 140, 141, 142

Hagman, Larry, 176

Haldeman, Bob, 32

Hanna, Lee, 171, 201–2

Harrison, Rex, 170

Hart, John, 24

Hartman, David, 173

Hartz, Jim, 127, 172–73

McGovern, George, 202

McHugh and Hoffman (consulting firm), 150, 162, 201

McKay, Jim, 221

Mackin, Cassie, 167, 182, 228, 231–32

McLaughlin, Marya, 7, 181

McLuhan, Marshall, 51

McManus, Jim, 261

McNamara, Bob, 261

MacNeil, Robert, 26, 232, 241, 249

"MacNeil-Lehrer Report," 165, 232, 277

McSherry, Bill, 137–38

Magid, Frank, 157, 158, 162, 166; on Harry Reasoner, 187; on Max Robinson, 232–33; on Barbara Walters, 168, 186–87

Mann, Al, 140

Mann, Ralph, 92, 93, 152, 215, 271

Mannes, Marya, 148

Manning, Gordon, 24, 126, 182

Marlow, Jess, 172

Martin, Murphy, 141

Marzolf, Marian, *Up from the Footnote,* 180

Mears, Walter, 194

Meredith, Don, 221

Meriwether, Lee Ann, 169

Miami News, 194

Mickelson, Sig, 53, 64–65, 107, 108

Midgley, Les, 162

Miller, John, 186

Millstein, Gilbert, 87, 93

Mini-Cam, 223

Minow, Newton, 81–82, 107

Monroe, Bill, 172

"Montauk meeting," 222, 230

Moore, Mary Tyler, 30

Moore, Tom, 147

Morgan, Edward P., 142

Morgan, Thomas, 135

Morton, Bruce, 8, 261

Moyers, Bill, 26, 148, 232, 267

Mudd, Daniel, 14, 15, 29

Mudd, Emma Jeanne (E. J.) (Spears), 14, 29, 39

Mudd, Jonathan, 14

Mudd, Kostka, 13

Mudd, Maria, 14

Mudd, Matthew, 14

Mudd, Roger, 102, 115, 119, 194, 203–4, 261; assignments of, 13–14, 15–16; and Tom Brokaw, 269, 271, 274; and Civil Rights Act filibuster, 16; compared with Dan Rather, 7–9, 13, 17, 18; credentials of, 7; and Cronkite successor, 6, 18–19, 21–25, 30–42 *passim,* 255–56; dedication to family of, 14–15; defection of, from CBS to NBC, 5, 41; and instant analysis directive, 22–23; and interview with Edward Kennedy, 14; political conventions handled by, 117–18; preoccupation with Washington of, 15–16, 17; his substitutions for Walter Cronkite, 114

Mulholland, Robert, 210, 214

Murrow, Edward R., 24, 29, 31, 62, 107, 238; and Walter Cronkite, 108, 123; early career of, 46–47, 49–50, 52; and Douglas